INTRODUCTION TO THE STUDY OF THE HOLY QURAN

MIRZA BASHIR-UD-DIN MAHMUD AHMAD

INTRODUCTION TO THE STUDY OF THE HOLY QURAN

By

HAḌRAT MIRZA BASHIR-UD-DIN MAHMUD AHMAD
(KHALIFATUL MASIH II)

1996
Islam International Publications Ltd.

Fifth Edition 1996
First Published in U.K. in 1985 (ISBN 0-85525-035-6)
by The London Mosque
Reprinted (Fourth Edition) in 1989 by
Islam International Publications Limited
'Islamabad', Sheephatch Lane
Tilford, Surrey GU10 2AQ U.K.
Reprinted Present Fifth Edition in 1996

Printed in U.K. by:
Biddles Limited
Woodbridge Road,
Guildford Surrey GU1 1DA

British Library Cataloguing in Publication Data:
Ahmad, Mirza Bashiruddin Mahmud, *1889-1965*
Introduction to the Study of the Holy Quran.
1. Islam. Koran. Critical Studies
I. Title II. Deebaachah Tafseer-ul-Quran.
English.
297'. 1226

ISBN 1-85372-203-0

A WORD FROM THE AUTHOR

ON the publication of the English Translation and Commentary of the Holy Quran Vol. I, friends expressed a wish that the introduction, which I wrote, be printed separately. In compliance with their desire, it is here presented in the form of a book, entitled "INTRODUCTION TO THE STUDY OF THE HOLY QURAN." It will thus be within the reach of a greater number of people, so that benefiting by it they may acquire the understanding of the teachings of the Holy Quran.

The criticisms of the Translation and Commentary of the Holy Quran, made by various scholars, will be dealt with subsequently.

MIRZA BASHIR-UD-DIN MAHMUD AHMAD,
(*Khalifatul Masih II*)

CONTENTS

PAGE

NEED OF A NEW TRANSLATION 1

NEED OF THE QURAN 6
Religion not a Product of Human Imagination .. 10
Islam Teaches Oneness of God and of Humanity .. 16
Meaning of Civilization and Culture 20
Different Periods of Civilization and Culture .. 23
Contradictions in the Old Testament 33
Contradictions in the New Testament 57
Contradictions in the Vedas 76
God's Promise to Abraham 79
Fārān—A Part of Arabia 89
The Quraish are Ishmael's Descendants 91
The Prophet Mentioned in Habakkuk 95
Prophet's Advent Foretold by Solomon 97
Isaiah's Prophecies 101
Prophecies of Daniel 116
Prophecies in the New Testament 120

THE HOLY PROPHET—A LIFE SKETCH.. 130
The Message of Islam 150
The Hijra 167
Pact Between Various Tribes of Medina 175
Battle of Badr 180
Battle of Uḥud 188
Encounter with Banū Muṣṭaliq 204
Battle of the Ditch 207
Banū Quraiẓa Punished 220
The Quran on War and Peace.. 229
The Prophet's Precepts about War 237
The Prophet Leaves for Mecca with 1,500 Companions 240
Treaty of Ḥudaibiya 244
Prophet's Letters to Various Kings (Letter to Heraclius) 246

PAGE
Letter to the King of Iran 250
Letter to the Negus 253
Letter to the Ruler of Egypt 254
Letter to Chief of Baḥrain 256
Fall of Khaibar 257
Battle of Mūta 263
The Prophet Marches on Mecca with Ten Thousand Followers 267
Fall of Mecca 270
The Prophet Forgives His Enemies 279
Battle of Ḥunain 282
The Expedition of Tabūk 291
The Last Pilgrimage 294
The Prophet Passes Away 302

THE PROPHET'S PERSONALITY AND CHARACTER .. 306

THE COMPILATION OF THE QURAN 354
Devices Adopted to Safe-guard Text of the Quran .. 355
The Quran Committed to Memory 360
The Quran Collected in One Volume 362
Standardized Copies of the Quran 363
Arrangement of Chapters and Verses 368

SOME PROPHECIES OF THE QURAN 372

CHARACTERISTICS OF THE QURANIC TEACHINGS .. 379
Belief in a Living God 380
Quranic Conception of Salvation 383
Miracles 385
Islamic Form of Government 396
The Quran on Slavery 398
The Human Soul 399
Quranic Plan of Spiritual Universe 402
God—The Ultimate Cause of All Creation 406
Principal Divine Attributes 409
Divine Attributes not Contradictory 419
Man—The Centre of the Universe 421
The Culmination of Process of Evolution 423

CONTENTS

PAGE

The Object of Man's Creation 425
The Law of Nature and the Law of Sharī'at .. 426
Quran the Perfect Scripture 430
Principles to Establish Social Order 431
Life after Death 432

AHMAD THE PROMISED MESSIAH 434

THE MESSIAH'S PROMISED SON 437

TRANSLATION INTO OTHER LANGUAGES.. 440

ACKNOWLEDGEMENTS 442

بِسْمِ اللّٰهِ الرَّحْمٰنِ الرَّحِيْمِ

INTRODUCTION TO THE STUDY OF
THE HOLY QURAN

NEED OF A NEW TRANSLATION AND A NEW COMMENTARY

In presenting this new Translation and Commentary of the Quran, we think it proper to point out that this is not a commercial enterprise nor does its main interest lie in its being new.

Our effort has been prompted by the belief that while a new translation is needed today by those who do not know Arabic, a new commentary is needed by all, whether they know Arabic or not and this for two reasons :

(*i*) Translations prepared by non-Muslims (with the exception of translations into Urdu and Persian) have all been prepared by authors who had little or no knowledge of the Arabic language and who were, therefore, unable even to understand the Arabic text, not to speak of being able to translate it. Some of them translated from other translations, and this made the meaning only more remote from the original.

(*ii*) For their interpretation of the text these translations rely not on a knowledge of the Arabic language, but on the older commentaries. A commentary, however, is largely a matter of individual opinion, part of which may be accepted by one person, part by another, and part by none at all. A translation based on a commentary may be said to reflect an individual opinion, not the true meaning of the text.

In view of these defects, there is genuine and pressing need of a new translation prepared by Arabic-knowing scholars and firmly based on a knowledge of the Arabic language, its canon and idiom.

I

PRESENT TRANSLATION FULFILS THE NEED

The present English Translation is intended to fulfil these two requirements and, God willing, it will be followed in due course by similar translations into other languages.

The Arabic language is a language with a philosophical design. Its words have been designed with a purpose. Its roots have been devised for the expression of elementary emotions and experiences, and these by slight variations in actual use give to Arabic words a significance both wide and deep. To turn them adequately into any other language is well-nigh impossible, and, as translation alone is not enough, we have to add explanatory notes to a translation to show the breadth of meaning hidden in the text. Our own Translation is no exception to the rule. It cannot hope to bring out the complete or even the approximate meaning of the original. It may only hope to bring out one of its possible meanings. To make up this deficiency, therefore, we have added explanatory notes to our Translation. But even these are not comprehensive. They do not bring out the full sense of the text, but they compensate to some extent for the limitations of the translation. Under Important Words we have indicated the breadth of meanings which the text possesses ; and, for this, we have drawn on lexicons regarded as standard not only by Muslims but also by Arabic-speaking non-Muslims. We trust that a study of this material will deepen the reader's insight into our Translation, and convince him that the sense we have sought to put into the Arabic original is not arbitrary but is based upon accepted Arabic usage and canon. The reader with no knowledge of Arabic should feel assured that our rendering, though unacceptable to some, is based on sound Arabic usage and can be dismissed only if evidence of other parts of the Quran or of sound Arabic usage points to the contrary.

SPECIAL FEATURES OF THIS COMMENTARY

Having said so much about our Translation, we wish to say something about our Commentary.

Commentaries of the Quran are already many, and an addition

to their number seems hard to justify. But we have good reasons for attempting and presenting a new Commentary. They are:

(*i*) As we have said, Arabic words possess an extraordinary breadth of meaning. A translation consequently can adopt only one of all possible meanings. It was necessary, therefore, to append Notes to the Translation, and indicate other possible meanings of the text.

(*ii*) All the large and systematic commentaries of the Quran are in Arabic, and it should be obvious that those who cannot read the Quran in Arabic can make no use of these commentaries.

(*iii*) Explanatory notes added to their translations by non-Muslim authors are inadequate for two reasons:

(*a*) They have been influenced by the writings of the opponents of Islam;

(*b*) Their authors had no knowledge of Arabic, or very little. They were unable to read the larger and more reliable commentaries. To these commentaries, therefore, European translators make no reference. They refer only to the minor and more popular commentaries. If there is a reference to any of the larger works, it is taken from another work, not from the original.

(*iv*) Comprehension of any systematic or scientific book requires knowledge not only of the language in which the book is written and of the commentaries on the book which experts in the language or in the subject may have written. It also requires close study of the book itself and insight into the terminology, idiom and fundamentals which the book employs and from which its contents derive their significance. Those who seek to interpret the book without a study of the book itself will have little help from the commentaries. European translators and commentators of the Quran do not seem to have made the necessary close study of the Holy Book. No wonder, therefore, that their comments often border on the ludicrous.

(*v*) Every age gives rise to new sciences in the light of which every book which professes to teach anything is exposed to a new criticism. The value of a book is either more securely established or it becomes more doubtful than ever. The Quran being no exception to the rule, a new commentary of it was necessary in the light of new knowledge. Without it we cannot judge how far the Quran is still effective as a teaching or how far it has surpassed its own record.

When the first commentaries of the Quran were written, the Bible in Arabic did not exist. There was not one complete copy. The fragments which had been translated into Arabic were not available to the commentators of the Quran. Whenever, therefore, they had to discuss parts of the Quran containing references to the Bible or the Mosaic tradition, they had to rely on hearsay or their own speculations. Needless to say, their comments are at times disappointing and at times ridiculous. European writers attribute their mistakes to the Quran and hold up the Holy Book to ridicule. They forget that these commentators did not know the Bible. They relied on popular accounts or on what they heard from Jewish and Christian scholars who passed on to the unsuspecting commentators of the Quran material drawn sometimes from their books of tradition instead of the Bible and sometimes from their own mischievous imagination. In this transaction the commentators no doubt betrayed simplicity and lack of caution, but the Jewish and Christian scholars betrayed lack of honesty and piety. European writers of our time, therefore, have far more reason to deplore the dishonesty of their forefathers than to ridicule the Muslim commentators of the Quran. But now it is different. Now knowledge of the Bible has become common. Arabic, Latin and Greek works have become accessible to Muslim scholars and we are able to comment in a new way upon parts of the Quran which contain references to the Bible and the Mosaic tradition.

(*vi*) Until our own time controversy between one religion and another related less to moral and social ideals and more to belief and ritual. Because of this the teaching of the Quran bearing on moral ideas and moral training and on social, economic, and political relations was never discussed. Today, however, the world thinks much more in terms of these practical matters. It was necessary, therefore, to attempt a commentary which should deal more adequately with the practical teaching of the Quran.

(*vii*) Being a revealed Book the Quran contains prophecies. A discussion of these prophecies is not possible until after they have been fulfilled. For this reason also we needed a new commentary which should enumerate prophecies of the Quran which have been fulfilled so far and which constitute an important part of the proof that the Quran is a revealed Book of God.

(*viii*) The Quran deals with all other religions and ideologies. It incorporates in itself the best part of their teaching, points to their weaknesses and supplies their deficiencies. Early Muslim commentators were ignorant of what these religions and ideologies taught and stood for. They were, therefore, unable to appreciate completely what the Quran had to teach about them. Now all the most obscure teachings have come to light so that the teaching of the Quran relating to other teachings has become evident to its devotees. To compensate for this shortcoming in the older commentaries, also, we needed a new commentary of the Quran.

For these reasons we feel that our Translation and Commentary not only does not call for apology but meets a genuine and important need. In presenting it we discharge a duty.

We hope that those who read our Translation and Commentary with care and without prejudice will feel constrained to view Islam from a new angle. We hope that they will become convinced that true Islam is not full of faults, as Western writers imagine it to be, but that it is rather a well laid out garden of the spirit where a visitor may dwell with every kind of fragrance and beauty and which affords a vision of the Paradise promised by all Teachers of religion.

OTHER REVEALED BOOKS

When the Quran was revealed about 1325 years ago there were in the world many religions and many religious books. In and near Arabia there were people who believed in the Old and the New Testaments. Many Arabs had become Christian or had developed a leaning towards Christianity. Arabs were being converted to the Jewish religion. Among converts were Ka'b b. Ashraf, a Medinite chief and a notorious enemy of Islam, and his father. Ka'b's father belonged to the Banū Ṭai' tribe. He became so enamoured of the Jewish faith that the Jew, Abū Rāfi' b. Abī Ḥaqīq, gave his daughter in marriage to him and Ka'b was born of this marriage (Al-Khamīs, Vol I). In Mecca itself, apart from Christian slaves, there were Meccans who leaned towards Christianity. Waraqa b. Naufal, cousin of Khadīja, the first wife of the Holy Prophet, entertained the Christian belief. He also had some knowledge of Hebrew and translated the Hebrew Gospels into Arabic. We have in Bukhārī :

> Waraqa b. Naufal had accepted Christianity in the period of darkness ; and used to translate the Gospels from Hebrew into Arabic (Bukhārī, ch. on *Bad'al Waḥy*).

At the other end of Arabia lived the Iranians, and they also believed in a Prophet and a book. Though the Zend-Avesta had suffered changes at human hands, it was yet held in reverence by many hundreds of thousands of believers and a powerful State was at its back. In India the Vedas had been adored for thousands of years. There was also the Gita of Sri Krishna and the teaching of the Buddha. Confucianism held sway in China but the influence of the Buddha was increasing.

NEED OF THE QURAN

In the presence of all these books and teachings, did the world need another book ? This is the question which should occur to everyone who starts upon a study of the Quran. Its answer will take many forms :

First, was not this division between religion and religion reason enough for the coming of yet another religion to unite all ? Secondly, was not the human mind to undergo a process of evolution similar to that which the human body had already gone through ? And, just as physical evolution had ultimately become established, were not mental and spiritual evolution destined towards an ultimate perfection which was the very end of human existence ? Thirdly, had not earlier books become so defective that a new book had now become a universal necessity which was met by the Quran ? Fourthly, did earlier religions regard their Messages as absolutely final? Did they not believe in continued spiritual progress? Did they not continuously assure their followers of a coming Message which would unite mankind and lead them to their ultimate objective?

The answer to these four questions is the answer to the question concerning the need of the Quran in the presence of earlier books and Messages.

We proceed to answer these questions one by one.

Was not division between religion and religion reason enough for the coming of a new Teaching which would unite all earlier teachings?

GOD OF THE BIBLE A NATIONAL GOD

Religion has a twofold purpose: (*i*) it enables man to meet his Maker; and (*ii*) it teaches him his duty towards his fellow-men. All religions existing at the advent of Islam were not only different but mutually contradictory. The Bible talked not of God, but of the God of Israel. We read in it again and again:

> And David said to Abigail, Blessed be the Lord God of Israel, which sent thee this day to meet me (I Samuel 25 : 32).
>
> And also thus said the king, Blessed be the Lord God of Israel, which hath given one to sit on my throne this day, mine eyes even seeing it (I Kings 1 : 48).
>
> Blessed be the Lord God of Israel for ever and ever. And all the people said, Amen, and praised the Lord (I Chronicles 16 : 36).
>
> And he said, Blessed be the Lord God of Israel, who hath with his hands fulfilled that which he spake with his mouth to my father David, saying . . . (II Chronicles 6 : 4).
>
> "God, the God of Israel, who only doeth wondrous things" (Psalms 72 : 18).

Jesus also regarded himself as a Teacher for Banī Isrā'īl. If others approached him, he would send them away. In Matthew 15: 21-26 we read:

> Then Jesus went thence, and departed into the coasts of Tyre and Sidon. And, behold, a woman of Canaan came out of the same coasts, and cried unto him, saying, Have mercy on me, O Lord, thou son of David; my daughter is grievously

> vexed with a devil. But he answered her not a word. And his disciples came and besought him, saying, Send her away; for she crieth after us. But he answered and said, I am not sent but unto the lost sheep of the house of Israel. Then came she and worshipped him, saying, Lord, help me. But he answered and said, It is not meet to take the children's bread, and to cast it to dogs.

Jesus also taught the apostles:

> Give not that which is holy unto the dogs, neither cast ye your pearls before swine, lest they trample them under their feet, and turn again and rend you (Matt. 7 : 6).

VEDAS ALSO A NATIONAL SCRIPTURE

Among the followers of the Vedas, the reading of the Vedas had become so exclusive a prerogative of the high castes that Gotama Rishi says:

> If a Sudra happens to hear the Vedas then it is the king's duty to drop molten lead and wax into his ears; if a Sudra were to recite the Vedic Mantras the king should cut off his tongue and if he try to read the Vedas, the king should cut his body (Gotama Smrti : 12).

The teaching about "foemen" in the Vedas is extreme and barbarous.

In the Atharva-Veda the orthodox are taught to put the non-Vedics in chains and to plunder their houses:

> Consume, with lion aspect, all their hamlets, with tiger aspect, drive away thy foemen. Sole lord and leader and allied with Indra, seize, conqueror, thine enemies' possessions. (Atharva-Veda IV, 22 : 7).

Similarly Vedic prayers addressed to the sun, moon, fire, Indra, and even grass, seek the destruction of the non-Vedic dharmis. Thus we have:

> Bewildering the senses of our foemen, seize thou their bodies and depart, O Apva. Attack them, set their hearts on fire and burn them: so let our foes abide in utter darkness.
> "Whetting thy bolt and thy sharp blade,
> "O Indra, crush thou the foe and scatter
> "Those who hate us" (Sama-Veda Part II, ix, iii, 9).

Blind, O my foemen, shall ye be even as headless serpents are : may Indra slay each best of you, when Agni's flame hath struck you down (Sama-Veda Part II, ix, iii, 8).

"Cleave through, O Darbha, amulet, my foes', my adversaries' heart ;

"Rise thou and batter down their heads" (Atharva-Veda XIX, 28 : 4).

We also have:

"Do not hold discourses with non-Vedic dharmis" (Gotama-dharm Sut. v).

Should anyone criticize the Vedas, turn him out of the country, that is, condemn him to a life-sentence (Manu Dharm Shastra).

Confucianism and Zoroastrianism also were national religions. They did not address their Messages to the whole world, nor did they try to teach on any large scale. Just as Hinduism regards India as God's favoured land, so does Confucianism regard China as God's own kingdom. There are only two ways to resolve this division and disagreement between religions : either we must hold that there are several gods, or, if God is one, we must prove Him so. Or we must have these conflicting religions replaced by one Teaching.

GOD IS ONE

The world is far advanced now. We do not need to labour over the point that if the world has a Maker, He is and can only be one Maker. The God of Israel, the God of the Hindus, the God of China and the God of Iran are not different. Nor is the God of Arabia, of Afghanistan and of Europe different. Nor is the God of the Mongols and the God of the Semites different. God is one, even as the law to which the world is subject is one law, and the system which links one part of it to another is one system. Science builds itself on the belief that all natural and mechanical changes are expressions of one law. The world has one principle—motion, as the materialistic philosophers assert. Or, it has one Maker. If this is true, expressions like the God of Israel, the God of the Arabs, the God of the Hindus, are meaningless. But if God is one, why should we have so many different religions ? Were they the product of the human brain ? Was it because of this that every nation and every people worshipped its own God? If these religions were not a human product, why and how came this division between religion and religion? If ever there was reason for this division, was it proper that the division should continue?

RELIGION NOT A PRODUCT OF HUMAN IMAGINATION

As for the question whether these religions were the product of human imagination, the answer is certainly that they were not and this for several reasons.

Religions well established in the world reveal some distinguishing features:

First, according to all ordinary standards the Founders were men of slender means. They had no power or prestige. Yet they addressed themselves to the great as well as the small and in due course they and their followers rose from a humble to a high position in the world. This proves that they were sustained and supported by a great Power.

Secondly, all Founders of religions have been persons highly honoured and valued for the purity of their lives even by those who later, on the announcement of their claims, became their enemies. It is inconceivable that those who did not lie about men, began suddenly to lie about God. The universal acknowledgement of the purity of their lives before the announcement of their claims is proof of the truth of these claims. The Quran stresses this point:

> I have indeed lived among you a whole lifetime before this. Will you not then understand? (10 : 17).

The verse represents the Holy Prophet as saying to his accusers, "I have lived for a lifetime among you, as one of you. You had the chance to observe me at close quarters; you have been witnesses to my truthfulness. How then dare you say that I have today suddenly begun to lie about God?"

Similarly the Quran says:

> Verily, Allah has conferred a favour on the Believers by raising among them a Messenger from among themselves (3 : 165).

The same point is stressed in the verse:

> "Surely, a Messenger has come unto you from among yourselves" (9 : 128).

That is, "a Messenger to you, who is one of you, not one whom you do not know, but one whom you well know and of whose purity of character you have yourselves been witnesses."

Even of Prophets other than the Holy Prophet of Islam, the Quran makes similar assertions. They were raised from among their own people. It could not be said of them that those whom these Prophets first addressed did not know them well enough. When the inmates of Hell are cast into Hell, God will address them, saying:

> Did not Messengers from among yourselves come to you, reciting unto you the Signs of your Lord, and warning you of the meeting of this day of yours? (39 : 72).

And:

> O Company of Jinn and men! did not Messengers come to you from among yourselves who related to you My Signs and who warned you of the meeting of this your day? (6 : 131).

In another place we read:

> And We sent among them a Messenger from among themselves, who said, "Serve Allah. You have no God other than He' (23 : 33).

Again:

> "And remember the day when We shall raise up a witness from every people" (16 : 85).

The word "witness" used here means a Prophet raised for a people. On the Day of Judgement, the Prophets will point to themselves as visible proof of what God's communications had done for them. God will put disbelievers to shame, saying, "See what My Prophet has attained to, and to what your disbelief has led!" All the Prophets, we are told, were raised from amongst their own people. The conditions under which each Prophet was brought up and the reactions of each Prophet to these conditions were well known to each people. Each people, therefore, was a witness of the piety and purity of its Prophet. Besides this we also have in the Quran verses such as the following:

"And unto 'Ād We sent their brother Hūd" (7 : 66)...
"And to Thamūd We sent their brother Ṣāliḥ" (7 : 74).
"And to Midian We sent their brother Shu'aib" (7 : 86).

The verses mean that Hūd, Ṣāliḥ and Shu'aib, were in close association with their respective peoples, so that those peoples could be said to know everything about them. Of Ṣāliḥ we read that when he announced himself as a Prophet to his people, he was told :

> O Ṣāliḥ, thou wast among us one in whom we placed our hopes. Dost thou forbid us to worship what our fathers worshipped ? (11 : 63).
>
> Similarly the people of Shu'aib told Shu'aib :
>
> O Shu'aib, does thy prayer bid thee that we should leave what our fathers worshipped, or that we cease to do with our property what we please. Thou art indeed intelligent and right-minded (11 : 88).

From these passages it is clear that, according to the Quran, the Holy Prophet himself, and Hūd, Ṣāliḥ, Shu'aib and other Prophets, were not obscure persons little known to their respective peoples. Their people well knew what sort of lives their Teachers led and whether they were not honest, God-fearing and pious individuals. Of none of them could it be said that a nondescript pretender had designs upon his own people

Thirdly, the Founders of religions did not possess those powers and accomplishments which ordinarily make for successful leadership. They knew little or nothing of the arts or culture of their time. Yet what each taught turned out to be something in advance of his time, something pertinent and seasonable. By adopting this teaching a people attained to a great height in civilization and culture, and retained the glory for many centuries. A true religious Teacher makes this possible. Yet it is inconceivable that a person innocent of ordinary accomplishments, as soon as he begins to lie about God, should come to have such tremendous powers that his teaching dominates all other teachings current in his time. Such a development is impossible without the help of a powerful God.

REVEALED TEACHINGS ALWAYS AGAINST CURRENT IDEAS

Fourthly, when we consider what these Founders of religions taught, we find that it has always been contrary to all contemporary trends. If this teaching had been in line with the tendencies of their times, it could be said that these Teachers only gave expression to those tendencies. Instead, what they taught was very different from anything they found current. A terrible controversy ensued and it seemed as though the country had been set ablaze. Yet those who chose to deny and controvert the teaching were ultimately themselves compelled to submit to it. This also proves that these Teachers were not a product of their times, but were Teachers, Reformers and Prophets in the sense in which they claimed to be.

In the time of Moses, how novel must have seemed his teaching about One God. When Jesus confronted in his time a materialism born of the worldliness of the Jews and of the vicious influence of Rome, how peculiar must have appeared his stress on the spirit? How out of place must have been his Message of forgiveness to a people who trembled under the tyranny of Roman soldiers, groaning all the while for legitimate vengeance? How out of time must have appeared Krishna who taught war, on the one hand, and, on the other, a withdrawal from the material world in order to cultivate the spirit. The Zoroastrian teaching, embracing all aspects of human life, must also have come as a shock to the licentiousness of that time. The Holy Prophet appeared in Arabia and addressed himself to Jews and Christians. How strange it must have appeared to those who believed that there was to be no teaching outside their own! Then he taught the Meccan idolaters that God was One, and that all men were equal. How peculiar must his teaching have seemed to a people who believed intensely in the superiority of their own race! To teach hardened drunkards and gamblers the evils of their ways, to criticize almost everything they believed or did, to give them a new teaching and then to succeed seems impossible. It is like being able to swim up-stream against a current rushing with tremendous force. It is utterly beyond human capacity.

Fifthly, the Founders of religions have all shown Signs and

miracles. Every one of them announced at the outset that his teaching would prevail and that those who might seek to destroy it would themselves be destroyed. They were without means and ill-equipped. Their teachings were contrary to firmly-established beliefs and habits of thinking and provoked the fiercest opposition of their people. Yet they succeeded, and what they had foretold came to pass. Why were their prophecies and their promises fulfilled? No doubt there have been others, generals and dictators, who have attained to apparently similar success. But it is not success which is in point. It is success which is foretold, which is attributed to God from the beginning, success on which is staked the Prophet's whole moral reputation and which is achieved in spite of the worst opposition. Napoleon, Hitler and Chingiz Khan rose high from humble positions. But they did not set themselves against any thought-current of their time. Nor did they declare that God had promised them victory in spite of opposition. Nor did they have to confront any wide-spread opposition. The ends they set out to achieve were adored by most of their contemporaries, who perhaps proposed different methods but not different ends. If they suffered defeat, they lost nothing. They still stood high in their peoples' esteem, and feared nothing. But it was different with Moses, Jesus, Krishna, Zoroaster and the Prophet of Islam. True, they did not fail. But if they had, they would have lost everything. They would not have been proclaimed as heroes, but would have been condemned as pretenders and intriguers. History would have taken scant notice of them and lasting disrepute would have been their reward. Between them and men like Napoleon or Hitler, therefore, there is a world of difference—the same difference as there is between their respective successes. There are not many people who have regard or reverence for Napoleon, Hitler or Chingiz Khan. Some regard them as heroes and are completely carried away by their deeds. But can they command true loyalty or obedience? Loyalty and obedience are given only to religious Teachers, such as Moses, Jesus, Krishna, Zoroaster and the Holy Prophet of Islam. Many millions of human beings throughout the ages have done what these Teachers bade them do. Many millions have denied themselves what these Teachers forbade. Their smallest thoughts, words, and deeds have been subject to what they were taught by their Masters. Do national heroes command even one iota of the loyalty and submission accorded to these Teachers ? These Teachers, therefore, were from God and what they taught was taught by God.

WHY TEACHINGS OF VARIOUS RELIGIONS DIFFER

But the question is: If these Teachers were all from God, why did their teachings differ so much one from another ? Would God teach different things at different times ? Even ordinary mortals try to be consistent and teach the same thing at different times. The answer to this question is that when conditions remain the same, it would be absurd to issue different directions. But when conditions change, variation of teaching is of the essence of wisdom. In the time of the Prophet Adam, it seems, human beings lived together in one part of the world ; one teaching, therefore, was enough for them. Possibly even up to Noah's time they continued to live in this way. According to the Bible, human tribes continued to live together in one part of the world up to Babylonian times. The Bible is not a book of history. But there is evidence which supports the Biblical account.

Among all nations of the world, even among savages inhabiting lonely islands, we find traces of the story of Noah's Flood. It seems unlikely that the whole of the world was first engulfed in a universal deluge, and then knowledge of it spread in all parts of the world. It seems more likely that in one part of the world there was a deluge which resulted in the dispersion of the population in different directions. If it is not proved that the world was one up to Babylonian times, history lends support to the view that it was one up to Noah's time. After Noah's time the population dispersed into different countries. The influence of Noah's teaching began to decline, because means of communication were so poor. A Teacher in one country could not communicate his Message to other countries. It was but appropriate then that God should have sent a

Prophet to each country, so that no country should be without His guidance. This made for division between religion and religion, because the human mind had not yet fully developed. As human intellect and understanding lacked the development to which they were to attain later, every country had a teaching sent to it appropriate to the level of development to which it had attained.

ISLAM TEACHES ONENESS OF GOD AND OF HUMANITY

But when the human race began to advance, and more and more countries began to be inhabited, and distances between them began to be annihilated, and means of communication began to improve, the human mind began to appreciate the need of a universal teaching, covering all the different situations of man. Through mutual contact men came to have insight into the fundamental oneness of the human race and the Oneness of their Creator and Guide. Then in the desert of Arabia, God sent His final Message to mankind through the Holy Prophet of Islam. No wonder, this Message begins by praising God, the Lord of the worlds. It speaks of God to Whom all manner of praise is due, Who sends His sustenance to all peoples and all countries, and in an equitable measure. He is not partial to any country or any people. Therefore the Message which begins thus inevitably ends by invoking the Lord of all mankind, their King and their God. The Prophet who brought this Message was a Second Adam. As in the time of the First Adam there was one revelation and one people, so in the time of this Second Adam the world again had one revelation and became one people. If, therefore, this world has been created by One God, and if God is equally interested in all peoples and all countries, it is imperative that ultimately these different peoples and different religious traditions should unite in one belief and one outlook. If the Quran had not come, the spiritual purpose for which mankind had been created would have been frustrated. If the world cannot be assembled around one spiritual centre, can we ever come to appreciate the Oneness of our Creator? A river has many tributaries but at last it becomes one broad stream and it is then that its might and beauty manifest themselves. The Messages which Moses, Jesus, Krishna, Zoroaster and other Prophets brought to different parts of the world are like tributaries which arise before a mighty river shapes its course. They were all good and wholesome. But it was necessary that they should flow at last into one river, and demonstrate the Oneness of God and promote the one ultimate purpose for which mankind had been created. If the Quran does not fulfil this purpose, where is the teaching which does? Not the Bible, because the Bible talks only of the God of Israel. Nor Zoroaster's, because Zoroaster conveys the light of God exclusively to the Iranian people. Nor the Vedas, because the Rishis prescribe the penalty of casting molten lead into the ears of Shudras—India's original inhabitants—who are bold enough to listen to the Vedic recitation. Nor does the Buddha fulfil this great purpose, because though the faith of the Buddha spread in China after his death, yet his own vision never travelled beyond the confines of India. Nor does the teaching of Jesus fulfil this purpose.

JESUS NOT A UNIVERSAL TEACHER

Jesus says:

> Think not that I am come to destroy the law, or the prophets. I am not come to destroy but to fulfil. For verily I say unto you, Till heaven and earth pass, one jot or one tittle shall in no wise pass from the law, till all be fulfilled (Matthew 5 : 17–18).

What Moses and the earlier Prophets have taught in this respect, we have described already. Christian missionaries have gone to all parts of the world, but Jesus himself had no such plan. The question is not what Christian believers are trying to do. The question is, what was the intention of Jesus himself? What was the design of God Who sent Jesus? This nobody can express better than Jesus himself and Jesus said clearly:

> "I am not sent but unto the lost sheep of the house of Israel" (Matthew 15 : 24).
>
> "For the Son of man is come to save that which was lost" (Matthew 18 : 11).

The teaching of Jesus, therefore, is only for Israel, not for others. It is said that Jesus exhorted his followers to go to other people :

> Go ye therefore, and teach all nations, baptizing them in the name of the Father, and of the Son, and of the Holy Ghost (Matthew 28 : 19).

But to argue from this that Jesus had commanded his followers to take his Message to peoples other than Israel is not correct. It means only this that the followers of Jesus were commanded by him to preach his Message to *all the tribes of Israel* and not to all nations and peoples as such. Jesus speaks in clear terms :

> Verily I say unto you, That ye which have followed me, in the regeneration when the Son of man shall sit in the throne of his glory, ye also shall sit upon twelve thrones, judging the twelve tribes of Israel (Matthew 19 : 28).
>
> "I am not sent but unto the lost sheep of the house of Israel" (Matthew 15 : 24).
>
> "It is not meet to take the children's bread, and to cast it to dogs" (Matthew 15 : 26).

Again we read:

> These twelve Jesus sent forth, and commanded them, saying, Go not into the way of the Gentiles, and into any city of the Samaritans enter ye not : but go rather to the lost sheep of the house of Israel (Matthew 10 : 5–6).

Nobody should imagine that the idea here is that Christian preachers should first go to Israelite towns, then to others. For, to go to the lost sheep of Israel does not mean only to visit their towns, but to convert them to Christianity. The idea, therefore, is that until the Israelites have become Christian, no attention is to be paid to others. Jesus makes it quite clear that the task of preaching to Israel and converting them will not be completed until his Second Coming. Thus we read :

> But when they persecute you in this city, flee ye into another : for verily I say unto you, Ye shall not have gone over the cities of Israel, till the Son of man be come (Matthew 10 : 23).

From this it is clear that Matthew 28 : 19 requires Christian preachers to establish Christianity in the towns of Israel and not merely to visit those towns. It is made quite clear that this duty of preaching to the Israelites will not be over until the Second Coming. In preaching to others, therefore, while the Second Coming of Jesus had yet to take place, Christian preachers are acting against the teaching of Jesus.

The apostles also regard it as incorrect to preach the Gospel to non-Israelites. Thus we read :

> Now they which were scattered abroad upon the persecution that arose about Stephen travelled as far as Phenice, and Cyprus, and Antioch, preaching the word to none but unto the Jews only (Acts 11 : 19).

Similarly, when the apostles heard that Peter in one place had preached the Gospel to non-Israelites, they were annoyed :

> And when Peter was come to Jerusalem, they that were of the circumcision contended with him, saying, Thou wentest into men uncircumcised, and didst eat with them (Acts 11 : 2–3).

Before the Holy Prophet of Islam, therefore, nobody addressed a Message to the whole of mankind; before the Quran, no book addressed itself to the whole of humanity. It is the Holy Prophet who declared :

> "Say, O mankind ! truly I am a Messenger to you all from Allah" (7 : 159).

The revelation of the Quran, therefore, was meant to remove those differences and divisions which had come to pass between religion and religion and people and people, and which had first arisen out of the inevitable limitations of earlier teachings. If the Quran had not come, these divisions would have endured. The world would never have known that it had but One Creator, nor would it have realized that its creation had one large purpose in view. Differences between religions prior to Islam seem to require rather than to resist the coming of a Teaching which should unite them all.

The second question is, was not the human mind to undergo the same process of evolution as the human body had already undergone ? And just as the human body had ultimately reached a certain stability of form, was not the mind (and soul) of man destined similarly to attain to a stability which was its ultimate end ?

MEANING OF CIVILIZATION AND CULTURE

In answer to this question we must remember that when we examine retrospectively the civilization and culture of different countries, we find that there have been many different periods through which those countries have passed. Some of these periods have been so advanced that between them and our time there seems to be little or no difference. If we disregard the mechanical achievements of the modern world, the achievements of some of the earlier periods of human history seem little different from the achievements of our own time. Both in civilization and culture such similarities exist. But if we go deep enough, we will find two important differences between earlier and modern periods.

Before we describe these two differences, we wish to make clear what we understand by civilization and by culture. According to us, civilization is a purely materialistic conception. When material progress takes place, there comes about a certain uniformity and a certain ease in human activities. This uniformity and ease constitute civilization. The output which results from human labour, and the means of transport needed to move this output from place to place constitute an advance in civilization. Similarly, all the methods which may be invented for the transfer of goods from hand to hand, all the schemes which may be instituted to promote education, industry, scientific research, constitute progress in civilization. Whatever may be done to maintain internal security and defence against external aggression constitutes civilization. All these are factors which influence human activities. A country which is advanced in respect of these factors confers upon its inhabitants a pattern of daily life quite different from that of other countries. It is this difference which constitutes a difference of civilization. In a country not agriculturally advanced the daily food of the inhabitants will be found to be quite different from the daily food of a country advanced in agriculture. An agriculturally advanced country encourages the consumption of many different kinds of foods. It will try to provide for a variety of needs as well as a variety of tastes. But an agriculturally backward country will not be able to provide any such variety. There will be no regard for individual differences in bodily health or refinement of taste. Whatever food the country produces as a whole will be provided, without any or many alternatives. Similarly, an industrially backward country will not be able to compare with an industrially advanced country, in dress, housing and furnishing and in other accessories to comfortable living. The industrially backward country will not be able to provide cloth enough for its inhabitants. The question as to what variety of cut the cloth might be shaped into will not even arise. The people of that country will not even know what a coat is, let alone different kinds of coats appropriate for different occasions. Even a shirt will be a luxury for them. Shoes made of kid skin will be beyond their conception. To insist on footwear made of untanned hide will be something of a luxury. The very idea of footwear will be something uncommon. The inhabitants will usually go barefooted, or they will be quite content with a piece of untanned and unshaped leather tied on their feet. We refer to these matters only incidentally. We cannot go into all the details, but very little detail is needed to prove that such differences in the external pattern of our lives are the result of difference in the degree of advancement which different peoples attain in agriculture, industry, science and education. The differences are so large that those who are used to one kind of living will have no desire to associate with those used to another kind of living. It is these differences which, according to us, constitute differences of civilization and it is these differences on which the issues of peace and war to a very large extent depend. It is these differences which in the long run give rise to imperialistic designs and lust for power.

Culture is different from civilization. Culture, in our view, is related to civilization precisely as the soul of man is related to his body. Differences of civilization are ultimately differences of material advance; but differences of culture spring from differences of spiritual advance. The culture of a people may be said to consist of those ideas and ideals which grow under the influence of religious or ethical teachings. A religious teaching provides the foundations. Followers of that teaching then build on those foundations. In building on those foundations, the followers may travel far from the original teaching, but they can never completely lose touch with the foundations. A person who executes the plan of a building may deviate as much as he likes from the original plan, yet he cannot ignore the main parts of that plan. In the same way religions and ideologies provide plans of living. What the votaries of those religions and ideologies build on the original plan develops into distinctive patterns of art and morality, so that the observer is bound to put followers of different religions into quite different classes. These differences are differences of culture. Differences of culture have become very important today. To advocate and to claim tolerance and breadth of view is very common today. In spite of this a nominal Christian, otherwise an atheist, will associate far more easily with a bigoted Christian than he will with a nominal Muslim, otherwise an atheist, or with a bigoted Muslim. There is no doubt that in our time political interests also dominate the mutual relations of peoples and these political interests spring from differences of civilization. But cultural differences are not less important. A European Muslim is very cordial to an Asiatic Muslim ; the cordiality he displays for a fellow-Muslim, he never displays for a fellow-European. A bigoted European Christian is cordial towards an atheist American. Is this due to strict religious bias ? No. If religious bias were the only factor at work, then a Christian would find himself nearer to a Muslim's heart than to that of an atheist. The truth is that between Christian and Christian, even though one of them be an atheist, there are ties of culture, a Christian culture we may call it. A Christian atheist is no longer Christian in his religious beliefs but his emotions and actions are not free from the influence of Christian culture. Influences which transmit themselves through many generations are not easily obliterated. A Christian artist who may have become an atheist in thought will still display a Christian influence in his paintings and his music. In fact, but for such influence, his art would seem as out of place as thistles in a rose garden.

DIFFERENT PERIODS OF CIVILIZATION AND CULTURE

We now wish to point out that periods of civilization and culture come at times in isolation and at times in combination. They come separately at one time and simultaneously at another. Occasionally a nation attains to a great civilization but not to a great culture; occasionally to a great culture but not to a great civilization. Rome in its glory was the bearer of a great civilization; but it had no culture. Its Art and its Philosophy did not spring from any foundational ideology. Every individual was free to grow in his own way and to interpret life without reference to any large and basic principles. During the first few centuries of its existence Christianity gave no civilization to the world but it gave culture of a very high order, a culture which sprang from a determinate outlook on life and which accordingly had its own characteristic features. Early Christians had their activities rooted in certain principles; their lives were defined by certain limits. These principles and limits were laid down for them by their religious teaching. On the other hand, the principles and limits within which the Roman mind worked were dictated by materialistic urges. In short, early Rome was an excellent example of a civilization and early Christianity a similar example of culture. Later, in Rome civilization and culture mingled together. When Rome became Christian, it had both a civilization and a culture, but its civilization was subordinate to its culture. At present Europe possesses both a civilization and a culture but, owing to the dominance of materialistic conceptions, its culture has become subordinate to its civilization. When we study the history of the world, we find that times during which religion has succeeded in promoting a true philosophy of morals or a true culture seem to have been very similar to our own time. Similarly, times during which a materialistic outlook on life has produced a true civilization seem to have been very similar to our own. But two differences seem to be outstanding. Civilizations and cultures which arose before the advent of Islam were not universal in their appeal or conception. They were not derived from a universal principle. Religion and civilization were not like branches shooting out of the same root. If they ever seemed to be so, they lacked true unity. In the Jewish religion, no doubt, an effort has been made to combine civilization and culture. In the Old Testament, to a very large extent, social ideas and ideals have been combined with material conceptions, and both centre around religion. But this attempt of the Old Testament can be described as a first attempt only and not a finally successful attempt. The same is true of the Hindu and the Zoroastrian religion. The thousand and one needs of human life seem to require an ideology and a system of thought which is elastic enough to serve as a guide for all occasions and all needs. Such an ideology the older religions do not provide. A wooden, inelastic teaching bearing on the needs of civilized society is also offered by them. But the innumerable needs of a wide human society cannot be met by an inelastic system of teaching. What distinguishes man from other animals is the very important fact that human beings, while they are so much alike, are at the same time so very different from one another. The animal world is distinguished by a dead uniformity. Buffaloes, cows, lions, tigers, hawks and fishes, in short, animals and birds whether they live on land, in water or in the air, are all alike in their external appearance as well as in the structure of their brain. They seem to obey one uniform law. But man is different. Human individuals come into the world with the same kind of body. They have the same kind of appearance, and their limbs and sense organs also seem to be very similar. But in respect of their mind and in respect of what they think and feel they are very different from one another. If we must have guidance for all these differently situated and differently constituted human individuals, it must be one, the rigidity of which is tempered by a due degree of flexibility.

JEWISH AND CHRISTIAN CULTURES

As the world has advanced, it has made effort after effort to approach this ideal. Moses gave to Israel both a religion and a civilization. But his teaching proved too rigid to answer to that variety of urges of which human nature is capable. As soon as the people of Israel began to think along new channels and to entertain new ideals and objectives and to break new ground, the teaching which Moses had left for them began to fail. Moses did not succeed in making good citizens out of the new generations of Israel. True, they continued to attach themselves to this teaching but they became either rebels or hypocrites. Christianity, therefore, could not but proclaim that the Law was a curse. Christianity was compelled to proclaim this, because it saw that the utterly rigid Law of Moses had made human beings either rebels or hypocrites. The Message of Jesus, however, was delivered many centuries after Moses. The Mosaic Law was like a coat made to the size of a child, which no longer fitted adult Israel. Jesus saw the futility of grown-up and able-bodied adults trying to put on frocks made for little children. The spirit of Jesus rebelled against this. We should rather say that from the depth of Jesus' heart came the voice of God to say: "This people has gone far ahead of the time when they received their teaching from Moses. This teaching was enough for them as long as they remained in their earlier condition. But now they need a new teaching, a new coat to fit their increased size." But the new teaching which Jesus proposed for Israel or, to be exact, the teaching which Christians coming centuries after Jesus attributed to him, may be summed up in the phrase, "The Law is a curse." There is no doubt that food which is above the digestive capacity of a person is a blight, not a blessing; but it would be wrong to conclude from this that the food as such is a blight and not a blessing. A small coat would seem strange on an able-bodied adult. So would a large coat on the body of a child. A small coat on the body of an adult and a large coat on the body of a child seem strange, but it cannot be said that the coat as such is funny. It seems to us, therefore, that to attribute to Jesus the teaching that "The Law is a curse" is cruel. All that Jesus must have said and meant was that the version of the Mosaic teaching current in the time of Jesus had become a curse for the people of that time. If he meant this, it was but truth. But the followers of Jesus have mutilated this piece of wisdom into something preposterous. In any case, whether Jesus said what we think he said or what Christians mistakenly think he said, there can be no doubt that in his time the human mind had advanced far from what it was in the time of Moses. It needed now a new guidance, a new ethics, a new civilization and a new culture. But while Israelite Teachers had tied man to a narrowly conceived teaching, Christian Teachers released man from all moral and religious obligations. Mosaic teaching restrained the mind of Israel from advancing beyond Moses' time, unless it was in the form of rebellion or hypocrisy. Christian teaching made man free from all obligations and induced the belief that the Law of God cannot raise man to any moral height. Man took over from God, as it were, the duty of planning for his salvation. The result was that the very religion which thought that the sacrifice of God was necessary for the salvation of man began to teach that for the moral advance of man the guidance of God was not necessary. We have a complete historic record only of the Israelite religion. Therefore we have taken our example from Israelite history. When a question relates to the end which a process of evolution seeks, we can answer it only by reference to historical records complete in all their stages. The history of the Israelite religion is witness to the fact that the human mind kept on growing for a long time. It traversed stage after stage but did not seem to reach any final end. Similarly, the history of the world is witness to the fact that the human mind has advanced through many periods of social progress, but has still failed to reach the conception of a large human brotherhood. Both lines of evidence seem to point to the fact that the human mind, like the human body, has had to pass through many evolutionary stages. But until the advent of Islam it did not reach any kind of finality in spiritual advance. In passing through different stages of social advance it was not able to rise above the limitations of nation or race and the idea of human equality and human brotherhood did not take root. It passed through many different periods of culture, but did not reach any satisfactory Law, a Law for all mankind. The Mosaic teaching no doubt made an attempt to bring together social and cultural ideals, but after a time it began to fail. It began to fail because what it had offered was not the last word on the subject. Jesus no doubt tried to make a change, but the change did not prove enough, and was not able to stand the tide of rebellion in which the human mind had then become involved. All that survived of the teaching of Jesus is the saying attributed to Christianity that the Law is a curse. This saying, taken in the form in which it occurs, offends the good sense of every thinking person. Unless it is suitably interpreted, the saying is itself a curse because it only serves to turn man away from God and to free him from His guidance. Therefore it seems that the end which the evolution of the human mind was seeking had not yet come. The process and stages through which human civilization and human culture had passed pointed to the fact that civilization and culture were subject to the same law of evolution to which the human body was for long subject. It seems certain, therefore, that human civilization and culture were to attain to an ultimate perfection in the same way in which the human body, after a long process of evolution, had attained to an ultimate perfection of form; and this alone indicates the need of Islam in the presence of other religions, the need of a religion which should provide an end to the evolution of human culture, an end which is embodied in the teaching of the Quran.

A PERTINENT QUESTION

The third question, an affirmative answer to which establishes the need of the Quran, is: Had the earlier books come to suffer from defects which called for a new book, which was the Quran?

In answer to this we must remember that the first criterion by which we can measure the usefulness of a book is freedom from external interference. A revealed book is superior to a man-made book because we can assume that the former will not lead us into error. God is sheer guidance. In a book revealed by Him, therefore, we may expect to find only light and truth, no darkness or error. If our conception of God does not imply such a trust in what He reveals, then that conception has no value. If communications from God also can err, then what ground have we for holding divine teaching superior to human teaching? Belief in a book entails belief that that book is free from error. It is possible, however, that a book originally revealed by God may come to suffer from human interference. If the contents of a book have suffered additions and subtractions at human hands, then that book can no longer serve as a guide.

When we examine the earlier revealed books from this point of view, we find them entirely unsatisfying. The followers of the Old Testament regard it as a revealed book. Christians also describe it as a Book of God, and Muslims also think that it was a revelation. But it is one thing for a book to be revealed, and quite another for that book to retain intact its revealed text. No doubt, all the three peoples—Jews, Christians and Muslims, agree that God spoke to the Prophets of the Old Testament. But they no longer believe, and external and internal evidence no longer support the view, that the record of the Old Testament as we possess it today constitutes the word of God as it was first revealed. From the history of Israel we learn that in the time of Nebuchadnezzar the books of Israel were burnt and destroyed. They were rewritten by the Prophet Ezra, and of Ezra we read in Jewish literature :

> "It was forgotten but Ezra restored it" [(Suk. 20a). Jew. Enc. Vol. 5, p. 322].

And again :

> Ezra re-established the text of Pentateuch, introducing therein the Assyrian or square characters [(Sanh. 21b.) Jew. Enc. Vol. 5, p. 322].

Similarly we read :

> He showed his doubts concerning the correctness of some words of the text by placing points over them. Should Elijah, said he, approve the text, the points will be disregarded ; should he disapprove, the doubtful words will be removed from the text [(Ab. R. N. xxxiv) Jewish Encyclopaedia, Vol. 5, p. 322].

From these quotations it is evident that the Torah, in whatever form it existed at the time—whether the form which Ezra gave to it or the form which it had received from earlier times —was a very uncertain and unreliable book. Its general text could no longer be regarded as the word of God preserved in pristine purity. The "Book of Ezra" is no longer included in the Bible as we know it today. Yet it is no less reliable than any of the other books of the Bible. It is called the "Greek Book of Ezra." In olden times it was put before the books of Ezra and Nehemiah. Later on Jerome, a notable Christian priest who was entrusted by the Pope with the task of editing the Bible, dropped it out of the Bible on the ground that its Hebrew original was no longer available. This book is described by some as the third book of Ezra and by some as the second book. In any event it seems that though this book was dropped out of the Bible, a great majority of Jews and Christians describe it as the "Book of Ezra." In verses 20-25 of the 14th chapter of this book we read :

> Behold, Lord, I will go, as thou hast commanded me and reprove the people which are present : but they that shall be born afterward, who shall admonish them ? thus the world is set in darkness, and they that dwell therein are without light. For thy law is burnt, therefore, no man knoweth the things that are done of thee, or the works that shall begin. But if I have found grace before thee, send the Holy Ghost into me, and I shall write all that hath been done in the world since the beginning, which were written in thy law, that men may find thy path, and that they which will live in the latter days may live. And he answered me, saying, Go thy way, gather the people together, and say unto them that they seek thee not for forty days. But look thou prepare thee many box trees, and take with thee Sarea, Dabria, Selemia, Ecanus, and Asiel, these five which are ready to write swiftly ; And come hither, and I shall light a candle of understanding in thine heart, which shall not be put out, till the things be performed which thou shalt begin to write (Apocrypha ; II ESDRAS, 14).

From this it appears that Ezra and the five scribes worked hard for forty days in seclusion and with the help of God composed 204 books. In verse 44 of this very chapter we read :

> "In forty days they wrote two hundred and four books" (Apocrypha ; II ESDRAS, 14).

From this we may conclude :

(*a*) that in the time of the Prophet Ezra, who lived about 450 years before Jesus, the Torah and the books of the other Prophets had become mixed up ;

(*b*) that no reliable copy of these books was then in existence ;

(*c*) that Ezra wrote down the books again.

True, we are told that the books were revealed. But *revealed* only means that God helped in their composition. It does not mean that the text, word for word, was revealed by God. We learn from Jewish history that Ezra himself rejected parts of the text on the ground of unreliability, and that he left the final decision about them to Elijah. The Torah as we know it today, therefore, is not the Torah which was revealed to Moses. It is the Torah which Ezra recorded from his memory, and about parts of which he himself was in doubt. We should even say that the present Torah is not even the one which Ezra wrote, for Ezra wrote 204 books, and we do not find 204 books in the Bible.

Of Ezra's memory, Christian scholars themselves express great doubts. Adam Clark, the well-known commentator of the Bible, says in his commentary (1891), under I Chronicles (7 : 6), that here Ezra mistakenly writes names of grandsons instead of sons and that to try to reconcile contradictions of this kind is useless (p. 168). In 7 :6 we read : The sons of Benjamin; Bela and Becher, and Jediael, three ; whereas in 8 : 1 we have : Now Benjamin begat Bela his firstborn, Ashbel the second, and Aharah the third, Nohah the fourth, and Rapha the fifth.

Jewish scholars take the view that Ezra did not quite know whether a given person was son or grandson of another person. When this is the view held by Jewish and Christian scholars of Ezra's memory, how can ordinary Jews and Christians and other ordinary people be satisfied about the spiritual value of a book with as little authority as the Bible ?

Let us now pass on to the internal evidence on the point. The most important and the most decisive argument in this connection is provided by Deuteronomy (34 : 5-6) :

> So Moses the servant of the Lord died there in the land of Moab, according to the word of the Lord. And he buried him in a valley in the land of Moab, over against Beth-peor : but no man knoweth of his sepulchre unto this day.

These verses show clearly that they were composed and added hundreds of years after the time of Moses. It does not stand to reason that God ever addressed Moses, saying, "Nobody knows about your sepulchre unto this day." Can such words be addressed to a living human being ? Can the words "unto this day" be used in a speech addressed to him?

Then in verse 8 we read:

> And the children of Israel wept for Moses in the plains of Moab thirty days: so the days of weeping and mourning for Moses were ended.

This verse also shows that it cannot have been revealed to Moses but is a later addition.

Then in verse 10 we read:

> And there arose not a Prophet since in Israel like unto Moses, whom the Lord knew face to face.

This also does not seem to be a revelation of Moses but an invention made many hundreds of years after his death and entered in the Book of Moses. It is possible that it is the work of Ezra, but it may equally be the work of somebody else.

For further internal evidence on the point that the Torah, as we know it, was compiled after the time of Moses, and that it contains the writings of other persons, we should read Genesis 14:14:

> And when Abram heard that his brother was taken captive, he armed his trained servants, born in his own house, three hundred and eighteen, and pursued them unto Dan.

Compare this passage with Judges 18:27-29, in which it is said that this city which is called Dan in the book of Genesis was first called Laish. About 80 years after Moses this city was conquered by Israel and renamed Dan. We read:

> And they took the things which Micah had made, and the priest which he had, and came unto Laish, unto a people that were as quiet and secure: and they smote them with the edge of the sword, and burnt the city with fire. And there was no deliverer, because it was far from Zidon, and they had no business with any man; and it was in the valley that lieth by Beth-rehob. And they built a city and dwelt therein. And they called the name of the city Dan, after the name of Dan their father, who was born unto Israel: howbeit the name of the city was Laish at the first.

The point is that a name which was proposed 80 years after Moses, could not possibly occur in the Book of Moses. It is quite clear, therefore, that the Book of Moses had additions made to it after his death and many writers entered in it their own thoughts and speculations.

This sort of editing is not confined to the Book of Moses. Other books of the Bible also suffer the same fate.

In Joshua 24 : 29 we read :

> And it came to pass after these things, that Joshua the son of Nun, the servant of the Lord, died, being an hundred and ten years old.

Similarly in Job 42 : 17 it is written :

> "So Job died, being old and full of days."

From these quotations it is quite obvious that the book of Joshua was not recorded by Joshua and the book of Job was not recorded by Job. They were instead the compilations of persons who came later, and who compiled these books from what they heard from other people. It is possible also that the Prophets whose teachings are recorded in the Bible collected the word of God as it was received by them, but the records left by them could not endure the ravages of time, and when they became extinct the people who came after wrote them again from their memory, and in doing so entered many of their own thoughts and judgements into them. Is it any wonder that these books, which on historical as well as on their own internal evidence are maimed and mutilated, ceased to give satisfaction to their readers ? Is it any wonder that therefore, God also withdrew His protection from them so that mankind began to look and long for a book which should be free from and immune to all kinds of human interference ? If even after these books had become contaminated, God had not revealed to the world a book which could be regarded as the very word of God, and protection of which from human interference could not be doubted, then we would have had to admit that God is not concerned to guide man and that He sows the seed of faith not in the soil which brings forth certainty and conviction but in the soil which brings forth uncertainty and doubt and that He wishes to confer upon belief not even the measure of certainty which disbelief enjoys. But can we entertain such a thought ? Is it worthy of God ? If it is not true, and it certainly is not true, that God is not concerned to guide man, then we have to look for the book which superseded the Bible and replaced this garbled and interpolated version of the word of God.

CONTRADICTIONS IN THE OLD TESTAMENT

Further internal evidence bearing on the proposition that books of the Bible no longer reproduce the original revelation is provided by the contradictions which exist between different parts of its text.

(1) For example in Genesis 1 : 27 we read :

> "So God created man in his own image."

And further on in 2 : 17 we read :

> "But of the tree of the knowledge of good and evil, thou shalt not eat of it."

These two quotations are contradictory. If they are to be reconciled, we have to assume that even God is ignorant of the knowledge of good and evil. Because Adam being the image of God, if he was ignorant of the knowledge of good and evil, then God also will have to be assumed as devoid of the power of discriminating good from evil, the possession of which, in fact, constitutes the highest divine attribute. All other attributes are subordinate to it. If man was incapable of distinguishing between good and evil, he was incapable of anything worthy. What is worthy and valuable is that which is done intentionally and out of full consciousness. What is done unintentionally and unconsciously is not morally valuable. If man is incapable of distinguishing between good and evil, then he is not a moral being, being unable either to choose good or to avoid evil.

Is God also devoid of this moral attribute according to Jewish and Christian scholars ? Does not God know what is good and what is evil ? If He does not know this, then why does He send the Prophets, and what does He seek to teach through them ? Is not God concerned to establish good and to destroy evil ? If we forget for the moment that the very object for which man has been created is that he should know good from evil, and if this knowledge is forbidden to him, then what need was there to create him ? If man could not have knowledge of good and evil, how could he be said to have been made in the image and likeness of God ? Without an insight into moral facts and moral distinctions man could not reproduce any likeness of God. If man was the image of God, it is wrong to think that he was forbidden to go near the tree of the knowledge of good and evil. If he was forbidden to go near the tree of knowledge of good and evil, then it is wrong to say that God created man in His own image.

(2) In Genesis 2 : 17 we read :

> For in the day that thou eatest thereof (the tree of the knowledge of good and evil) thou shalt surely die.

In Genesis 2 : 9 we read :

> And out of the ground made the Lord God to grow every tree that is pleasant to the sight, and good for food ; the tree of life also in the midst of the garden and the tree of knowledge of good and evil.

This verse can mean only one of two things : either that there was one tree which was capable of giving life as well as the knowledge of good and evil ; or that there were two trees, one with life-giving powers and the other which gave the knowledge of good and evil. If, according to the verse, there was but one tree, then Genesis 2 : 17 is proved false, because verse 9 endows the tree with life-giving powers, not with death-like properties. If, according to Genesis, there were two trees and not one, then these two verses become contradictory. If Adam had eaten of the tree of the knowledge of good and evil, death was not inevitable, because he could also have eaten of the life-giving tree. In fact, according to the Bible, when Adam ate of the tree of knowledge he could also have eaten of the life-giving tree. If the consequence of eating the fruit of one tree was certain death, the consequence of eating the fruit of the other tree was eternal life. The situation in which Adam was placed is hard to understand ; one tree offered him eternal life, another offered death.

We know from the Bible that Adam and his wife ate of the tree of life. We read in Genesis 3 : 2-3 :

> And the woman said unto the serpent, We may eat of the fruit of the trees of the garden : But of the fruit of the tree which is in the midst of the garden, God hath said, Ye shall not eat of it, neither shall ye touch it, lest ye die.

From these verses it appears that Adam and his wife ate the fruit of all trees except the tree of knowledge. If this account of the Bible is true, then Adam and his wife certainly ate the fruit of the tree of life, and if they did eat of this tree of life, how could they die? Yet we read in Genesis 3 : 22 :

> And the Lord God said, Behold, the man is become as one of us, to know good and evil : and now, lest he put forth his hand, and take also of the tree of life, and eat, and live for ever.

This verse shows that Adam had eaten nothing of the tree of life, and it is impossible for us to determine which of the verses is true. Is it the one which says that Adam did not eat of the tree of life or the one in which Adam's wife is reported to have said that, except the tree of knowledge, they ate of all the trees in the garden? Nor is it possible for us to say whether eating of the tree of knowledge results in certain death or eating of the tree of life results in eternal life.

All these statements contradict one another, and the word of God cannot contain such contradictions. It is certain that these statements were added to the Bible by writers who entertained contradictory ideas. A book which contains such contradictory statements cannot be attributed to an ordinary rational human being, much less to God. But Moses was an honoured Prophet of God, and the Torah was certainly a revelation of God received by him. We have, therefore, to assume that those contradictions are later additions. Because of them, no blame attaches to God or to Moses. Only we must say that when God decided to replace the Bible by a book of lasting value, He withheld His protection from the Bible and it was no longer safe from human interference and from the ravages of time.

(3) In Genesis 22 : 14 we read :

> And Abraham called the name of that place Jehovah-jireh : as it is said to this day, In the mount of the Lord it shall be seen.

But in Exodus 6 : 2-3 we read :

> And God spake unto Moses, and said unto him, I am the Lord, And I appeared unto Abraham, unto Isaac, and unto Jacob, by the name of God Almighty, and by my name JEHOVAH was I not known to them.

The contradiction between these two passages is obvious. The passage from Exodus says that the name Jehovah was first revealed to Moses. Before his time no Prophet, Abraham,

Isaac or Jacob, had his name revealed to him. But the passage from Genesis says that this name was revealed even to Abraham and that he named a mount after it Jehovah-jireh.

(4) Similarly in Numbers 33 : 38 we have :

> And Aaron the priest went up into mount Hor at the commandment of the Lord, and died there, in the fortieth year after the children of Israel were come out of the land of Egypt, in the first day of the fifth month.

But in Deuteronomy 10 : 6 we read :

> And the children of Israel took their journey from Beeroth of the children of Jaakan to Mosera ; there Aaron died, and there he was buried ; and Eleazar his son . . .

It is evident that one and the same person could not die in two different places. There can be no doubt that these two contradictory passages were entered in the Bible by two different scribes who have written down their own speculations in it and presented them as the word of God.

(5) In I Samuel 16 : 10-13 we read that David was the eighth son of Jesse :

> Again, Jesse made seven of his sons to pass before Samuel. And Samuel said unto Jesse, The Lord hath not chosen these. And Samuel said unto Jesse, Are here all thy children ? And he said, There remaineth yet the youngest, and behold, he keepeth the sheep. And Samuel said unto Jesse, Send and fetch him : for we will not sit down till he come hither. And he sent, and brought him in. Now he was ruddy, and withal of a beautiful countenance, and goodly to look to. And the Lord said, Arise, anoint him : for this is he. Then Samuel took the horn of oil, and anointed him in the midst of his brethren : and the Spirit of the Lord came upon David from that day forward. So Samuel rose up, and went to Ramah.

But in I Chronicles 2 : 13-15 we read that David was the seventh son of Jesse. Thus :

> And Jesse begat his first-born Eliab, and Abinadab the second, and Shimma the third, Nethaneel the fourth, Raddai the fifth, Ozem the sixth, David the seventh.

This contradiction also shows that historians of different persuasions have entered their views into the Bible, so that the Bible, as we know it today, cannot be regarded as a Book of God preserved in its original purity.

(6) In II Samuel 6 : 23 we read :

> "Therefore Michal the daughter of Saul had no child unto the day of her death."

But in II Samuel 21 : 8 we read :

> . . . and the five sons of Michal the daughter of Saul, whom she brought up for Adriel the son of Barzillai the Meholathite.

The same book describes Michal as childless in one place and the mother of five sons in another.

(7) Similarly in II Chronicles 21 : 19-20 we read that king Jehoram ascended the throne at the age of thirty-two, reigned for eight years, remained dethroned for two years and then died of some fearful disease, *i.e.*, he lived altogether for forty-two years. But in the same book (22 : 1-2) we read :

> And the inhabitants of Jerusalem made Ahaziah his youngest son king in his stead : for the band of men that came with the Arabians to the camp had slain all the eldest. So Ahaziah the son of Jehoram king of Judah reigned. Forty and two years old was Ahaziah when he began to reign, and he reigned one year in Jerusalem.

The first passage states quite clearly that Jehoram was forty-two years of age at the time of his death. But the second passage asserts that the youngest son of Jehoram, Ahaziah, was also forty-two when he ascended the throne on the death of his father. Were father and son of the same age and were the other sons of Jehoram, who were killed in battle by the Arabians, older than their father ? Can any rational human being make these contradictory statements ? The father dies at the age of forty-two years and his youngest son of the same age becomes king after him. Such statements will not be found even in an ordinary book, let alone a book revealed by God. There can be no doubt that these contradictions did not exist in the original revelation. They were not to be found in the utterances of the Prophets. Being contradictions they cannot be attributed to a single author. We have to assume that many authors entered their thoughts into the Book of God, hoping to have them treated as revelations. One author believed that Jehoram was forty-two years of age when he died ; so he wrote accordingly. Another thought that Jehoram was one hundred years of age at the time of his death, and at that time his youngest son was forty-two years of age; so he wrote accordingly. These statements are contradictory. We have to admit that the writer who believed that Jehoram died at forty-two did not believe his son Ahaziah to be also forty-two at the time of his father's death, but possibly only fourteen or fifteen. We have also to admit that the writer who believed Ahaziah to be forty-two years of age at the time of his enthronement did not believe that his father at that time was also forty-two years of age. The question is, what spiritual benefit can accrue from such a book? What faith or trust can such a book inspire in its readers? If the claim had been that the Torah is a collection of statements made by many hundreds of thousands of Jewish writers, even then the book would have possessed some value. But we find that, on the one hand, this book is offered as the very word of God, and that, on the other, it contains thousands of contradictions. This unwarranted claim on behalf of the Bible takes away even such value as it would have possessed, had no such claim been made on its behalf. Such a book cannot serve as a guide, and who can say that after such a book we did not need another?

SAVAGE TEACHING OF THE OLD TESTAMENT

Not only are there contradictions; we also find that occasionally the most savage teaching is attributed to the Bible, a teaching which cannot be attributed to a Beneficent and Merciful God.

(1) In Exodus 21 : 20-21 we read:

> And if a man smite his servant, or his maid, with a rod, and he die under his hand; he shall be surely punished. Notwithstanding, if he continue a day or two, he shall not be punished: for he is his money.

How severe is this teaching on slaves. A cruel man belabours his slave or bondwoman so much that the victim dies after one or two days. Yet the Bible does not award any punishment to this cruel man because slaves and bondwomen are their master's property. Could such a teaching endure for all time? Was it not deserving of supersession by a teaching which was to abolish the institution of slavery, which was to restrain the masters of human slaves from being cruel to them? This teaching was no doubt provided by Islam. Not only did Islam lay down laws for the abolition of slavery but also laid down the rule that slaves and bondwomen who failed to obtain their liberty were not to be treated harshly. On one occasion Abū Mas'ūd Anṣārī was beating a slave of his. From behind he heard a voice saying, "Abū Mas'ūd, the power which God has over you is much greater than the power which you have over this slave." Abū Mas'ūd turned back and saw the Holy Prophet approaching. His whip dropped out of his hand. He said, "O Prophet of God, I free this slave in the name of God". And the Prophet replied, "Had you not done so, the fire of Hell would have scorched your face" (Muslim: *Kitāb-al-Imān*). Similarly, another Companion of the Prophet says, "We were seven brothers and we had one bondwoman. The youngest of us gave her a slap on the face. The Holy Prophet on hearing of this ordered the release of this bondwoman, because, he said, a master who beats his slave is not fit to keep one." (Bukhārī; *Kitab al'-Itq*).

The Holy Prophet himself set a high example in this respect. On the occasion of his first marriage, his wife Khadīja made over to him all her property including all her slaves. The Prophet declared that he could not make a human being his slave and, saying this, he set at liberty all the slaves he had received as a present from his wife, and during the rest of his life he never kept a slave.

(2) In Leviticus 20: 27 we read:

> A man also or woman that hath a familiar spirit, or that is a wizard, shall surely be put to death: they shall stone them with stones; their blood shall be upon them.

Similarly in Exodus 22: 18 we read:

> "Thou shalt not suffer a witch to live."

How irrational is this teaching and how unjust if witchcraft here only means tricks performed by a class of professional entertainers. We should regard it as an innocent calling. In the busy and anxious lives that men often lead, fun and amusement provide welcome relief. It is then that these professional entertainers divert attention from serious pursuits to their own feats. To regard this innocent calling punishable with death is unjust. If magic and witchcraft call up the mystery man of fairy tales who transforms a man into a bull, a woman into a bird, then this teaching of the Bible is both stupid and savage. Such mystery men have never existed, and to accuse anybody of such impossible powers and then to order his death is extreme savagery.

(3) In Deuteronomy 7 : 2 we read :

> And when the Lord thy God shall deliver them before thee ; thou shalt smite them, and utterly destroy them ; thou shalt make no covenant with them, nor shew mercy unto them.

About a vanquished enemy how cruel is this teaching. To put to death all members of the enemy after their defeat, not to enter into any understanding with them and to refuse to show any mercy to them may be the conduct of cruel earthly kings. It cannot be attributed to a Beneficent and Merciful God.

Certainly such teaching must have been invented by unrelenting Jews who came after Moses and entered this teaching into the Bible and made it so foul.

IRRATIONAL TEACHING OF THE OLD TESTAMENT

The Old Testament contains many irrational statements.

(1) In Leviticus 11: 6 we read :

> And the hare, because he cheweth the cud, but divideth not the hoof ; he is unclean unto you.

Similarly, in Numbers 22 : 28 it is said that Balaam's ass talked to him.

In Genesis 46 : 27 we read that the number of the Israelites when they entered Egypt was three score and ten, but two hundred and fifteen years later, that is to say in the time of Moses, they had multiplied so much that the adult males alone numbered six hundred thousand. In Exodus 12 : 37 this is the claim made :

> And the children of Israel journeyed from Rameses to Succoth, about six hundred thousand on foot that were men beside children.

If, keeping in view the adult male population, we estimate the strength of the whole population, it turns out to be approximately twenty-five hundred thousand. But it would be a great exaggeration and against all reasonable probability. In two hundred and fifteen years a group of seventy souls could not grow into two million five hundred thousand. Historical facts also are against this estimate. When Moses migrated from Egypt to Canaan and had to go into the wilderness for forty years, what did this large population of two million five hundred thousand live on ? Could they have found in the wilderness food and drink enough to keep them alive for forty long years ? True, as the Bible says, they had quails and honey-dew sent to them from heaven' But even according to the Bible this sustenance from heaven descended only occasionally. How then did this large population obtain their food when it did not descend from heaven ?

We also learn from the Bible that the tribes obtained water each from one spring. But can we believe that two million five hundred thousand souls could obtain water enough for their needs from a few springs. The lands through which they passed contain no streams or rivulets. There are springs here and there, but a spring does not have any large dimensions. How can springs provide water for two million five hundred thousand souls ? A book which contained such irrational statements could not satisfy human intellect. No doubt it was a book from God. It was written by His Prophets. But it has lost its original character. It has become mutilated and has been changed out of all recognition. To regard a book which has suffered in this way as the very word of God is to invite ridicule against God and religion. It was but necessary that after such a book we should have had another which should be free from human interference and immune to irrational interpolation. About the number of Israel the Quran comes to our rescue and points out the truth. It says :

> Dost thou not know of those who went forth from their homes, and they were thousands, fearing death (2 : 244).

According to the Quran the people of Israel who fled from Egypt for fear of Pharaoh numbered a few thousand, and this seems but true because two million five hundred thousand Jews could not live in fear of small Palestinian tribes. In the best of days Palestine did not have a population of more than two or three million. Even modern Palestine has a population between a million and a million and a half. Any proposed additions to this population are resented intensely by the Arabs. In ancient times transport of food was unknown. Large populations could not be supported by lands which had no produce of their own. The population of Palestine could not be more than a few thousand. In the chronicles of wars between Israelites and their enemies their number did not amount to more than a few hundred or a few thousand. If Moses led two million and a half Israelites into Palestine, then quite apart from the days in the wilderness, even in normal times food enough for such large numbers could not be found. As for the opposition this large population confronted in Palestine, no war was needed to put an end to it. Their large numbers were enough to drive out the original population.

(2) Similarly we read in Exodus 32 : 1-6 :

> And when the people saw that Moses delayed to come down out of the mount, the people gathered themselves together unto Aaron, and said unto him, Up, make us gods, which shall go before us ; for as for this Moses, the man that brought us up out of the land of Egypt, we wot not what is become of him. And Aaron said unto them, Break off the golden ear-rings, which are in the ears of your wives, of your sons, and of your daughters, and bring them unto me. And all the people brake off the golden ear-rings which were in their ears, and brought them unto Aaron. And he received them at their hand, and fashioned it with a graving tool, after he had made it a molten calf : and they said, These be thy Gods, O Irsael, which brought thee up out of the land of Egypt. And when Aaron saw it, he built an altar before it ; and Aaron made proclamation, and said, Tomorrow is a feast to the Lord. And they rose up early on the morrow, and offered burnt offerings, and brought peace offerings ; and the people sat down to eat and to drink, and rose up to play.

It is inconceivable, however, that a person who has heard the voice of God should begin to attribute Godly powers to others. One who sees an elephant cannot regard it as a rat. One who sees the sun cannot regard it as a candle. A man who sees another man cannot regard him as a worm. No more is it possible for a Prophet who has seen God and heard His voice to regard a calf of gold as God. Such misjudgement we do not expect even from an insane person, let alone a Prophet of God. The rank and file of Israel were pardonable. They had not seen God nor had they heard His voice. They had heard only Moses and Aaron speak to them and had come to believe in what they heard. So they accepted whatever Samiri taught them about the golden calf. It is impossible, however, to exonerate Aaron. He had seen God and had heard His voice. How could he be fooled by Samiri and come to regard as God a calf of gold made by human hands ? Is it possible that the Omniscient God Who knows the inmost secrets of human hearts could have appointed for the reformation of Israel a man who was destined to prove as weak as Aaron did according to this account ? Even ordinary kings are capable of selecting good generals and viceroys, and it redounds to their credit if they do so ; yet no king can read the hearts of his generals. But according to the Bible, God knows all secrets and knows more than any man or any king. Yet He chose Aaron and entrusted to him the task of reforming the people and spoke to him and revealed Himself to him. But when Samiri presented his ungodly teaching to Aaron, Aaron submitted himself to this teaching and on a suggestion by his people made a calf of gold, placed it on an eminence and declared it to be their god ! Aaron forgot the true God for fear of his people, forgot what he had been charged with teaching, forgot his duty, forgot all his wisdom and, like an ignorant and superstitious man, began to bow his head before a lifeless object. Those who entered their speculations into the Bible must have possessed feeble minds. But the fact that they thought that those who came later would not be able to detect these interpolations defeats comprehension. It remains true, however, that after such serious interferences the Torah could not retain the status of a revealed book. It needed another book to bring out its absurdities and reassure the world that Aaron was not an ungodly or a superstitious person. That book is the Quran. It exonerated Aaron of the charge of ungodliness. Instead of being ungodly himself, he restrained his people from this foul tendency. We read in the Quran :

> And Aaron had said to them before : O my people, you have only been tried by means of it (the calf), and surely the Gracious

God is your Lord; so follow me and obey my command (20 : 91).

From this it is evident that even before Moses returned from Mount Sinai, Aaron had warned the Israelites that the calf of gold had been set up to mislead them, that the Lord was the God Who had provided them with all the goods of life even before they were born. He had told them that the calf had been made before their very eyes. It was up to them, therefore, to follow Aaron, to obey him and to shun all forms of ungodliness.

It is up to all reasonable persons to consider whether the book revealed to Moses should continue to command our faith, when it begins to contradict established truths and to inculcate irrational beliefs. Should we not look for a book which should tell us the truth about events of the time of Moses, even though it should come two thousand years after him.

(3) In Genesis 19 : 26 we read:

> "But his wife looked back from behind him, and she became a pillar of salt."

This seems like magic. Such an account is worthy of stories told to children about ghosts and fairies. They have no place in a Book of God. The account which the Quran has given of this incident steers clear of all superstition. It says:

> "She (Lot's wife) was of those who stayed behind" (7 : 84).

She was not converted into a pillar of salt or any such thing. Only she refused to go with Lot and sacrificed love of God to love of relations.

In the Quran are narrated events belonging to the time of Moses. The present Torah narrates them in a wrong manner but the Quran, coming two thousand years later, is able to correct these narratives. The errors which the Quran points out are readily acknowledged by reason.

PROPHETS DEFAMED BY THE BIBLE

There have also crept into the Bible statements which are immoral in their import. It seems impossible to attribute actions reported in them either to God or His Prophets.

(1) In Genesis 9 : 20-22 we read:

> And Noah began to be an husbandman, and he planted a vineyard: And he drank of the wine, and was drunken; and he was uncovered within his tent. And Ham, the father of Canaan, saw the nakedness of his father, and told his two brethren without.

This account presents Noah in a most unbecoming manner. According to it Noah planted a vineyard, drank the wine, was undressed in his tent, his son Ham saw him naked and told his brothers about it. The account is wholly uncomplimentary to Noah, and yet of Noah we read in Genesis 6 : 9 :

> "Noah was a just man and perfect in his generations, and Noah walked with God."

It is inconceivable that such a man would commit the indecency of becoming undressed before his own children. Then it offends our moral judgement to think that the indecency should be committed by Noah but curses should be heaped upon Ham. Ham's fault, even according to the Biblical account, was to see his father undressed and yet he hardly could do otherwise. When he found his father drunken and naked, he could not possibly avoid seeing him as such and yet according to the Bible Noah said, "Cursed be Canaan" (Genesis 9 : 25).

Actually Canaan is not to blame at all. Canaan was the son of Ham who committed the unavoidable indecency of seeing his naked father. Yet Noah had not a word to say in condemnation of Ham. He curses Canaan, who is not to blame at all. Is it because Ham was his son and Canaan his grandson! Such conduct offends our moral consciousness and cannot be attributed to a Prophet. To attribute it to a Prophet is a matter of shame for one who makes the attempt. We can well understand, however, that these things were not revealed to Moses by God, nor did Moses have them written down in his book. Jewish scholars who describe Prophets as thieves and robbers must have entered these things into the Book of Moses as a cover for their own sins. Their unholy interference with a Book of God made it necessary that God should reveal another book which should be free from the absurdities and falsehoods which had crept into the old.

(2) In Genesis 19 : 30–36 we read :

> And Lot went up out of Zoar, and dwelt in the mountain, and his two daughters with him; for he feared to dwell in Zoar: and he dwelt in a cave, he and his two daughters. And the firstborn said unto the younger, Our father is old, and there is not a man in the earth to come in unto us after the manner of all the earth. Come, let us make our father drink wine, and we will lie with him, that we may preserve seed of our father. And they made their father drink wine that night: and the firstborn went in, and lay with her father; and he perceived not when she lay down, nor when she arose. And it came to pass on the morrow, that the firstborn said unto the younger, Behold I lay yesternight with my father: let us make him drink wine this night also; and go thou in, and lie with him, that we may preserve seed of our father. And they made their father drink wine that night also: and the younger arose, and lay with him; and he perceived not when she lay down nor when she arose. Thus were both the daughters of Lot with child by their father.

No comment is necessary on this terrible narrative. It offends our sense both of the factual and the moral. But the present Torah does not hesitate to attribute this to a Prophet. From this we have to conclude that the Torah, as we know it today, is not the Torah revealed to Moses. It must have been composed later by Jewish scholars at a time when they had developed hatred for the sons, real or supposed, of Lot, Moab and Ammon. The faith of these Jewish scholars had become so weak, their hearts had become so hardened that to defame Moab and Ammon they did not hesitate to attribute to the Prophet Lot conduct which is reprehensible in the extreme and the attribution of which to any Prophet is entirely in-intolerable. Is the Christian and the Jewish world today prepared to hear such things attributed to the Prophets of God. If they are, it is only further evidence that we should have had a book which corrected the depraved mentality of our day.

(3) In Deuteronomy 25 : 5–6 we read:

> If brethren dwell together, and one of them die, and have no child, the wife of the dead shall not marry without unto a stranger: her husband's brother shall go in unto her, and take her to him to wife, and perform the duty of an husband's brother unto her. And it shall be, that the firstborn which she beareth shall succeed in the name of his brother which is dead, and his name be not put out of Israel.

This teaching is ridiculous and depraved in the extreme. It allows a widow to submit to her husband's brother and bear children who should succeed in the name of the deceased. Can children produced by one person perpetuate the name of another? If children born to one's brother can perpetuate one's name, what need is there for the brother to have marital relations with one's widow? If a brother's son can be treated as one's own son, there is no need to allow the brother to have immoral relations with one's wife. Far better would it have been for the Bible to declare that of the sons of the brother one may be attributed to the dead brother. This would have been reasonable enough. But it seems that as Jewish scholars invented a foul accusation against Lot, so God made them enter into the Torah an injunction the effects of which should recoil upon the Jewish scholars who had tried to defame Prophet Lot. God's vengeance was dire but well deserved. Jewish women were led by injunctions invented by Jewish scholars to do what Jewish doctors had attributed to Lot. These defects of the Old Testament clearly point to the need of a perfect book which should be free from these defects, and that book is the Quran.

THE NEW TESTAMENT EXAMINED

We have seen that the Old Testament has suffered interpolations and changes in form as well as matter. It is possible no longer to use it as a guide. Let us turn now to an examination of the New Testament.

The books collected into the New Testament do not constitute the utterances of Jesus nor of his disciples. Jesus was a Jew and so were his disciples. If any of Jesus' utterances were to be found preserved in their originality, they could only be in the Hebrew language. So also with the utterances of his disciples. But no copy of the New Testament in ancient Hebrew exists in the world. The old copies are all in Greek. Christian writers try to cover this grave defect by saying that in the time of Jesus the language in general use was Greek. This is impossible for more reasons than one. Nations do not easily give up their language. It is for them as valuable an inheritance as any property or other possession. In Eastern Europe there are people who for three or four hundred years have lived under Russian rule, but their languages remain intact to this day. France has ruled over Morocco and Spain over Algiers for a long time. Yet the language of these subject peoples is still Arabic. Two thousand years have passed since the time of Jesus. Yet the Jews have not forgotten their language. Even today in parts of Europe and America, Jews speak Yiddish, a corrupt form of ancient Hebrew. If this long time spent amongst other peoples has not destroyed the Jewish language, could a brief association with the Romans destroy it? Let us remember that Roman rule in Palestine had begun only about fifty years before the advent of Jesus. This is not long enough for a people to forget their language. But there are other important considerations also to be kept in view:

(*i*) Nations which attain to any importance in history do not give up their language, and the Jews were a very important people indeed.

(*ii*) The religion of the jews was recorded in Hebrew, and for this reason particularly, it was impossible for them to give up their language.

(*iii*) In the scale of civilization and refinement, the Jews did not regard themselves as inferior to the Romans, but rather superior, and this must have made them proud of their language and reluctant to give it up.

(*iv*) The Jews entertained hope for the return of their political power. Nations which fear the future become pessimistic and therefore tend to lose pride in their language. But the Jews in the time of Jesus were awaiting the advent of their King who was to re-establish Jewish rule. Looking forward to such a future, they could not have been so negligent in protecting their language.

(*v*) Jewish authors of that time wrote in their own language or in some corrupt form of it. If their language had changed, we should have had books of the time written in a language other than Hebrew.

(*vi*) The oldest manuscripts of the New Testament are in Greek. But in the time of Jesus, the Roman Empire had not become divided into two halves. The centre of the Empire was still Rome. The Roman and Greek languages are very difficult. If Roman influence had at all penetrated Jewish life, it should have resulted in the assimilation of Latin (and not Greek) words into the Hebrew language. Yet the oldest manuscripts of the Gospels are all in Greek. This proves that the Gospels were written down at a time when the Roman Empire had become divided and its eastern possessions had become part of the Greek Empire, so that the Greek language had begun to exert its influence on Christianity and its literature.

(*vii*) Phrases such as the following which are preserved in the Gospels in their original form are all Hebrew phrases.

(1) "Hosanna" (Matthew 21 : 9);
(2) "Eli, Eli, Lama Sabachthani" (Matthew 27 : 46);
(3) "Rabbi" (John 3 : 2);
(4) "Talitha cumi" (Mark 5 : 41).

(*viii*) From The Acts (2 : 4–13) it appears that even after the crucifixion, Jews spoke Hebrew :

> And they were all filled with the Holy Ghost and began to speak with other tongues, as the Spirit gave them utterance. And there were dwelling at Jerusalem Jews, devout men, out of every nation under heaven. Now when this was noised abroad, the multitude came together, and were confounded, because that every man heard them speak in his own language. And they were all amazed and marvelled, saying one to another, Behold, are not all these which speak Galilaeans ? And how hear we, every man in our own tongue, wherein we were born ? Parthians, and Medes, and Elamites, and the dwellers in Mesopotamia, and in Judaea, and Cappadocia, in Pontus, and Asia, Phrygia, and Pamphylia, in Egypt, and in the parts of Libya about Cyrene, and in strangers of Rome, Jews and proselytes, Cretans and Arabians, we do hear them speak in our tongues the wonderful works of God. And they were all amazed, and were in doubt, saying one to another, What meaneth this ? Others mocking said, These men are full of new wine.

It is evident that at this time the language spoken in Palestine was Hebrew. Speaking any other language was extraordinary. Among the names mentioned is Rome, which means that the Roman language was not spoken in Palestine and whoever spoke it seemed a stranger. We are not concerned here with the merits of the narrative but we only wish to point out that this passage from The Acts proves conclusively that even after the crucifixion the language of the Jews was Hebrew. Those who knew other languages were exceptions. When some of the disciples spoke these other languages—among them Latin, some people thought they were drunk and talking nonsense. If the country as a whole used Roman or Greek, no such reaction was possible.

It is clear, therefore, that the language which Jesus and his disciples spoke was Hebrew, not Latin or Greek. So copies of the New Testament written down in Latin or Greek must have been written down long after the time of Jesus, at a time when Christianity had begun to penetrate into Roman territory and Roman imperialist power had become divided into the Italian and Greek parts. Books of this kind, composed one or two hundred years after Jesus by unknown authors and attributed by them to Jesus and his disciples, can be of little use to any believer today. It was necessary, therefore, that we should have had another book sent to us from Heaven, free from these defects and one which readers could regard with certainty as the very word of God.

JESUS' OWN ADMISSION

Jesus declares clearly that he had come not to destroy but to fulfil the older books. Thus in Matthew (5 : 17–18) we read :

> Think not that I am come to destroy the law, or the prophets : I am not come to destroy, but to fulfil. For verily I say unto you, Till heaven and earth pass, one jot or one tittle shall in no wise pass from the law, till all be fulfilled.

From this it is evident that the mission of Jesus was to restore Mosaic teaching, but the New Testament as we have it today teaches that the Mosaic teaching was abrogated completely by Jesus. It is quite clear, therefore, that the present New Testament is not what Jesus taught and preached. The teaching of Jesus must have been a reproduction of the teaching of Moses, except for what the Scribes and Pharisees had themselves added to it. But the New Testament seeks to correct not only what the Scribes and Pharisees had invented but also what Moses and subsequent Prophets had taught in their time.

This position is contradictory. One part of the New Testament teaches one thing, another part quite another. When a book contradicts itself, it cannot be the work of the same author, at any rate, of a sane author. The books of the New Testament are said to have been dictated by the disciples of Jesus, and we cannot say that the disciples were not sane. The great disciples of Prophets always possess a high degree of sanity. We must, therefore, conclude that the disciples did not dictate any such thing. They talked as they went about. Those who heard them passed on the substance of what they heard to others. When these others sat down to record what they had heard, they added many of their own thoughts. The result was the New Testament as we know it today, a bundle of contradictions.

TESTIMONY OF CHRISTIAN SCHOLARS

After citing the internal evidence on the confused character of the New Testament, we cite the testimony of Christian scholars :

(*i*) In the commentary of the Bible by Horn (1882) we have that the facts relating to the composition of the Gospels, which have reached us from the ancient historians of the Church, are so uncertain and so slender that no definite conclusion can be drawn from them. Even the best authorities seem to accept as gospel truth the speculations current in their time, and, out of sheer reverence, those who come after accept their authority. The narratives, partly false and partly true, pass from one writer to another and after a time begin to be treated as though they were above criticism. (Vol. 4, Pt. 2, chap. 2).

(*ii*) In the same volume we have that the first Gospel seems to have been recorded in the year 37 or 38 or 41 or 43 or 48 or 61–62 or 64 A.D. ; the second at any time from 56 to 65 A.D., probably between 60 and 63 ; the third in 53 or 63 or 64 ; and the fourth in 68 or 69 or 70 or 97 or 98 A.D. The evidence with regard to the Epistle to the Hebrews, the second Epistle of Peter and the second and third Epistles of John, the Epistle of James and the Epistle of Jude, the Revelation of St. John the divine and the first Epistle of

John, is so confused that we had better not speak of it. These have been attributed to the disciples without any sound reasons.

(*iii*) Eusebius in his *History of the Church* writes that the first Epistle of Peter is genuine. His second Epistle has never been part of the Holy Book, but has been current in reading (Vol. 4, chap. 3).

(*iv*) In the same book (ch. 25) we read that the Epistle of James and the Epistle of Jude and the second Epistle of Peter and the second and third Epistles of John have all been held in great doubt. It is not known whether these were composed by the writers of the Gospels or by others with their names.

(*v*) In the Encyclopaedia Biblica (Vol. iv. p. 4980) we have :

> The NT was written by Christians for Christians ; it was moreover written in Greek for Greek-speaking communities, and the style of writing (with the exception, possibly, of the Apocalypse) was that of current literary composition. There has been no real break in the continuity of the Greek-speaking Church and we find accordingly that few real blunders of writing are met with in the leading types of the extant texts. This state of things has not prevented variations ; but they are not for the most part accidental. An overwhelming majority of the 'various readings' of the MSS of the NT were from the very first intentional alterations. The NT in very early times had no canonical authority, and alterations and additions were actually made where they seemed improvements.

That is to say, the New Testament was written by Christians for Christians. Moreover, it was written in Greek for Greek-speaking peoples, and the style was in keeping with current taste. There has been no break in the continuity of the Greek-speaking Church. There are, therefore, no serious errors of transcription in the current versions, though we cannot say there are not contradictions. The contradictions, however, are not accidental, but deliberate. It seems that from the very beginning some authors entered these alterations into the text of the New Testament.

The truth seems to be that the new Testament in the beginning was not regarded seriously as a revealed book. Improvements were, therefore, made unhesitatingly wherever these seemed possible.

(*vi*) Again we read :

> What is certain is that by the middle of the fourth century, Latin biblical MSS exhibited a most confusing variety of text, caused at least in part by revision from later Greek MSS as well as by modifications of the Latin phraseology. This confusion lasted until all the 'Old Latin' texts were supplanted by the revised version of Jerome (383–400 A.D.) which was undertaken at the request of Pope Damasus and ultimately became the Vulgate of the Western Church (Enc. Bib. p. 4993, Vol. IV).

What is absolutely certain, is, that in the middle of the fourth century, the Latin copy of the Bible was in a most confused state. The confusion was the result of a comparison with the Greek copy and of a change in Latin terminology. These confusions remained until Jerome's revised version, prepared under orders of the Pope between 383 and 400 A.D., took the place of the old Latin version among Christians.

(*vii*) Similarly we have :

> More important than these external matters are the variations which in course of time crept into the text itself. Many of these variations were mere slips of the eye, ear, memory, or judgement on the part of a copyist, who had no intention to do otherwise than follow what lay before him. But transcribers, especially early transcribers, by no means aimed at that minute accuracy which is expected of a modern critical editor. Corrections were made in the interest of grammar or of style. Slight changes were adopted in order to remove difficulties, additions came in, especially from parallel narratives in the Gospels, citations from the Old Testament were made more exact or more complete. That all this was done in perfect good faith, and simply because no strict conception of the duty of a copyist existed, is especially clear from the almost entire absence of deliberate falsification of the text in the interests of doctrinal controversy. It may suffice to mention, in addition to what has been already said, that glosses, or notes originally written on the margin, very often ended by being taken into the text, and that the custom of reading the Scriptures in public worship naturally brought in liturgical additions, such as the doxology of the Lord's Prayer ; while the commencement of an ecclesiastical lesson torn from its proper context had often to be supplemented by a few explanatory words, which soon came to be regarded as part of the original (Enc. Brit. 12th edition, p. 646, Vol. III).

(*viii*) Again we have :

> It appears from what we have already seen, that a considerable portion of the NT is made up of writings not directly apostolic (Enc. Brit. 12th edition, p. 643, Vol. III).

(*ix*) And again :

> Yet, as a matter of fact, every book in the NT, with the exception of the four great Epistles of St. Paul, is at present more or less the subject of controversy, and interpolations are asserted even in these (Enc. Brit. 12th edition, p. 643, Vol. III).

(*x*) The New Testament is not free even today from interpolations and alterations. As examples we have the following :

(1) In John (5 : 2–5) we had :

> Now there is at Jerusalem by the sheep market a pool, which is called in the Hebrew tongue Bethesda, having five porches. In these lay a great multitude of impotent folk, of blind, halt, withered, waiting for the moving of the water. For an angel went down at a certain season into the pool, and troubled the water : whosoever then first after the troubling of the water stepped in was made whole of whatsoever disease he had. And a certain man was there, which had an infirmity thirty and eight years. When Jesus saw him lie, and knew that he had been now a long time in that case, said he unto him, Wilt thou be made whole ?

For hundreds of years we had this account reproduced in the Gospels. Nobody ever thought that it was unreliable. But when there began controversies between the Muslims and the Christians in the nineteenth century, verse 4 and part of v. 3 were deleted from the above passage in the Revised Version published in 1881, out of fear of Muslim criticism, and it was noted on the margin that many ancient authorities insert, wholly, or in part, the words deleted from the text. The question is, when this portion was found in many ancient authorities, why was the change made. Moreover, the very fact that a certain verse is found in certain copies and is missing in others is a proof of the fact that the original text has been tampered with. There can be only two alternatives. Either we will have to admit that the verse was not found in the original text. In that case, we will have to conclude that certain scribes took the liberty of introducing the words on their own account. Or we will have to admit that the verse did exist in the original text. In that case we will have to infer that certain scribes intentionally expunged the verse from the text. In both cases the text will be considered as having been tampered with.

(2) In I John (5 : 7–8) we had :

> For there are three (that bear record in heaven, the Father, the word, and the Holy Ghost : and these three are one and there are three) that bear witness (in earth), the spirit, and the water, and the blood : and these three agree in one.

The above passage formed part of the New Testament for centuries, but when the Christians entered into conflict with the Muslims and the latter began to hurl attacks at such passages, the former altered the text of their sacred Scriptures and the words within brackets were expunged from the Revised Version published in 1881. Now the question is, if the words so expunged did not form part of the original text and were introduced into the text by somebody, it means that in 1881 Christian scholars admitted that Christian Scriptures had been subject to interpolations. But if the old copies were correct and the present change has been made in the text for expediency's sake, it means that process of tampering with the Christian Scriptures still continued.

(3) In Matthew (17 : 14–21) we have :

> And when they were come to the multitude, there came to him a certain man, kneeling down to him, and saying, Lord, have mercy on my son : for he is lunatic, and sore vexed : for oft times he falleth into the fire, and oft into the water. And I brought him to thy disciples, and they could not cure him. Then Jesus answered and said, O faithless and perverse generation, how long shall I be with you ? how long shall I suffer you ? bring him hither to me. And Jesus rebuked the devil ; and he departed out of him : and the child was cured from that very hour. Then came the disciples to Jesus apart, and said, Why could not we cast him out ? And Jesus said unto them, Because of your unbelief : for verily I say unto you, If ye have faith as a grain of mustard seed, ye shall say unto this mountain, Remove hence to yonder place ; and it shall remove ; and nothing shall be impossible unto you. Howbeit this kind goeth not out but by prayer and fasting.

Christian exponents seem to be convinced that after faith in

Jesus, nothing further is required in the way of good works, to attain the pleasure and love of God. But from the passage of Matthew quoted above it appears that this great end cannot be achieved except by prayer and fasting. Prayer and fasting, therefore, are important instruments for the assimilation of the grace of God. Because the disciples of Jesus did not make use of these instruments, they were unable, according to the Gospel narrative, to cast out a bad spirit, in spite of the fact that they had declared faith in Jesus. Muslim critics used this passage for a vital criticism. They said that mere faith in Jesus was not enough. Good works were also necessary and Jesus himself had stressed the importance of prayer and fasting, and had made use of them as instruments of spiritual advancement. If prayer and fasting were also necessary, then faith in Jesus could not be enough, and could not release man from the obligation to do good. This criticism was so vital that Christian exponents found themselves unable to give any reply. The only way of escape they found was in deleting the verse from the Gospel. Accordingly, in the Revised Version of the Gospel according to Matthew, we do not find this verse at all. The whole verse has been deleted and it has been proved that the Gospel text is still subject to human interference.

It is said that in Mark (9 : 29) the word 'prayer' is still retained ; and that if the change had been made from any bad motive, the word 'prayer' should not have been retained in Mark. But this plea does not hold good. Muslim criticism was not based on the word 'prayer', for prayer is still offered by Christians. The objection was based on the word 'fasting'. The verse that has been deleted showed that Jesus was in the habit of fasting and that he looked upon fasting as necessary for spiritual advancement ; so the Law could not be regarded as a curse. In order to avoid this criticism, the whole verse was deleted from Matthew and the word 'fasting' was deleted from Mark. It is also possible that one party of the revisers thought it necessary to omit the whole verse, while another party thought it sufficient to omit only the word 'fasting'.

CONTRADICTIONS IN THE NEW TESTAMENT

Then there are contradictions in the Gospel accounts and such contradictions also prove that the Gospels do not constitute a revelation of God or that human interference has changed the original revelation out of all recognition. Any ordinary author possessing an ordinary measure of consistency will not allow contradictions in what he writes. How then can we tolerate contradictions in a Book of God ? We give here some examples :

(*i*) With regard to the birth of Jesus we find from Matthew (1 : 1–22) and Luke (1 : 32–33) that the Messiah was to be one of ordinary human beings. Only, he was to be called son of God. From the Gospel of John (1 : 1), however, we find that the Messiah is the word which was ever with God and was, in fact, God, so that all have been made out of him.

(*ii*) From Matthew (3 : 13–17), Mark (1 : 9–12) and Luke (3 : 21, 22 and 4 : 1) it appears that Jesus received baptism from John and after receiving baptism from him, he left him at once or on the same day. But in the Gospel of John there is no mention of any baptism and the meeting between Jesus and John is said to have lasted two days.

(*iii*) From John (1 : 19–44) it appears that Jesus after remaining with John and his disciples for a few days went straight to Galilee. But from Matthew (4 : 1), Mark (1 - 12) and Luke (4 : 1), it appears that Jesus, after receiving baptism from John, went to the woods to have a trial of strength with Satan, and remained there for forty days.

(*iv*) From John (1 : 35–51) it appears that, soon after meeting John, Jesus made two of John's disciples, one Andrew and the other un-named, his own disciples and on the way to Galilee he made Simon Peter and Nathanael his disciples. But from Matthew (4 : 12–22), Mark (1 : 12–20) and Luke (4 : 14–15 ; 5 : 1–11) it appears that, after meeting John and remaining for forty days in the woods Jesus fasted, and on hearing of the imprisonment of John went to Galilee, and preached there in many places and for many days, and beside the lake at Galilee he admitted Simon Peter, Andrew, John and James as his disciples. That is to say, the place where, according to the Gospel of John, these persons were admitted as his disciples by Jesus is not the place where, according to the other Gospels, the admission of these disciples took place. The time also at which the admission took place according to John is not the time given by the other Gospels. The other Gospels put the time about two months later.

(*v*) In John (4 : 3 and 43–45) we are given to understand that the native place of Jesus was Judaea, and that Jesus, believing that a Prophet is not honoured in his native place, left it for Galilee where he was much honoured. But, in contradiction to this, in Matthew (13 : 54–58), Luke (4 : 24) and Mark (6 : 4) we are told that the native place of Jesus was not Judaea but Galilee. Not honoured in Galilee, he said, no Prophet had been honoured in his own place.

(*vi*) In John (3 : 22–26 and 4 : 1–3) we are told that even before John was put in prison, Jesus had started preaching his Message and baptizing people. But in Matthew (4 : 12–17) and Mark (1 : 14–15), we are told that Jesus started preaching after John's imprisonment.

(*vii*) According to Luke (3 : 23) Joseph, the husband of Mary, was the son of Heli ; but according to Matthew (1 : 16) he was the son of Jacob.

(*viii*) According to Luke (3 : 31) Jesus descended from David through Nathan but Matthew (1 : 6) traces the ancestry of Jesus through Nathan's brother, Solomon the King.

(*ix*) In the genealogy given by Matthew we have from Joseph to Abraham forty-one persons, but in the genealogy given by Luke we have fifty-six persons. Besides this, the names also in the two genealogies do not correspond.

(*x*) In Luke (24 : 50–51) we are told that Jesus was carried up into heaven at Bethany. But in The Acts (1 : 12) we read that the ascension took place on a mount called Olivet.

(*xi*) Luke (24 : 21–29, 36 and 51) says that on the day on which Jesus rose from the dead, or the night following, he ascended to the sky. But in The Acts (1 : 3) we read that Jesus ascended to the sky forty days after he rose from the dead.

(*xii*) In Matthew (10 : 10) we read that Jesus told his disciples to provide "nor script for your journey, neither two coats, neither shoes nor yet staves", but Mark (6 : 8–9) says that Jesus told his disciples that they should take nothing for their journey save a staff only. Mark, however, admits that Jesus ordered the disciples to be shod with sandals. From this it appears that according to Matthew, Jesus forbade the wearing even of shoes and the carrying of staves but according to Mark the disciples had orders to carry staves and to wear shoes.

SUPERSTITIONS IN THE GOSPELS

A study of the New Testament shows that it is not free from the element of superstition.

(*i*) In Mark (1 : 12–13) we have :

> And immediately the spirit driveth him into the wilderness. And he was therein the wilderness forty days, tempted of Satan ; and was with the wild beasts ; and the angels ministered unto him.

The incidents recorded here are nothing but delusions. The laws of God are against them. On this earth man lives in the company of men and not in that of animals or satans or angels. It is inconceivable that the laws of God were different at that time. We do not have satans living visibly with men in this world, nor do we find angels doing visible service for men. To witness such things in dreams and visions is a different matter. Such experiences were had by persons in the past, and they can be had even today. But neither did we in the past nor do we at the present time have human beings living with animals such as wolves and lions. Nor do we have Satan coming to a human being and carrying him off with him, so that the man follows him and obeys him against his will, rebelling only occasionally. Nor do we have angels coming and doing such services as baking bread, cooking and fetching water. In fairy tales we do have such accounts, but what place can they have in a religious book ? If the New Testament were a book like Kipling's *Jungle Book*, it would have been a different matter altogether. But the New Testament is a book for the religious guidance of man. What use can such a book have for fairy tales of this kind ? Jesus was a virtuous and pious man. We cannot attribute such a fantastic thing to him. He was an honoured Prophet of God and was sent for the guidance of his people. It is impossible that he should have taught such things. It is impossible that his teaching should have upset the mental balance of his followers and driven them from the path of reason into the morass of superstition. We are constrained, therefore, to say that these superstitious elements were added to the Gospels at some later time. Jesus is not responsible for them, nor are his disciples. The responsibility for the introduction of these superstitions into the text of the Gospels lies on those Christians who came later, who were no longer spiritually sensitive, and who preferred popular applause to strict truth.

(*ii*) In Mark (5 : 1–14) we read :

> And they came over unto the other side of the sea, into the country of the Gadarenes. And when he was come out of the ship, immediately there met him out of the tombs a man with an unclean spirit, who had his dwelling among the tombs ; and no man could bind him, no, not with chains : because that he had been often bound with fetters and chains, and the chains had been plucked asunder by him, and the fetters broken in pieces : neither could any man tame him. And always night and day, he was in the mountains, and in the tombs, crying, and cutting himself with stones. But when he saw Jesus afar off, he ran and worshipped him, and cried with a loud voice, and said, What have I to do with thee, Jesus, thou Son of the Most High God ? I adjure thee by God, that thou torment me not. For he said unto him, Come out of the man, thou unclean spirit. And he asked him, What is thy name ? And he answered, saying, My name is Legion : for we are many. And he besought him much that he would not send them away out of the country. Now there was there nigh unto the mountains a great herd of swine feeding. And all the devils besought him, saying, Send us into the swine, that we may enter into them. And forthwith Jesus gave them leave. And the unclean spirits went out, and entered into the swine : and the herd ran violently down a steep place into the sea (they were about two thousand) ; and were choked in the sea. And they that fed the swine fled, and told it in the city, and in the country. And they went out to see what it was that was done.

This passage contains so many superstitious ideas that the reader is left wondering as to how they ever crept into the Gospel account. We are told, firstly, that a man had become so violently insane that he could not be held by the strongest chains. Medical science and ordinary human experience belie such a statement. There certainly can be chains strong enough to hold and restrain the most violent maniac. Did not people in those days know how to make chains strong enough to hold human beings ?

Secondly, we are told in this passage that the maniac would cut himself with stones. Such a thing is most amazing. For years apparently, a man goes on cutting himself with stones and yet he does not die.

Thirdly, we are told that Jesus addressed this man, saying, "Come out of the man, thou unclean spirit." Such a thing would only be said by persons entrapped in primitive and ignorant ways. It would not be said by a Prophet. If unclean spirits could ever enter human beings, why do we not see such phenomena today ? Have we no means of tracing unclean spirits ? True, medical science today identifies mental diseases as neurasthenia, hysteria, insanity and so on, but medical science attributes them to other factors, not to unclean spirits. The Gospel account, however, tells us that a rational, truthful, person like Jesus thought that when a person goes mad it is because an unclean spirit enters him. To attribute such a superstitious thought to a Prophet seems cruel to us. It is to project one's own superstitions on to a great Teacher. Jesus himself could never have said such a thing. Nor could his disciples. It is certainly a fabrication of later times.

But the superstitious thought is deepened further. We are told that Jesus asked the unclean spirit his name, and the spirit answered, "My name is Legion : for we are many." That is to say, it was not one spirit but an army of them.

We are told further that the spirits begged Jesus not to send them away out of the country. But Jesus did not agree, upon which the evil spirits begged him to send them into a herd of swine, that they might enter into them. To this Jesus readily agreed. The unclean spirits then went away and entered into the swine and the herd ran violently down a precipice into the sea. And in this way two thousand of them were drowned.

How superstitious and stupid does this passage seem ! We are told that the evil spirits wanted leave to quit the body of man and enter into the swine. A further question is : This herd of swine must have been somebody's property and what right did Jesus have to destroy another man's property ? If it is said that the son of God had right over all manner of property, then the question is, why call God the God of love ? If God as Master of everything can destroy things in the possession of ordinary human beings, then what law or order do we have in the world ? And what evidence do we have for the beneficence of God ?

Besides this, there is another serious superstition taught in this passage. We are told that when the evil spirits entered into the swine, the swine ran over a steep precipice into the sea. The question is, why this difference of behaviour ? When the evil spirits entered a man, he did not hurl himself into the sea. But when they entered into a herd of two thousand swine, they all ran into the sea and died. The whole passage is superstitious and stupid. Anybody who is convinced of the greatness and rationality of Jesus cannot attribute these things to him or to his disciples. He will have to conclude that such passages have been added to the New Testament account by later writers.

(*iii*) It appears from the New Testament account that Jesus used to restore the dead to life. Thus in John (11 : 43–44) we read :

> And when he thus had spoken, he cried with a loud voice, Lazarus, come forth. And he that was dead came forth, bound hand and foot with grave-clothes : and his face was bound with a napkin. Jesus saith unto them, Loose him, and let him go.

Similarly in Matthew (27 : 51–53) we have :

> And, behold, the veil of the temple was rent in twain from the top to the bottom ; and the earth did quake, and the rocks rent ; and the graves were opened ; and many bodies of the saints which slept arose, and came out of the graves after his resurrection, and went into the holy city, and appeared unto many.

Can any rational being be persuaded to believe these accounts ? If the dead could ever be restored to life, why not today ? If it is said that this was the special prerogative of Jesus, our reply is that this is not true because Jesus himself said that if his followers had faith as small as a grain of mustard seed, they would be able to show Signs greater than those shown by him.

We have in John (14 : 12–14) :

> Verily, verily, I say unto you, he that believeth on me, the works that I do shall he do also ; and greater works than these shall he do ; because I go unto my Father. And whatsoever ye shall ask in my name, that will I do, that the Father may be glorified in the Son. If ye shall ask anything in my name, I will do it.

The question is, can Christians today restore the dead to life.

(*iv*) In Matthew (14 : 25–27) we have :

> And in the fourth watch of the night Jesus went unto them, walking on the sea. And when the disciples saw him walking on the sea, they were troubled, saying, It is a spirit ; and they cried out for fear. But straightway Jesus spake unto them, saying, Be of good cheer ; it is I ; be not afraid.

This also is rank superstition. What man can ever walk on water ?

(*v*) in Luke (11 : 24–26) we have :

> When the unclean spirit is gone out of a man, he walketh through dry places, seeking rest ; and finding none, he saith, I will return unto my house whence I came out. And when he cometh, he findeth it swept and garnished. Then goeth he, and taketh to him seven other spirits more wicked than himself ; and they enter in, and dwell there ; and the last state of that man is worse than the first.

What abject superstition is this ? What possible meaning can such accounts have ? Can they be attributed to a man like Jesus ? To tell a lie is bad enough. To coin a superstition is about as bad. But to attribute lies and superstitions to God and His Prophets is cruel. The unwary and ignorant writers of the Gospels have been responsible for perpetrating this cruelty. In doing so, they have ruined the Gospels and made them unworthy as religious books.

DOUBTFUL ETHICS OF THE NEW TESTAMENT

(*i*) In Mark (11 : 12–14) we have :

> And on the morrow, when they were come from Bethany, he was hungry : and seeing a fig tree afar off having leaves, he came, if haply he might find anything thereon : and when he came to it, he found nothing but leaves ; for the time of figs was not yet. And Jesus answered and said unto it, No man eat fruit of thee hereafter for ever. And his disciples heard it.

From this it appears that (*a*) Jesus who lived in a country where the fig tree was to be found in abundance did not know when figs were in season ; (*b*) he was, it seems, so devoid of good manners that instead of being sorry for his own mistake, he proceeded to curse a lifeless tree, saying, "No man eat fruit of thee hereafter." We Muslims do not believe Jesus to be God. We regard him only as a Prophet of God. But even we cannot believe that he could have said what is here attributed to him. We cannot but be amazed at those who regard him as the son of God, and as the best exemplar of morals, and who yet tolerate these descriptions which attribute unmannerly conduct to him. They never stop to think whether such things could ever be said by Jesus and whether they were not wrongly attributed to him by others.

Christian apologists today tend to explain away this passage. They suggest that the curse applies not to the fig tree but to the Jewish nation and only means that Jews hereafter will not be able to bring forth any fruit. The explanation is lame. Those who are conversant with ordinary literary forms cannot be impressed by such explanations. If the fig tree was to be used as metaphor, was it necessary that Jesus should have walked up to one, at a time when he was suffering from hunger ? According to the passage in Mark, Jesus saw the fig tree full of leaves, and he decided to go near it, hoping he would find some fruit. It was after he had seen it closely and found nothing but leaves (the time of figs had not yet come) that he cursed the tree. Jesus, in short, goes to the tree to satisfy his hunger. The tree has leaves on it and Jesus hopes to find some fruit. The narrator adds that the time of figs had not yet come. All this shows that this incident was not meant as a metaphor. The narrator makes it quite clear that Jesus went to the tree because he was hungry, and was hoping to find some fruit. But the time of fruit had not yet come. It is possible that this particular tree was late in yielding fruit, or that it suffered from some disease and failed to yield fruit. Jesus, however, became annoyed and cursed the tree. If all this is correctly reported, have we not reason to ask whether those who curse inanimate objects like trees, rivers, mountains or stones, can be regarded as rational beings ? Did the writer who attributed this to

Jesus think that generations of readers who would come after would swallow this caricature of a sane and decent person like Jesus. Christian devotees may be fooled by such a narrative, but we Muslims cannot attribute these things to Jesus, not because he was in any way different from the other Prophets, but because we do not expect such things from even ordinary decent and well-behaved persons.

(*ii*) In Matthew (7 : 6) we have :

> Give not that which is holy unto the dogs, neither cast ye your pearls before swine, lest they trample them under their feet, and turn again and rend you.

What is here described as "holy" and as "pearls" is really the revelation and Signs of God. "Dogs" and "swine" in the verse mean the people who had refused to believe in Jesus. There is no doubt that the Signs of God are holier than the holiest things. They are more precious than pearls. But there is no doubt either that things which are holy and precious as pearls are meant just for those who are devoid of them. Signs of God have to be shown to those who are devoid of faith in Him. The Prophets do not bring faith only to those who already have it. This is apparent from history that Prophets have never appeared except in time of great disbelief. They have appeared only when the world is enwrapped in darkness, and their mission is to guide the world from darkness to light. Their Message is addressed to those groping in the dark. It is for them that they come into the world. It does not seem possible that a beloved of God should describe as dogs and swine those whose only fault is that the light of faith has not yet dawned upon them. It is impossible that a Prophet should say that the Signs of God should not be narrated to disbelievers for fear lest they trample them under their feet. If a Prophet were to say such a thing, how will disbelievers ever come to believe ? The attribution of such a saying to Jesus is cruel. It amounts to saying that the very people for whom he had come were described by him as dogs and swine and this for no fault of theirs, nor for any mischief which they had committed, but only because the truth had not yet become manifest to them. Contrast with this the example of the Holy Prophet of Islam. In the Quran (26 : 4) we read :

"Maybe thou wilt kill thyself by over-exertion in thy work because they believe not."

The verse describes how anxious the Prophet was to take his Message to all disbelievers. If we contrast the Jesus of the Gospels with the Holy Prophet of Islam, we find a world of difference. One is prepared to work himself to death for the sake of those who will not believe ; the other would turn away from them, calling them dogs and swine and ordering his disciples not to recite the Signs of God to them.

There is no doubt that the Holy Prophet of Islam transcends all the other Prophets in his moral example. But we cannot believe that Jesus was as devoid of good morals as the Gospels make him out to be. True, he had not reached the spiritual heights which the Holy Prophet of Islam had. Nevertheless, he was a Prophet of God and had been sent by Him to teach people morals and the ways of the spirit. His example must have distinguished him from millions of other human beings, but woe to the writer who attributes such unmannerly conduct to him.

In this connection we cannot omit to mention the incident relating to the woman of Canaan mentioned in Matthew (15 : 21–26) and Mark (7 : 24–27). This woman approached Jesus in great humility. In accordance with the custom of her people she fell at his feet and wanted only guidance from him. But Jesus, according to the Gospel writer, said, "It is not meet to take the children's bread and cast it unto the dogs."

With what longing and expectation this poor woman must have approached Jesus. And she went not to beg for bread or cloth or for any such material thing ; all she wanted was spiritual guidance. She wanted from him just what Jesus had come to give. But the Gospel narratives say that Jesus sent this woman away. Not only this. He abused a woman to her face, called her dog and dishonoured her. Jesus, if the Gospel account is true, did not dishonour this woman from Canaan only. He dishonoured the entire fair sex, and proved by his own utterance that he had nothing to give to poor women. All his thoughts were concentrated on the well-being of the Jewish race. He would prefer having his feet anointed by a sinning Jewish woman (Luke 7 : 36–38) to saying a word of comfort to a non-Jewish woman. If Christians accept this part of the Gospel narrative as true, they are quite welcome. But we for our part cannot believe that his disciples could have said such a thing about him. These things according to us are fabrications of later writers. And they were made at a time when the real Jesus had disappeared from the world and an imaginary Jesus was being manufactured by ignorant writers.

(*iii*) In John (2 : 1–4) we have :

> And the third day there was a marriage in Cana of Galilee ; and the mother of Jesus was there ; and both Jesus was called, and his disciples, to the marriage. And when they wanted wine, the mother of Jesus saith unto him, They have no wine. Jesus saith unto her, Woman, what have I to do with thee ? mine hour is not yet come.

Similarly in Matthew (12 : 47-48) we have :

> Then one said unto him, Behold, thy mother and thy brethren stand without, desiring to speak with thee. But he answered and said unto him that told him, Who is my mother and who are my brethren ?

These passages from John and Matthew show that Jesus did not have much regard even for his mother, a relationship which is held in the highest respect and esteem by all decent persons. Will an ordinary Christian today address his mother saying, "Woman, what have I to do with thee ?" Will any Christian today dismiss his mother contemptuously and yet be counted as decent ? Then why did the Gospel writers single out Jesus for such a ridiculous description ? Respect for mothers is a common virtue even among primitive communities. It is a species of good manners which the worst of human beings display. But if the Gospel narrative is to be believed, this last Teacher of Israel, this hero of the Mosaic tradition, who came to lead a people from darkness into light and teach them good morals, was rude to his mother and behaved insolently towards her. According to Christian belief, Jesus was the son of God, not a human being. If Jesus was the son of God, why was he born in the lap of Mary. If he had accepted being born in Mary's lap, and had subjected her to a mother's travails for nine months, and had sucked at her breast for two years, and had for years burdened her with the duty of his upbringing, could he not have repaid a mother's debt by showing the courtesy and respect due to her ? The truth seems to be that these are only apologies. Christians do not hold Jesus in half the reverence in which they hold the fabricated Gospels. The fabricated Gospels are their own creation and Jesus was a creation of God. They are not prepared to adopt the straight course of admitting that the Gospel accounts are mistaken They would rather have Jesus defamed than reject the Gospel accounts. But rational and decent human beings who have pondered over the life of Jesus and tried to grasp his purifying example cannot but admit that the Gospels as we find them today are full of fabrications and errors. They contain elements which do not promote, but which tend instead to destroy, the spiritual cravings of man. With the Gospels in such a plight, it was necessary that God should have sent to the world a new revelation free from errors and capable of inculcating in man not only high morals but also a high spiritual outlook. That revelation is the Quran.

INTERPOLATIONS IN THE VEDAS

The third religion important in respect of numbers is Hinduism. In accordance with the teaching of the Quran we hold the certain belief that the Hindu religion had its origin in divine revelation and, because the Hindus regard the Vedas as their religious books, we are constrained also to believe that the Vedas contain revelations received by Hindu Prophets. But the state in which the Vedas are to be found at the present time is most confusing. We do not even know the names of persons who received these revelations. Vedic mantras in the beginning mention some names, but these names, according to Hindu scholars themselves, are not the names of the recipients of the revelations, but of those who collected them. The historical value of the Vedas, therefore, is very significant.

The Vedic scholars hold the following opinions about the Vedas :

(1) Pandit Vedic Muni in his *Veda Sarvasva* writes :

> In truth, the confusion to which this Atharva-Veda has been reduced is without parallel in the other Vedas. Even after Sayana-

charya many *Suktas* have been added to it. A fine method of interpolation has been invented. In the first stage the interpolated passage is marked out from the text by the words *Atha* (beginning) and *Iti* (end). When the readers get used to the change the words *Atha* and *Iti* are dropped out and the interpolated passage becomes part of the general text. Just as in the Rig-Veda collection the *Valkhilya Suktas* are being added, so at the end of the Atharva-Veda are being added the *Kuntapa Suktas*. If you ask "From where have these *Suktas* from the fifth Anu-vaka to *Kuntapa* come ?", you have no reply. Ignorance is so rampant that at the end the words, "Atharva-Veda Samhita Samapta" are thought to be a sufficient guarantee that all that has gone before constitutes the Ahtarva collection. Nobody stops to inquire who the collector and publisher are, and what capacity they have for the task (p. 97).

(2) Pandit Mahesh Chandra Prashad writes in his *Sanskrit Sahitya ka Itihas*:

Vaja Saneyi Shukla Yajur-Veda Samhita is a strange collection. In this the Vedas and Brahmanas are as separate parts. There are altogether forty chapters, but most people are convinced that of these eighteen only are genuine, the rest having been added later. Chapters one to eighteen correspond to *Bhaga Taittiriya Samhita* and *Krishna Yajur-Veda* in prose and verse. Of these eighteen chapters we have an explanation, word for word, in their Brahmanas. But in the case of the remaining chapters we have explanations only of a few mantras here and there. Katyayana regards chapters twenty-six to thirty-five as interpolations. Chapters nineteen to twenty-five contain an account of sacrifices. They do not tally with the *Taittiriya Samhita*. Chapters twenty-six to twenty-nine largely consist of mantras relating to the same sacrificial rites which have been mentioned in the earlier chapters, from which it appears that most certainly they have been added later (p. 160).

(3) Pandit Shanti Dev Shastri writes in *The Ganga* (Feb. 1931):

In the first place there was no certain finding as to whether the Vedas are *three* or *four*. According to Manu Smrti and Shatapatha Brahmana, Rig-Veda, Yajur-Veda and Sama-Veda are the only Vedas and they make the number three. But according to Vaja Saneyi Upanishad, Brahamana Upanishad and Mundaka Upanishad the Vedas are four in number (p. 232).

(4) Pandit Hirday Narain writes in *The Ganga* (Jan. 1931):

In *Charana Vyuha* and other writings of Shaunaka Rishi the account given of the exact number of the Vedic mantras, their words and letters does not apply to the present editions of the Vedas, from which it appears that the Vedas have suffered many additions and subtractions.

(5) Pandit Shanti Dev Shastri writes in *The Ganga* (Feb. 1931):

When *Charana Vyuha* of Shaunaka Rishi was composed, the *Shakalya Samhita* in the Rig-Veda collection had 153,826 words, 432,000 letters and 10,622 mantras. But today you do not find these numbers (p. 231).

(6) Dr. Tarapad Chaudhri writes in *The Ganga* (Jan. 1932):

Besides these, you have in the Vedas, words which quite obviously strike you as foreign to the general text. It seems that the text has been tampered with by the unconscious fault of those who dictated as well as of those who transcribed it (p. 74).

(7) Pandit Vedic Muni in his *Veda-Sarvasva* writes:

The time of the composition of *Gopatha Brahmana* is just the time when the advocates of sacrifices held the field. At that time the votaries of the Rig-Veda, Yajur-Veda, Sama-Veda and Atharva-Veda were engaged in a fierce controversy and busy in making interpolations on different excuses. The mantras of the Rig-Veda which they fancied they each entered into their own respective Vedas. Everybody thought himself above criticism and hated everybody else. Not only this. Differences which had crept into the different manuscripts had divided the votaries of the different Vedas among themselves. The votaries of *Vashkala Samhita* had separated from the votaries of *Shakalya Samhita*, the votaries of *Madhyandina Samhita* from *Kanva Samhita* and *Shaunaka Samhita* from *Pippalada Samhita*. Each regarded his own fancied text as the best and the purest and all the others as corrupt and fabricated. The many differences in the texts of the Vedas which we find today took their birth in these evil times (pp. 105–6).

(8) The same authority goes on to say:

Besides these, parts of Brahmana Granthas have also been added to the Vedas, which the discerning reader can detect at once. The Atharva-Veda is in the same plight. Our doctors of theology should ponder over the situation. That a religious book should be in such a sad state is very regrettable (*op. cit.*, p. 108).

(9) Further on he writes:

It has already been pointed out that we have at present two versions of the Atharva-Veda. One is *Pippalada Samhita*, the other *Shaunaka Samhita*. Of the two the *Pippalada Samhita* is the more reliable. But this has not been pointed out, nor has Sayanacharya written a commentary on it. Printed copies of the *Shaunaka Samhita* are available in three different editions issued by three different presses. Of these, two give the bare text and the third Sayanacharya's commentary in addition to the text. One of the bare texts has been issued by the Vedic Press, Ajmer, the other by the Bombay Press, the Printer being Sevak Lal. All the three editions differ in both chapter and verse (*op. cit.*, p. 109).

(10) The Arya Samaj scholar, Pandit Raghunundan Sharma, writes in his book *Sahitya Bhushana Vaidic Sampatti*:

As far as we know, no evidence has ever been provided as to where exactly interpolations have been made in the Vedas. Nor is it proved that the places where interpolations have been shown to exist were not known to Vedic scholars. Places where interpolations exist have been known for a long time (since the time of the Brahmana Granthas). They are not interpolations, but only annotations which, owing to the oversight of copyists and printers, have entered into the text and become apparently a part of it. *Valkhilya Suktas* in the Rig-Veda (altogether eleven chapters and eighty mantras), *Khil* or *Brahmana Bhaga* in the Yajur-Veda (several chapters), *Aranyaka* and *Mahanamni* chapters (two chapters and sixty-five mantras) in the Sama-Veda, and *Kuntapa Sukta* (ten chapters and one hundred and fifty mantras) in the Atharva-Veda—these are interpolations well known to all, and for which there is ample evidence. Besides these, there are passages in the Yajur-Veda and Atharva-Veda which have been interpolated and which can easily be identified as interpolations. In short, just as variations in the various versions are well known, and pure versions are nevertheless available, in the same way the interpolations in the Vedas are also well known. . . . We find that the *Vaja Saneyi Smahita* (the current version of the Yajur-Veda) has one thousand nine hundred mantras which number includes the *Shakvari* mantras, because we are told . . . that one hundred less than two thousand mantras are those of *Vaja Saneyi* and the number includes those of *Shakvari*. If it is *Vaja Saneyi Samhita*, it should include only *Vaja Saneyi* mantras. But we find that the current version of *Vaja Saneyi* contains one thousand nine hundred and seventy-five mantras. From this it is evident that *Shakvari* mantras are certainly included in the

> number one thousand nine hundred. The remaining seventy-five have been added from somewhere outside (p. 570–71).

These statements show clearly that the Vedas are not free from fabrications. The older as well as the more modern Vedic scholars all seem to agree that the Vedas had had other mantras added to them. To say, as modern scholars tend to say, that the Vedic scholars have traced the interpolations and separated them from the genuine part of the text, is not of much avail. If Vedic scholars had become convinced that some specific mantras were fabrications, why did they not drop them out of the text ? The fact that even the fabricated mantras continue to be included in the text shows that Vedic scholars were not quite convinced of their spurious character. The Arya Samaj writer in the end admits that only one thousand nine hundred mantras of the Yajur-Veda are original, the remaining seventy-five being later additions. Even about the one thousand nine hundred mantras he admits that they include some of the *Shakvari* mantras. These statements, with the significant qualifications, show that nobody really knows the truth and that everybody is trying to speculate. But can speculations be made the foundation of spiritual aspirations ?

The truth seems to be that the genuineness of the Atharva-Veda has ever been in doubt, and the Yajur-Veda and the Rig-Veda also are so similar in their composition that it is most likely that the two have freely borrowed from each other. When confusion is so rife, who can say what mantra is genuine revelation and what is not, what is a fabrication and what is not ? A book open to so much doubt cannot serve as a guidance for man. It must be replaced by another book free from all confusion and immune to human interference, upon which man can rely and which he can regard as a revelation with the same certainty with which he can regard "the choir of heaven and the furniture of earth" and indeed his own existence. Only such a book can inspire man with confidence in his search after God. Such a book is the Quran.

SAVAGE TEACHING OF THE VEDAS

We quote some examples of the savage teaching of the Vedas :

(*i*) In Atharva-Veda (iv, 22 : 7) we have :

Consume, with lion aspect, all their hamlets, with tiger aspect, drive away thy foemen.

Sole lord and leader and allied with Indra, seize, conqueror, thine enemies' possessions.

(*ii*) In Sama-Veda (Part II, ix, iii, 8) we have :

Blind, O my foemen, shall ye be even as headless serpents are : May Indra slay each best of you, when Agni's flame hath struck you down.

(*iii*) In Sama-Veda (11 : 1) we have :

O god Indra, may the Soma juice given by us make you happy and intoxicated. Grant to us wealth and power and our enemies defeat and disgrace.

(*iv*) In Sama-Veda we have :

Ye slay our Arya foes, O Lords of heroes, slay our Dasa foes : Ye drive all enemies away (Part II, ii, ii, 8).

"Trample him down beneath thy feet, him who watches for and aims at us" (Part II, iv, i, 16).

(*v*) In Atharva-Veda (XIX, 28 : 4–10) we have :

Cleave through, O Darbha, amulet, my foes', mine adversaries' heart. Rise thou and batter down their heads like growth that covereth the earth. Cleave thou my rivals, Darbha, cleave the men who fain would fight with me. . . . Tear thou my rivals, Darbha. . . . Hew thou my rivals, Darbha. . . . Cleave thou my rivals, Darbha. . . . Pierce thou my rivals, Darbha. . . . Pierce the men who hate me, Amulet.

(*vi*) In Atharva-Veda (XIX, 29 : 1–9) we have :

Split thou my rivals, Darbha. . . . Crush thou my rivals, Darbha, ... Burn thou, my rivals. . . . Consume thou my rivals. . . . Slay thou my rivals, Darbha. . . . Slay all who wish me evil.

(vii) In Yajur-Veda (27 : 2) we have :

"Agni, be those uninjured who adore thee, thy priests be glorious and none beside them."

(*viii*) In Yajur-Veda (11 : 80) we have :

Agni, him who would seek to injure us, the man who looks on us with hate, turn thou to ashes.

Besides the Vedas, other Hindu books also contain the same

sort of teaching. In the Manu Smrti, admitted by all Hindu schools as a reliable Hindu Scripture, we have :*

(*i*) Whatever man of the three highest classes, having addicted himself to heretical books, shall treat with contempt those two roots of law, he must be driven as an atheist and a scorner of revelation from the company of the virtuous (II : 11).

Are the critics of the Vedas to be banished from the country ?

(*ii*) A man of the lowest class, who shall insolently place himself on the same seat with one of the highest, shall either be banished with a mark on his hinder parts, or the king shall cause a gash to be made on his buttock (VIII : 281)..

(*iii*) A Brahman may seize without hesitation, if he be distressed for a subsistence, the goods of his Sudra-slave ; for as that slave can have no property, his master may take his goods (VIII : 417).

(*iv*) But a man of the servile class whether bought or unbought, he may compel to perform servile duty ; because such a man was created by the Self-Existent for the purpose of serving Brahmans (VIII : 413).

(*v*) A Sudra, though emancipated by his master, is not released from a state of servitude ; for, of a state, which is natural to him, by whom can he be divested ? (VIII : 414).

(*vi*) Should he (a Sudra), through pride, give instructions to priests concerning their duty, let the king order some hot oil to be dropped into his mouth and ear (VIII : 272).

From these passages from Manu it is obvious that according to the Hindu religion, the grace and beneficence of God are confined to a few chosen castes. For some human beings it is a sin to recite the Vedas or listen to their recitation, and if they break the rule and seek either to recite, listen to or memorize any part of the Vedas, dire punishment amounting even to death is the penalty they have to pay.

This sort of teaching shows conclusively that the Vedic Dharma was meant for a few people. It was not a universal Message. Brahmans, Kshatryas, and Vaishyas do not constitute the whole of humanity. For other sections of mankind what does Hindu teaching offer ? Is there no guidance for them ? Can the universal providence of God be reconciled to the idea of guiding one part of His creation and omitting the other, leading one part to Heaven and the other part to Hell ? Such teaching is not only savage. It is repugnant and dis-

* The quotations are from the translation by Sir William Jones, 1869.

honourable to God. Our God is full of grace and universal beneficence. Every part of the world is under His providence. Those who live on the surface of the earth, or those who live under it or those who live in the air, all grow and fulfil their destinies under the universal sustenance of God. He has endowed all sections of mankind with the same powers, the same urges and the same emotions. The urges which raise men in the spiritual scale have been distributed equally over the whole of humanity. No people have been dealt with scantily, neither Europeans, nor Americans, nor Japanese, nor any other Asiatics. Hindus are not superior to others in respect of spiritual aspirations or mental capacities. God could not have omitted large sections of His own creation from His guidance, and chosen a sixth of the human race for it. The existence of such a teaching declares openly that the time of this teaching is over. We need now a book which should address itself to the whole of humanity, which should collect Arab and non-Arab, Jew and Gentile, Brahman and non-Brahman in one fold, and inculcate a universal feeling, and teach us not to treat the humble and the downtrodden as unworthy, but as even more deserving of our sympathy, compassion and care. It was this need of a new book which the Quran came to fulfil.

SUPERSTITIONS IN THE VEDAS

The Vedas are full of superstitions. Elements like fire are called gods. True, it is said that these are not gods but only names of the attributes of God. But it is true also that the Vedas teach, as pious duties, practices like lighting fire and burning oil, ghee and other such articles in it (Rig-Veda II. 10 : 4), and no doubt is left that oil, ghee, etc., are food for Agni, the fire-god. If Agni is an attribute of God, what is the point in lighting fire and feeding it with expensive inflammables ? The ceremonial must be a superstition even if Agni is only an attribute. If, on the other hand, Agni is regarded as God, and the ceremonial suggests that it is, then the whole thing, the ceremonial as well as the belief behind it, is nothing but rank superstition.

In the Rig-Veda (II, 11 : 11) we have :

> Drink thou, O Hero Indra, drink the Soma; let the joy-giving juices make thee joyful.

Now Indra is the name either of God or of His angels. If Indra is the name of God, it is a most primitive thought which prompts one to offer Soma juice to God. If, on the other hand, Indra is the name of an angel or a spirit, even then the offering of Soma juice is a mean superstition. For God is hidden, and His angels are spiritual beings. They need no drinks.

In the same place (11 : 15) we read:

> Let those enjoy in whom thou art delighted. Indra, drink Soma for thy strength and gladness.

To think that Soma juice will bring power to God or His angels is ridiculous in the extreme.

It is not one or two verses which teach superstitions of this kind. Hundreds of such verses can be quoted. We have, in some of them, descriptions of gods crossing the skies, mounted on clouds or on chariots.

A large part of the Vedas consists of immoral suggestions. These pertain to matters of sex and are so brazen that we fear quotation would offend the reader's sense of decency. Sex impulses and sex organs are described with a detail which would be nauseating even in a book of medicine.

For these reasons, we can say that though there are parts of the Vedas which point to their origin in divine revelation, there are others which prove that they have suffered from human fabrication. Because of this, the Vedas can no longer be treated as a guide for human conduct. We need, instead, a book free from all such defects. That book is the Quran.

CONTRADICTIONS IN THE VEDAS

Like the Bible the Vedas contain interpolations made by different persons in different periods. No wonder there are many contradictions in their text, and here are some examples:

(*i*) The Vedas raise the question, who made the sun? To this quite different answers are proposed in different parts of the Vedas. In the Rig-Veda (IX, 96 : 5) we are told that the sun was made by the Soma god.

But in the Rig-Veda (VIII, 36 : 4) we are told the sun was made by the god Indra.

The same book teaches one thing in one chapter and quite another in another chapter. It teaches in one chapter that the sun was made by the Soma god, and in another, that it was made by the god Indra. When we turn to the other Vedas the contradiction becomes more and more serious.

In the Yajur-Veda (31 : 12) we read that the sun was made by Brahma from his eye.

The Atharva-Veda further contradicts this. In it (XIX, 27 : 7) we find that all the gods joined together and made the sun.

This is different from, and contradicts, all the other accounts.

(*ii*) The Vedas teach that the sun at first was on the earth, it was then taken to the skies. This account may be ridiculous from the point of view of astronomical science; we are concerned only to point out that even this extraordinary statement is couched in very different terms in different parts of the Vedas.

In Krishna Yajur-Veda Taittiriya Samhita (7 : 1) we read that the sun was on the earth and gods then carried it on their backs to the heavens and placed it there.

In the Rig-Veda (X, 156 : 4) we read that the fire-god carried the sun and placed it in the sky.

But in the Rig-Veda itself in another place (VIII, 12 : 30) we read that god Indra alone carried the sun to heaven.

And in yet another place (X, 62 : 3) it is stated that the sun was carried unaided by the Atri Rishi to heaven.

In the Atharva-Veda (XIII, 2 : 12) it is given that the sun was carried unaided by the Atri Rishi to heaven that it should create the months.

> In Shukla Yajur-Veda (4 : 31) we have that it was the god Varuna who set the sun on the sky. The belief that the sun was carried from the earth to the heavens is ridiculous enough. But contradictory versions of it are even more ridiculous. The Rig-Veda alone gives three contradictory accounts. One is that the sun was taken by the fire-god from the earth to the heaven. A second is that it was the god Indra who did so. A third is that the sons of Angira Rishi performed this feat. The Yajur-Veda also gives contradictory versions. According to one, all the gods joined hands and carried the sun to the heaven. According to the other, this duty was performed unaided by the god Varuna. The Atharva-Veda gives quite a

different account, declaring that it was the Rishi Atri who carried out the task.

(*iii*) Of the creation of heaven and earth, we have many accounts in the Vedas. But these accounts contradict one another as much as the accounts of ghosts and fairies do in children's tales.

In the Sama-Veda, Purva Archik (VI. 1 : 4), we have that the heaven and the earth were made by the Soma god.

But in the Rig-Veda (VIII, 26 : 4) we find that the heaven and the earth were made by the god Indra living on the Soma juice.

In another place in the Rig-Veda (II, 40 : 1) we have that the heaven and the earth were made by Soma and Pushan.

In the Yajur-Veda (13 : 4) it is written that the heaven and the earth were made by Brahma.

NUMBER OF VEDIC GODS

We believe, as we have said before, that the Vedas were originally a revelation of God and as such they taught nothing but the Unity and Oneness of God. But the Vedas, as we know them today, are not the Vedas which were revealed to the Rishis. The Vedas today are full of polytheistic descriptions and these descriptions are to be found in such abundance that what little in the Vedas still bears on the Unity of God is relegated to the background. We give below a few examples :

In the Yajur-Veda (7 : 19) we are told that there are in all thirty-three gods, eleven on the earth, eleven in the sky, eleven in the waters.

In the Rig-Veda (III, 9 : 9) we are told that the total number of gods is three thousand, three hundred and forty. This, because, according to the Rig-Veda, three thousand three hundred and thirty-nine gods went to the fire-god and fed him with ghee. On his joining the big company the total number of gods became three thousand three hundred and forty. Accordingly in the Rig-Veda (X, 52 : 6) the total number of gods is three thousand three hundred and forty. This divergence in the number of gods present in different parts of the Vedas is amazing in the extreme ; according to the Yajur-Veda thirty-three and according to the Rig-Veda three thousand three hundred and forty! To have departed from the conception of One God was dangerous enough. But such wide divergence in the number of gods proposed in different parts of the Vedas seems worse than dangerous. Contradictions of this kind compel us to conclude that though the original Vedas were most certainly revealed, the present Vedas no longer retain their original character, and are incapable of giving satisfaction to those who are in quest of spiritual solace. They need to be replaced by another book which should be free from all immoral, contradictory, savage and superstitious teaching. That book, we claim, is the Quran.

GOD'S PROMISE TO ABRAHAM

A fourth question, the answer to which should throw light on the question relating to the need of the Quran, is : Did earlier religions regard themselves as final ? Or did they believe in a kind of spiritual progression which was due to culminate in a universal teaching for the guidance of mankind ?

In answer to this, we must admit that a continuous narrative, in which the story of one Prophet is linked with that of another, is to be found only in the Bible. In reconstructing the stories of the Prophets, the help we derive from the Bible is invaluable. No other book revealed before the Quran can give us this help. To answer the question whether earlier teachings and earlier Prophets did or did not foretell the coming of a perfect Teaching and a perfect Prophet after them, we have to turn to the Bible.

When we do so, we find that God made many promises to the Patriarch Abraham. He was born in Ur of the Chaldees. From there he migrated with his father to Canaan, His father stopped on the way at Haran and died there. On his father's death Abraham was commanded by God to leave Haran and go to Canaan and had the following revelation :

> And I will make of thee a great nation, and I will bless thee, and make thy name great ; and thou shalt be a blessing : And I will bless them that bless thee, and curse him that curseth thee ; and in thee shall all families of the earth be blessed (Genesis 12 : 2–3).

And again (Genesis 13 : 15):

> "For all the land which thou seest, to thee will I give it, and to thy seed for ever."

And again (Genesis 16 : 10–12):

> And the angel of the Lord said unto her (*i.e.* to Hagar), I will multiply thy seed exceedingly, that it shall not be numbered for multitude. And the angel of the Lord said unto her, Behold, thou art with child, and shalt bear a son, and shalt call his name Ishmael; because the Lord hath heard thy affliction. And he will be a wild man; his hand will be against every man, and every man's hand against him; and he shall dwell in the presence of all his brethren.

And again (Genesis 17 : 9–11):

> And God said unto Abraham, Thou shalt keep my covenant therefore, thou, and thy seed after thee in their generations. This is my covenant which ye shall keep, between me and you and thy seed after thee; Every man-child among you shall be circumcised. And ye shall circumcise the flesh of your foreskin; and it shall be a token of the covenant betwixt me and you.

And (Genesis 17 : 14):

> And the uncircumcised man-child whose flesh of his foreskin is not circumcised, that soul shall be cut off from his people; he hath broken my covenant.

Further on (Genesis 17 : 16), we are told that Abraham's wife Sarah also was promised a son:

> And I will bless her, and give thee a son also of her; yea, I will bless her, and she shall be a mother of nations; kings of people shall be of her.

Of the progeny of Sarah (through Isaac) we are told (Genesis 17 : 19):

> And I will establish my covenant with him for an everlasting covenant, and with his seed after him.

Of Ishmael (Genesis 17 : 20–22) we read:

> And as for Ishmael, I have heard thee (refers to Abraham's prayer in Genesis 17 : 18—"O that Ishmael might live before thee"): Behold, I have blessed him, and will make him fruitful, and will multiply him exceedingly; twelve princes shall he beget, and I will make him a great nation. But my covenant will I establish with Isaac, which Sarah shall bear unto thee at this set time in the next year. And he left off talking with him, and God went up from Abraham.

Again (Genesis 21 : 13) :

> "And also of the son of the bondwoman will I make a nation, because he is thy seed."

Again of Ishmael, God said to Hagar (Genesis 21 : 17–18) :

> For God hath heard the voice of the lad where he is. Arise, lift up the lad, and hold him in thine hand ; for I will make him a great nation.

Again (Genesis 21 : 20–21) :

> And God was with the lad ; and he grew, and dwelt in the wilderness, and became an archer. And he dwelt in the wilderness of Paran : and his mother took him a wife out of the land of Egypt.

From these quotations it is obvious that Abraham had two sons, Ishmael and Isaac, Ishmael being the elder and Isaac the younger. God promised Abraham that He would multiply and bless his progeny. The promise applies to both Isaac and Ishmael. From the quotations it also appears that Ishmael lived in the wilderness of Paran, that the land of Canaan was given over to the sons of Abraham, and that the external sign of the covenant which God made with Abraham was circumcision of all males. All these promises were fulfilled. The progeny of Isaac multiplied exceedingly. From among them arose the Prophets, Moses, David, Ezekiel, Daniel and Jesus. For two thousand years they ruled over Canaan. Their hold on it was never really abolished, though for a short time it became weak. After the seventh century A.D., however, the sons of Isaac, and those who observed the letter of the Law of Moses had to withdraw from Canaan. The sons of Ishmael, instead, became its political as well as its spiritual leaders. The fact that the sons of Israel had to surrender the land of Canaan shows that they had become unworthy of the promise which God had made to them through Abraham. This promise was that Israel would remain in possession of this land until the Last Day, and the promise was true. The Last Day in the divine promise, therefore, cannot mean the day which is to mark the end of the world, but the day on which the Law of Moses was to be superseded by the promulgation of a new Law for the guidance of the world. In the language of divine revelation the advent of a new Law is often described as the birth of a new heaven and a new earth. Just as a new heaven and a new earth cannot be created without a large-scale upheaval—usually associated with the Last Day—so the establishment of a new Law must entail a large-scale upheaval of the people who receive that Law. Therefore, when the prophecy said that the sons of Israel would retain their hold over Canaan until the Last Day, it meant that their hold would continue until the advent of a new Law-giving Prophet. In the utterances of David we have a hint of this meaning of the prophecy. The promise contained in Genesis that Israel would retain possession of Canaan until the Last Day is expressed differently. Thus in Psalms (37 : 29) we read :

> "The righteous shall inherit the land, and dwell therein for ever."

The promise of eternal possession is not for Israel as such but for the righteous. This utterance of David, in fact, was a clear warning that the days of Israel's dominance were numbered. The Prophet seemed to point out that the divine promise, after a time, was to be understood not in a racial but in a spiritual sense ; that the sons of Ishmael were going to inherit the promises made to Abraham by inheriting the truth and a new covenant was going to be initiated through them. If our interpretation of the prophecy is not correct, then the question is, Why did God make the sons of Ishmael—and believers in the Message of the Quran—dominant in Palestine ? The prophecy was quite clear. The sons of Isaac were to hold Palestine until the Last Day. The question is, Why did they not ? Why did God allow a transfer of political power from the sons of Isaac to the sons of Ishmael ? If the transfer had lasted for a short time, it would have made no difference to the prophecy. The rise and fall in the fortunes of nations are a common phenomenon. But the transfer of which we speak proved a permanent one. More than one thousand three hundred years have passed, and Palestine is still in the possession of Muslims, the sons of Ishmael. European powers and the U.S.A. are trying hard to alter this, but so far, at any rate, they have not succeeded. If at all they succeed in their designs, the success is bound to be short-lived. Either the new Israelite settlers will become converted to Islam and regain possession of Palestine through a new covenant ; or they will have to quit Palestine once again. Palestine is for those who keep the covenant which Abraham made with God. Christians, no doubt, claim to fulfil the covenant. But they forget that the covenant lays down an important external sign. That sign is circumcision of the male population. Only Ishmaelites have kept the sign both before and since the revelation of the Quran.

In short, the prophecy of Abraham promised blessings to both Isaac and Ishmael. According to this promise, the sons of Isaac were established over Canaan and the sons of Ishmael over Arabia. But when the Last Day arrived for the sons of Isaac, then, in terms of the prophecy of David, the promise was transferred from Israel to Ishmael. The claim of Israel was now only a racial claim. The claim of Ishmael was spiritual. On the basis of their racial claim the sons of Ishmael held Mecca and the territory around (2 : 125–29). On the basis of their spiritual claim they added Canaan to their possessions after the religious deterioration of Israel.

THE PROPHECY IN DEUTERONOMY

When Moses went to Mount Horeb under the command of God, he addressed the Israelites saying :

> The Lord thy God will raise up unto thee a Prophet from the midst of thee, of thy brethren, like unto me ; unto him ye shall hearken (Deuteronomy 18 : 15).

God spoke to Moses saying :

> I will raise them up a Prophet from among their brethren, like unto thee, and will put my words in his mouth ; and he shall speak unto them all that I shall command him. And it shall come to pass, that whosoever will not hearken unto my words which he shall speak in my name, I will require it of him. But the prophet, which shall presume to speak a word in my name, which I have not commanded him to speak, or that shall speak in the name of other gods, even that prophet shall die (Deuteronomy 18 : 18–20).

From these passages it is evident that Moses prophesied about a Law-giving Prophet who was to appear after him, and who was to be from among the brethren of Israel.

That he was to be a Law-giver, and not an ordinary Prophet is obvious from the words "like unto Moses". As Moses was a Law-giver, the Prophet, who was to be like Moses, was also to be a Law-giver. The Promised Prophet is described as one who "shall speak unto them all that I shall command him." From this also it appears that the Promised Prophet was to be a Law-giving Prophet. The promulgation of a new Law means the initiation of a new movement, a new nation. A Prophet who promulgates a new Law, therefore, is no ordinary Teacher or Reformer. He has to present a comprehensive teaching, incorporating fundamental principles as well as detailed rules. Without it a new nation cannot be raised. But a Prophet who does not bring a new Law has only to explain and to annotate an already existing Law. It is not necessary for him to present all that he receives from God to his people. It is possible that some of his revelations may be meant only for his personal edification, which he is under no obligation to pass on to his people. The prophecy also lays down that the Promised Prophet will "speak in my name", and those who will not listen to him, God will "require it" of them ; that is, those who turn a deaf ear will incur punishment. We are also told that any one who pretends to fulfil the prophecy will be put to death.

If we keep in view all the terms of the prophecy, we are bound to conclude that until at least the time of Jesus no Prophet had appeared in the world who could be said to have answered to the description of the Promised Prophet. All the Prophets who appeared between Moses and Jesus, therefore, may be ignored, when we set out in search of the Prophet who could be said to have fulfilled this prophecy. They have left no following and no people who could espouse their claims. Only Jesus remains who has a large following, and who is regarded by his followers as the last Teacher sent by God into this world. But when we apply, one by one, the terms of the prophecy to Jesus, we find that not one of them applies to him :

First, the Promised Prophet was to be a Law-giving Prophet. Was Jesus a Law-giver ? Did he bring a new Law into the world to replace an old one ? Jesus said clearly :

> Think not that I am come to destroy the law, or the prophets : I am not come to destroy, but to fulfil. For verily I say unto

> you, Till heaven and earth pass, one jot or one tittle shall in no wise pass from the law, till all be fulfilled (Matthew 5 : 17–18).

The followers of Jesus went so far as to declare :

> And the law is not of faith : but, The man that doeth them shall live in them. Christ hath redeemed us from the curse of the law, . . . (Galatians, 3 : 12–13).

Jesus laid no claim to giving a new Law, and his disciples regard the Law as a curse. How then can Jesus and his followers be said to fulfil the prophecy in Deuteronomy ?

Secondly, the Promised Prophet was to be raised not from among Israel but from among their brethren and Jesus was an Israelite.

Christian exponents, confronted with this fact, are wont to say that Jesus had no earthly father, so he can be said to be one of the brethren of Israel. But such a construction would be untenable. The prophecy speaks of *brethren*, which means they were to constitute a race or a people from among whom the Promised Prophet was to rise. Jesus stands alone, as son of God. If there were other sons of God, he might have answered to the description of the prophecy. But, apart from this, it is clearly laid down in the Bible that Christ was to be of the seed of David (Psalms, 132 : 11 ; Jeremiah, 23 : 5). Jesus may shed his Israelite origin because he had no earthly father : but he will not then remain a son of David, so that the prophecy of the Psalms relating to Christ will not apply to him.

Thirdly, the prophecy says: "I will put my words in his mouth." But the Gospels do not consist of words which God put in Jesus' mouth. They only tell us the story of Jesus and what he said in some of his public addresses and what his disciples said or did on different occasions.

Fourthly, the Promised One was to be a Prophet, while the Christian view is that Jesus was not a Prophet, but the son of God. How, then, can Jesus answer to the description of the prophecy ?

Fifthly, we have in the prophecy : "Words which he shall speak in my name." Strange as it may seem, there is in the Gospels not a single example of words which Jesus may be said to have received from God with the command to pass them on to the people whom he taught.

Sixthly, we have in the prophecy : "He shall speak unto them all that I shall command." The Promised Prophet, according to this, was to give to the world a complete and comprehensive teaching. But Jesus claimed no such mission for himself. He regarded himself as the forerunner of a greater Teacher yet to come. Thus we have (John, 16 : 12–13) :

> I have yet many things to say unto you, but ye cannot bear them now. Howbeit when he, the Spirit of truth, is come, he will guide you into all truth : for he shall not speak of himself ; but whatsoever he shall hear, that shall he speak : and he will shew you things to come.

From these verses it appears that the prophecy in Deuteronomy was not fulfilled in Jesus. We cannot but conclude, therefore, that both the Old and the New Testaments foretold the coming of a Prophet after Jesus who was to guide the world "unto all truth", and who was to establish the name of God on earth for all time. Our claim is that the revelation of the Quran and the advent of the Holy Prophet mark the fulfilment of the prophecy in Deuteronomy. The following facts bear this out :

(*i*) The Holy Prophet Muhammad was a descendant of Ishmael. The descendants of Ishmael were the brethren of the descendants of Isaac, the Israelites.

(*ii*) The Holy Prophet is the only one claiming to be a Prophet like Moses. We have in the Quran (73 : 16) :

> Verily We have sent to you a Messenger, who is a witness over you, even as We sent a Messenger to Pharaoh.

The Quran definitely likens the Holy Prophet to Moses.

(*iii*) The prophecy described the Promised One as a Prophet. The Holy Prophet claimed to be a Prophet only. Jesus, we are told, on the other hand, did not claim to be a Prophet. We read in Mark (8 : 27-30) :

> He asked his disciples, saying unto them, Whom do men say that I am ? and they answered, John the Baptist : but some say, Elias ; and others, One of the prophets. And he saith unto them, But whom say ye that I am ? And Peter answereth and saith unto him. Thou art the Christ. And he charged them that they should tell no man of him.

That is to say, Jesus denies being either John the Baptist, or Elias, or one of the Prophets. But the prophecy in Deuteronomy speaks of the Promised One as a Prophet like Moses. The prophecy, therefore, applies to the Prophet of Islam and not to Jesus.

(*iv*) The prophecy speaks of "words I will put in his mouth." The Gospels do not contain any such words. On the contrary, the Holy Prophet of Islam brought to the world the Quran which is from beginning to end only the word of God, which God put into his mouth. The Quran describes itself as the word of God (2 : 76).

(*v*) The prophecy said that the Promised One would speak all that he was commanded. We have quoted the Gospels to prove that Jesus did not pass on everything he received from God, and that there was to be another after him, who was to do so. The Holy Prophet of Islam fully answers to this description. We have in the Quran (5 : 68): "O Messenger! convey to the people what has been revealed to thee from thy Lord." The verse seems to say, "O Prophet, there is an ancient prophecy about you which said that when you come into the world you would give to it all the truths you received from your God. Therefore preach to the world whatever is revealed to you, whether it likes it or not." Similarly, the verse revealed on the completion of the revelation of the Quran says:

> This day have I perfected your religion for you and completed My favour upon you and have chosen for you Islam as religion (5 : 4).

That is to say, "Through the revelation of the Quran, faith has been made perfect and the gift of guidance made complete for you, and peace and tranquillity have been appointed for you as your religion." It was the Holy Prophet of Islam, therefore, who taught everything and kept back nothing. In the time of Jesus, people were not ready to receive and to believe in everything that was worth while. But in the time of the Holy Prophet of Islam man had traversed all the stages of spiritual evolution and the time had come for all the truths to be revealed to the world.

(*vi*) The prophecy speaks of "words which he shall speak in my name". This part of the prophecy also was fulfilled in the Holy Prophet of Islam. He is the only one who spoke in the name of God, because every Chapter of the revealed Book brought by him begins with the words : "In the name of Allah, the Gracious, the Merciful." This great sign, duly incorporated in the Quran, also proves that the last stride in the spiritual advance of humanity, foretold by Moses, was registered with the advent of the Holy Prophet of Islam.

(*vii*) The prophecy laid down the important criterion :

> But the prophet, which shall presume to speak a word in my name, which I have not commanded him to speak, or that shall speak in the name of other gods, even that prophet shall die (Deuteronomy 18 : 20).

In this verse the world was taught how to distinguish the Promised One of the prophecy from those who should only pretend to fulfil the prophecy. It was necessary that a clear criterion should be laid down. The Promised One had to be charged with the important mission of initiating the last stage in the spiritual advance of man. If pretenders to this office should arise, the world would run great risks. To ward off these risks, God laid down the criterion that a pretender would incur divine punishment and meet with death and defeat. The Holy Prophet of Islam laid claim to this office very early in his career, and in the clearest terms. When he announced his claim, he was friendless and weak. The enemy was large in numbers and was strong, and he left no stone unturned to bring to nought his message and his mission and spared no pains to put an end to his life. Mighty rulers also set themselves against him but it was they, not the Prophet who suffered discomfiture and disgrace. The Holy Prophet died full of success. When he died, the whole of Arabia had declared faith in him ; and after his death his first Successors in a few years spread Islam throughout the whole of the then known world.

Moses was a true Prophet. The prophecy in Deuteronomy was a revelation from God. But was the Holy Prophet bound to succeed in the way he did ? And were his enemies, who thirsted for his blood, bound to fail in the way they did ? No, neither the Holy Prophet's success nor the failure of his enemies was an accident. On the other hand, it seems that the Quran had in view the terms of the prophecy in Deuteronomy when it declared before all Arabia and early in the career of the Holy Prophet :

"And Allah will protect thee from men" (5 : 68).

Similarly, addressing the enemies of the Prophet, the Quran declared :

> He is the Knower of the unseen ; and He reveals not His secrets to any one, except him whom He chooses, namely a Messenger of His. And then He causes an escort of guarding angels to go before him and behind him (72 : 27–28).

That is to say, the Prophet, having been charged with an important mission, would not be left unprotected. Enemies would never be able to kill him.

These verses proved that the success which the Holy Prophet attained was not an accident of good fortune. He declared early, through revelations received by him from God and recorded to this day in the Quran, that God would protect him from the murderous attacks of his enemies. He warned the world that because he was not a pretender but the Prophet promised in the prophecy in Deuteronomy, he would not be killed.

In short, one thousand nine hundred years before the advent of the Prophet of Islam, Moses declared that his own Law was, in the divine scheme, not the last Law ; that the world was to have a fuller Law later on ; and that, for this, God would send in the Latter Days another Messenger of His. This Messenger was to teach all truths ; it was he who was to mark the last stage in the spiritual advance of man. The world had to wait for another book and another Prophet. If, therefore, the Quran and the Holy Prophet have come after the Bible and after the Prophets Moses and Jesus, and if they claim to have come from God as guidance to man, their claim must be treated as just and true. It must be taken as the fulfilment of ancient prophecies. The revelation of the Quran was not a gratuitous revelation, a redundance in the presence of those revelations. Indeed, if the Quran had not been revealed, promises made by God through His Messengers would have gone unfulfilled, and the world would have become afflicted with doubt and disbelief.

FĀRĀN—PART OF ARABIA

In Deuteronomy (33 : 2) we have :

> And he said, the Lord came from Sinai, and rose up from Seir unto them ; he shined forth from mount Paran and he came with ten thousands of saints : from his right hand went a fiery law for them.

In this verse Moses is promised three manifestations of the glory of God. The first of these appeared from Sinai, to which a reference is made in Exodus (19 : 20) :

> And the Lord came down upon mount Sinai, on the top of the mount : and the Lord called Moses up to the top of the mount ; and Moses went up.

This manifestation of divine glory appeared in the time of Moses. The world witnessed the blessings which came with it. Time passed. The second manifestation promised in the prophecy was to take place from Seir. Seir is that part of the world round about which the miracles of Jesus took place. "Rising up from Seir", therefore, points to the advent of Jesus. Christian exponents of the Gospels identify Seir with Sinai but this is a mistake. Seir is part of Palestine. The name has many corrupt forms. One of thess serves as the name of a people who are descendants of the Prophet Jacob and are known as Banū Āsher. Another serves as a name for the north western part of Palestine. Seir, therefore, stands for the second manifestation of divine glory, to wit, the one especially associated with Palestine. To identify Seir with Sinai and to attribute both manifestations to Moses, is wrong also because Moses never crossed into Canaan. He died at a spot from where he could only see its borders. After Moses and before Jesus no manifestation of divine glory took place which could rank with that of Sinai. "Rising up from Seir", therefore, means the advent of Jesus which took place right in Canaan, and through which, as it were, God showed His face for a second time. The third manifestation of divine glory was to take its rise from Paran, and Paran (Arabic Fārān) is the name of the hills which lie between Mecca and Medina. Arab geographers always called this territory Fārān. A halting place on the way from Mecca to Medina is called the Valley of Fāṭima. When caravans pass through it, children from the neighbourhood meet them and sell them flowers. Asked where the flowers come from, the children answer : "Bariyyat Fārān", (Faṣl al-Khiṭāb) that is, the wilderness of Fārān. Fārān, therefore, is part of Arabia, the Ḥijāz to be exact. According to the Old Testament, Ishmael lived in this part. Thus in Genesis (21 : 20–21) we have :

> And God was with the lad (Ishmael) ; and he grew, and dwelt in the wilderness, and became an archer. And he dwelt in the wilderness of Paran ; and his mother took him a wife out of the land of Egypt.

THE QURAISH ARE ISHMAEL'S DESCENDANTS

The Biblical description of Paran is somewhat different from that of Arab geographers. According to the Bible, Paran is a territory adjacent to Canaan. But a territory made up of woods and hills must be a large one, sometimes extending over hundreds and thousands of miles. It cannot be just a strip of land situated within another territory or on its edge. The Biblical description can only mean that the woods and hills of Paran rise from somewhere near Canaan. It cannot mean that Paran is the southern periphery of Canaan. The Bible, however, admits that Abraham had a son called Ishmael and that he lived in Paran. The testimony of the sons of Ishmael who inhabited it, must be regarded as paramount. The Israelites should have little to say on the point. Their knowledge of history and geography was not good. They could not give an adequate account of the route they followed in their own journey from Egypt to Canaan. How could they pronounce on the geographical facts of other territories ? Only one people today trace their descent from Ishmael and they are the Quraish. They live in Arabia, and Mecca is their centre. If the Quraish claim is a pretence, it is difficult to find a motive for it. The claim could not advance their racial status, for the Israelites still looked down upon them. Nothing could make a desert people trace their descent to Ishmael unless the descent was a fact.

Also, if the Arab claim is false, where did the descendants of Ishmael disappear ? According to the Bible, Ishmael had twelve sons, and these twelve again, according to the Bible, were to multiply exceedingly.

Thus in Genesis (21 : 13) we have :

> And also of the son of the bondwoman (*i.e.*, Ishmael) will I make a nation, because he is thy seed.

Again in Genesis (21 : 18) we have :

> "Arise, lift up the lad, and hold him in thine hand ; for I will make him a great nation."

Again in Genesis (17 : 20) God says to Abraham :

> And as for Ishmael, I have heard thee : Behold, I have blessed him, and will make him fruitful, and will multiply him exceedingly ; twelve princes shall he beget, and I will make him a great nation.

That is to say, the descendants of Ishmael, were to multiply exceedingly and were to become a great nation. If the claim of the Arabs to be the descendants of Ishmael is false, equally must these Biblical prophecies be false. For there is not another nation in the world which claims descent from Ishmael. It is only when the claim of the Arabs is accepted, that the Biblical prophecies relating to Ishmael can be proved true ; for they all apply to the Arabs.

The strongest historical evidence consists of stable national traditions. For hundreds of years a people have regarded themselves as descendants of Ishmael and no other people in the world so regard themselves. Better evidence than this there cannot be.

According to the Bible, the Ishmaelites lived in Paran, and Paran, according to Arab geographers, is the territory extending from Mecca to the northern border of Arabia. Paran, therefore, is part of Arabia as certainly as the Quraish are the descendants of Ishmael. The divine glory which was to rise from Paran was, therefore, to rise from Arabia.

That the Ishmaelites had settled in Arabia is proved by further evidence from the Bible. In Genesis (25 : 13–16) we have the names of the twelve sons of Ishmael as follows :

> 1. Nebajoth. 2. Kedar. 3. Adbeel. 4. Mibsam. 5. Mishma. 6. Dumah. 7. Massa. 8. Hadar. 9. Tema. 10. Jetur. 11. Naphish. 12. Kedemah.

In accordance with ancient custom, we should expect their descendants to be named after their respective ancestors. The descendants of Jacob, for instance, would be named after their ancestor. Countries also have been named after their people. In the light of these customs a survey of the population of Arabia reveals that the names of the twelve sons of Ishmael are found spread in different parts of Arabia. The descendants of Ishmael fill the entire length and breadth of the country.

The first son of Ishmael was Nebajoth. The territory peopled by his descendants, according to geographers is between thirty and thirty-eight degrees North, and thirty-six to thirty-eight degrees East. The Rev. Katripikari (Khuṭubāt Ahmadiyya) admits this and says the descendants of Nebajoth occupied the territory between Palestine and Yanbū', the port for Medina.

Kedar was the second son. His descendants also constitute part of the Arab population. The literal meaning of Kedar is "of camels", which points to their Arabian habitation. They are to be found in the territory between the Ḥijāz and Medina. Ptolemy and Pliny, in the course of their description of the people of the Ḥijāz, speak of the tribes Kedars and Gedors (the latter seems to be a corrupt form of Kedar). There are Arabs today who claim descent from Kedar.

The third son was Adbeel. According to Josephus, the Adbeels also lived in this part of Arabia. The fourth was Mibsam. We cannot find any traces of this tribe in ordinary geography books. But it is possible that their name has become corrupted into some unrecognizable form. The fifth son was Mishma, and the Mishmas are to be found to this day in Arabia. The sixth was Dumah. A well-known spot in Arabia is still called Dumah, and Arab geographers have always traced this name to that of the sixth son of Ishmael. The seventh son was Massa, whose name is to be found intact in a Yemenite tribe. Their archaeological remains can also be identified. Katripikari mentions this. The eighth son was Hadar after whom we have the famous town Ḥudaida in Yemen.

The ninth son was Tema. From Najd to the Ḥijāz the territory is called Tema and it is all peopled by the descendants of Tema. In fact they seem to have spread right up to the Persian Gulf.

The tenth son was Jetur (Arabic Yaṭūr). The Jeturs can also be traced in Arabia and are known as Jedūrs. The sounds "j" and "y" often interchange, as do "t" and "d".

The eleventh son was Naphish, and Forster thinks that the authority of Josephus and the Old Testament supports the view that the descendants of Naphish lived in the wilds of Arabia.

The twelfth son was Kedemah. The habitation of the descendants of Kedemah is known to lie, according to the famous geographer, Mas'ūdī, in Yemen. The tribe known as Aṣḥāb al-Rass and mentioned also in the Quran are descendants of Ishmael, and they were two tribes, one called Kedamah and the other Yamin. According to some authorities the second one was called Ra'wīl, not Yamin.

Historical and geographical evidence, therefore, shows that the descendants of Abraham have lived in Arabia. All of them held Mecca and the Ka'ba in great reverence, and from this it appears that Ishmael first settled in Mecca, and this is the part which, according to both Arab and Old Testament records, is called Paran (or Arabic Fārān). The testimony of the revelation of Isaiah (21 : 13–17) supports the same view :

> The burden upon Arabia. In the forest in Arabia shall ye lodge, O ye travelling companies of Dedanim. The inhabitants of the land of Tema brought water to him that was thirsty, they prevented with their bread him that fled. For they fled from the swords, from the drawn sword, and from the bent bow, and from the grievousness of war. For thus hath the Lord said unto me, Within a year, according to the years of an hireling, and all the glory of Kedar shall fail : And the residue of the number of archers, the mighty men of the children of Kedar, shall be diminished : for the Lord God of Israel hath spoken it.

This prophetic passage is a picture of the Battle of Badr which took place about a year after the Holy Prophet's migration from Mecca to Medina. In this battle the sons of Kedar, the people of Mecca and the territories around, suffered a grievous defeat at the hands of Muslims. Unable to withstand the fierceness of Muslim swordsmen and archers, the Meccans sustained a disgraceful defeat. Mark the words with which the passage begins : "The burden upon Arabia". Herein Tema and Kedar are respectively spoken of as an Arabian territory and an Arabian tribe. According to this text, revealed seven hundred and fourteen years before Jesus to the Prophet Isaiah, the descendants of Ishmael lived in the Ḥijāz.

In short, from whatever side we may approach this question, there is abundant evidence that the Quraish were the descendants of Ishmael and that Paran of the Bible (Arabic Fārān) is the land in which they lived. The manifestation of divine glory that was due to take place from Paran was the advent of the Holy Prophet Muhammad, prophesied by Moses.

THE HOLY PROPHET MENTIONED IN HABAKKUK

This advent was also prophesied by Habakkuk (3 : 3–7) six hundred and twenty-six years before Jesus. Thus we have :

> God came from Teman, and the Holy One from mount Paran. Selah. His glory covered the heavens, and the earth was full of his praise. And his brightness was as the light ; he had horns coming out of his hands : and there was the hiding of his power. Before him went the pestilence, and burning coals went forth at his feet. He stood, and measured the earth : he beheld, and drove asunder the nations ; and the everlasting mountains were scattered, the perpetual hills did bow : his ways are everlasting. I saw the tents of Cushan in affliction ; and the curtains of the land of Midian did tremble.

Here we have a mention of Tema and of a Holy One from Paran. From the prophecies of Moses and Habakkuk it is evident that the advent of Jesus was not to mark the last stage in the spiritual development of man. It was to be followed by the advent of another Prophet to mark the third manifestation of divine glory. This prophet was to manifest both the Beauty and the Majesty of God and bring a fiery Law into the world, not merely a Message of forgiveness.

The Holy One to appear from the land of Tema and Mount Paran is the Holy Prophet Muhammad, and his fiery Law is the Quran which has the virtue of consuming to ashes the stuff of which sins and satanic machinations are made. Moses truly said that the Promised One, rising from Paran, would be accompanied by ten thousand saints. As all the world knows, it was the Holy Prophet of Islam who rose from Paran and marched into Mecca with ten thousand followers. Could Jesus be said to have fulfilled this great prophecy or David or

Moses? Did any of them rise from Paran? Did any of them march to victory with ten thousand saintly followers? Jesus had only twelve disciples, one of whom sold him for a little money. Another cursed him for fear of being maltreated. Ten remained faithful but, according to the Gospel account, even they dispersed when Jesus was put on the Cross. Had they stood by their Master's side, even then a following of ten could not have equalled a following of ten thousand. And then the Biblical prophecy says clearly that the ten thousand would be with the Promised Prophet. But the Gospels tell us that the ten disciples of Jesus who remained abandoned him when he was put on the Cross.

According to Habakkuk, one sign of the Promised One was to be the amount of praise showered upon him. Thus Habakkuk (3 : 3) says, "and the earth was full of his praise."

It does not seem to us a mere accident that the Holy Prophet of Islam was named Muhammad (literally, the Praised One). When his enemies denounced him, they were worried by the contradiction entailed in denouncing the Praised One. So they changed his name from Muhammad to Mudhammam, from the Praised One to the denounced one. When the Prophet's Companions got exasperated at the denunciations and abuse hurled at him he would say, "Hold your peace; they abuse not me but someone else called Mudhammam." Only a man with a name as beautiful as his personality and character could answer to the description which Habakkuk had given of the Promised One. No less significant is the tradition of devotional verse which has grown in Islam, and which has resulted in an important branch of the poetry written by Muslims of all countries.

Habakkuk also says:

> "Before him went the pestilence, and burning coals went forth at his feet" (3 : 5).

This sign of the Promised One was also fulfilled in the Prophet of Islam. True, the prophecy speaks of pestilence, that is, a disease in epidemic form. But it is large scale destruction and death which a pestilence brings which is here meant. Because the enemies of the Holy Prophet suffered large scale destruction and death in their encounters with him, he may be said to have fulfilled even this part of the prophecy.

Again it says :

> "He stood and measured the earth : he beheld, and drove asunder the nations" (3 : 6).

This part of the prophecy, like the others, can apply neither to Moses nor to Jesus. Moses died while he was still fighting his enemies, while Jesus was put on the Cross. The Prophet who beheld and drove asunder the nations was the Prophet of Islam. Truly did he say of himself, "My presence is awe-inspiring, and I have been helped not a little by it. People fear me from a distance of one month's journey" (Bukhārī).

Again :

> "The everlasting mountains were scattered, the perpetual hills did bow" (3 : 6).

This part of the prophecy also applies to the Holy Prophet of Islam. For his enemies were completely routed. Mountains and hills only mean powerful enemies.

Again we have in Habakkuk (3 : 7) :

> "I saw the tents of Cushan in affliction : and the curtains of the land of Midian did tremble."

This part of the prophecy clearly shows that the Promised Prophet was to belong to somewhere outside Syria. For it is the hordes in Cushan and Midian which are to be afflicted and frightened on the appearance of the armies of the Promised One. The description cannot apply to Moses or Jesus. It applies only to the Prophet of Islam. When a small army of his, in the time of his First Successor, Abū Bakr, advanced towards Palestine, notwithstanding the fact that Canaan was then under the Roman Kaiser, master of half the known world at the time, the superior forces of the Kaiser were crushed by the inferior Muslim forces. "The tents of Cushan were in affliction and the curtains of the land of Midian did tremble." The people of these lands found their salvation in laying down their arms before the servants of the Holy Prophet Muhammad.

THE PROPHET'S ADVENT FORETOLD BY SOLOMON

(*a*) In the Song of Solomon (5 : 10–16) we have :

> My beloved is white and ruddy, the chiefest among ten thousand. His head is as the most fine gold, his locks are

> bushy, and black as a raven. His eyes are as the eyes of doves by the rivers of waters, washed with milk, and fitly set. His cheeks are as a bed of spices, as sweet flowers: his lips like lilies, dropping sweet smelling myrrh. His hands are as gold rings set with the beryl: his belly is as bright ivory overlaid with sapphires. His legs are as pillars of marble, set upon socks of fine gold: his countenance is as Lebanon, excellent as the cedars. His mouth is most sweet: yea, he is altogether lovely. This is my beloved, and this is my friend, O daughters of Jerusalem.

This prophecy promises a Prophet who would be superior to others, and would possess a rank higher than others. We say this because the rapturous description in the Song of Solomon comes in reply to the question:

> "What is thy beloved more than another beloved?" (5 : 9).

We are told that this beloved would stand out like a flag among ten thousand men. As a flag symbolizes an army, the description, therefore, applies to some great occasion on which this beloved would command a following of ten thousand.

We are also told:

> "His lips like lilies, dropping sweet smelling myrrh" (5 : 13).

Now myrrh is a kind of gum, of bitter taste but sweet-smelling and very useful, a germ-killer and a cicatrizer, used in disinfectant preparations, in treating wounds and making scents and perfumes.

We are also told that "he is altogether lovely" (mark the Hebrew *Mahamaddīm*). It means his person and character would be such as to compel love and admiration.

This prophecy clearly applies to the Holy Prophet of Islam. It was he who headed ten thousand saints and marched victorious from the heights of Paran into the valley of Mecca, exactly as had been foretold by Moses. It was he whose teaching proved like myrrh for the world, bitter in taste but beautiful in its effects. It contained principles and rules all of which were calculated to promote the well-being of man, and which yet tasted bitter to some nations. And it is he who is called (and is true to the description) Muhammad.

Christian writers are wont to say that the beloved promised in this prophecy has been called *Mahamaddīm* not *Muhammad*.

But this objection does not go very far. The Old Testament name for God is *Elohīm*. In Hebrew it is common to show consideration and reverence by using a plural for a single person. We do the same in Urdu. Lecturing in Urdu, a lecturer might easily conclude his tribute to the Prophet by saying *Yeh hain hamáre Muhammad*, meaning, These are our Muhammad!

(*b*) In the Song of Solomon, we have another prophecy about the Holy Prophet of Islam. This is in 4 : 9–12. In these verses Solomon addresses his beloved as both sister and spouse (4 : 9 ; 4 : 10 ; 4 : 12). The simultaneous use of the two forms of address—sister and spouse—is not without significance. "Sister" indicates that the Promised Prophet would be an Ishmaelite, one of the brethren of the Israelites ; and "spouse" indicates that the Message of the Promised Prophet will not be confined to his own people, as were the Messages of all the Israelite Prophets. It would be open to other nations and peoples as well. We should not be misled by the feminine form of address used here. The passage is couched in poetical language, full of metaphors. The last line of the chapter uses the masculine form, which is contradictory, but significant. Thus we have :

> "Let my beloved come into his garden, and eat his pleasant fruits" (4 : 16).

The prophecy (4 : 9–12), therefore, applies only to the Holy Prophet of Islam. Jesus was not one of the brethren of Israel, nor was his teaching addressed to any people other than Israel.

(*c*) We also have in the Song of Solomon (1 : 5–6) :

> I am black, but comely, O ye daughters of Jerusalem, as the tents of Kedar, as the curtains of Solomon. Look not upon me, because I am black.

From this description it appears that Solomon foretold the advent of a Prophet who would come from the south, and he (or his people) would be black of skin as compared with the descendants of Isaac. It is well known that the people of Syria and Palestine have a fairer complexion than the people of Arabia. The Prophet of Islam was an Arab.

(*d*) In the same place another sign of the Promised One is given as follows :

> My mother's children were angry with me ; they made me the keeper of the vineyards ; but mine own vineyard have I not kept (1 : 6).

This is a description of the people to which the Promised One was to belong. The Arabs, at the advent of the Prophet of Islam, were an unambitious people. They accepted employment under Romans and Iranians, but of their own country they thought but little. The Holy Prophet came and Arabia rose from her slumber. The result was an Arab-led world movement embracing every conceivable side of human progress—spiritual, intellectual, political. The Arabs became the keepers not only of their own vineyard, but of the vineyards of the whole world.

(*e*) The Song of Solomon also contains a warning for Israel : they are told not to meddle with the Promised Prophet. Thus in 2 : 7 we have :

> I charge you, O ye daughters of Jerusalem, by the roes, and by the hinds of the field, that ye stir not up, nor awake my love, till he please.

The theme is continued in the Song in 3 : 5 and in 8 : 4. These passages only mean that when the Promised Prophet appeared, Jews and Christians, two branches of Israel, would oppose and oppress him ; but as the Prophet would be a God-appointed Prophet, they would not succeed, but would instead suffer an ignominious defeat. Solomon, accordingly, warned his people saying :

> "I charge you, that ye stir not up, nor awake my love, till he please."

The Israelites, both Jews and Christians, were advised to do nothing to the Promised Prophet. When his influence spread to their land, they should accept him. It would not do to oppose him and to try to stem the tide of his influence. Opposition would spell the opponents' own destruction. For a people who meddle with a Prophet's mission become liable to divine punishment. The warning proved true. Jews and Christians became meddlesome and brought divine punishment upon themselves. If a people remain passive and show no hostility to a Prophet, he adopts no violent steps against them but confines himself to teaching and preaching. Occasionally, a Prophet draws the sword, but only against those who first draw the sword against him. He makes war only upon those who first make war upon him and seek to put down by force and oppression the Message sent by God. The Holy Prophet's example illustrates this point. It was the risk entailed by thoughtless hostility to a true Message against which Solomon warned.

These prophecies cannot possibly apply to Jesus. Jesus did not appear from the south of Palestine. Nor was he one of the brethren of Israel. Nor did he have the means to resist and to destroy the opposition of Israel. The prophecies apply only to the Prophet of Islam. He is the beloved of the Song of Solomon. The Song is, in fact, a rapturous description of the Prophet.

ISAIAH'S PROPHECIES

The book of Isaiah also is full of prophecies about the Holy Prophet of Islam. They all point to the advent of another great Prophet, the harbinger of peace and contentment for the whole world. In accordance with the divine way, however, the prophecies contain a symbolic element which has to be interpreted before the meaning of the prophecies can be unravelled. The use in them of such names as Jerusalem, Zion, etc., is only symbolic. But Christian writers have been misled by these symbols into thinking that the prophecies relate to Jesus. Names *qua* names do not constitute any part of the prophecies. If the general content of the prophecies does not apply to Jesus, the names Jerusalem or Israel or Zion will not justify the application. True, the names also have a meaning, but a meaning which fits into the main content of the prophecies. As such the names Jerusalem and Israel will only mean "My holy places" or "My select people", not Jerusalem or Israel *per se*.

(*a*) The first prophecy we wish to quote from Isaiah is contained in 4 : 1–3. It is as follows :

> And in that day seven women shall take hold of one man, saying, We will eat our own bread, and wear our own apparel : only let us be called by thy name to take away our reproach. In that day shall the branch of the Lord be beautiful and glorious

> and the fruit of the earth shall be excellent and comely for them that are escaped of Israel. And it shall come to pass that he that is left in Zion, and he that remaineth in Jerusalem shall be called holy, even every one that is written among the living in Jerusalem.

Once it is agreed that Zion and Jerusalem in this prophecy are but symbols, the entire content of the prophecy is seen to apply to the Holy Prophet of Islam and to no one else. The prophecy says that the Promised Prophet will bring with him wealth and splendour, that he will have treasures of the earth laid at his feet, that his people will be called holy and that polygamous marriages will be the rule at the time. Do these signs apply to Jesus and his disciples ? Did they bring with them a period of wealth and splendour ? Were the treasures of the earth laid at their feet ? Was polygamy in demand by their society ? No. The signs apply only to the Holy Prophet of Islam, his followers and his time. Jesus is supposed to have disapproved of polygamous marriages. But the Holy Prophet of Islam sanctioned and even commanded these under certain conditions. It was in his time that wars had to be fought in defence of religion and the youth of the nation had to lay down their lives. The number of widows increased and young women had difficulty in finding husbands. The Holy Prophet, accordingly, ordered polygamous marriages to prevent immorality and to make up for lost man-power.

(*b*) In Isaiah (5 : 26–30) we have :

> And he will lift up an ensign to the nations from far, and will hiss unto them from the end of the earth : and, behold, they shall come with speed swiftly : None shall be weary nor stumble among them ; nor shall slumber nor sleep ; neither shall the girdle of their loins be loosed, nor the latchet of their shoes be broken : whose arrows are sharp, and all their bows bent, their horses' hoofs shall be counted like flint, and their wheels like a whirlwind : Their roaring shall be like a lion, they shall roar like young lions : yea, they shall roar, and lay hold of the prey, and shall carry it away safe, and none shall deliver it. And in that day they shall roar against them like the roaring of the sea : and if one look unto the land, behold darkness and sorrow, and the light is darkened in the heavens thereof.

A time was to come, according to this prophecy, when somewhere outside Palestine, a man would raise a flag. This man would call the nations of the world who would swiftly answer his call and gather around him. Those who responded to him would shun sloth and indolence and make great sacrifices for their cause. They would take part in wars and their horses' hoofs would emit fire like flint. Their attacks on their enemy would resemble a whirlwind. They would completely overpower their enemy whom no one would be able to save. And why should they do all this? Because they would see that the world was full of darkness and a big change called for.

This prophecy applies in its entirety to the Holy Prophet of Islam. There is a reference to it in the Quran also. In accordance with it, the Holy Prophet appeared away from Palestine in Mecca, and raised his flag in Medina; it was he who announced to the world:

> "Say, 'O mankind, truly I am a Messenger to you all'" (7 : 159).

It was his voice to which men and women from the ends of the earth responded with great alacrity. In Jesus' life not one convert came from outside Israel. All his disciples came from within a radius of forty to fifty miles. But believers in the Prophet of Islam came from Yemen and Najd and Iran, and among them were idol-worshippers and Jews and Christians. They made such great sacrifices at the Prophet's call and exerted themselves for it so ungrudgingly that the worst enemies of Islam feel constrained to pay a tribute to their spirit of devotion and sacrifice. God Himself pays a tribute to them in the Quran thus:

> "Allah is well pleased with them and they are well pleased with Him" (9 : 100).
>
> "There are some of them who have fulfilled their vow, and some who still wait" (33 : 24).

The Prophet's followers had to take part in wars and to make use of bows and arrows. Their horses' hoofs were like flint and their wheels like the whirlwind. To this also there is a clear reference in the Quran:

> By the panting chargers of the warriors, striking sparks of fire, making raids at dawn, and raising clouds of dust therewith, and penetrating thereby into the centre of the enemy forces (100 : 2–6).

This is a description of the warriors of early Islam, and how truly does it correspond to the prophecy of Isaiah.

We have in one part of the prophecy :

> And if one look unto the land, behold darkness and sorrow. and the light is darkened in the heavens thereof (Isaiah 5 : 30),

The Quran refers to this in 30 : 41 thus :

> "Corruption has appeared on land and sea." That is, both human wisdom and divine teaching have become dark and both point to the need of a new Teacher, bearer of a new Message from God.

Also in 65 : 11–12 we have :

> Allah has indeed sent down to you an admonition—a Messenger who recites unto you the clear Signs of Allah, that he may bring those who believe and do good deeds out of darkness into light.

(*c*) In Isaiah (8 : 13–17) we have :

> Sanctify the Lord of hosts himself ; and let him be your fear, and let him be your dread. And he shall be for a sanctuary ; but for a stone of stumbling and for a rock of offence to both the houses of Israel, for a gin and for a snare to the inhabitants of Jerusalem. And many among them shall stumble, and fall, and be broken, and be snared, and be taken. Bind up the testimony, seal the law among my disciples. And I will wait upon the Lord, that hideth his face from the house of Jacob, and I will look for him.

The prophecy clearly foretells the appearance of a Holy One whose coming will prove a trial for both Houses of Israel, a snare and a gin for the inhabitants of Jerusalem, who will be defeated and disgraced if they choose to oppose him. His advent will mark the supersession of the Mosaic Law and God will turn away His face from the House of Jacob.

Christian writers are silent on this point. Maybe they take the two Houses of Israel to mean the two factions, one of which supported and the other opposed the son of Solomon and set up a rival rule. But this will not do, because the prophecy speaks of a holy man and of events which will take place in his time. This holy man can either be Jesus or some one coming after Jesus, because there has been no outstanding religious personality between Isaiah and Jesus who may have confronted Israel with a crucial Message. But did Jesus confront Israel with any such Message? And did Israel suffer defeat and disgrace on opposing this Message? And did Jesus seal the Law for his disciples and announce its supersession by another Law? As for this, Jesus' declaration is quite clear. He said:

> Think not that I am come to destroy the law, or the prophets: I am not come to destroy, but to fulfil. For verily I say unto you, Till heaven and earth pass, one jot or one tittle shall in no wise pass from the law, till all be fulfilled (Matthew 5: 17–18).

Jesus settled the point not for his own time only but also for the future. He said significantly:

> Can the children of the bride-chamber fast, while the bridegroom is with them? As long as they have the bridegroom with them, they cannot fast. But the days will come when the bridegroom shall be taken away from them, and then shall they fast in those days (Mark 2: 19–20).

From these declarations it is obvious that, according to Jesus, even after his death, the Mosaic Law was to remain binding upon his disciples. Were this not so, he could have said that the days of fasting were over. Instead of this he not only fasted himself, but he also prophesied that his disciples would begin to fast after him. Sealing the Law, therefore, does not mean abolition of the Law as such or repudiation of the very idea of determinate religious duties. It means that in the time of the Promised Holy Man, the Mosaic Law would become superseded and a new Law would become established in its place. If this interpretation of ours is not true, why were we told that God would turn away His face from the House of Jacob? Did not Jesus belong to the House of Jacob? If he did not so belong, he could not be a descendant of David. And if he was not a descendant of David, he could not be the Christ of the prophecy. For Christ was to be a descendant of David:

(*d*) In Isaiah (9: 6–7) we have:

> For unto us a child is born, unto us a son is given: and the government shall be upon his shoulder: and his name shall be called Wonderful, Counsellor, The mighty God, The everlasting Father, The Prince of Peace. Of the increase of his government and peace there shall be no end, upon the throne of David, and

> upon his kingdom, to order it, and to establish it with judgement and with justice from henceforth even for ever. The zeal of the Lord of hosts will perform this.

The prophecy promises the advent of a king who will have five names or titles : (1) Wonderful. (2) Counsellor. (3) The mighty God. (4) The everlasting Father. (5) The Prince of Peace. The prosperity and peace in his empire will know no bounds ; he will sit on the throne of David for ever and perpetuate its good name by judgement and justice.

Annotators of the Gospels say in their headnotes to this chapter that this prophecy relates to the birth of Jesus. But of the signs mentioned in this prophecy, not one applies to Jesus. Did he for instance, ever become king ? Were the names enumerated in the prophecy—Wonderful, Counsellor, mighty God, everlasting Father, Prince of Peace, ever applied to him ? Wonderful, he might have been called, because of his peculiar birth. But the description does not seem to have been proposed. His deniers regarded his birth as illegitimate, so they could not describe him as Wonderful. His supporters, on the other hand, were in doubt about his ancestry. According to some he was a son of David. We have :

> If he be the King of Israel, let him now come down from the cross, and we will believe him. The thieves also, which were crucified with him, cast the same in his teeth (Matthew 27 : 42, 44).

Jesus gave no exhibition of his "might", nor was he ever described as "mighty" by anybody. Both friend and foe denied this of him. Were this not the case, his disciples would not have deserted him and fled. Says Matthew (26 : 56) :

> "Then all the disciples forsook him, and fled."

Does a mighty one meet with such a fate ?

The fourth name is everlasting Father, and this also does not apply to Jesus. For, as we have shown already, he foretold another who would come after him.

The fifth name is Prince of Peace and even this cannot apply to Jesus. He never became king, so he never could bring peace to the world. Instead, he remained oppressed by the Jews and was ultimately put on the Cross by them.

The prophecy lays down as a sign, "Of the increase of his

government and peace, there shall be no end". Jesus never attained to any government and, therefore, never could witness its increase.

Another sign is, "Upon the throne of David, and upon his kingdom, to order it, and to establish it with judgement and with justice from henceforth even for ever," and even this does not apply to Jesus.

These signs apply to the Holy Prophet of Islam. It was he who had to shoulder the responsibilities of State and who, quite against his will, found himself a king. It is an irony of fate that Jesus, who never became king, constantly dreamed of being one (Matthew, 21 : 4, 5 and 27 : 11 ; Luke, 23 : 1–3). The Holy Prophet was king ; yet he hated being one, and constantly warned his followers against imitating the ways of Kaiser and Chosroes.

One name of the Promised One is Wonderful. Jesus admits that the bearer of this name was to come after him. We have this admission in the parable of the vineyard (Matthew, 21 : 33–44). The parable is : A householder planted a vineyard and let it out to husbandmen. He then sent his servants to collect the fruit, but the husbandmen beat or killed or stoned the servants one by one. He sent more servants, but they also were maltreated like the others. He then sent his son, but the husbandmen killed the son. Having said so much, Jesus asked :

> When the lord therefore of the vineyard cometh, what will he do unto those husbandmen ? (21 : 40).

And those who heard answered :

> He will miserably destroy those wicked men, and will let out his vineyard unto other husbandmen, which shall render him the fruits in their seasons (21 : 41).

But Jesus said again :

> Did ye never read in the scriptures, The stone which the builders rejected, the same is become the head of the corner ; this is the Lord's doing, and it is marvellous in our eyes. Therefore say I unto you, the kingdom of God shall be taken from you, and given to a nation bringing forth the fruits thereof. And whosoever shall fall on this stone shall be broken : but on whomsoever it shall fall, it will grind him to powder (21 : 42–44).

That is to say, after the son had been slain, there would be another one sent by God, the one who would prove "the head of the corner", and who would seem "marvellous" in the eyes of Jesus and of all others. The Marvellous One, therefore, would come after the son is slain. It can only be the Holy Prophet of Islam who appeared after Jesus who was put on the Cross.

The third name of the Promised One is Counsellor. The name applies pre-eminently to the Holy Prophet. A nation turned to him for advice. He, in turn, held regular consultation with his people, and made it obligatory on the State to consult the people in all important matters. That the Prophet was a much-consulted person is evident from the Quran. We have:

> O ye who believe, when you consult the Messenger, give alms before your consultation. That is better for you and purer. But if you find not anything to give, then know that Allah is Forgiving, Merciful (58 : 13).

The rule about giving in charity before consulting, makes it clear that consulting the Prophet had become a regular institution, and a voluntary fee had been introduced to raise money for the poor. The rule was meant for those who could afford it. The Prophet had come to have so many calls on his time that it seemed possible and desirable to make a suitable charge on individual applicants. The charge was justified because the Prophet's time had to be devoted to the benefit of mankind at large; if individuals applied for the use of his time, it was meet they should pay something into the public treasury. Consulting the Prophet, therefore, had become a regular institution. The Prophet more than anybody else deserves to be called the Counsellor. The Prophet also instituted the system of consultation as an essential condition of good government.

Says the Quran:

> "And whose affairs are decided by mutual consultation" (42 : 39).

General measures and administrative rules are not to be initiated until the people's representatives have been consulted. Following this injunction, the Holy Prophet laid down consultation as an important duty of the Khalīfa, or elected head of Muslims. He is reported to have said, "There is no Khilāfat without consultation". (Izālat al-Khifā 'an Khilāfat al-Khulafā). A State administered without consulting the people would be un-Islamic. Compared with this, what did Jesus do as counsellor? He never consulted on any considerable scale. Nor did he encourage counselling as an institution. The Holy Prophet, therefore, was the Counsellor of the prophecy and not Jesus.

The third name in the prophecy is mighty God. The Old Testament points to a resemblance between God and Moses. Thus in Exodus (7 : 1) we have:

> "And the Lord said unto Moses, See, I have made thee a God to Pharaoh."

And again in Exodus (4 : 16):

> "And thou shalt be to him (Aaron) instead of God."

In the Bible Jesus is called son of God and Moses a "like of God". Whenever, therefore, a human being is spoken of as a "like of God", it would mean Moses or some one like Moses. Moses we have shown above, foretold of a prophet like himself (Deut. 18 : 18), and he is no other than the Holy Prophet of Islam, he being the one who really answers to the description of the prophecy. It is the Prophet of Islam, therefore, who can most legitimately be called God or, better, a Manifestation of God. We have references relevant to this in the Quran. At the Battle of Badr, the Prophet took a handful of gravel and threw it at the enemy. This proved a signal for a dust-storm which discomfited the enemy and contributed to his defeat. Of this, God says to the Prophet:

> "And thou threwest not when thou didst throw, but it was Allah Who threw" (8 : 18).

Similarly at the time of entering Islam, new believers used to take the oath of allegiance to the Prophet. Referring to this God says in the Quran:

> "Verily those who swear allegiance to thee indeed swear allegiance to Allah" (48 : 11).

The Prophet does service for God. The term "God" of the prophecy, therefore, applies to the Prophet rather than to anybody else. So does the expression "mighty". For it was he who was able to subjugate all his enemies in his lifetime and to smash all opposition.

The fourth name in the prophecy is everlasting Father. This also applies to the Prophet and to no one else. It was he who claimed unambiguously a lasting character for his teaching. For he foretold the second coming of Christ, but the second coming of Christ was to be in the person of one of the Prophet's own followers, not one whose coming could violate his spiritual dominion. Referring to this God says in the Quran :

> And We have not sent thee save as a bringer together of all mankind—a bearer of glad tidings and a warner ; but most men know not. And they say, "When will this promise be fulfilled, if you speak the truth ?" Say, "For you is an appointed day from which you cannot remain behind a single moment nor can you get ahead of it" (34: 29-31).

The expression "all mankind" here points to the universal and everlasting character of the Message of Islam. It is to be addressed to all nations in all ages. Disbelievers taunt the Prophet about the day promised here and ask when it will be ; that is, when will the universal and everlasting character of Islam be demonstrated to the world ? God says in reply that the day will come as appointed.

The day is referred to also in 32 : 6, thus :

> He would plan the divine ordinance from the heaven unto the earth, then shall it go up. to Him in a day the duration of which is a thousand years according to what you reckon.

The thing planned is Islam. In course of time its influence will begin to decline. In a thousand years it will have ascended back to heaven. The special divine support which it enjoyed in the beginning will disappear and its fortunes will be at the mercy of the natural forces of the world. From the Quran as well as the Ḥadīth it appears that the expansion of Islam was to go on for the first three hundred years, after which was to set in the period of its decline. The decline was to go on for one thousand years. Reading together the two passages—34 : 29–31 and 32 : 6—it becomes quite clear that for a long time people would remain unconvinced of the universal and everlasting character of the Message of Islam ; but after one thousand three hundred years facts and conditions would emerge which would leave the world in no doubt about it. The passages read together point to the second coming of the Messiah—promised in both the Quran and the Ḥadīth—and remind us that the second coming will take place in the person of a follower of the Prophet of Islam. As the advent of the Promised Messiah would have been prophesied by other Prophets also, his rise from among the followers of the Holy Prophet would prove conclusively that the spiritual dominion of the Prophet of Islam was everlasting, that there were to be no heavenly Teachers now except from among his followers. The Law and Teaching of the Holy Prophet would remain unsuperseded by any other Law or Teaching. Besides, in the Promised Messiah's time there was great stress to be laid on the duty of preaching, resulting ultimately in the spread of Islam all over the world. When this happens, the universal and everlasting character of Islam will be established beyond doubt. The everlasting Father of the prophecy of Isaiah, therefore, is the Prophet of Islam and none other.

The fifth name in the prophecy is Prince of Peace. Prince also means king ; a prince is potential king. We may, therefore, take the expression to mean King of Peace, and as such it can apply only to the Prophet of Islam. The religion which he founded is called Islam, which literally means, "peace".

We do not know in what sense Jesus can be regarded as Prince of Peace. At least one meaning of this expression would be that the person so called has an abundance of the quality called peace. Prince of Peace would, therefore, be a person who has peace in his natural gifts and is able to give peace to others. There is no evidence of this in the case of Jesus. He never had the power to administer forgiveness to his enemies. True, he preached forgiveness and taught his followers to turn the other cheek. But between profession and performance there is a world of difference, and what is really valuable is performance, not profession. Of this performance, we have evidence only in the Holy Prophet. How cruelly he was treated by his people. There are no excesses which were not committed against him and his followers. Many among his closest relations and friends were murdered mercilessly. The prophet's own person was a witness to these barbarities. He was their target on many different occasions and in many different ways. He had to leave his home town and seek shelter elsewhere, as had his friends and followers. Almost all of them had to suffer the pangs of separation from their near and dear ones. Some were torn asunder while tied to two camels running in opposite directions. Women were killed by spears thrust in their private parts. Slaves who believed in him were stripped and dragged on burning sand and gravel. They were persecuted and asked to renounce their faith. The bodies of Muslims killed in battle were mutilated. In short, early Muslims—men and women, old and young, dead and living—had to suffer to the utmost and in a variety of ways. But at last God made them triumphant. The Holy Prophet, with ten thousand followers, re-entered Mecca as a victor. The cruel enemy was at his feet, thinking no punishment too much for what he had done. Yet all that the Prophet said to them was, "This day, I forgive you all" (Hishām). The Prophet had the power to avenge the wrongs done to him and his followers. But he chose to forgive, and to desist even from any injury to their sentiments. When Muslims were advancing towards Mecca, a Muslim general was heard to say that on that day they would repay the Meccans in their own coin (Bukhārī). The Prophet deposed the general, saying that such remarks were calculated to hurt the Meccans. Do we meet with any such thing in the life of Jesus ? Or in the lives of his disciples ? Or, in the whole of Christian history ? There is no doubt that Christians also suffered much persecution and hardship, and were a weak people. But the time came when they were installed in power. How did they then treat their enemies ? Is not history dyed red with the blood of their enemies ? How then can Jesus be called Prince of Peace ? He himself could not afford peace to others. His followers were able to afford it, but did not give it. Instead, they gave death and destruction. The Prophet of Islam had the power to punish his enemies for wrongs many times more savage than those perpetrated by Jews against Jesus. Still he chose to forgive. The Prophet was, therefore, the Prince of Peace of Isaiah's prophecy.

The seventh sign of the Promised One according to Isaiah (9: 7) was:

> "Of the increase of his government and peace, there shall be no end."

The sign clearly applies to the Prophet of Islam and not to Jesus. Jesus did not attain to any political power. The Prophet did, and his followers became rulers of the whole of the then known world ; and so well did they rule that it is impossible to find a parallel.

The eighth sign was :

> Upon the throne of David, and upon his kingdom, to order it, and to establish it with judgement and with justice from henceforth even for ever (9 : 7).

Did Jesus ever ascend the throne of David ? It may be he did so three hundred years later, when the Roman Emperor became Christian. But the prophecy lays down that the throne is to be retained for ever. The hold of Jesus lasted for about three hundred years when it ended with the rise of Islam, and now for one thousand three hundred years, Palestine—the throne of David—has been in the possession of Muslims. What is nearer to the expression "for ever" in the prophecy—three hundred years or one thousand three hundred ? No doubt, today a Christian power holds Palestine. But it is significant from our standpoint that the British are there not as rulers but as holders of a mandate. A temporary lapse in the Muslim possession cannot contradict the prophecy.

The rule which the Prophet of Islam established in the world through his followers was full of judgement and justice, to use the words of the prophecy. We have historical evidence to prove this. In the time of 'Umar, the Second Khalīfa of Islam, a Muslim army had to withdraw temporarily from Christian territory under the pressure of superior Roman forces. Before they did, they collected the inhabitants and told them that they could no longer protect their lives and property ; so they were returning to them the money they had realized from them as tax. The Christian inhabitants of Jerusalem were so impressed by this singular act of good judgement and justice that they came out with the Muslim army, wailing and praying for the Muslims' speedy return

(The Caliphate and Futūḥ). Little wonder Isaiah says of the Promised One:

> Upon the throne of David, and upon his kingdom, to order it and to establish it with judgement and with justice (9 : 7).

(*e*) In Isaiah (19 : 21-25) we have:

> And the Lord shall be known to Egypt, and the Egyptians shall know the Lord in that day; and shall do sacrifice and oblation; yea, they shall vow a vow unto the Lord, and perform it. And the Lord shall smite Egypt: he shall smite and heal it; and they shall return even to the Lord, and he shall be intreated of them, and shall heal them. In that day shall there be a highway out of Egypt to Assyria, and the Assyrian shall come into Egypt, and the Egyptian into Assyria, and the Egyptians shall serve with the Assyrians. In that day shall Israel be the third with Egypt and with Assyria, even a blessing in the midst of the land; whom the Lord of hosts shall bless, saying, Blessed be Egypt my people, and Assyria the work of my hands, and Israel mine inheritance.

This prophecy speaks of a time when God would manifest Himself to the people of Egypt who would, therefore, come to know Him and would make sacrifices and offerings to Him; Egypt and Syria would unite, the inhabitants of each would visit the other; and both would join in a common form of worship.

This prophecy also was fulfilled in the Holy Prophet of Islam. The people of Egypt did become Christian, but only for a short time of their history. Now for one thousand three hundred years Egyptians have been Muslims. In the words of Isaiah, God says to the Egyptians: "Blessed be Egypt, my people." Let the Egyptians speak for themselves. Do they owe allegiance to Jesus or to the Prophet of Islam?

We then have:

> "And Assyria the work of my hands."

Similarly let the Assyrians speak for themselves. Do they attribute themselves to Jesus or the Prophet of Islam?

And we have:

> "And Israel mine inheritance."

Who holds Palestine, the land of Israel?

No doubt, under European and American influence Jews are entering Palestine. But the Jews are not the followers of Jesus. And in any case Muslims still form a majority in this land of Israel, and Christians still a minority. If Jews take possession of the land it will only mean a temporary lapse in the Muslim possession, and whether it is Jews or Muslims who possess the land, Jesus can have no claim on the prophecy.

The prophecy speaks of "a highway out of Egypt into Assyria", i.e., a sign of active contact between the two countries. The prophecy pictures the inhabitants of the two countries visiting and befriending each other and joining in a common mode of worship. Who brought all this about ; was it Jesus ? Christians were in possession of both Egypt and Assyria and a majority of the inhabitants of these countries, at one time, were Christian. But during this time, did the conditions arise of which the prophecy speaks ? According to the prophecy the two countries were to develop such intimate contact that for all practical purposes they were to become one people, with one language and one faith. Some contact between two neighbouring countries is normal and natural. But the contact between Egypt and Assyria was to be different ; it was to result in welding two peoples into one, and to give them a common nationality. Such a fusion between the two never occurred in the time of Christian rule. Under Rome, Egypt and Syria were parts of the same empire, but the mode of administration in the two countries remained different. Egypt was a semi-independent kingdom, and Assyria was under a Roman Governor. The Egyptian Church also was different from the Assyrian Church. In Egypt, under the influence of the Alexandrian Church, Christianity had assumed a form different from that of the Palestinian or Syrian Church. The Egyptians worshipped in their own language, Coptic, and Syrians in a corrupt mixture of Hebrew and Greek. Under Islam conditions became quite different. For centuries Egypt and Syria remained under one rule. Both began to speak and still speak one language. Both adopted and still keep up a common mode of worship. Both developed a common consciousness. Syrian scholars went to Egypt and were honoured as Egyptian savants. Egyptian scholars went to Syria and were honoured as Syrian savants. Even today, while the Muslim world under European diplomacy lies dismembered, the Arab League is a united body of Egyptians, Syrians and Palestinians. The three seem to share and to be proud of a common nationality. This prophecy of Isaiah, therefore, was fulfilled in and through the Holy Prophet of Islam and his followers. To apply this to Jesus and the Christian Church seems utter extravagance.

(*f*) In Isaiah (62 : 2) we have :

> "And thou shalt be called by a new name, which the mouth of the Lord shall name."

Quite evidently, the prophecy foretells of a new movement, with a new name, and the new name will not be one assumed by the movement, but one proposed for it by God in His revealed word. Annotators of the Bible apply this prophecy to the Christian Church, notwithstanding the common knowledge that the names Christian and Christianity, or the many names by which Christian sects are known, were never proposed by God in His revealed word but were assumed by the people. There is one people alone in all the world who have a name given to them by God, and they are Muslims. Thus the Quran says :

> "He named you Muslims both before and in this Book" (22 : 79).

This is a clear reference to the prophecies of Isaiah. The verse of the Quran seems to say, "We foretold that your name will not be one of your choice but one of Our choice. Accordingly, today, We give you the name—Muslim." The name is derived from *salām* which means Peace, and this is in keeping with one of the titles of the Promised Prophet—"Prince of Peace". The prophecy was marvellous. Equally marvellous is the fact that only Muslims claim to have received their name from God in His own revealed word. Isaiah foretold that a Prophet would come the name of whose followers would be chosen by God and announced in His revealed word. The Holy Prophet of Islam is that Prophet ; his followers have been named Muslims by God, and his religion Islam.

PROPHECIES OF DANIEL

According to the book of Daniel, chapter 2, Nebuchadnezzar, King of Babylon, had a dream, which he forgot soon after. Then he called upon the wise men of his time to tell him both the dream and its meaning. None of them, however, was able to do so. Daniel prayed to God and had the dream and its meaning revealed to him.

The dream was as follows :—

> Thou, O king, sawest, and behold a great image. This great image, whose brightness was excellent, stood before thee; and the form thereof was terrible. This image's head was of fine gold, his breast and his arms of silver, his belly and his thighs of brass, his legs of iron, his feet part of iron and part of clay. Thou sawest till that a stone was cut out without hands, which smote the image upon his feet that were of iron and clay, and brake them to pieces. Then was the iron, the clay, the brass, the silver, and the gold, broken to pieces together, and became like the chaff of the summer threshing floors; and the wind carried them away, that no place was found for them: and the stone that smote the image became a great mountain, and filled the whole earth (Daniel 2 : 31–35).

The interpretation which Daniel gave of the dream was the following :

> Thou, O king, art a king of kings : for the God of heaven hath given thee a kingdom, power, and strength, and glory. And wheresoever the children of men dwell, the beasts of the field and the fowls of the heaven hath he given into thine hand, and hath made thee ruler over them all. Thou art this head of gold. And after thee shall arise another kingdom inferior to thee, and another third kingdom of brass, which shall bear rule over all the earth. And the fourth kingdom shall be strong as iron; forasmuch as iron breaketh in pieces and subdueth all things : and as iron that breaketh all these, shall it break in pieces and bruise. And whereas thou sawest the feet and toes, part of potters' clay, and part of iron, the kingdom shall be divided; but there shall be in it of the strength of the iron, forasmuch as thou sawest the iron mixed with miry clay. And as the toes of the feet were part of iron, and part of clay, so the kingdom shall be partly strong, and partly broken. And whereas thou sawest iron mixed with miry clay, they shall mingle themselves with the seed of men; but they shall not cleave one to another, even as iron is not mixed with clay. And in the days of these kings shall the God of heaven set up a kingdom, which shall never be destroyed : and the kingdom shall not be left to other people, but it shall break in pieces and consume all these kingdoms, and it shall stand for ever. Forasmuch as thou sawest that the stone was cut out of the mountain, without hands, and that it brake in pieces the iron, the brass, the clay, the silver, and the

> gold; the great God hath made known to the king what shall come to pass hereafter: and the dream is certain, and the interpretation thereof sure (Daniel 2 : 37–45).

In Daniel's interpretation, the gold head is the king of Babylon; the silver breast and arms the kingdoms of Persia and Midia which arose after the kingdom of Babylon; the brass thighs stand for the Greek Empire under Alexander, which became dominant after Persia and Midia; and the iron legs stand for the Roman Empire which attained to power on the decline of the Alexandrian Empire. About this last, the dream says:

> "His feet (*i.e.*, the image's) part of iron and part of clay" (2 : 33).

The description points to the fact that the Roman Empire would cover parts of Europe as well as Asia. Iron legs denote the European part of the Roman Empire and point to the strength of a single nationality and a single faith. But the feet, says the dream, were partly of iron, partly of clay. This meant that the European power was to subjugate parts of Asia and thus become an imperial power. Imperial powers command large territories and vast resources, but they also suffer from the inherent weakness which comes from lack of cohesion among their peoples. The dream evidently means that in latter years the Roman Empire would begin to decline because of this lack of cohesion. The dream, however, proceeds to say more important things:

> Thou sawest till that a stone was cut out without hands, which smote the image upon his feet that were of iron and clay, and brake them to pieces. Then was the iron, the clay, the brass, the silver, and the gold, broken to pieces together, and became like the chaff of the summer threshing floors; and the wind carried them away, that no place was found for them: and the stone that smote the image became a great mountain, and filled the whole earth (Daniel 2 : 34–35).

Here we have a prediction of the rise of Islam. Early Islam clashed first with Rome and then with Iran. When they clashed with Rome, Rome had conquered the Alexandrian Empire of Greece and had become more powerful than ever; and when they clashed with Iran, Iran had extended its power over Babylon. When their clashes resulted in the destruction of both Rome and Iran, then did the iron, the clay, the brass, the silver, and the gold, break to pieces together, and became like the chaff of the summer threshing floors. The order of events in the dream and their interpretation by Daniel leave no doubt as to their meaning.

Everybody knows that Babylon was succeeded by Persia and Midia and the power of Persia and Midia was broken by Alexander and the Empire of Alexander was replaced by that of Rome which from its Eastern seat of authority at Constantinople laid the foundation of a mighty Europo-Asiatic Empire. This Asiatic Roman Empire was defeated and destroyed by the Holy Prophet and his Companions. Once receiving a report that the Roman armies intended to attack the Muslims, he led an expedition in person to the Syrian border. But no regular fighting then took place. Irregular skirmishes and raids, however, continued till regular fighting was resumed in the time of Abū Bakr which resulted in the total discomfiture and annihilation of the Roman Empire in the time of 'Umar, the Second Khalīfa, when the Persian Empire also suffered defeat at the hands of Muslim armies. Thus both these once mighty empires shrank into diminutive and distant States.

We have references to the "stone" of Daniel's prophecy in Isaiah and Matthew. In Isaiah 8 : 14 we read of a Holy One :

> And he shall be for a sanctuary ; but for a stone of stumbling and for a rock of offence to both the houses of Israel, for a gin and for a snare to the inhabitants of Jerusalem.

And in 8 : 15 :

> And many among them shall stumble, and fall and be broken, and be snared, and be taken.

And from Matthew, chapter 21, it appears that the Promised One—the stone of the prophecy—is not Jesus, but another coming after Jesus, and in 21 : 44 we have a fine description of the stone :

> And whosoever shall fall on this stone shall be broken : but on whomsoever it shall fall, it will grind him to powder.

Similarly in Psalms 118 : 22 we have :

> "The stone which the builders refused is become the head stone of the corner."

To this there is reference also in Matthew (21 : 42) :

> Jesus saith unto them, Did ye never read in the scriptures, The stone which the builders rejected, the same is become the head of the corner : this is the Lord's doing, and it is marvellous in our eyes.

As we have shown above, Jesus himself denies all claim to this prophecy, which applies to one coming after the son is slain. Christians today fondly apply the prophecy to their Church. But this attempt will not avail. According to Daniel, the thighs of the image were made of brass, the legs (*i.e.*, the Roman Empire) of iron and the feet of iron and clay ; the stone smote the image upon his feet. Early Islam, that is to say, was to clash with the borders of the Asiatic part of the Roman Empire and smash it to pieces. The Roman Empire was the temporal expression of the Christian Church. The stone of the prophecy, therefore, was to clash with the Church. The stone could not be the Church, for the Church could not clash with the Church. Nor could it be Jesus. For Jesus came long before the Eastern Roman Empire. Whoever destroyed the might of the Roman Empire, fulfilled this prophecy. The prophecy, therefore, applies to the Holy Prophet of Islam and his followers, and to no one else.

The prophecy goes on to say :

> The stone that smote the image became a great mountain, and filled the whole earth (Daniel 2 : 35).

This is exactly what happened. The Holy Prophet and his band of devotees defeated the Kaiser and the Chosroes, and Muslims became rulers over the whole of the then known world. The stone did become a great mountain ; for a thousand years the direction of world affairs remained in the hands of Muslims.

PROPHECIES IN THE NEW TESTAMENT

We turn now to prophecies about the Prophet of Islam which are recorded in the New Testament. In Matthew (21 : 33–46) we read :

> Hear another parable : There was a certain householder, which planted a vineyard, and hedged it round about, and digged a winepress in it, and built a tower, and let it out to husbandmen, and went into a far country : And when the time of the fruit

drew near, he sent his servants to the husbandmen, that they might receive the fruits of it. And the husbandmen took his servants, and beat one, and killed another, and stoned another. Again, he sent other servants more than the first; and they did unto them likewise. But last of all he sent unto them his son, saying, They will reverence my son. But when the husbandmen saw the son, they said among themselves, This is the heir; come, let us kill him, and let us seize on his inheritance. And they caught him and cast him out of the vineyard, and slew him. When the lord therefore of the vineyard cometh, what will he do unto those husbandmen? They say unto him, He will miserably destroy those wicked men, and will let out his vineyard unto other husbandmen which shall render him the fruits in their seasons. Jesus saith unto them, Did ye never read in the scriptures, The stone which the builders rejected, the same is become the head of the corner; this is the Lord's doing, and it is marvellous in our eyes? Therefore say I unto you, The Kingdom of God shall be taken from you, and given to a nation bringing forth the fruits thereof. And whosoever shall fall on this stone shall be broken; but on whomsoever it shall fall, it will grind him to powder. And when the chief priests and Pharisees had heard his parables, they perceived that he spake of them. But when they sought to lay hands on him, they feared the multitude, because they took him for a prophet.

We have referred to this prophecy before. In this beautiful parable Jesus has presented an epitome of the history of Prophets. The passage leaves no doubt that vineyard means the world; husbandmen mean mankind at large; fruits which the householder wishes to collect mean virtue, piety and devotion to God; servants mean Prophets who have been coming into the world one after the other; son means Jesus who appeared after a long line of Prophets. The son was dishonoured and slain by the husbandmen. Having said this, Jesus goes on to speak of "the stone which the builders rejected, the same is become the head of the corner." The stone which had been rejected is the progeny of Ishmael, whom the sons of Isaac used to treat with contempt. According to the prophecy, one from among the sons of Ishmael was to appear and become the head of the corner, "the Seal of the Prophets", to use the well-known expression of the Quran—no ordinary Prophet, but one who would bring a final and complete Law from God. The advent of an Ishmaelite for the grand office would seem strange too. Yet (as Jesus says) God would take away His kingdom from the Israelites and give it to the Ishmaelites, who would prove a nation bringing forth the fruits thereof, that is, a people who would keep alive the worship of God in the world. Everybody should be able to see that the only outstanding Prophet who came after Jesus and who could be said to answer to this description is the Holy Prophet of Islam. He it was who came into conflict with Judaism and Christianity and completely shattered the influence of both. He it was whose race was hated. Of him alone could it be truly said, "Whosoever fell on him was broken and on whomsoever he fell was ground to powder."

(*b*) In Matthew (23 : 38–39) we have :

> Behold, your house is left unto you desolate. For I say unto you, Ye shall not see me henceforth, till ye shall say, Blessed is he that cometh in the name of the Lord.

The verses mean that Jesus is going to depart from his people and his people will not be able to see him again, until they declare :

> "Blessed is he that cometh in the name of the Lord."

There is a prophecy here of two advents. One after the departure of Jesus ; this was to be like the advent of God. The other was the second advent of Jesus himself. It is made clear that until the one who "cometh in the name of the Lord" has come, the second coming of Jesus will not take place. We have proved above that one who comes in the name of the Lord is the one resembling Moses.

The prophecy of Jesus and the certain fact of the advent of Islam and its Holy Prophet leave no doubt that in the divine scheme the advent of Jesus was not to mark the last great stage in spiritual advance. The last stage was to be marked by the advent of one coming "in the name of the Lord." It cannot be said that after him Jesus is to come again, so the last stage in spiritual advance will still be marked by Jesus. The point is made clear by Jesus himself. Did he not say :

> Ye shall not see me henceforth, till ye shall say, Blessed is he that cometh in the name of the Lord (Matthew 23 : 39).

Only they will see, receive and acknowledge Jesus on his

second coming who will first have accepted and acknowledged "the like of Moses". A denier of "the like of Moses" will not be able to recognize Jesus when he comes a second time. And why not? Because Jesus when he comes again will be found among the followers of "the like of Moses". Only they will be able to believe in the second coming of Jesus who will first have believed in "the like of Moses". Jesus, therefore, when he comes a second time, will be no independent Teacher. He will be a strict follower and an image of "the like of Moses". The last stage of spiritual advance, therefore, will be marked by this "like of Moses", and by no one else.

(*c*) We read in John (1 : 20–21) that people went to John the Baptist, and asked him if he were the Christ of the prophecy and he said, No. Then they

> "asked him, what then? Art thou Elias? And he saith, I am not" (1 : 21).

Then they asked him:

> "Art thou that prophet? And he answered, No" (1 : 21).

And then they said:

> Why baptizest thou then, if thou be not that Christ, nor Elias, neither that prophet? (1 . 25).

It is evident from this that three prophecies were current in the time of Jesus: (*i*) the second coming of Elias; (*ii*) the birth of Christ; (*iii*) the coming of that Prophet, that is, the Promised One of the prophecy in Deuteronomy. The three were believed to be separate persons.

Now Jesus has declared that John himself is Elias. Thus in Matthew (11 : 14) we have:

> "And if ye will receive it, this is Elias, which was for to come."

From Luke (1 : 17) it also appears that before the birth of John, his father Zacharias had the revelation:

> "And he shall go before him in the spirit and power of Elias."

Then in Mark (9 : 13) we have Jesus declaring:

> "That Elias is indeed come."

And again in Matthew (17 : 12):

> That Elias is come already, and they knew him not, but have done unto him whatsoever they listed.

From all these passages, it is clear that according to the Gospels, the second coming of Elias had taken place in John. As for Christ, it is agreed that he is no other than Jesus of the New Testament. Only "that Prophet" remains. He is neither John, nor Jesus, because he is different from both, a third. It is also known that "that Prophet" had not appeared until the time of Jesus. So it is clear that "that Prophet" of the Bible had to appear, according to the testimony of the Gospels, some time after Jesus. After Jesus, no one has claimed to be "that Prophet" and indeed no one seems to fulfil the signs attributed to "that Prophet" except the Holy Prophet of Islam.

(*d*) In Luke (24 : 49) we have :

> And, behold, I send the promise of my Father upon you ; but tarry ye in the city of Jerusalem, until ye be endued with power from on high.

From this verse also it appears that after Jesus there was to be another. And who is he except the Holy Prophet ? No one excepting him has ever made the claim.

(*e*) In John (14 : 26) we have :

> But the Comforter, which is the Holy Ghost, whom the Father will send in my name, he shall teach you all things, and bring all things to your remembrance, whatsoever I have said unto you.

This prophecy also is true only of the Prophet of Islam. True, it says "whom the Father will send in my name". But "in my name" can only mean, "he will bear testimony to my truth". The Holy Prophet testified to the truth of Jesus as a divine and honoured Teacher and Prophet, and declared them mistaken and misguided who thought him accursed. The prophecy says clearly, "He shall teach you all things." The words are reminiscent of those used in the prophecy in Deuteronomy. The description applies only to the Holy Prophet ; and it was his teaching which brought comfort to the world.

(*f*) In John (16 : 7–14) we have :

> Nevertheless I tell you the truth ; It is expedient for you that I go away : for if I go not away, the Comforter will not come unto you ; but if I depart, I will send him unto you. And when he is come, he will reprove the world of sin, and of righteousness, and of judgement : of sin, because they believe not on me ;

> of righteousness, because I go to my Father, and ye see me no more ; of judgement, because the prince of this world is judged. I have yet many things to say unto you, but ye cannot bear them now. Howbeit when he, the Spirit of truth, is come, he will guide you into all truth ; for he shall not speak of himself ; but whatsoever he shall hear, that shall he speak : and he will shew you things to come. He shall glorify me : for he shall receive of mine, and shall shew it unto you.

The prophecy lays down that the Comforter will come after the departure of Jesus. When the Comforter comes, he will reprove the world of sin and truth and justice. Of sin, because he will accuse the Jews of disbelief in Jesus. Of truth, because he will correct the erroneous belief in the resurrection of Jesus, and because he will assure the world that Jesus of Nazareth —the Teacher who appeared to Israel—will not again come into the world in person. Of justice, because he will put an end to all satanic forces. The prophecy also says that when the Spirit of truth comes, he will guide them into all truth, that the book revealed to him will contain no human word, that he will foretell things to come, and that he will glorify Jesus and clear him of all charges.

This prophecy unmistakably applies to the Holy Prophet. It says quite clearly that unless Jesus departs, the Comforter cannot come. From The Acts (3 : 21–22) it also appears that the Prophet promised in Deuteronomy 18 : 18 is to appear sometime between the departure of Jesus and his second coming. The Comforter, therefore, is no other than the Promised One of Deuteronomy 18 : 18. The prophecy says that the Promised One will reprove the deniers of Jesus. The Promised One could not be a Christian. It is but usual for followers to reprove the deniers of their Prophet. The prophecy must relate to one who would belong to another people, with no racial or religious connection with Jesus but being truthful and God-sent, he should respect the cause of all true Prophets and promote respect and reverence for them all. The Prophet of Islam was an Ishmaelite, not a Christian or Jew. But how he defends the honour of Jesus ! Referring to the Jews the Quran (4 : 158–161) says :

> And their saying, 'We did kill the Messiah, Jesus, son of Mary, the Messenger of Allah' ; whereas they slew him not,

> nor crucified him, but he was made to appear to them like one crucified ; and those who differ therein are certainly in a state of doubt about it : they have no definite knowledge thereof, but only follow a conjecture ; and they did not convert this conjecture into a certainty ; on the contrary, Allah exalted him to Himself. And Allah is Mighty, Wise ; and there is none among the People of the Book but will believe in it before his death ; and on the day of Resurrection, he (Jesus) shall be a witness against them. So, because of the transgression of the Jews, We forbade them pure things, which had been allowed to them, and also because of their hindering many men from Allah's way.

The excesses of the Jews were their disbelief, their cruel charge against Mary, and their utterly false claim that they had put to death Jesus, a Messenger of God. The truth about this claim was that they had failed to kill Jesus either by the sword or by crucifixion. They had only strong suspicion that Jesus had died on the Cross. But it was only a suspicion, not a certain belief. They themselves continued to differ among themselves and had no agreed view as to what had really happened to Jesus. Possessing no certain knowledge, they merely speculated. But this is certain that they failed in their design to put Jesus to death. Allah, on the other hand, saved him from an accursed death on the Cross and admitted him to the circle of His favoured ones, and Allah is both Powerful and Wise. Every follower of the Book will continue to affirm his belief in the death of Jesus on the Cross, but on the Judgement Day Jesus himself will depose against them all and accuse them of affirming a falsehood. Because of these excesses of the Jews, God withdrew from them those heavenly blessings which formerly seemed their birthright. The passage speaks for itself.

A second sign in the prophecy of John (16 : 7–14) is that the Promised One will correct the erroneous belief in the resurrection of Jesus and prove that Jesus, the Israelite, will not come to the world again. This duty was duly performed by the Holy Prophet of Islam ; he exposed the error that Jesus rose from the dead and ascended to heaven where he was still alive. Says the Quran (5 : 117–119) :

> And when Allah will say, "O Jesus, son of Mary, didst thou say to men, 'Take me and my mother for two gods beside Allah ? ' " he will answer, "Holy art Thou. I could never say

> that to which I had no right. If I had said it, Thou wouldst have surely known it. Thou knowest what is in my mind, and I know not what is in Thy mind. It is only Thou Who art the Knower of hidden things. I said nothing to them except that which Thou didst command me—'Worship Allah, my Lord and your Lord.' And I was a witness over them as long as I remained among them, but since Thou didst cause me to die, Thou hast been the watcher over them; and Thou art witness over all things. If Thou punish them, they are Thy servants; and if Thou forgive them, Thou surely art the Mighty, the Wise."

The interrogation and the reply are to take place on the Judgement Day. The passage declares that Jesus is dead, and not alive in heaven; only his followers raised him to godhead after he had died and departed from this world. Ascending to heaven only means that, having done his duty he had gone to his Maker, honoured and successful.

The prophecy (John 16 : 7–14) also said that Satan and satanic forces will be smashed at the hands of the Promised One. Of all the Prophets, the Prophet of Islam stands preeminent in the designing of measures against all satanic forces and influences and for the promotion of purity and piety in human life. We cannot go into a detailed exposition of such points here. The reader will find it elsewhere in this work. We may only say that at least one visible proof of this claim of ours on behalf of the Prophet is the prayer for protection against the influence of Satan which the Prophet taught his followers, and on the frequent use of which he insisted, *viz.*, *I seek refuge with Allah from Satan, the rejected.* The prayer is in habitual use by Muslims. We know of nothing like it in the teachings of other Prophets. Muslims, more than any other people, are alive to their daily duty of defeating the designs of Satan. They, more than any other people, have been taught this duty. They, more than any other people, are deserving of the promise contained in the prophecy. Their Prophet, therefore, will be said to have fulfilled the prophecy. To kill Satan, however, is not to kill him outright, so that his influence no longer remains in the world. This has never happened and never will happen. Satanic influences and temptations must remain. Without them faith will have no value. To kill Satan therefore is to reduce evil influences and propensities to a minimum, and to promote good influences and dispositions to a maximum. The Church cannot lay claim to this part of the prophecy because the Church has declared the Law a curse and cast doubt over the very conceptions of good and evil. The words in the prophecy—"he will guide you into all truth"—we have already explained in our discussion of the prophecy contained in Deuteronomy 18 : 18.

Of the promise—"he will show you things to come"—we need only say that no other Prophet has told the world of things to come so much as has the Prophet of Islam.

Of the sign—"he shall not speak of himself, but whatsoever he shall hear, that shall he speak"—we should say that the description can apply only to the Prophet of Islam. The New and the Old Testaments do not contain a single book in which man's word has not been mixed with God's. The Quran is nothing but the word of God from beginning to end. Not a word even of the Prophet is to be found in it, let alone anybody else's.

The last sign in the prophecy—"he will glorify me"—also applies to the Holy Prophet. For it is he who cleared Jesus of the charge that, having died on the Cross, he met an accursed death ; and of the charge that, having claimed Godhead for himself, Jesus had been guilty of disobedience and disloyalty to God ; and of the other foul charges which the Jews had brought against him.

(*g*) In The Acts (3 : 21–24) we have :

> Whom the heaven must receive until the times of restitution of all things, which God hath spoken by the mouth of all his holy prophets since the world began. For Moses truly said unto the fathers, A Prophet shall the Lord your God raise up unto you of your brethren, like unto me ; him shall ye hear in all things whatsoever he shall say unto you. And it shall come to pass, that every soul, which will not hear that prophet, shall be destroyed from among the people. Yea, and all the prophets from Samuel and those that follow after, as many as have spoken, have likewise foretold of these days.

The verses contain a reference to the prophecy in Deuteronomy and the clear hint that until the Prophet promised in the prophecy in Deuteronomy has come, the second coming of

Jesus will not take place. The prophecy in Deuteronomy said that the Promised Prophet would bring a new Law. Reference to this in The Acts means clearly that the teaching of Jesus will be superseded by the teaching of the Promised One. A new Law can have no other meaning. The Prophet promised in the prophecy in Deuteronomy (and in this passage from The Acts), therefore, was to mark the last stage in the spiritual advance of man. For he was to supersede Moses and Jesus and give the world a new Teaching and a new Law.

The passage from The Acts points to another significant sign of the Promised One. It says :

> All the prophets from Samuel and those that follow after, as many as have spoken, have likewise foretold of these days (3 : 24).

The prophecy of Moses we have already cited. As Jesus came after Samuel, this verse from The Acts can only mean that from Moses to Jesus every Prophet has foretold the advent of a Prophet, which means that until this Prophet appears the spiritual foundations on which man must build will not have been completely laid. As this Prophet, according to the signs of the Bible, is no other than the Holy Prophet of Islam, we must admit that the Holy Prophet is the Promised One of all Prophets and his Law is the Law prophesied by all Prophets. Who can then say that even while the Old and the New Testaments existed in the world the Quran was a redundance ? All the earlier Prophets have pointed to the need of the Quran and prophesied about it. No reasonable plea can be urged by their followers now against the Quran. We can only say that if they deny the need of the Quran, they will cast doubts on the truth of their own Prophets and the truth of the prophecies which they made. Did not Moses say :

> When a prophet speaketh in the name of the Lord, if the thing follow not, nor come to pass, that is the thing which the Lord hath not spoken, but the Prophet hath spoken it presumptuously ; thou shalt not be afraid of him (Deut. 18 : 22).

THE HOLY PROPHET—A LIFE SKETCH

WE have now answered the question concerning the need for the revelation of the Quran in the presence of other religious books. We wish now to give a life-sketch of the Holy Prophet. The connection between a revelation and its recipient is intimate, and we cannot hope to understand the one without the other.

The philosopher is able to dissociate what a person says from the person saying and to think of each in isolation from the other. An Arabic proverb regards what a person says as more important than the person saying it. But the great majority of ordinary human beings make no distinction between the two and regard both as equally important. With regard to a revealed book it seems particularly important that, when we study it we should keep in view the life and character of the person who received the book from God and communicated it to his generation. A religious teaching, however well-argued, is not accepted by a people unless it captivates them by a strong personality appeal. This is because religious Law is different in aim from secular law. The State stands for stability and order. It seeks to establish external obedience; for this it is enough to have laws which secure external good behaviour. Motives do not matter so long as there is no visible departure from the law. Bad motives are not punished by any court of law unless they result in bad conduct. But from the standpoint of religion, motives are as important as the actions which result from them. They are even more important. Actions are also important—they are the symptoms and signs of invisible motives. But an improvement in visible actions is no guarantee of improvement in invisible motives. An improvement in invisible motives, however, is a guarantee of improvement in visible actions. Fire without warmth is impossible; so is purity of heart impossible without purity of conduct. Temporary lapses or indolence there may be; but in general, purity of heart must lead to purity of conduct.

Now purity of heart is best promoted by concrete example. A good law appeals to our understanding and reason; but a good example appeals to our motives and sentiments. A good law rouses us to think, but a good example rouses us to action. When thinking becomes refined, it may or may not result in a refinement of our physical and spiritual character. It may result only in spasms of good conduct—not in a steady and stable character. The point is illustrated by the difference between ordinary altruistic conduct and altruistic conduct which springs from natural instincts such as the maternal instinct. One springs largely from reason, the other largely from emotions. Conduct which springs from reason cannot compete with conduct which springs from emotions or dispositions which grow out of emotions.

A mother's love and care for her child spring from emotions or from dispositions, shaped out of emotions. The philosopher's regard for his neighbour springs from reasoned altruism. Reasoned conduct is not constant or consistent, because reflection often tends to fail and all the relevant facts cannot always be attended to before action is ordered. Hesitation and deliberation, the essentials of all reasoned conduct, also tend to be prolonged. But conduct which springs from emotions or from tendencies shaped out of emotions is spontaneous, constant and consistent. A mother may seem over-sacrificing, but rational appeals will not dissuade her from the path laid down for her by nature. When the child is in trouble, she will not sit and deliberate, but will at once set about doing what she thinks is good for the child. All her thoughts will bend to this end. It seems, therefore, that themes of moral reclamation will not succeed unless human individuals can be taught to act from dispositions and sentiments rooted in their natural emotions and impulses. When the call comes for action, response should not be held back by undue deliberation. It should spring spontaneously from within each individual and should not have to be forced from without by appeals to reason.

True, emotions are usually accorded a place second to reason. But this is because we only think of uncultured or misguided emotions. Conduct which becomes related to emotions only reduces or abolishes the period of hesitation and deliberation intervening between a call for action and the action itself. The elimination of this period is necessary if actions are to be quick and numerous. A person who deliberates too much or too often wastes time which should be spent in action. But the person who grasps a truth and then converts that truth into an emotion never hesitates to respond whenever there is a call for action. Such a person can never be beaten by one given to deliberating. His output is twenty times more than the output of the other. Spontaneity and apparent impulsiveness cannot reduce the value of his actions. For he does not really act from impulses: he deliberates and acquires insight into ends and means. This insight he welds into his emotions. He acts spontaneously and apparently unthinkingly, but his actions have a rational basis and are the result of deliberation. Only for him deliberation once concluded, does not have to be gone through again and again. To deliberate overmuch or to deliberate again and again cannot be rational. Any large-scale reclamation or reconstruction of the world, therefore, will have to wait not on intellectual clarity and intellectual conviction, but will have to be linked with the normal emotions and impulses of man. The greatest possible intellectual clarity will not rid us of doubts and uncertainties. There is one way to escape doubts, and that is to grasp a truth and then to assimilate it into our character. When this is done, truths no longer strike us as objects for apprehension or enjoyment, but serve as signals and guides for action and achievement. For the ordinary man this assimilation of truths into everyday character is not possible save under the influence of practical examples. Reasoning may stimulate our understanding; it cannot stimulate self-denial which only a living exemplar of self-sacrifice and self-denial can. Words used in prayers may be most appropriate and persuasive, but nothing will induce the absorption needed in prayer more than the sight of an actual worshipper absorbed in prayer.

But we should not be misunderstood. An example can be misleading and dangerous. It must be examined before it can be allowed to influence us. Unless it has been examined and found satisfying, imitation of it will only result in habit-ridden individuals and a custom-ridden society. What we need, therefore, is both a reasoned teaching and a spotless practical exemplar. Thank God, Books revealed by Him have been revealed to Prophets, not dropped from above. Books appeal to our understanding, Prophets to our heart. No wonder, Prophets make a much deeper impression on the world than do philosophers ; they succeed where philosophers fail. Philosophers seek to clarify our thinking, not to convert us by their good example. But Prophets do both. They excite our intellect through their books and our hearts through their example. Their recorded teaching sharpens our understanding, while the signs of divine existence witnessed in their persons promote certainty, faith and fervour.

It seems to us, therefore, that in this General Introduction we should give some account of the life and character of the Holy Prophet of Islam.

LIFE OF THE PROPHET AN OPEN BOOK

The life of the Holy Founder of Islam is like an open book, to any part of which one may turn and meet with interesting details. The life of no other Teacher or Prophet is as well-recorded and as accessible to study as is the life of the Holy Prophet. True, this abundance of recorded fact has given malicious critics their opportunity. But it is also true that when the criticisms have been examined and disposed of, the faith and devotion which result cannot be inspired by any other life. Obscure lives escape criticism, but they fail to produce conviction and confidence in their devotees. Some disappointments and difficulties are bound to remain. But a life as rich in recorded detail as the Prophet's inspires reflection and, then, conviction. When criticism and false constructions have been liquidated, such a life is bound to endear itself to us completely and for ever.

It should be evident, however, that the story of a life so open and so rich cannot even briefly be told. Only a glimpse of it can be attempted. But even a glimpse is worth while. A religious book, as we say, can have little appeal unless a study of it can be supplemented by a knowledge of its Teacher. The point has been missed by many religions. The Hindu religion, for instance, upholds the Vedas, but of the Rishis who received the Vedas from God it is able to tell us nothing. The need to supplement a message by an account of the messenger does not seem to have impressed itself upon Hindu exponents. Jewish and Christian scholars, on the other hand, do not hesitate to denounce their own Prophets. They forget that revelation which has failed to reclaim its recipient cannot be of much use to others. If the recipient is intractable the question arises, why did God choose him ? Must He have done so ? Neither supposition seems reasonable. To think that revelation fails to reclaim some recipients is as unreasonable as to think that God has no alternative except to choose incompetent recipients for some of His revelations. Yet ideas of this kind have found their way into different religions, possibly because of the distance which now divides them from their Founders or because human intellect, until the advent of Islam, was incapable of perceiving the error of these ideas. How important and valuable it is to keep together a book and its Teacher was realized very early in Islam. One of the Prophet's holy consorts was the young 'Ā'isha. She was thirteen to fourteen years of age when she was married to the Prophet. For about eight years she lived in wedlock with him. When the Prophet died she was about twenty-two years of age. She was young and illiterate. Yet she knew that a teaching cannot be divorced from its teacher. Asked to describe the Prophet's character, she answered at once that his character was the Quran (Abū Dāwūd). What he did was what the Quran taught ; what the Quran taught was nothing else than what he did. It redounds to the glory of the Prophet that an illiterate young woman was able to grasp a truth which escaped Hindu, Jewish and Christian scholars.

'Ā'isha expressed a great and an important truth in a crisp little sentence : it is impossible for a true and honest teacher to teach one thing but practise another, or to practise one thing but teach another. The Prophet was a true and honest Teacher. This is what 'Ā'isha evidently wanted to say. He practised what he preached and preached what he practised. To know him is to know the Quran and to know the Quran is to know him.

ARABIA AT THE TIME OF THE PROPHET'S BIRTH

The Prophet was born in Mecca in August 570 A.D. He was given the name Muhammad which means, the Praised One. To understand his life and character we must have some idea of the conditions which obtained in Arabia at the time of his birth.

When he was born the whole of Arabia, with exceptions here and there, believed in a polytheistic form of religion. The Arabs traced their descent to Abraham. They knew that Abraham was a monotheistic Teacher. In spite of this, they entertained polytheistic beliefs and were given to polytheistic practices. In defence, they said that some human beings are outstanding in their contact with God. Their intercession on behalf of others is accepted by God. God is High and Exalted. To reach Him is difficult for ordinary human beings. Only perfect human beings can reach Him. Ordinary human beings, therefore, must have others to intercede on their behalf befor they can reach God and attain to His pleasure and His help. With this attitude they were able to combine their reverence for Abraham, the monotheist, with their own polytheistic beliefs. Abraham, they said, was a holy man. He was able to reach God without intercession. But ordinary Meccans were not able to reach God without the intercession of other holy and righteous persons. To seek this intercession, the people of Mecca had made idols of many holy and righteous persons, and these they worshipped and to these they made offerings in order to please God through them. This attitude was primitive and illogical. It was full of defects and gaps. But the people of Mecca were not worried by these. They had not had a monotheistic Teacher for a long time, and polytheism, once it takes root in any society, spreads and knows no bounds. The number of gods begins to increase. At the time of the Prophet's birth, it is said that in the Ka'ba alone, the Sacred Mosque of all Islam and the house of worship built by Abraham and his son Ishmael, there were three hundred and sixty idols. It seems that for every day of the lunar year the Meccans had an idol. In other places and in other big centres there were other idols, so that we can say that every part of Arabia was steeped in polytheistic belief. The Arabs were devoted to the culture of speech. They were much interested in their spoken language and were very keen on its advance. Their intellectual ambitions, however, were scant. Of History, Geography, Mathematics, etc., they knew nothing. But as they were a desert people and had to find their way about in the desert without the assistance of landmarks, they had developed a keen interest in Astronomy. There was in the whole of Arabia not a single school. It is said that in Mecca only a few individuals could read and write.

From the moral point of view the Arabs were a contradictory people. They suffered from some extreme moral defects but at the same time they possessed some admirable qualities. They were given to excessive drinking. To become drunk and to run wild under the effect of drink was for them a virtue, not a vice. Their conception of a gentleman was one who should entertain his friends and neighbours to drinking bouts. Every rich man would hold a drinking party at least five times in the day. Gambling was their national sport. But they had made of it a fine art. They did not gamble in order to become rich. Winners were expected to entertain their friends. In times of war, funds were collected through gambling. Even today we have the institution of prize-bonds to raise money for war. The institution has been resuscitated in our time by the people of Europe and America. But they should remember that in this they only imitate the Arabs. When war came, Arabian tribes would assemble and hold a gambling party. Whoever won had to bear the greater part of the expenses of the war.

Of the amenities of civilized life, the Arabs knew nothing. They found compensation in drinking and gambling. Their chief occupation was trade, and to this end they sent their caravans to far-off places. In this way they traded with Abyssinia, Syria and Palestine. They had trade relations even with India. The rich among them were great admirers of Indian swords. Their clothing needs were supplied largely by Yemen and Syria. The trading centres were the towns. The rest of Arabia, excepting Yemen and some northern parts, was Bedouin. There were no permanent settlements, no permanent places of habitation. The different tribes had divided the country between them so that members of a tribe wandered about freely in their part of the country. When the water supply in any place was exhausted, they would move on to some other place and settle down. Their capital consisted of sheep, goats and camels. From the wool they made cloth, and from the skins they made tents. What was left over they sold in the market. Gold and silver were not unknown, but they were certainly very rare possessions. The poor and the common folks made ornaments of cowries and sweet-smelling substances. Seeds of melons were cleaned, dried and strung together to make necklaces. Crime and immoralities of various kinds were rampant. Theft was rare but dacoity was common. To attack and to dispossess one another was regarded a birthright. But, at the same time, they honoured their word more than any other people. Should an individual go to a powerful leader or tribe and ask for protection, that leader or tribe was honour-bound to protect that individual. If this was not done, the tribe lost caste throughout Arabia. Poets commanded great prestige. They were honoured as national leaders. Leaders were expected to possess great powers of speech and even to be able to compose verse. Hospitality had developed into a national virtue. A forlorn traveller on arrival at the headquarters of a tribe would be treated as an honoured guest. The best animals would be slaughtered for him and the utmost consideration shown. They did not care who the visitor was. It was enough that a visitor had arrived. The visit meant an increase of status and prestige for the tribe. It became the tribe's duty, therefore, to honour the visitor. By honouring him it honoured itself. Woman in this Arab society had no status and no rights. Among them it was thought honourable to put baby girls to death. It is a mistake, however, to think that infanticide was practised on a country-wide scale. Such a dangerous institution could not flourish throughout a country. That would have meant the extinction of the race. The truth is that in Arabia—or for that matter in India or any other country where infanticide has ever existed, it has been confined only to certain families. The Arab families who practised it either had an exaggerated notion of their social status or they were constrained in other ways. Possibly they were unable to find suitable young men for their daughters to marry; knowing this, they put to death their baby girls. The evil of this institution lies in its savageness and its cruelty, not in the results which it has in terms of a nation's population. Different methods were used for killing baby girls, among them burying alive and strangulation.

Only the real mother was regarded as a mother in Arab society. Step-mothers were not regarded as mothers and there was no ban on a son's marrying his step-mother on the death of his father. Polygamous marriages were very common, and there was no limit to the number of wives a man could take. More than one sister could also be taken to wife by the same person at one and the same time.

The worst treatment was meted out by combatant sides to one another in war. Where hatred was strong, they did not hesitate to split the bodies of the wounded, take out parts and eat them in cannibal fashion. They did not hesitate to mutilate the bodies of their enemies. Cutting off the nose or ears, or plucking out an eye was a common form of cruelty practised by them. Slavery was widespread. Weak tribes were made slaves. The slave had no accepted status. Every master did as he liked with his slaves. No action could be taken against a master who maltreated his slave. A master could murder his slave without having to answer for it. If one master murdered another's slave, even then the penalty was not death. All that was required of him was to compensate the aggrieved master suitably. Women-slaves were used to satisfy sexual desires. The children born of such unions were also treated as slaves. Women-slaves who became mothers remained slaves. In terms of civilization and social advance the Arabs were a very backward people. Kindness and consideration to one another were unknown. Woman had the worst status possible. Still the Arabs possessed some virtues. Individual bravery, for instance, sometimes reached a very high level.

It was among such people that the Holy Prophet of Islam was born. His father 'Abdullah had died before his birth. Accordingly, he and his mother Āmina had to be looked after by the grandfather, 'Abd al-Muṭṭalib. The child Muhammad was suckled by a countrywoman who lived in a place near Ṭā'if.

It was a custom in Arabia in those days to hand over children to women in the country, whose duty it was to bring up the children, to train their speech and to give them a good start in bodily health. When the Prophet was in his sixth year, his mother died while travelling from Medina to Mecca and had to be buried *en route*. The child was brought to Mecca by a woman-servant and handed over to the grandfather. When he was in his eighth year, his grandfather also died, after which Abū Ṭālib, his uncle, became his guardian, this being the wish expressed in a will by the grandfather. The Prophet had two or three opportunities to travel out of Arabia. One of these occurred when at the age of twelve he went in the company of Abū Ṭālib to Syria. It seems that this journey took him only to the south-eastern towns of Syria, for in historical references to this journey there is no mention of places like Jerusalem. From now onwards until he grew up to young manhood he remained in Mecca. From very childhood he was given to reflection and meditation. In the quarrels and rivalries of others he took no part, except with a view to putting an end to them. It is said that the tribes living in Mecca and the territories around, tired of unending blood-feuds, resolved to found an association the purpose of which was to help victims of aggressive and unjust treatment. When the Holy Prophet heard of this, he gladly joined. Members of this association gave an undertaking in the following terms:

> They will help those who were oppressed and will restore them their rights, as long as the last drop of water remained in the sea. And if they do not do so, they will compensate the victims out of their own belongings (Rauḍ al-Unuf by Imām Suhailī).

It seems that no other member of this association was ever called upon to discharge the undertaking solemnly entered into by members of this association. But opportunity came to the Holy Prophet when he had announced his Mission. His worst enemy was Abū Jahl, a chief of Mecca. He preached social boycott and public humiliation of the Prophet. About that time a person from outside came to Mecca. Money was due to him from Abū Jahl, but Abū Jahl refused to pay. He mentioned this to people in Mecca. Some young men, out of sheer mischief, suggested that he should approach the Prophet. They thought that the Prophet would refuse to do anything for fear of the general opposition to him and particularly for fear of the opposition of Abū Jahl. If he refused to help this man, he would be said to have broken his pledge to the association. If, on the other hand, he did not refuse and chose to approach Abū Jahl for the restitution of this loan, Abū Jahl was certain to turn him away with contempt. This man went to the Prophet and complained to him about Abū Jahl. The prophet, hesitating not a minute, stood up, went with the man and knocked at Abū Jahl's door. Abū Jahl came out and saw that his creditor was standing with the Prophet. The Prophet mentioned the loan and suggested its payment. Abū Jahl was taken aback and, making no excuses, paid at once. When the other chiefs of Mecca heard of this they reproved Abū Jahl, telling him how weak and self-contradictory he had proved. He preached the social boycott of the Prophet, yet he himself accepted direction from the Prophet and paid a loan on his suggestion. In self-defence, Abū Jahl pleaded that any other person would have done the same. He told them that as he saw the Prophet standing at his door, he also saw two wild camels standing one on each side, ready to attack. We cannot say what this experience was. Was it a miraculous appearance designed to upset Abū Jahl or was it the awe-inspiring presence of the Prophet which produced this hallucination? A man hated and oppressed by a whole town had taken the courage to go alone to the leader of that town and demand the restitution of a loan. Maybe this very unexpected sight frightened Abū Jahl and for a moment made him forget what he had sworn to do against the Prophet, and forced him to do as the Prophet suggested (Hishām).

HOLY PROPHET'S MARRIAGE WITH KHADĪJA

When the Prophet was about twenty-five years old, his reputation for integrity and fellow-feeling had spread over the whole of the town. People would point admiring fingers at him and say, here was a man who could be trusted. This reputation reached the ears of a rich widow who approached the Prophet's uncle, Abū Ṭālib, to let his nephew lead a trading caravan of hers to Syria. Abū Ṭālib mentioned this to the Prophet and the Prophet agreed. The expedition met with great success and brought unexpected profits. The rich widow, Khadīja, was convinced that the success of the caravan was due not only to the conditions of the market in Syria, but also to the integrity and efficiency of its leader. She interrogated her slave, Maisara, on this subject, and Maisara supported her view and told her that the honesty and sympathy with which this young leader of the caravan had managed her affairs would not be shown by many persons. Khadīja was much impressed by this account. She was forty years of age and had already been widowed twice. She sent a woman friend of hers to the Prophet to find out whether he would be persuaded to marry her. This woman went to the Prophet and asked why he had not married. The Prophet replied he was not rich enough to do so. The visitor suggested whether he would agree, if a rich and respectable woman were found whom he could marry. The Prophet asked who this woman could be, and the visitor said she was Khadīja. The Prophet apologized, saying that Khadīja was too highly placed for him. The visitor undertook to deal with all difficulties. In that case, said the Prophet, there was nothing for him to say but to agree. Khadīja then sent a message to the Prophet's uncle. Marriage between the Prophet and Khadīja was settled and solemnized. A poor man orphaned in childhood had his first peep into prosperity. He became rich. But the use he made of his riches is an object-lesson to all mankind. After the marriage Khadīja felt that she was rich and he was poor and that this inequality between them would not make for happiness. So she proposed to make over her property and her slaves to the Prophet. The Prophet, making sure that Khadīja was in earnest, declared that as soon as he had any of Khadīja's slaves, he would set them free. And he did so. Moreover, the greater part of the property which he received from Khadīja he distributed among the poor. Among the slaves whom he thus set free was one Zaid. He appeared to be more intelligent and more alert than others. He belonged to a respectable family, had been kidnapped as a child and sold from place to place until he reached Mecca.

Young Zaid, newly freed, saw at once that it was better to sacrifice freedom for the sake of slavery to the Prophet. When the Prophet set the slaves free, Zaid refused to be freed and asked leave to continue to live with the Prophet. He did so, and as time went on his attachment to the Prophet grew. But in the meantime Zaid's father and his uncle were on his track and they ultimately heard that he was in Mecca. In Mecca they traced him in the house of the Prophet. Coming to the Prophet, they asked for the liberty of Zaid and offered to pay as much ransom as the Prophet should demand. The Prophet said that Zaid was free and could go with them as he liked. He sent for Zaid and showed him his father and uncle. After the parties had met and dried their tears, Zaid's father told him that he had been freed by his kind Master and, as his mother was much afflicted by the separation, he had better return home. Zaid replied, "Father ! who does not love his parents ? My heart is full of love for you and mother. But I love this man Muhammad so much that I cannot think of living elsewhere than with him. I have met you and I am glad. But separation from Muhammad I cannot endure." Zaid's father and his uncle did their utmost to persuade Zaid to return home with them but Zaid did not agree. Upon this the Holy Prophet said, "Zaid was a freed man already, but from today he will be my son." Seeing this affection between Zaid and the Prophet, Zaid's father and uncle went back and Zaid remained with the Prophet (Hishām).

THE PROPHET RECEIVES HIS FIRST REVELATION

When the Prophet was over thirty years of age, love of God and love of His worship began to possess him more and more. Revolting against the mischiefs, misdeeds and the many vices of the people of Mecca, he chose a spot two or three miles away for his meditations. This was on top of a hill, a sort of cave shaped out of stone. His wife Khadīja would prepare food enough for several days, and with this he would repair to the cave Ḥirā. In the cave he would worship God day and night. When he was forty years of age, he saw a vision. It was in this very cave. He saw some one commanding him to recite.

The Prophet said in reply he did not know what or how to recite. The figure insisted and at last made the Prophet recite the following verses :

> Recite thou in the name of thy Lord Who created, created man from a clot of blood. Recite ! And thy Lord is the Most Beneficent, Who taught man by the pen, taught man what he knew not (96 : 2–6).

These verses, the first ever revealed to the Prophet, became part of the Quran as did other verses which were revealed later. They have tremendous meaning. They command the Prophet to stand up and be ready to proclaim the name of the One God, the One Creator—of the Prophet and of all others—Who has made man and sowed the seed of His own love and that of fellow-men in his nature. The Prophet was commanded to proclaim the Message of this God, and was promised help and protection by Him in the proclamation of this Message. The verses foretold a time when the world would be taught all manner of knowledge through the instrumentality of the pen, and would be taught things never heard of before. The verses constitute an epitome of the Quran. Whatever the Prophet was to be taught in later revelations is contained in embryo in these verses. The foundation was laid in them of a great and heretofore unknown advance in the spiritual progress of man. The meaning and explanation of these verses will be found in their place in this Commentary. We refer to them here because their revelation constitutes a great occasion in the life of the Prophet. When the Prophet received this revelation, he was full of fear of the responsibility which God had decided to place on his shoulders. Any other person in his place would have been filled with pride—he would have felt that he had become great. The Prophet was different. He could achieve great things but could take no pride in his achievement. After this great experience he reached home greatly agitated, his face drawn. On Khadīja's enquiry, he narrated the whole experience to her and summed up his fears, saying, "Weak man that I am, how can I carry the responsibility which God proposes to put on my shoulders." Khadīja replied at once :

> God is witness, He has not sent you this Word that you should fail and prove unworthy, that He should then give you up.

> How can God do such a thing, while you are kind and considerate to your relations, help the poor and the forlorn and bear their burdens ? You are restoring the virtues which had disappeared from our country. You treat guests with honour and help those who are in distress. Can you be subjected by God to any trial ? (Bukhārī).

Having said this, Khadīja took the Prophet to her cousin, Waraqa bin Naufal, a Christian. When he heard the account Waraqa said :

> "The angel who descended on Moses, I am sure, has descended on you" (Bukhārī).

FIRST CONVERTS

Waraqa evidently referred to the prophecy in Deuteronomy 18 : 18. When the news reached Zaid, the Prophet's freed slave, now about thirty years of age, and his cousin 'Alī, about eleven, they both declared their faith in him. Abū Bakr, friend of his childhood, was out of town. As he returned he began to hear of this new experience which the Prophet had had. He was told that his friend had gone mad and had begun to say that angels brought him messages from God. Abū Bakr trusted the Prophet completely. He did not doubt for a minute that the Prophet must be right—he had known him to be both sane and sincere. He knocked at the Prophet's door and on admission into his company asked him what had happened. The Prophet, fearing lest Abū Bakr should misunderstand, began a long explanation. Abū Bakr stopped the Prophet from doing so, and insisted that all he wanted to know was whether an angel had really descended upon him from God and had given him a Message. The Prophet wanted to explain again, but Abū Bakr said he wanted to hear no explanation. He wanted only an answer to the question whether he had had a Message from God. The Prophet said, "Yes" and Abū Bakr at once declared his faith. Having declared his faith, he said, argument would have detracted from the value of his faith. He had known the Prophet long and intimately. He could not doubt him, and he wanted no argument to be convinced of his truth. This small group of the Faithful then were the first believers of Islam : a woman full of years, an eleven-year-old boy, a freed slave living among strangers, a young friend and the Prophet himself. This was the party which made the silent resolve to spread the light of God all over the world. When the people and their leaders heard of this, they laughed and declared that these men had gone mad. There was nothing to fear and nothing to worry about. But as time went on, the truth began to dawn and as the Prophet Isaiah (28 : 13) said long ago, precept upon precept, precept upon precept ; line upon line, line upon line ; here a little, and there a little ; began to descend upon the Prophet.

THE FAITHFUL PERSECUTED

God began to talk to Muhammad in "another tongue". The youth of the country began to wonder. Those in search of truth became excited. Out of scorn and derision began to grow approval and admiration. Slaves, young men, and hapless women began to collect around the Prophet. In his Message and in his teaching there was hope for the degraded, the depressed and the young. Women thought the time for the restoration of their rights was near. Slaves thought the day of their liberation had come and young men thought the avenues of progress were going to be thrown open to them. When derision began to change into approval and indifference into attachment, the chiefs of Mecca and the officials began to take fright. They assembled and took counsel. They decided that derision was no method to deal with this menace. A more serious remedy had to be applied. The new influence had to be put down by force. It was decided that persecution and some form of boycott must be instituted. Practical steps were soon taken, and Mecca was pitched against Islam in a serious conflict. The Prophet and his small following were no longer considered mad, but a growing influence which, if allowed to grow unimpeded, would prove a danger to the faith, prestige, customs and traditions of Mecca. Islam threatened to pull down and rebuild the old structure of Meccan society, to create a new heaven and a new earth, the coming of which must mean the disappearance of the old heaven of Arabia and its old heart. Meccans could no longer laugh at Islam. It was a question now of life and death for them. Islam was a challenge and Mecca accepted the challenge, as enemies of Prophets had always accepted the challenge of their Prophets. They decided not to meet argument by argument but to draw the sword and put down the dangerous teaching by force ; not to match the good example of the Prophet and his followers by their own, nor to reply to kind words in kind, but to maltreat the innocent and to abuse those who spoke kindly. Once again in the world a conflict started between belief and disbelief ; the forces of Satan declared war on the angels. The Faithful, still a handful, had no power to resist the onslaughts and violence of the disbelievers. A most cruel campaign began. Women were butchered shamelessly. Men were slaughtered. The slaves who had declared their faith in the Prophet were dragged over burning sands and stones. Their skins became hardened like those of animals. A long time after, when Islam had become established far and near, one of these early converts named Khabbāb bin Al-Arat had his body exposed. His friends saw his skin hardened like an animal's and asked him why it was so. Khabbāb laughed and said it was nothing ; only a memory of those early days when slaves converted to Islam were dragged through the streets of Mecca over hard and hot sands and stones (Musnad, Vol. 5, p. 110).

The slaves who believed came from all communities. Bilāl was a negro, Ṣuhaib a Greek. They belonged to different faiths. Jabr and Ṣuhaib were Christians, Bilāl and 'Ammār, idol-worshippers. Bilāl was made to lie on hot sand, loaded with stones, and boys were made to dance on his chest, and his master, Umayya bin Khalf, tortured him thus and then asked him to renounce Allah and the Prophet and sing the praises of the Meccan gods, Lāt and 'Uzzā. Bilāl only said, *Aḥad*, *Aḥad* . . . (God is One).

Exasperated, Umayya handed Bilāl over to street boys, asking them to put a cord round his neck and drag him through the town over sharp stones. Bilāl's body bled, but he went on muttering, *Aḥad*, *Aḥad*. . . . Later, when Muslims settled in Medina and were able to live and worship in comparative peace, the Holy Prophet appointed Bilāl a *Mu'adhdhin*, the official who calls the worshippers to prayers. Being an African,

Bilāl missed the (*h*) in the Arabic *Ash-hadu* (I bear witness). Medinite believers laughed at his defective pronunciation, but the Prophet rebuked them and told them how dear Bilāl was to God for the stout faith he showed under Meccan tortures. Abū Bakr paid ransom for Bilāl and many other slaves and secured their release. Among them was Ṣuhaib, a prosperous merchant, whom the Quraish continued to belabour even after his release. When the Holy Prophet left Mecca to settle down in Medina, Ṣuhaib wanted to go with him. But the Meccans stopped him. He could not take away from Mecca, they said, the wealth he had earned in Mecca. Ṣuhaib offered to surrender all his property and earnings and asked whether they would then let him go. The Meccans accepted the arrangement. Ṣuhaib reached Medina empty-handed and saw the Prophet, who heard him and congratulated him, saying, "This was the best bargain of your life."

Most of these slave-converts remained steadfast in outer as well as inner professions of faith. But some were weak. Once the Holy Prophet found 'Ammār groaning with pain and drying his tears. Approached by the Prophet, 'Ammār said he had been beaten and compelled to recant. The Prophet asked him, "But did you believe at heart ?" 'Ammār declared that he did, and the Prophet said that God would forgive his weakness.

'Ammār's father, Yāsir, and his mother, Samiyya, also were tormented by disbelievers. On one such occasion the Prophet happened to pass by. Filled with emotion, he said, "Family of Yāsir, bear up patiently, for God has prepared for you a Paradise." The prophetic words were soon fulfilled. Yāsir succumbed to the tortures, and a little later Abū Jahl murdered his aged wife, Samiyya, with a spear.

Zinnīra, a woman slave, lost her eyes under the cruel treatment of disbelievers.

Abū Fukaih, Ṣafwān bin Umayya's slave, was laid on hot sand while over his chest were placed heavy and hot stones, under pain of which his tongue dropped out.

Other slaves were mishandled in similar ways.

These cruelties were beyond endurance. But early believers bore them because their hearts were made stout by assurances received daily from God. The Quran descended on the

Prophet, but the reassuring voice of God descended on all believers. Were not this so, the Faithful could not have withstood the cruelties to which they were subjected. Abandoned by fellow-men, friends and relations, they had none but God with them, and they cared not whether they had anyone else. Because of Him, the cruelties seemed nothing, abuse sounded like prayers and stones seemed like velvet.

The free citizens who believed were not less cruelly treated. Their elders and chiefs tormented them in different ways. 'Uthmān was a man of forty, and prosperous. Yet when the Quraish resolved upon general persecution of Muslims, his uncle, Ḥakam, tied him up and beat him. Zubair bin al-'Awwām, a brave young lad who later became a great Muslim general, was wrapped up in a mat by his uncle, smoked from underneath and tortured by suffocation. But he would not recant. He had found Truth and would not give it up.

Abū Dharr, of the tribe of Ghaffār, heard of the Prophet and went to Mecca to investigate. The Meccans dissuaded him, saying that they knew Muhammad well and that his Movement was only a selfish design. Abū Dharr was not impressed; so he went to the Prophet, heard the Message of Islam straight from him and was converted. Abū Dharr asked if he could keep his faith secret from his tribe. The Prophet said he could do so for a few days. But as he passed through the streets of Mecca he heard a party of Meccan chiefs abuse the Holy Prophet and make vile attacks. No longer could he keep his faith secret, and he declared at once: "I bear witness that there is no God but Allah, and that there is no one like Allah; and Muhammad is His Servant and Prophet." This cry raised in an assembly of disbelievers seemed to them an effrontery. They rose in wrath and belaboured him until he fell down senseless. The Prophet's uncle 'Abbās, not a convert yet, passed by and began to remonstrate on behalf of the victim. "Your food caravans pass through Abū Dharr's tribe," he said, "and angered at your treatment, his people can starve you to death." The following day Abū Dharr stayed at home. But the day after he went again to the same assembly and found them abusing the Holy Prophet as before. He went to the Ka'ba and found people doing the same. He could not restrain himself, stood up and made a loud declaration of his faith. Again he was severely handled. The same thing happened a third time, and Abū Dharr went back to his tribe.

The Holy Prophet himself was no exception to the cruel treatment meted out to the Faithful. On one occasion he was in prayer. A party of disbelievers put a mantle round his neck and dragged him; his eyes seemed protruded. Abū Bakr happened to come and rescued him, saying, "You seek to kill him, because he says, God is his Master?" On another occasion he lay prostrate in prayer and they laid the entrails of a camel on his back. He could not rise until the weight was removed. On yet another occasion he was passing through a street and a group of street boys followed him. They went on slapping his neck and telling the people that he called himself a Prophet. Such was the hatred and enmity against him, and such was his helplessness.

The Prophet's house was stoned from surrounding houses. Garbage and the remains of slaughtered animals were thrown into his kitchen. On many occasions dust was thrown on him while he was praying so that he had to retire to a safe spot for his public prayers.

These cruelties, perpetrated against a weak and innocent group and their honest, well-meaning but helpless Leader, were not wasted, however. Decent men saw all this and became drawn to Islam. The Prophet was once resting on Ṣafā, a hill near the Ka'ba. The Meccan chief Abū Jahl, the Prophet's arch-enemy, passed by and began to pour vile abuse on him. The Prophet said nothing and went home. A woman-slave of his household was a witness to this distressing scene. Ḥamza, the Prophet's uncle, a brave man feared by all his townsmen, returned home from a hunt in the jungle and entered the house proudly, his bow hung on his shoulder. The woman-slave had not forgotten the morning scene. She was disgusted to see Ḥamza walk home thus. She taunted him, saying that he thought himself brave and went about armed but knew not what Abū Jahl had done to his innocent nephew in the morning. Ḥamza heard an account of the morning incident. Though not a believer, he possessed nobility of character. He may have been impressed by the Prophet's Message, but not to the extent of joining openly. When he heard of this wanton attack by Abū Jahl, he could not hold back. His hesitancy about the new Message was gone. He began to feel that so far he had been too casual about it. He made straight for the Ka'ba, where the chiefs of Mecca were wont to meet and confer. He took his bow and struck Abū Jahl hard. "Count me from today a follower of Muhammad," he said. "You abused him this morning because he would say nothing. If you are brave, come out and fight me." Abū Jahl was dumbfounded. His friends rose to help but, afraid of Ḥamza and his tribe, Abū Jahl stopped them, thinking an open fight would cost too dearly. He was really to blame, he said, about the morning incident (Hishām and Ṭabarī).

THE MESSAGE OF ISLAM

Opposition continued to mount. At the same time the Prophet and his followers were doing all they could to make plain to the Meccans the Message of Islam. It was a many-sided Message and of great ultimate significance, not only for Arabs but for the whole world. It was a Message from God. It said:

> The Creator of the world is One. None else is worthy of worship. The Prophets have ever believed Him to be One, and taught their followers so. Meccans should give up all images and idols. Did they not see that the idols could not even remove the flies which dropped on the offerings laid at their feet? If they were attacked they could not repel. If they had a question put to them, they could not answer. If they were asked for help, they could do nothing. But the One God helped those who asked for His help, answered those who addressed Him in prayer, subjugated His enemies, and raised those who abased themselves before Him. When light came from Him, it illumined His devotees. Why then did the Meccans neglect Him and turn to lifeless images and idols and waste their lives? Did they not see that their want of faith in the One True God had made them utterly superstitious and incompetent? They had no idea of what was clean and what was unclean, of right and wrong. They did not honour their mothers. They treated savagely their sisters and daughters, and denied them their due. They did not treat their wives well. They tormented widows, exploited orphans, the poor

and the weak, and sought to build their prosperity on the ruins of others. Of lying and cheating they were not ashamed, nor of burgling and loot. Gambling and drinking were their delight. For culture and national advance they did not care. How long were they going to ignore the One True God, and continue to lose and lose, and suffer and suffer ? Had they not better reform ? Had they not better give up all forms of exploitation of one another, restore rights to whom they were due, spend their wealth on national needs and on improving the lot of the poor and the weak, treat orphans as a trust and regard their protection as a duty, support widows and establish and encourage good works in the whole community, cultivate not merely justice and equity, but compassion and grace ? Life in this world should be productive of good. "Leave good works behind", the Message further said, "that they may grow and bear fruit after you are gone. There is virtue in giving to others, not in receiving from them. Learn to surrender that you may be nearer to your God. Practise self-denial for the sake of your fellow-men, that you may multiply your credit with God. True, the Muslims are weak, but do not go after their weakness, Truth will triumph. This is the decree of Heaven. Through the Prophet a new measure and a new criterion of good and evil, of right and wrong, will be set up in the world. Justice and mercy will reign. No constraint will be allowed in the matter of religion, and no interference. The cruelties to which women and slaves have been subjected will be obliterated. The Kingdom of God will be instituted in place of the kingdom of Satan."

When this Message was preached to the people of Mecca and the well-meaning and reflective among them began to be impressed by it, the elders of Mecca took a serious view of what was happening. They went in a deputation to the Prophet's uncle, Abū Ṭālib, and addressed him thus :

You are one of our chiefs and for your sake we have so far spared your nephew, Muhammad. The time has come, however, when we should put an end to this national crisis, this conflict in our midst. We ask and demand that he should desist from saying anything against our idols. Let him proclaim that God is One, but let him not say anything against our idols. If he agrees to this, our conflict and controversy with him will be over. We urge you to persuade him. But if you are unable to do so, then one of two things must happen. Either you will have to give up your nephew, or we, your people, will give you up (Hishām).

Abū Ṭālib was confronted with a hard choice. To give up his nephew was hard. Equally hard was it to be disowned by his people. Arabs had little in the way of money. Their prestige lay in their leadership. They lived for their people, and their people for them. Abū Ṭālib was much upset. He sent for the Prophet and explained to him the demand made by the elders of Mecca. "If you do not agree," he said with tears in his eyes, "then either I have to give you up or my people will give me up." The Prophet was in evident sympathy with his uncle. Tears came to his eyes and he said :

> I ask you not to give up your people. I ask you not to stand by me. Instead, you may give me up and stand by your people. But the One and Only God is my witness when I say that even if they were to place the sun on my right and the moon on my left, I would not desist from preaching the truth of the One God. I must go on doing so until I die. You can choose your own pleasure (Hishām and Zurqānī).

This reply, firm, straight and sincere, opened the eyes of Abū Ṭālib. He sank deep in thought. Though he did not have the courage to believe, he thought he was lucky to have lived to see this grand demonstration of belief and regard for duty. Turning to the Prophet, he said :

> "My nephew, go your way. Do your duty. Let my people give me up. I am with you" (Hishām).

EMIGRATION TO ABYSSINIA

When tyranny reached its extreme limit the Prophet assembled his followers, and pointing to the west told them of a land across the sea where men were not murdered because of a change of faith, where they could worship God unmolested, and where there was a just king. Let them go there ; maybe the change would bring them relief. A party of Muslim men, women and children, acting on this suggestion, went to Abyssinia. The migration was on a small scale and very pathetic. The Arabs regarded themselves as keepers of the Ka'ba, and so they were. To leave Mecca was for them a great wrench, and no Arab could think of doing so unless living in Mecca had become absolutely impossible. Nor were the Meccans prepared to tolerate such a movement. They would not let their victims escape and have the least chance to live elsewhere. The party, therefore, had to keep its preparations for the journey a close secret and to depart without even saying good-bye to their friends and relations. Their departure, however, became known to some and did not fail to impress them. 'Umar, subsequently the Second Khalīfa of Islam, was still a disbeliever, a bitter enemy and persecutor of Muslims. By sheer chance, he met some members of this party. One of these was a woman, Umm 'Abdullah. When 'Umar saw household effects packed up and loaded on animals, he understood at once that it was a party leaving Mecca to take refuge elsewhere. "Are you going?" he asked. "Yes, God is our witness," replied Umm 'Abdullah. "We go to another land, because you treat us most cruelly here. We will not return now until Allah pleases to make it easy for us." 'Umar was impressed and said, "God be with you." There was emotion in his voice. This silent scene had upset him. When the Meccans got to know of it, they sent a party in chase. This party went as far as the sea but found that the Muslims had already embarked. Not being able to overtake them, they decided to send a delegation to Abyssinia to excite the king against the refugees and to persuade him to hand them over again to Meccans. One of the delegates was 'Amr bin al-'Āṣ, who later joined Islam and conquered Egypt. The delegation went to Abyssinia, met the king and intrigued with his court. But the king proved very firm and, in spite of the pressure which the Meccan delegation and his own courtiers were able to put upon him, he refused to hand over the Muslim refugees to their persecutors. The delegation returned disappointed, but in Mecca they soon thought of another plan to force the return of Muslims from Abyssinia. Among the caravans going to Abyssinia they set afloat the rumour that all Mecca had accepted Islam. When the rumour reached Abyssinia, many Muslim refugees joyfully returned to Mecca but found on arrival that the rumour which had reached them was a fabrication. Some Muslims went back again to Abyssinia but some decided to stay. Among the latter was 'Uthmān bin Maẓ'ūn, son of a leading Meccan chief. 'Uthmān received protection from a friend of his father, Walīd bin Mughīra, and began to live in peace. But he saw that other Muslims continued to suffer brutal persecution. It made him very unhappy. He went to Walīd and renounced his protection. He felt he should not have such protection while other Muslims continued to suffer. Walīd announced this to the Meccans.

One day, Labīd, poet-laureate of Arabia, sat among the chiefs of Meccas, reciting his verse. He read a line which meant that all graces must ultimately come to an end. 'Uthmān boldly contradicted him and said, "The graces of Paradise will be everlasting." Labīd, not used to such contradictions, lost his temper and said, "Quraish, your guests were not insulted like this before. Whence has this fashion begun?" To appease Labīd, a man from among the audience rose and said, "Go on and take no notice of this fool". 'Uthmān insisted that he had said nothing foolish. This exasperated the Quraishite, who sprang upon 'Uthmān and gave him a sharp blow, knocking out an eye. Walīd was present at the scene. He was a close friend of 'Uthmān's father. He could not endure such treatment of his deceased friend's son. But 'Uthmān was no longer under his formal protection and Arab custom now forbade him to take sides. So he could do nothing. Half in anger, half in anguish he turned to 'Uthmān, and said, "Son of my friend, you would have saved your eye, had you not renounced my protection. You have to thank yourself for it." 'Uthmān replied, "I have longed for this. I lament not over the loss of one eye, because the other waits for the same fate. Remember, while the Prophet suffers, we want no peace" (Ḥalbiyya, Vol. 1, p. 348).

'UMAR ACCEPTS ISLAM

About this time, another very important event took place. 'Umar, who later became the Second Khalīfa of Islam, was still one of the fiercest and the most feared enemies of Islam. He felt that no effective step had yet been taken against the new Movement and decided to put an end to the Prophet's life. He took his sword and set out. A friend was puzzled to see him going and asked where he was going and with what intent. "To kill Muhammad," said 'Umar.

"But would you be safe from his tribe after this? And do

you really know how things are going? Do you know that your sister and her husband have joined Islam?"

It came like a bolt from the blue and greatly upset 'Umar. He decided to go and have done with his sister and her husband first. As he reached their house he heard a recitation going on inside. The voice was that of Khabbāb who was teaching them the Holy Book. 'Umar entered the house swiftly. Khabbāb, alarmed by the hurried steps, had already hid himself. 'Umar's sister, Fāṭima, put away the leaves of the Quran. Confronting her and her husband, 'Umar said, "I hear you have renounced your own faith," and, saying this, he raised his hand to strike her husband, who was incidentally his own cousin. Fāṭima threw herself between 'Umar and her husband; so 'Umar's hand fell on Fāṭima's face and struck her on the nose, from which blood flowed freely. The blow made Fāṭima all the braver. She said, "Yes, we are Muslims now and shall remain so; do what you may." 'Umar was a brave man, though rough. His sister's face, dyed red by his own hand, filled him with remorse. Soon he was a changed man. He asked to be shown those leaves of the Quran they were reading from. Fāṭima refused lest he should tear them up and throw them away. 'Umar promised not to do so. But, said Fāṭima, he was not clean. 'Umar offered to have a bath. Clean and cooled, he took the leaves of the Quran in his hand. They contained a portion of the Chapter *Ṭā Hā*. And he came upon the verses:

> "Verily I am Allah; there is no God beside Me. So serve Me, and observe prayer for My remembrance. Surely the Hour is coming, and I am going to manifest it, that every soul may be recompensed for its endeavour" (20 : 15, 16).

The firm assertion of God's existence, the clear promise that Islam would soon establish genuine worship in place of the customary one current in Mecca—these and a host of other associated ideas must have moved 'Umar. He could contain himself no longer. Faith welled up in his heart and he said, "How wonderful, how inspiring!" Khabbāb came out of his hiding, and said, "God is my witness, only yesterday I heard the Prophet pray for the conversion of 'Umar or 'Amr ibn Hishām. Your change is the result of that prayer." 'Umar's mind was made up. He asked where the Prophet was and made straight for him at Dār Arqam, his bare sword still in his hand. As he knocked at the door, the Prophet's Companions could see 'Umar through the crevices. They feared lest he should have some evil design. But the Prophet said, "Let him come in." 'Umar entered, sword in hand. "What brings you ?" inquired the Prophet. "Prophet of God," said 'Umar, "I am here to become a Muslim." *Allāhu Akbar*, cried the Prophet. *Allāhu Akbar*, cried the Companions. The hills around Mecca echoed the cries. News of the conversion spread like wild fire and henceforward 'Umar, the much-feared persecutor of Islam, himself began to be persecuted along with other Muslims. But 'Umar had changed. He delighted now in suffering as he had delighted before in inflicting suffering. He went about Mecca, a much harassed person.

PERSECUTION INTENSIFIES

Persecution became more and more serious and more unbearable. Many Muslims had already left Mecca. Those who stayed behind had to suffer more than ever before. But Muslims swerved not a bit from the path they had chosen. Their hearts were as stout as ever, their faith as steadfast. Their devotion to the One God was on the increase and so was their hatred for the national idols of Mecca. The conflict had become more serious than ever. The Meccans convened another big meeting. At this they resolved on an all-out boycott of the Muslims. The Meccans were to have no normal dealings with Muslims. They were neither to buy from them, nor to sell them anything. The Prophet, his family and a number of relations who, though not Muslims, still stood by him, were compelled to take shelter in a lonely place, a possession of Abū Ṭālib. Without money, without means and without reserves, the Prophet's family and relations suffered untold hardships under this blockade. For three years there was no slackening of it. Then at last, five decent members of the enemy revolted against these conditions. They went to the blockaded family, offered to annul the boycott, and asked the family to come out. Abū Ṭālib came out and reproved his people. The revolt of the five became known all over Mecca, but good feeling asserted itself again, and Meccans decided they must cancel the savage boycott. The boycott was over, but not its consequences. In a few days the Prophet's faithful wife, Khadīja, met her death, and a month later his uncle, Abū Ṭālib.

The Holy Prophet had now lost the companionship and support of Khadīja, and he and the Muslims had lost the good offices of Abū Ṭālib. Their passing away naturally also resulted in the loss of some general sympathy. Abū Lahab, another uncle of the Prophet, seemed ready at first to side with the Prophet. The shock of his brother's death and regard for his dying wish were still fresh in his mind. But the Meccans soon succeeded in antagonizing him. They made use of the usual appeals. The Prophet taught that disbelief in the Oneness of God was an offence, punishable in the Hereafter ; his teaching contradicted everything they had learnt from their forefathers, and so on. Abū Lahab decided to oppose the Prophet more than ever. Relations between Muslims and Meccans had become strained. A three-year boycott and blockade had enlarged the gulf between them. Meeting and preaching seemed impossible. The Prophet did not mind the ill-treatment and the persecution ; these were nothing so long as he had the chance to meet and address people. But now it seemed that he had no such chance in Mecca. General antagonism apart, the Prophet now found it impossible to appear in any street or public place. If he did, they threw dust at him and sent him back to his house. Once he returned home, his head covered with dust. A daughter wept as she removed the dust. The Prophet told her not to weep for God was with him. Ill-treatment did not upset the Prophet. He even welcomed it as evidence of interest in his Message. One day, for instance, the Meccans by a general intrigue said nothing to him nor did they ill-treat him in any way. The Prophet retired home disappointed, until the reassuring voice of God made him go to his people again.

THE PROPHET GOES TO TĀ'IF

It seemed that in Mecca now nobody would listen to him

and this made him sad. He felt he was stagnating. So he decided to turn elsewhere for the preaching of his Message, and he chose Ṭā'if, a small town about sixty miles to the south-east of Mecca and famed for its fruit and its agriculture. The Prophet's decision was in keeping with the traditions of all Prophets. Moses turned now to the Pharaoh, now to Israel, and now to Midian. Jesus, similarly, turned now to Galilee, now to places across the Jordan, and now to Jerusalem. So the Holy Prophet of Islam, finding that Meccans would ill-treat but not listen, turned to Ṭā'if. In polytheistic beliefs and practices Ṭā'if was not behind Mecca. The idols to be found in the Ka'ba were not the only, nor the only important, idols in Arabia. One important idol, al-Lāt, was to be found in Ṭā'if; because of it Ṭā'if also was a centre of pilgrimage. The inhabitants of Ṭā'if were connected with those of Mecca by ties of blood; and many green spots between Ṭā'if and Mecca were owned by Meccans. On arrival at Ṭā'if, the Prophet had visits from its chiefs but none seemed willing to accept the Message. The rank and file obeyed their leaders and dismissed the teaching with contempt. This was not unusual. People immersed in worldly affairs always regard such a Message as something of an interference and even an offence. Because the Message is without visible support—such as numbers or arms—they also feel they can dismiss it with contempt. The Prophet was no exception. Reports of him had already reached Ṭā'if, and here he now was, without arms or following, a lone individual with only one companion, Zaid. The towns folk thought him a nuisance which should be ended, if only to please their chiefs. They set vagabonds of the town and street boys at him who pelted him with stones and drove him out of the town. Zaid was wounded and the Prophet began to bleed profusely. But the pursuit continued until this defenceless party of two was several miles out of Ṭā'if. The Prophet was sorely grieved and dejected when an angel descended upon him and asked if he would like his persecutors to be destroyed. "No," said the Prophet. "I hope that of these very tormentors would be born those who would worship the One True God." (Bukhārī, *Kitāb Bad' al-Khalq*.)

Exhausted and dejected, he stopped at a vineyard owned by

two Meccans who happened to be present. They were among his persecutors at Mecca, but on this occasion they became sympathetic. Was it because a Meccan had been ill-treated by the people of Ṭā'if, or was it because a spark of human kindness suddenly glowed in their hearts? They sent to the Prophet a tray full of grapes with a Christian slave, 'Addās by name and belonging to Nineveh. 'Addās presented the tray to the Prophet and his companion. While he looked wistfully at them, he became more curious than ever when he heard the Prophet say, "In the name of Allah, the Gracious, the Merciful." His Christian background was enlivened and he felt he was in the presence of a Hebrew Prophet. The Prophet asked him where he belonged and 'Addās said Nineveh, upon which the Prophet said, "Jonah, son of Amittai, who belonged to Nineveh, was a holy man, a Prophet like me." The Prophet also told 'Addās of his own Message. 'Addās felt charmed and believed at once. He embraced the Prophet with tears in his eyes and started kissing his head, hands and feet. The meeting over, the Prophet turned again to Allah and said:

> Allah, I submit my plaint to Thee. I am weak, and without means. My people look down upon me. Thou art Lord of the weak and the poor and Thou art my Lord. To whom wilt Thou abandon me—to strangers who push me about or to the enemy who oppresses me in my own town? If Thou art not angered at me, I care not for my enemy. Thy mercy be with me. I seek refuge in the light of Thy face. It is Thou Who canst drive away darkness from the world and give peace to all, here and hereafter. Let not Thy anger and Thy wrath descend on me. Thou art never angry except when Thou art pleased soon after. And there is no power and no refuge except with Thee (Hishām and Ṭabarī).

Having said this prayer, he set back for Mecca. He stopped *en route* at Nakhla for a few days and set out again. According to Meccan tradition he was no longer a citizen of Mecca. He had left it because he thought it hostile and could not return to it except with the permission of the Meccans. Accordingly, he sent word to Muṭ'im bin 'Adī—a Meccan chief, to ask if Meccans would permit him to come back. Muṭ'im, though as bitter an enemy as any other, possessed nobility of heart. He collected his sons and relatives. Arming themselves, they went to the Ka'ba. Standing in the courtyard he announced he was permitting the Prophet to return. The Prophet then returned, and made a circuit of the Ka'ba. Muṭ'im, his sons and relatives, with swords unsheathed, then escorted the Prophet to his house. It was not protection in the customary Arabian sense which had been extended to the Prophet. The Prophet continued to suffer and Muṭ'im did not shield him. Muṭ'im's act amounted to a declaration of formal permission for the Prophet to return.

The Prophet's journey to Ṭā'if has extorted praise even from the enemies of Islam. Sir William Muir, in his biography of the Prophet, writes (speaking of the journey to Ṭā'if):

> There is something lofty and heroic in this journey of Muhammad to Aṭ-Ṭā'if; a solitary man, despised and rejected by his own people, going boldly forth in the name of God, like Jonah to Nineveh, and summoning an idolatrous city to repent and support his mission. It sheds a strong light on the intensity of his belief in the divine origin of his calling (Life of Muhammad by Sir W. Muir, 1923 edition, pp. 112–113).

Mecca returned to its old hostility. The Prophet's home town again became hell for him. But he continued to tell people of his Message. The formula, "God is One", began to be heard here and there. With love and regard, and with a sense of fellow-feeling, the Prophet persisted in the exposition of his Message. People turned away but he addressed them again and again. He made his proclamation, whether the people cared or not, and persistence seemed to pay. The handful of Muslims who had returned from Abyssinia and had decided to stay, preached secretly to their friends, neighbours and relations. Some of these were persuaded to declare themselves openly and to share the sufferings of other Muslims. But many, though persuaded at heart, did not have the courage to confess openly; they waited for the kingdom of God to come to the earth.

In the meantime revelations received by the Prophet began to hint at the near possibility of migration from Mecca. Some idea of the place they were to migrate to was also given to him. It was a town of wells and date-groves. He thought of Yamāma. But soon the thought was dismissed. He then waited in the assurance that whatever place they were destined to go to would certainly become the cradle of Islam.

ISLAM SPREADS TO MEDINA

The annual Ḥajj drew near, and from all parts of Arabia pilgrims began to arrive in Mecca. The Prophet went wherever he found a group of people, expounded to them the idea of One God and told them to give up excesses of all kinds and prepare for the Kingdom of God. Some listened and became interested. Some wished to listen but were sent away by the Meccans. Some who had already made up their minds, stopped to ridicule. The Prophet was in the valley of Minā when he saw a group of six or seven people. He found that they belonged to the Khazraj tribe, one in alliance with the Jews. He asked them if they would listen to what he had to say. They had heard of him and were interested; so they agreed. The Prophet spent some time telling them that the Kingdom of God was at hand, that idols were going to disappear, that the idea of One God was due to triumph, and piety and purity were once again going to rule. Would they not, in Medina, welcome the Message? The group became much impressed. They accepted the Message and promised, on their return to Medina, to confer with others and report next year whether Medina would be willing to receive Muslim refugees from Mecca. They returned and conferred with their friends and relations. There were, at the time, two Arab and three Jewish tribes at Medina. The Arab tribes were the Aus and the Khazraj and the Jewish tribes the Banū Quraiẓa, the Banū Naḍīr, and the Banū Qainuqā'. The Aus and the Khazraj were at war. The Quraiẓa and the Naḍīr were in alliance with the Aus and the Qainuqā' with the Khazraj. Tired of unending warfare, they were inclined to peace. At last they agreed to acknowledge the Khazraj Chief, 'Abdullah bin Ubayy bin Salūl, as King of Medina. From the Jews, the Aus and the Khazraj had heard of prophecies in the Bible. They had heard Jewish tales of the lost glory of Israel and of the advent of a Prophet "like unto Moses." This advent was near at hand, the Jews used to say. It was to mark the return to power of Israel and the destruction of their enemies. When the people of Medina heard of the Prophet, they became impressed and began to ask if this Meccan Prophet was not the Prophet they had heard of from the Jews. Many young men readily believed. At the next Ḥajj twelve men from Medina came to Mecca to join the Prophet. Ten of these belonged to the Khazraj and two to the Aus tribe. They met the Prophet in the valley of Minā and, holding the Prophet's hand, solemnly declared their belief in the Oneness of God and their resolve to abstain from all common evils, from infanticide, and from making false accusations against one another. They also resolved to obey the Prophet in all good things. When they returned to Medina, they started telling others of their New Faith. Zeal increased. Idols were taken out of their niches and thrown on the streets. Those who used to bow before images began to hold their heads high. They resolved to bow to none except the One God. The Jews wondered. Centuries of friendship, exposition and debate had failed to produce the change which this Meccan Teacher had produced in a few days. The people of Medina would go to the few Muslims in their midst and make inquiries about Islam. But the few Muslims could not cope with the large numbers of inquiries, nor did they know enough. They decided, therefore, to address a request to the Prophet to send them some one to teach Islam. The Prophet agreed to send Muṣ'ab, one of the Muslims who had been in Abyssinia. Muṣ'ab was the first missionary of Islam to go out of Mecca. At about this time, the Prophet had a grand promise from God. He had a vision in which he saw that he was in Jerusalem and Prophets had joined behind him in congregational worship. Jerusalem only meant Medina, which was going to become the centre of the worship of the One God. Other Prophets congregating behind the Prophet of Islam meant that men following different Prophets would join Islam, and Islam would thus become a universal religion.

Conditions in Mecca had now become most critical. Persecution had assumed the worst possible form. Meccans laughed at this vision and described it as wishful thinking. They did not know that the foundations of the New Jerusalem had been laid. Nations of the East and the West were agog. They wanted to hear the Last Great Message of God. In those very days the Kaiser and the Chosroes of Iran went to war with each other. Chosroes was victorious. Syria and Palestine were overrun by Iranian armies. Jerusalem was destroyed. Egypt and Asia Minor were mastered. At the mouth of the Bosphorus, only ten miles from Constantinople, Iranian generals were able to pitch their tents. Meccans rejoiced over Iranian victories and said the judgement of God had been delivered—the idol-worshippers of Iran had defeated a People of the Book. At that time, the Holy Prophet received the following revelation :

> The Romans have been defeated in the land nearby, and they, after their defeat, will be victorious in a few years—Allah's is the command before and after that—and on that day will the believers rejoice with the help of Allah. He helps whom He pleases ; and He is the Mighty, the Merciful. Allah has made this promise. Allah breaks not His promise, but most men know not (30 : 3–7).

The prophecy was fulfilled in a few years. The Romans defeated the Iranians and recovered the territories they had lost to them. The part of the prophecy which said, "On that day the believers shall rejoice with the help of God", was also fulfilled. Islam began to advance. The Meccans believed they had put an end to it by persuading people not to listen to Muslims but to show active hostility instead. Right at this time the Prophet received in his revelations news of victories for Muslims, and destruction for Meccans. The Prophet announced the following verses :

> And they say, "Why does he not bring us a Sign from his Lord ?" Has there not come to them the clear evidence in what is contained in the former books ? And if We had destroyed them with a punishment before it, they would have surely said, "Our Lord, wherefore didst Thou not send to us a Messenger that we might have followed Thy commandments before we were humbled and disgraced ?" Say, "Each one is waiting ; wait ye, therefore, and you will know who are the people of the right path and who follow true guidance" (20 : 134–136).

The Meccans complained of lack of Signs. They were told that the prophecies about Islam and the Prophet recorded in earlier books should be enough. Had Meccans been destroyed before the Message of Islam could be explained to them, they would have complained of lack of chance to consider the Signs.

The Meccans must, therefore, wait.

Revelations promising victory for believers and defeat for disbelievers were being received every day. When the Meccans looked at their own power and prosperity and at the powerlessness and poverty of Muslims, and then heard of the promises of divine help and of Muslim victories in the Prophet's daily revelations, they wondered and wondered. Were they mad or was the Prophet mad? They were hoping that persecution would compel the Muslims to give up their faith and return to the Meccans, that the Prophet himself and his closest followers would begin to have doubts about his claims. But instead of this they had to listen to confident affirmations like the following:

> Nay, I swear by all that you see, and by all that you see not that it is surely the message brought by an honoured Messenger. And it is not the word of a poet; little is it that you believe; nor is it the utterance of a soothsayer; little is it that you heed. It is a revelation from the Lord of the worlds. And if he had forged any sayings in Our name, We would surely have seized him by the right hand, and then surely would We have severed his life-artery, and not one of you could have held Us off from him. And surely it is an admonition for the God-fearing. And, surely, We know that some of you reject Our Signs. And, surely, it is a source of anguish for the disbelievers. And, surely, it is the true certainty. So glorify the name of thy Lord, the Great (69 : 39–53).

Meccans were warned that all their fond hopes would be smashed. The Prophet was neither a poet, nor a soothsayer nor a pretender. The Quran was a reading for the pious. True, it had its deniers. But it also had its secret admirers, those who were jealous of its teaching and its truths. The promises and prophecies contained in it would all be fulfilled. The Prophet was asked to ignore all opposition and go on celebrating his Mighty God.

The third Ḥajj arrived. Among the pilgrims from Medina was a large party of Muslims. Owing to Meccan opposition these Muslims from Medina wished to see the Prophet in private. The Prophet's own thoughts were turning more and more to Medina, as a likely place for migration. He mentioned this to his closest relations but they tried to dissuade him from all thoughts of this kind. They pleaded that though Mecca was full of opposition, it offered the support of several influential relations. The prospects at Medina were all uncertain and, should Medina prove as hostile as Mecca, would the Prophet's Meccan relations be able to help ? The Prophet, however, was convinced that migration to Medina had been decreed. So he rejected the advice of his relations and decided to migrate to Medina.

FIRST PLEDGE OF 'AQABA

After midnight, the Prophet again met the Muslims from Medina in the valley of 'Aqaba. His uncle 'Abbās was with him. The Muslims from Medina numbered seventy-three, out of whom sixty-two belonged to the Khazraj tribe and eleven to the Aus. The party included two women, one being Umm 'Ammāra, of the Banū Najjār. They had been taught Islam by Muṣ'ab, and were full of faith and determination. They all proved to be pillars of Islam. Umm 'Ammāra is an example. She instilled in her children undying loyalty to Islam. One of her sons, Ḥabīb, was taken prisoner by Musailima, the Pretender, in an encounter after the Prophet's death. Musailima tried to unsettle Ḥabīb's faith. "Do you believe Muhammad to be a Messenger of God ?" he asked. "Yes," was the reply. "Do you believe me to be a Messenger of God ?" asked Musailima. "No," replied Ḥabīb. Upon this Musailima ordered one of his limbs to be cut off. This done, he asked Ḥabīb again, "Do you believe Muhammad to be a Messenger of God ?" "Yes," replied Ḥabīb. "Do you believe me to be a Messenger of God ?" "No." Musailima ordered another limb to be cut off Ḥabīb's body. Limb after limb was cut off in this way and Ḥabīb's body was reduced to many pieces. He died a cruel death, but left behind an unforgettable example of personal heroism and sacrifice for the sake of religious conviction (Ḥalbiyya, Vol. 2, p. 17).

Umm 'Ammāra accompanied the Prophet in several wars.

This party of Medina Muslims, in short, attained to great

distinction for their loyalty and faith. They came to Mecca not for wealth, but for faith; and they had it in abundance.

Moved by family ties and feeling legitimately responsible for the safety of the Prophet, 'Abbās thus addressed the party:

> O Khazraj, this my relation is respected here by his people. They are not all Muslims, yet they protect him. But he has chosen now to leave us and go to you. O Khazraj, do you know what will happen? All Arabia will be against you. If you realize the risks entailed by your invitation, then take him away; if you do not, then give up your intention and let him stay here.

The leader of this party Al-Barā' replied assuredly:

> We have heard you. Our resolution is firm. Our lives are at the disposal of the Prophet of God. We are decided, and only await his decision (Ḥalbiyya, Vol. 2, p. 18).

The Prophet gave a further exposition of Islam and its teaching. Explaining this, he told the party that he would go to Medina if they would hold Islam as dear as they held their wives and children. He had not quite finished when this party of seventy-three devotees cried, Yes, Yes, in one voice. In their zeal they forgot that they could be overheard. 'Abbās cautioned them to speak low. But the party was full of faith. Death now was nothing in their eyes. When 'Abbās cautioned the party, one of them said aloud, "We are not afraid, O Prophet of God. Permit us, and we can deal with the Meccans right now and avenge the wrongs they have done you." But the Prophet said he had not yet been commanded to fight.

The party then took the oath of fealty and the meeting dispersed.

The Meccans did get to know of this meeting. They went to the Medina encampment to complain against these visitors to their chiefs. 'Abdullah bin Ubbay bin Salūl—Chief of chiefs—knew nothing of what had happened. He assured the Meccans that it must be some false rumour which they had heard. The people of Medina had accepted him as their leader and could not do anything without his knowledge and permission. He did not know that the people of Medina had cast off the rule of Satan and accepted the rule of God instead.

THE HIJRA

The party returned to Medina and the Prophet and his followers started preparations for migration. Family after family began to disappear. Muslims, certain that the Kingdom of God was near, were full of courage. Sometimes a whole lane would be emptied in the course of a night. In the morning Meccans would see the doors locked and realize that the residents had migrated to Medina. The growing influence of Islam amazed them.

At last not a single Muslim remained in Mecca save a few slave converts, the Prophet himself, Abū Bakr and 'Alī. The Meccans realized that their prey was about to escape. The chiefs assembled again and decided they should now kill the Prophet. By a special divine design, it seems, the date they appointed for killing the Prophet was appointed for his escape. When the Meccan party was collecting in front of the Prophet's house with intent to kill, the Prophet was moving out in the secrecy of the night. The Meccans must have feared anticipation of their foul design by the Prophet. They proceeded cautiously and when the Prophet himself passed by, they took him for someone else, and withdrew to avoid being noticed. The Prophet's closest friend Abū Bakr had been informed of the Prophet's plan the day before. He duly joined and then both left Mecca, and took shelter in a cave called Thaur, about three or four miles from Mecca over a hill. When the Meccans learnt of the Prophet's escape, they collected and sent a force in pursuit. Led by a tracker, they reached Thaur. Standing at the mouth of the cave in which the Prophet and Abū Bakr sat hiding, the tracker said that Muhammad was either in the cave or had ascended to heaven. Abū Bakr heard this and his heart sank. "The enemy has nearly got us," he whispered. "Fear not, God is with us," replied the Prophet. "I fear not for myself," went on Abū Bakr, "but for you. For, if I die, I am but an ordinary mortal; but if you die, it will mean death to faith and spirit" (Zurqānī). "Even so, fear not," assured the Prophet, "We are not two in this cave. There is a third—God" (Bukhārī).

Meccan tyranny was destined to end. Islam was to have the

chance to grow. The pursuers were deceived. They ridiculed the tracker's judgement. It was too open a cave, they said, for anybody to take shelter in, for with snakes and vipers it was none too safe. If they had but bent a little, they could have sighted the two. But they did not, and dismissing the tracker, they returned to Mecca.

For two days the Prophet and Abū Bakr waited in the cave. On the third night, according to plan, two fleet camels were brought to the cave, one for the Prophet and the guide ; the other for Abū Bakr and his servant, 'Āmir bin Fuhaira.

SURĀQA PURSUES THE PROPHET

Before setting out, the Prophet looked back at Mecca. Emotions welled up in his heart. Mecca was his birthplace. He had lived there as child and man and had received there the divine Call. It was the place where his forefathers had lived and flourished since the time of Ishmael. With these thoughts, he had a last long look at it and then said, "Mecca, thou art dearer to me than any other place in the world, but thy people would not let me live here." Upon this Abū Bakr said, "The place hath turned out its Prophet. It only awaiteth its destruction." The Meccans, after the failure of their pursuit, put a prize on the heads of the two fugitives. Whoever captured and restored to the Meccans the Prophet or Abū Bakr dead or alive was to have a reward of a hundred camels. The announcement was made among the tribes around Mecca. Tempted by the reward, Surāqa bin Mālik, a Bedouin chief, started in pursuit of the party and ultimately sighted them on the road to Medina. He saw two mounted camels and, feeling sure they were bearing the Prophet and Abū Bakr, spurred on his horse. The horse reared and fell before it had gone very far and Surāqa fell with it. Surāqa's own account of what happened is interesting. He says :

> After I fell from the horse, I consulted my luck in the superstitious fashion common with Arabs by a throw of the arrows. The arrows boded ill-luck. But the temptation of the reward was great. I mounted again and resumed my pursuit and nearly overtook the party. The Prophet rode with dignity, and did not look back. Abū Bakr, however, looked back again and

again (evidently out of fear for the safety of the Prophet). As I neared them, my horse reared again, and I fell off. I consulted the arrows again; and again they boded ill-luck. My horse's hoofs sank deep into the sand. Mounting again and resuming the pursuit seemed difficult. I then understood that the party was under divine protection. I called out to them and entreated them to stop. When near enough I told them of my evil intention and of my change of heart. I told them I was giving up the pursuit and returning. The Prophet let me go, but made me promise not to reveal their whereabouts to anybody. I became convinced that the Prophet was a true one, destined to succeed. I requested the Prophet to write me a guarantee of peace to serve me when he became supreme. The Prophet asked 'Āmir bin Fuhaira to write me a guarantee, and he did. As I got ready to return with it, the Prophet received a revelation about the future and said, "Surāqa, how wilt thou feel with the gold bangles of the Chosroes on thy wrists?" Amazed at the prophecy I asked, "Which Chosroes? Chosroes bin Hormizd, the Emperor of Iran?" The Prophet said, "Yes" (Usud al-Ghāba).

Sixteen or seventeen years later the prophecy was literally fulfilled. Surāqa accepted Islam and went to Medina. The Prophet died, and after him, first Abū Bakr, and then 'Umar became the Khalīfās of Islam. The growing influence of Islam made the Iranians jealous and led them to attack the Muslims but, instead of subjugating the Muslims, they were themselves subjugated by them. The capital of Iran fell to the Muslims who captured its treasures, including the gold bangles which the Chosroes wore at State functions. After his conversion, Surāqa used to describe his pursuit of the Prophet and his party and to tell of what passed between him and the Prophet. When the spoils of the war with Iran were placed before 'Umar, he saw the gold bangles and remembered what the Prophet had told Surāqa. It was a grand prophecy made at a time of utter helplessness. 'Umar decided to stage a visible fulfilment of the prophecy. He, therefore, sent for Surāqa and ordered him to put on the gold bangles. Surāqa protested that the wearing of gold by men had been forbidden by Islam. 'Umar said that this was true, but that the occasion was an exception. The Prophet had foreseen Chosroes' gold bangles on his wrists; therefore he had to wear them now, even on pain of punishment. Surāqa was objecting out of deference to the

Prophet's teaching; otherwise he was as eager as anyone else to provide visible proof of the fulfilment of the great prophecy. He put on the bangles and Muslims saw the prophecy fulfilled (Usud al-Ghāba). The fugitive Prophet had become a king. He himself was no longer in this world. But those who succeeded him could witness the fulfilment of his words and visions.

THE PROPHET ARRIVES AT MEDINA

To return to our narrative of the Hijra. After the Prophet had dismissed Surāqa he continued his journey to Medina unmolested. When he reached Medina, the Prophet found the people waiting impatiently. A more auspicious day could not have dawned for them. For, the sun which had risen for Mecca had come instead to shine on Medina.

News that the Prophet had left Mecca had reached them, so they were expecting his arrival. Parties of them went miles out of Medina to look for him. They went in the morning and returned disappointed in the evening. When at last the Prophet did reach Medina, he decided to stop for a while in Qubā, a nearby village. A Jew had seen the two camels and had decided that they were carrying the Prophet and his Companions. He climbed an eminence and shouted, "Sons of Qaila, he for whom you waited has come." Everyone in Medina who heard this cry rushed to Qubā, while the people of Qubā, overjoyed at the arrival of the Prophet in their midst sang songs in his honour.

The utter simplicity of the Prophet is illustrated by an incident which took place at this time at Qubā. Most people in Medina had not seen the Prophet before. When they saw his party sitting under a tree, many of them took Abū Bakr for the Prophet. Abū Bakr, though younger, had a greyer beard and was better dressed than the Prophet. So they turned to him and sat in front of him, after showing him the obeisance due to the Prophet. When Abū Bakr saw that he was being mistaken for the Prophet, he rose, took his mantle and hung it against the sun and said, "Prophet of God, you are in the sun. I make this shade for you" (Bukhārī). With tact and courtesy he made plain to visitors from Medina their error. The

Prophet stopped at Qubā for ten days, after which the people of Medina took him to their city. When he entered the town, he found that all the people, men, women and children, had turned out to receive him. Among the songs they sang was:

> Moon of the fourteenth night has risen on us from behind al-Widā'. So long as we have in our midst one who calls us to God, it is incumbent upon us to tender our thanks to God. To you who have been sent to us by God we present our perfect obedience (Ḥalbiyya).

The Prophet did not enter Medina from the eastern side. When the people of Medina described him as a "moon of the fourteenth night", they meant that they were living in the dark before the Prophet came to shed his light upon them. It was a Monday when the Prophet entered Medina. It was a Monday when he left the cave Thaur and, strange as it may seem, it was a Monday on which he took Mecca about ten years later.

ABŪ AYYŪB ANṢĀRĪ AS PROPHET'S HOST

While the Prophet was in Medina, everybody longed to have the honour of being his host. As his camel passed through a lane, families would line up to receive him. With one voice they would say, "Here we are with our homes, our property and our lives to receive you and to offer our protection to you. Come and live with us." Many would show greater zeal, go forward and hold the reins of the camel and insist on the Prophet's dismounting in front of their doors and entering their houses. Politely the Prophet would refuse saying, "Leave my camel alone. She is under the command of God; she will stop where God wants her to stop." Ultimately it stopped on a site which belonged to orphans of the Banū Najjār tribe. The Prophet dismounted and said, "It seems that this is where God wants us to stop." He made enquiries. A trustee of the orphans came forward and offered the site for the use of the Prophet. The Prophet replied that he would not accept the offer unless he were allowed to pay. A price was settled and the Prophet decided to build a mosque and some houses on it. This settled, the Prophet asked who lived nearest to the site. Abū Ayyūb Anṣārī came forward and said that his house was the nearest and that his services were at the Prophet's disposal. The Prophet asked him to prepare a room in his house for him. Abū Ayyūb's house was double-storeyed. He offered to let the Prophet have the upper storey. But the Prophet preferred to have the lower storey for the convenience of his visitors.

The devotion which the people of Medina had for the Prophet showed itself again. Abū Ayyūb agreed to let the Prophet have the lower storey, but refused to go to sleep on a floor under which lived the Prophet. He and his wife thought it discourteous to do so. A pitcher of water was accidentally broken and water flowed on the floor. Abū Ayyūb, fearing lest some water should drip through to the room occupied by the Prophet, took his quilt and with it dried up the water before any could drip through. In the morning he called on the Prophet and narrated the events of the night before, upon hearing which the Prophet agreed to occupy the upper storey. Abū Ayyūb prepared meals and sent them up. The Prophet ate whatever he wanted and Abū Ayyūb whatever remained. After a few days, others demanded a share in entertaining the Prophet. Until the Prophet settled in his own house and made his own arrangements he was entertained by the people of Medina in turn. A widow had an only son named Anas, aged about eight or nine. She brought the boy to the Prophet and offered him for the Prophet's personal service. This Anas became immortalized in the annals of Islam. He became a very learned man, and also rich. He attained to over one hundred years of age and in the days of the Khalīfās was held in great esteem by everybody. Anas is reported to have said that although he went into the service of the Prophet as a boy and remained with him until the Prophet died, never did the Prophet speak unkindly to him, nor did he ever admonish him, nor did he ever set him a duty harder than he could perform. During his stay in Medina, the Prophet had only Anas with him. The testimony of Anas, therefore, reveals the Prophet's character as it developed in the days of his growing power and prosperity at Medina.

Later, the Prophet sent his freedman Zaid to Mecca to fetch his family and relations. The Meccans had been stupefied by the sudden and well-planned departure of the Prophet and his followers. For some time, therefore, they did nothing to vex him. When the Prophet's family and the family of Abū Bakr left Mecca they raised no difficulty. The two families reached Medina unmolested. In the meantime the Prophet laid the foundations of a mosque on the site he had bought for the purpose. After this, he built houses for himself and for his Companions. About seven months were spent on their completion.

LIFE UNSAFE AT MEDINA

Within a few days of the Prophet's arrival in Medina, the pagan tribes there became interested in Islam and a majority of them joined. Many, not persuaded at heart, also joined. In this way a party joined the fold of Islam who were not Muslims at heart. Its members played a very sinister part in subsequent history. Some of them became sincere Muslims. Others remained insincere and kept intriguing against Islam and Muslims. Some refused to join at all. But they could not stand the growing influence of the New Faith, so they migrated from Medina to Mecca. Medina became a Muslim town. In it was established the worship of the One God. There was not a second town in the world then which could make this claim. It was no small joy to the Prophet and his friends that within a few days of their migration a whole town had agreed to give up the worship of idols and to establish instead the worship of the One Invisible God. But there was no peace yet for Muslims. In Medina itself a party of Arabs had only outwardly joined Islam. Inwardly, they were the sworn enemies of the Prophet. Then there were the Jews, who continuously intrigued against him. The Prophet was aware of these dangers. He remained alert and urged his friends and followers to be on their guard. He often remained awake the whole night (Bārī, Vol. 6, p. 60). Tired by night-long vigilance he once expressed a desire for help. Soon he heard the sound of armour. "What is this?" he asked. "It is Sa'd bin Waqqāṣ, O Prophet, who has come to do sentinel duty for you" (Bukhārī and Muslim). The people of Medina were alive to their great responsibility. They had invited the Prophet to come and live in their midst and it was now their duty to protect him. The tribes took counsel and decided to guard the Prophet's house in turn.

In the unsafety of his person and in the absence of peace for his followers, there was no difference between the Prophet's life at Mecca and his life at Medina. The only difference was that at Medina Muslims were able to worship in public in the mosque which they had built in the name of God. They were able to assemble for this purpose five times in the day without let or hindrance.

Two or three months passed. The people of Mecca recovered from their bewilderment and started making plans for the vexation of Muslims. They soon found that it did not fulfil their purpose merely to trouble Muslims in and around Mecca. It was necessary to attack the Prophet and his followers at Medina and turn them out of their new refuge. Accordingly they addressed a letter to 'Abdullah bin Ubayy ibn Salūl, a leader of Medina, who, before the Prophet's arrival, had been accepted as king of Medina by all parties. They said in this letter that they had been shocked at the prophet's arrival at Medina and that it was wrong on the part of the people of Medina to afford refuge to him. In the end they said:

> Now that you have admitted our enemy in your home, we swear by God and declare that we, the people of Mecca, will join in an attack on Medina unless you, the people of Medina, agree to turn him out of Medina or give him a joint fight. When we attack Medina, we will put to the sword all able-bodied men and enslave all women (Abū Dāwūd, *Kitāb al-Kharāj*).

'Abdullah bin Ubayy ibn Salūl thought this letter a God-send. He consulted other hypocrites in Medina and persuaded them that if they allowed the Prophet to live in peace among them they would invite the hostility of Mecca. It behoved them, therefore, to make war upon the Prophet, if only in order to appease the Meccans. The Prophet got to know of this. He went to 'Abdullah bin Ubayy ibn Salūl and tried to convince him that such a step would prove suicidal. Many people in Medina had become Muslims and were prepared to lay down their lives for Islam. If 'Abdullah declared war upon Muslims, the majority of the people of Medina would fight on the side of

Muslims. Such a war would, therefore, cost him dear and spell his own destruction. 'Abdullah, impressed by this advice, was dissuaded from his plans.

At this time, the Prophet took another important step. He collected the Muslims and suggested that every two Muslims should become linked together as two brothers. The idea was well received. Medinite took Meccan as his brother. Under this new brotherhood, the Muslims of Medina offered to share their property and their belongings with the Muslims of Mecca. One Medinite Muslim offered to divorce one of his two wives and to have her married to his Meccan brother. The Meccan Muslims declined to accept the offers of the Muslims of Medina out of regard for the needs of the latter. But the Muslims of Medina remained insistent, and the point had to be referred to the Prophet. The Muslims of Medina urged that the Meccan Muslims were their brothers ; so, they had to share their property with them. The Meccan Muslims did not know how to manage land. But they could share the produce of the land if not the land itself. The Meccan Muslims declined with thanks this incredibly generous offer, and preferred to stick to their own vocation of trade. Many Meccan Muslims became rich again. But Muslims of Medina ever remember their offer to share their property with Meccan Muslims. Many a time when a Medinite Muslim died, his sons divided the inheritance with their Meccan brothers. For many years the practice continued, until the Quran abolished it by its teaching about the division of inheritance (Bukhārī and Muslim).

PACT BETWEEN VARIOUS TRIBES OF MEDINA

Besides uniting Meccan and Medinite Muslims in a brotherhood, the Holy Prophet instituted a covenant between all the inhabitants of Medina. By this covenant, Arabs and the Jews were united into a common citizenship with Muslims. The Prophet explained to both Arabs and Jews that before the Muslims emerged as a group in Medina, there were only two groups in their town, but with Muslims now, there were three groups. It was but proper that they should enter into an agreement which should be binding upon them all, and which should assure to all of them a measure of peace. Eventually an agreement was arrived at. The agreement said :

> Between the Prophet of God and the Faithful on the one hand, and all those on the other, who voluntarily agree to enter. If any of the Meccan Muslims is killed, the Meccan Muslims will themselves be responsible. The responsibility for securing the release of their prisoners will also be theirs. The Muslim tribes of Medina similarly will be responsible for their own lives and their prisoners. Whoever rebels or promotes enmity and disorder will be considered a common enemy. It will be the duty of all the others to fight against him, even though he happens to be a son or a close relation. If a disbeliever is killed in battle by a believer, his Muslim relations will seek no revenge. Nor will they assist disbelievers against believers. The Jews who join this covenant will be helped by Muslims. The Jews will not be put to any hardship. Their enemies will not be helped against them. No disbeliever will give quarter to anybody from Mecca. He will not act as a trustee for any Meccan property. In a war between Muslims and disbelievers he will take no part. If a believer is maltreated without cause, Muslims will have the right to fight against those who maltreat. If a common enemy attack Medina, the Jews will side with the Muslims and share the expenses of the battle. The Jewish tribes in covenant with the other tribes of Medina will have rights similar to those of Muslims. The Jews will keep to their own faith, and Muslims to their own. The rights enjoyed by the Jews will also be enjoyed by their followers. The citizens of Medina will not have the right to declare war without the sanction of the Prophet. But this will not prejudice the right of any individual to avenge an individual wrong. The Jews will bear the expenses of their own organization, and Muslims their own. But in case of war, they will act with unity. The city of Medina will be regarded as sacred and inviolate by those who sign the covenant. Strangers who come under the protection of its citizens will be treated as citizens. But the people of Medina will not be allowed to admit a woman to its citizenship without the permission of her relations. All disputes will be referred for decision to God and the Prophet. Parties to this covenant will not have the right to enter into any agreement with the Meccans or their allies. This, because parties to this covenant agree in resisting their common enemies. The parties will remain united in peace as in war. No party will enter into a separate peace. But no party will be obliged to take part in war. A party, however, which commits any excess will be liable to a penalty. Certainly

God is the protector of the righteous and the Faithful and Muhammad is His Prophet (Hishām).

This is the covenant in brief. It has been prepared from scraps to be found in historical records. It emphasizes beyond any doubt that in settling disputes and disagreements between the parties at Medina, the guiding principles were to be honesty, truth and justice. Those committing excesses were to be held responsible for those excesses. The covenant makes it clear that the Prophet of Islam was determined to treat with civility and kindness the other citizens of Medina, and to regard them and deal with them as brethren. If disputes and conflicts arose later, the responsibility rested with the Jews.

As we have already said, two or three months passed away before Meccans could renew their planned hostility against Islam. An occasion was provided by Sa'd bin Mu'ādh, chief of the Aus tribe of Medina, who arrived at Mecca for the circuit of the Ka'ba. Abū Jahl saw him do this and said, "After giving protection to this apostate Muhammad, do you expect you can come to Mecca and circuit the Ka'ba in peace? Do you think you can protect and save him? I swear by God, that had it not been for Abū Sufyān, you could not have returned safe to your family."

Sa'd bin Mu'ādh replied, "Take it from me, if you Meccans stop us from visiting and circuiting the Ka'ba, you will have no peace on your road to Syria." At about that time Walīd bin Mughīra, a Meccan chief, became seriously ill. He apprehended that his end had come. The other chiefs of Mecca were sitting around. Walīd could not control himself and began to cry. The Meccan chiefs wondered at this and asked him why he was crying. "Do you think I am afraid of death? No, it is not death I fear. What I fear is lest the Faith of Muhammad should spread and even Mecca go under him." Abū Sufyān assured Walīd that as long as they lived they would resist with their lives the spread of this Faith (Khamīs, Vol. 1).

MECCANS PREPARING TO ATTACK MEDINA

From this narration of events it is quite clear that the lull in Meccan hostility was only temporary. The leaders of

Mecca were preparing for a renewed attack on Islam. Dying chiefs bound their survivors to oaths of hostility against the Prophet, and roused them to war against him and his followers. The people of Medina were invited to take up arms against the Muslims and were warned that, if they refused to do so, the Meccans and their allied tribes would attack Medina, kill their men and enslave their women. If the Prophet had stood aside and done nothing for the defence of Medina, he would have incurred a terrible responsibility. The Prophet, therefore, instituted a system of reconnaissance. He sent parties of men to places round about Mecca to report on signs of preparations for war. Now and then, there were incidents—scuffles and fights—between these parties and Meccans. European writers say these incidents were initiated by the Prophet and that, therefore, in the wars which ensued, he was the aggressor. But we have before us the thirteen years of Meccan tyranny, their intrigues for antagonizing the people of Medina against the Muslims, and the threatened attack upon Medina itself. Nobody who remembers all this can charge the Prophet with the responsibility for initiating these incidents. If he sent out parties of Muslims for purpose of reconnaissance, it was in self-defence. Thirteen years of tyranny were justification enough for the preparations of Muslims for self-defence. If wars ensued between them and their Meccan enemy, the responsibility did not lie with Muslims. The slender grounds on which Christian nations today declare war against one another are well known. If half of what the Meccans did to Muslims is done today to a European people, they would feel justified in going to war. When the people of one country organize on a large scale the killing of another, when one people compels another to leave their homes, does it not give the victims the right to make war ? After Muslims had migrated to Medina, no further ground was needed for them to declare war on the Meccans. But the Prophet declared no war. He showed tolerance and confined his defensive activities to reconnaissance. The Meccans, however, continued to irritate and harass the Muslims. They excited the people of Medina against them and interfered with their right of pilgrimage. They changed their normal caravan routes and started going through tribal areas around Medina, to rouse the tribes against the Muslims. The peace of Medina was threatened ; so it was the obvious duty of Muslims to accept the challenge of war which the Meccans had been throwing down for fourteen years. Nobody under the circumstances could question the right of Muslims to accept this challenge.

While the Prophet was busy reconnoitring, he was not neglecting the normal and spiritual needs of his following in Medina. A great majority of the people of Medina had become Muslims, by outward profession as well as by inward faith. Some had joined by outward profession only. The Prophet, therefore, started instituting the Islamic form of government in his small following. In earlier days, Arabs had settled their disputes by the sword and by individual violence. The prophet introduced juridical procedures. Judges were appointed to settle claims which individuals or parties brought against one another. Unless a judge declared a claim to be just and true, it was not admitted. In the old days intellectual pursuits had been looked upon with contempt. The Prophet took steps to promote literacy and love of learning. Those who could read and write were asked to teach others the same arts. Injustice and cruelty were ended. The rights of women were established. The rich were to pay for the needs of the poor and for improving the social amenities of Medina. Labourers were protected from exploitation. For weak and incompetent heirs, arrangements were made for the appointment of trustees. Loan transactions began to be committed to writing. The importance of fulfilling all undertakings began to be impressed. The excesses committed against slaves were abolished. Hygiene and public sanitation began to receive attention. A census of the population was undertaken. Lanes and highways were ordered to be widened, and steps were taken to keep them clean. In short, laws were instituted for the promotion of an ideal family and social life. The savage Arabs for the first time in their history were introduced to the rules of politeness and civilized existence.

BATTLE OF BADR

While the Prophet planned for the practical institution of laws which were to serve not only his own generation of Arabs but all mankind for all time to come, the people of Medina made their plans for war. The Prophet planned for a law which was to bring to his own people and all the others peace, honour and progress; his Meccan enemy planned for the destruction of that law. The Meccan plans eventually resulted in the Battle of Badr. It was the eighteenth month after the Hijra. A commercial caravan led by Abū Sufyān was returning from Syria. Under pretence of protecting this caravan, the Meccans raised a large army and decided to take it to Medina. The Holy Prophet came to know of these preparations. He also had revelations from God which said that the time to pay back the enemy in his own coin had come. He went out of Medina with a number of followers. Nobody at the time knew whether this party of Muslims would have to confront the caravan which was coming from Syria or the army which was coming from Mecca. The party numbered about three hundred. A commercial caravan in those days did not consist only of camels loaded with merchandise. It also included armed men who guarded the caravan and escorted it through its journey. Since tension had arisen between Meccans and the Muslims of Medina, the Meccan chiefs had begun to take special care about arming the escort. History records the fact of two other caravans which passed by this route a short while before. In one of these, two hundred armed men were provided as guard and escort, and in the other three hundred. It is wrong to suggest, as Christian writers do, that the Prophet took three hundred followers and set out to attack an undefended commercial caravan. The suggestion is mischievous and unfounded. The caravan which was now coming from Syria was a large one and, considering its size and the armed escort provided for other caravans, it seems reasonable to think that about four to five hundred armed guards must have been provided to serve as its escort. To say that the Muslim party of three hundred poorly-armed men were led by the Prophet to attack such a well-armed caravan in the hope of looting it is unjust in the extreme. Only rank prejudice and determined ill-will against Islam can prompt such a thought. If the Muslim party was out to confront only this caravan, their adventure could have been described as an adventure of war, although war in self-defence, for the Muslim party from Medina was small and ill-armed and the Meccan caravan was large and well-armed, and for a long time they had been carrying on a campaign of hostility against the Muslims of Medina.

In point of fact the conditions under which this small party of Muslims set out of Medina were far more grave. As we have said, they did not know whether it was the caravan from Syria or the army from Mecca which they would have to confront. The uncertainty under which the Muslims laboured is hinted at in the Quran. But the Muslims were prepared for both. The uncertainty under which the Muslims left Medina redounds to the credit of their faith and their tremendous sincerity. It was after they had gone some distance from Medina that the Prophet made it known to them that they would have to confront the large Meccan army rather than the small Syrian caravan.

Speculations had reached Muslims about the size of the Meccan army. The most moderate of these speculations placed the number at one thousand, all of them seasoned soldiers skilled in the art of war. The number accompanying the Prophet was only three hundred and thirteen, and of these many were unskilled and inexperienced, and most were ill-armed. A great majority of them went on foot, or mounted on camels. There were only two horses in the whole party. This party, which was as poorly equipped with the weapons of war as it was raw in experience, had to confront a force three times its number, consisting mostly of experienced fighters. It was quite obviously the most dangerous thing ever undertaken in history. The Holy Prophet was wise enough to ensure that nobody took part in it without due knowledge and without his will and heart in it. He told his party clearly that it was no longer the caravan they had to confront but the army from Mecca. He asked the party for their counsel. One after another, his Meccan followers stood up and assured the Prophet of their loyalty and zeal, and of their determination to fight the

Meccan enemy who had come to attack the Muslims of Medina in their homes. Every time the Prophet heard a Meccan Muslim, he asked for more counsel and more advice. The Muslims of Medina had been silent. The aggressors were from Mecca, with blood relations to many of those Muslims who had migrated with the Prophet to Medina and who were now in this small party. The Muslims of Medina were afraid lest their zeal to fight the Meccan enemy should injure the feelings of their Meccan brethren. But when the Prophet insisted on more and more counsel, one of the Medinite Muslims stood up and said, "Prophet of God, you are having all the counsel you want, but you continue to ask for more. Perhaps you refer to us, the Muslims of Medina. Is that true?"

"Yes," said the Prophet.

"You ask for our counsel," he said, "because you think that when you came to us, we agreed to fight on your side only in case you and your fellow emigrants from Mecca were attacked in Medina. But now we seem to have come out of Medina, and you feel that our agreement does not cover the conditions under which we find ourselves today. But O Prophet of God, when we entered into that agreement we did not know you as well as we do now. We know now what high spiritual station you hold. We care not for what we agreed to. We now stand by you, whatever you ask us to do. We will not behave like the followers of Moses who said, 'Go you and your God and fight the enemy, we remain here behind.' If we must fight, we will and we will fight to the right of you, to the left of you, in front of you and behind you. True, the enemy wants to get at you. But we assure you that he will not do so, without stepping over our dead bodies. Prophet of God, you invite us to fight. We are prepared to do more. Not far from here is the sea. If you command us to jump into it, we will hesitate not." (Bukhārī, *Kitāb al-Maghāzī*, and Hishām).

This was the spirit of devotion and sacrifice which early Muslims displayed, and the like of which is not to be found in the history of the world. The example of the followers of Moses has been cited above. As for the disciples of Jesus, we know they abandoned Jesus at a critical time. One of them gave him away for a paltry sum. Another cursed him, and the remaining ten ran away. The Muslims who joined the Prophet from Medina had been in his companionship only for a year and a half. But they had attained to such strength of faith that, had the Prophet but ordered, they would have plunged themselves heedlessly into the sea. The Prophet took counsel. But he had no doubt at all as to the devotion of his following. He took counsel in order to sift the weaklings and send them away. But he found that the Meccan and the Medinite Muslims vied with one another in the expression of their devotion. Both were determined that they would not turn their backs to the enemy, even though the enemy was three times their number and far better equipped, armed and experienced. They would rather put their faith in the promises of God, show their regard for Islam, and lay down their lives in its defence.

Assured of this devotion by both Meccan and Medinite Muslims, the Prophet advanced. When he reached a place called Badr, he accepted the suggestion of one of his followers and ordered his men to settle near the brook of Badr. The Muslims took possession of this source of water, but the land on which they took up their positions was all sand, and therefore unsuitable for the manoeuvres of fighting men. The followers of the Prophet showed natural anxiety over this disadvantage. The Prophet himself shared the anxiety of his followers and spent the whole night praying. Again and again he said :

> My God, over the entire face of the earth just now, there are only these three hundred men who are devoted to Thee and determined to establish Thy worship. My God, if these three hundred men die today at the hands of their enemy in this battle, who will be left behind to glorify Thy name ? (Ṭabarī).

God heard the supplication of His Prophet. Rain came over-night. The sandy part of the field which the Muslims occupied became wet and solid. The dry part of the field occupied by the enemy became muddy and slippery. Maybe the Meccan enemy chose this part of the field and left the other for the Muslims because their experienced eye preferred dry ground to facilitate the movements of their soldiers and cavalry. But the tables were turned upon them by a timely act of God. The rain which came over-night made the sandy part of the field which was in the possession of the Muslims hard and the hard field where the Meccans had encamped slippery. During the night the Prophet had a clear intimation from God that important members of the enemy would meet with their death. He even had individual names revealed to him. The spots at which they were to drop dead were also revealed. They died as they were named and dropped where it had been foretold.

In the battle itself this little party of Muslims displayed wonderful daring and devotion. One incident proves this. One of the few generals which the Muslim force included was 'Abd al-Raḥmān bin 'Auf, one of the chiefs of Mecca and an experienced soldier in his own way. When the battle began, he looked to his right and to his left to see what kind of support he had. He found to his amazement, that he had only two lads from Medina on his flanks. His heart sank and he said to himself, "Every general needs support on his sides. More so I on this day. But I only have two raw boys. What can I do with them ?" 'Abd al-Raḥmān bin 'Auf says he had hardly finished saying this to himself when one of the boys touched his side with his elbow. As he bent over to hear the boy, the latter said, "Uncle, we have heard of one Abū Jahl, who used to harass and torment the Prophet. Uncle, I want to fight him ; tell me where he is." 'Abd al-Raḥmān had not yet replied to this youthful inquiry, when his attention was similarly drawn by the boy on the other side, who asked him the same question. 'Abd al-Raḥmān was not a little amazed at the courage and determination of these two boys. A seasoned soldier, he did not think that even he would select the commander of the enemy for an individual encounter. 'Abd al-Raḥmān raised his finger to point at Abū Jahl—armed to the teeth and standing behind the lines protected by two senior generals, with drawn swords. 'Abd al-Raḥmān had not dropped his finger, when the two boys dashed into the enemy ranks with the speed of an eagle, making straight for their chosen target. The attack was sudden. The soldiers and guards were stupefied. They attacked the boys. One of the boys lost an arm. But they remained unnerved and unbeaten. They attacked Abū Jahl, with such violence that the great commander fell to the ground, mortally wounded. From the spirited determination of these two boys, one can judge how deeply the followers of the Prophet, both old and young, had been stirred by the cruel persecution to which they and the Prophet had been subjected. We only read about them in history, but yet are deeply stirred. The people of Medina heard of these cruelties from eye-witnesses. The feelings they must have had, can well be imagined. They heard of Meccan cruelties on the one hand and of the forbearance of the Prophet on the other. No wonder their determination mounted high to avenge the wrongs done to the Prophet and to the Muslims of Mecca. They looked only for an opportunity to tell the Meccan tormentors that if the Muslims did not retaliate, it was not because they were powerless ; it was because they had not been permitted by God to do so. How determined this small Muslim force was to die fighting can be gauged from another incident. Battle had not yet been joined when Abū Jahl sent a Bedouin chief to the Muslim side to report on their numbers. This chief returned and reported that the Muslims were three hundred or more. Abū Jahl and his followers were glad. They thought the Muslims easy prey. "But," said the Bedouin chief, "my advice to you is—Don't fight these men, because every one of them seems determined to die. I have seen not men but death mounted on camels" (Ṭabarī and Hishām). The Bedouin chief was right—those who are prepared to die do not easily die.

A GREAT PROPHECY FULFILLED

The time of the battle drew near. The Prophet came out of the little hut in which he had been praying, and announced :

> "The hosts will certainly be routed and will show their backs."

These were the words revealed to the Prophet some time before in Mecca. Evidently they related to this battle. When Meccan cruelty had reached its extreme limit, and Muslims were migrating to places where they could have peace, the Prophet had the following verses revealed to him by God :

> And surely to the people of Pharaoh also came Warners. They rejected all Our Signs. So We seized them as the seizing of One Who is Mighty and Omnipotent. Are your disbelievers better than those ? Or have you an exemption in the Scriptures ? The hosts will certainly be routed and will show their backs. Nay, the Hour is their appointed time ; and the Hour will be most calamitous and most bitter. Surely the offenders will be in bewilderment and flaming fire. On the day when they will be dragged into the Fire on their faces and it will be said to them, "Taste ye the touch of burning" (54 : 42-49).

These verses are part of Sūra Al-Qamar and this Sūra, according to all reports, was revealed in Mecca. Muslim authorities place the date of its revelation somewhere between the fifth and tenth year of the Prophet's Call, that is, at least three years before the Hijra (*i.e.* the year of the Prophet's migration from Mecca to Medina). More likely, it was revealed eight years before. European authorities have the same view. According to Noldeke, the whole of this Chapter was revealed after the fifth year of the Prophet's Call. Wherry thinks this date a little too early. According to him, the Chapter belongs to the sixth or seventh year before the Hijra, or after the Prophet's Call. In short, both Muslim and non-Muslim authorities agree that this Chapter was revealed years before the Prophet and his followers migrated from Mecca to Medina. The prophetic value of the Meccan verses is beyond dispute. There is in these verses a clear hint of what was in store for the Meccans in the battlefield of Badr. The fate they were going to meet is clearly foretold. When the Prophet came out of his hut, he reiterated the prophetic description contained in the Meccan Chapter. He must have been put in mind of the Meccan verses, during his prayers in the hut. By reciting one of the verses he reminded his followers that the Hour promised in the Meccan revelation had come.

And the Hour had really come. The Prophet Isaiah (21 : 13–17) had foretold this very hour. The battle began, even though Muslims were not ready for it and non-Muslims had been advised against taking part in it. Three hundred and thirteen Muslims, most of them inexperienced and unused to warfare, and nearly all of them unequipped, stood before a number three times as large, and all of them seasoned soldiers.

In a few hours, many noted chiefs of Mecca met their end. Just as the Prophet Isaiah had foretold, the glory of Kedar faded away. The Meccan army fled in miserable haste, leaving behind their dead as well as some prisoners. Among the prisoners was the Prophet's uncle, 'Abbās, who generally stood by the Prophet during the days at Mecca. 'Abbās had been compelled to join the Meccans and to fight the Prophet. Another prisoner was Abu'l 'Āṣ, a son-in-law of the Prophet. Among the dead was Abū Jahl, Commander-in-chief of the Meccan army and, according to all accounts, arch-enemy of Islam.

Victory came, but it brought mixed feelings to the Prophet. He rejoiced over the fulfilment of divine promises, repeated during the fourteen years which had gone by, promises which had also been recorded in some of the earliest religious writings. But at the same time he grieved over the plight of the Meccans. What a pitiable end had they met ! If this victory had come to another in his place, he would have jumped with joy. But the sight of the prisoners before him, bound and handcuffed, brought tears to the eyes of the Prophet and his faithful friend Abū Bakr. 'Umar, who succeeded Abū Bakr as the Second Khalīfa of Islam, saw this but could not understand. Why should the Prophet and Abū Bakr weep over a victory ? 'Umar was bewildered. So he made bold to ask the Prophet, "Prophet of God, tell me why you weep when God has given you such a grand victory. If we must weep, I will weep with you, or put on a weeping face at least." The Prophet pointed to the miserable plight of the Meccan prisoners. This was what disobedience of God led to.

The Prophet Isaiah spoke again and again of the justice of this Prophet, who had emerged victorious from a deadly battle. Of this there was a grand demonstration on this occasion. Returning to Medina the Prophet rested for the night on the way. The devoted followers who watched him could see that he turned from side to side and could not sleep. They soon guessed that it was because he heard the groans of his uncle, 'Abbās, who lay nearby, bound tight as a prisoner of war. They loosened the cord on 'Abbās. 'Abbās stopped groaning. The Prophet, no longer disturbed by his groans, went to sleep.

A little later he woke up and wondered why he no longer heard 'Abbās groan. He half thought 'Abbās had gone into a swoon. But the Companions guarding 'Abbās told him they had loosened the cord on 'Abbās to let him (the Prophet) sleep undisturbed. "No, no," said the Prophet, "there must be no injustice. If 'Abbās is related to me, other prisoners are related to others. Loosen the cords on all of them or tie the cord tight on 'Abbās also." The Companions heard this admonition and decided to loosen the cords on all the prisoners, and themselves bear the responsibility for their safe custody. Of the prisoners, those who were literate were promised freedom if they each undertook to make ten Meccan boys literate—this being their ransom for liberty. Those who had nobody to pay ransom for them, obtained their liberty for the asking. Those who could afford to pay ransom, were set free after they had paid it. By setting the prisoners free in this way, the Prophet put an end to the cruel practice of converting prisoners of war into slaves.

BATTLE OF UḤUD

When the Meccan army fled from Badr they announced that they would attack Medina again and avenge upon the Muslims for what the Meccans had suffered in the battle ; and only a year later they did attack Medina again in full force. They felt so humiliated and disgraced at their defeat that the Meccan chiefs forbade surviving relations to weep over those who had died in the battle. They also laid down that profits from commercial caravans would be constituted into a war fund. With full preparations, therefore, an army of three thousand under the command of Abū Sufyān attacked Medina. The Prophet held a council and asked his followers whether they would meet the enemy in Medina or outside. He himself favoured the former alternative. He preferred to let the Muslims stay in Medina and let the enemy come and attack them in their homes. This, he thought, would place the responsibility for aggression and attack on the enemy. But at the council were many Muslims who had not had the chance to take part in the Battle of Badr, and who now longed to fight for God.

They insisted on having a straight and open fight and on having the chance to die fighting. The Prophet accepted the general advice (Ṭabaqāt).

While this was being debated, the Prophet related a vision of his. He said, "I had a vision. I saw a cow, and I also saw my sword with its point broken. I saw the cow being butchered, and that I had put my hand inside a coat of armour. I also saw myself riding a ram." The Companions asked the Prophet how he interpreted the vision.

"The butchering of the cow" said the Prophet, "indicates that some of my Companions will be killed in battle. The broken point of my sword indicates that some important one among my relations will meet his death, or maybe, I myself will suffer pain or injury of some kind. Putting my hand in a coat of armour seems to mean that if we stay in Medina it is better for us. The fact that I have seen myself riding a ram means that we will overpower the commander of the disbelievers, and that he will die at our hands" (Bukhārī, Hishām and Ṭabaqāt).

It was made clear by this vision and its interpretation that it was better for Muslims to stay in Medina. The Prophet, however, did not insist upon this, because the interpretation of the vision was his own, not a part of revealed knowledge. He accepted the advice of the majority and decided to go out of Medina to meet the enemy. As he set out, the more zealous section of his following realizing their mistake, approached the Prophet and said, "Prophet of God, the way you advised seems better. We ought to stay in Medina and meet the enemy in our streets."

"Not now," said the Prophet. "Now the Prophet of God has put on his armour. Come what may, now we shall go forward. If you prove steadfast and persevering, God will help you" (Bukhārī and Ṭabaqāt). So saying, he went forward with a force of a thousand. At a small distance from Medina they camped for the night. It was the Prophet's custom to let his fighting force rest a while before they met the enemy. At the time of the morning prayers, he made a round. He found that some Jews also had joined the Muslims. They pretended they had treaties of alliance with the Medina tribes. As the Prophet had had knowledge of Jewish intrigues, he sent off the Jews. As soon as he did so, 'Abdullah bin Ubayy ibn Salūl, chief of the hypocrites, withdrew with his three hundred followers. He said the Muslim army was now no match for the enemy. To take part in the battle was now certain death. The Prophet had made a mistake in sending off his own allies. The result of this eleventh-hour desertion was that only seven hundred Muslims were left under the Prophet's command. The seven hundred stood against an army more than four times their number, and many more times better in equipment. In the Meccan army were seven hundred fighters in armour ; in the Muslim army only one hundred. The Meccans had a mounted force of two hundred horses, Muslims had only two horses. The Prophet reached Uḥud. Over a narrow hilly pass there, he posted a guard of fifty, charged with the duty of repelling any attack on it by the enemy or any attempt to possess it. The Prophet told them clearly their duty. It was to stand where they had been posted, and not to move from the spot until they were commanded to do so, no matter what happened to the Muslims. With the remaining six hundred and fifty men, the Prophet went to do battle with an army about five times as large. But, with the help of God, in a short time the six hundred and fifty Muslims drove away three thousand skilled Meccan soldiers. The Muslims ran in pursuit. The hilly pass on which fifty Muslims had been posted was in the rear. The guard said to the commander, "The enemy is beaten. It is time we took some part in the battle and won our laurels in the next world." The commander stopped them, reminding them of the clear orders of the Prophet. But the men explained that the Prophet's order was to be taken in the spirit and not in the letter. There was no meaning in continuing to guard the pass while the enemy was running for life.

VICTORY CONVERTED INTO DEFEAT

Arguing thus they left the pass and plunged into the battle. The fleeing Meccan army included Khālid bin Walīd, who later became a great Muslim general. His keen eye fell on the unguarded pass. There were only a few men guarding it now. Khālid shouted for another Meccan general 'Amr bin al-'Āṣ, and asked him to have a look at the pass behind. 'Amr did so, and thought it the chance of his life. Both generals stopped their men and climbed on to the hill. They killed the few Muslims who were still guarding the pass and from the eminence started an attack upon the Muslims. Hearing their war cries, the routed Meccan army collected itself again, and returned to the field. The attack on the Muslims was sudden. In their pursuit of the Meccan army they had dispersed over the whole of the field. Muslim resistance to this new attack could not be assembled. Only individual Muslim soldiers were seen engaging the enemy. Many of these fell fighting. Others fell back. A few made a ring round the Prophet. They could not have been more than twenty in all. The Meccan army attacked this ring fiercely. One by one, the Muslims in the ring fell under the blows of Meccan swordsmen. From the hill, the archers sent volleys of arrows. At that time, Ṭalḥa, one of the Quraish and the Muhājirīn (Meccan Muslims who had taken refuge in Medina), saw that the enemy arrows were all directed to the face of the Prophet. He stretched out his hand and held it up against the Prophet's face. Arrow after arrow struck Ṭalḥa's hand, yet it did not drop, athough with each shot it was pierced through. Ultimately it was completely mutilated. Ṭalḥa lost his hand and for the rest of life went about with a stump. In the time of the Fourth Khalīfa of Islam when internal dissensions had raised their head, Ṭalḥa was tauntingly described by an enemy as the handless Ṭalḥa. A friend of Ṭalḥa replied, "Handless, yea, but do you know where he lost his hand ? At the Battle of Uḥud, in which he raised his hand to shield the Prophet's face from the enemy's arrows."

Long after the Battle of Uḥud friends of Ṭalḥa asked him, "Did not your hand smart under the arrow shots and the pain make you cry ?" Ṭalḥa replied, "It made me smart, and it almost made me cry, but I resisted both because I knew that if my hand shook but slightly, it would expose the Prophet's face to the volley of enemy arrows." The few men who were left with the Prophet could not have stood the army which they faced. A party of the enemy advanced forward and pushed them off. The Prophet then stood alone like a wall, and soon a stone struck his forehead and made a deep gash in it. Another blow drove the rings of his helmet into his cheeks. When the arrows were falling thick and fast and the Prophet was wounded he prayed, "My God, forgive my people for they know not what they are doing" (Muslim). The Prophet fell on the dead, the dead who had lost their lives in his defence. Other Muslims came forward to defend the Prophet from more attacks. They also fell dead. The Prophet lay unconscious among these dead bodies. When the enemy saw this, they took him for dead. They withdrew in the certainty of victory, and proceeded to line up again. Among the Muslims who had been defending the Prophet and who had been pushed by the avalanche of enemy forces, was 'Umar. The battlefield had now cleared. 'Umar who saw this, became certain that the Prophet was dead. 'Umar was a brave man. He proved it again and again ; best of all, in fighting simultaneously the great Empires of Rome and Iran. He was never known to blench under difficulties. This 'Umar sat on a stone with drooping spirits, crying like a child. In the meantime another Muslim, Anas bin Naḍr by name, came wandering along in the belief that the Muslims had won. He had seen them overpower the enemy but, having had nothing to eat since the night before, had withdrawn from the battlefield, with some dates in his hand. As soon as he saw 'Umar crying, he stood amazed and asked, " 'Umar, what is the matter with you that instead of rejoicing over a magnificent victory won by the Muslims, you are crying?"

'Umar replied, "Anas, you do not know what has happened. You only saw the first part of the battle. You do not know that the enemy captured the strategic point on the hill and attacked us fiercely. The Muslims had dispersed, believing they had won. There was no resistance to this attack by the enemy. Only the Prophet with a handful of guards stood against the entire enemy and all of them fell down fighting."

"If this is true," said Anas, " what use is sitting here and crying ? Where our beloved Master has gone, there must we go too."

Anas had the last date in his hand. This he was about to

put in his mouth but, instead, he threw it away saying, "O date, except thee, is there anything which stands between Anas and Paradise ?"

Saying this, he unsheathed his sword and flung himself into the enemy forces, one against three thousand. He could not do much, but one believing spirit is superior to many. Fighting valiantly, Anas at last fell wounded, but he continued to fight. Upon this the enemy horde sprang barbarously upon him. It is said that when the battle was over, and the dead were identified, Anas's body could not be identified. It had been cut into seventy pieces. At last a sister of Anas identifying it by a mutilated finger said, "This is my brother's body" (Bukhārī).

Those Muslims who made a ring round the Prophet but were driven back, ran forward again as soon as they saw the enemy withdrawing. They lifted the Prophet's body from among the dead. Abū 'Ubaida bin al-Jarrāḥ caught between his teeth the rings which had sunk into the Prophet's cheeks and pulled them out, losing two teeth in the attempt.

After a little while, the Prophet returned to consciousness. The guards who surrounded him sent out messengers to tell Muslims to assemble again. A disrupted force began to assemble. They escorted the Prophet to the foot of the hill. Abū Sufyān, the enemy commander, seeing these Muslim remnants, cried aloud, "We have killed Muhammad." The Prophet heard the boastful cry but forbade the Muslims to answer, lest the enemy should know the truth and attack again and the exhausted and badly-wounded Muslims should have again to fight this savage horde. Not receiving a reply from the Muslims, Abū Sufyān became certain the Prophet was dead. He followed his first cry by a second and said, "We have also killed Abū Bakr." The Prophet forbade Abū Bakr to make any reply. Abū Sufyān followed by a third, and said, "We have also killed 'Umar." The Prophet forbade 'Umar also to reply. Upon this Abū Sufyān cried that they had killed all three. Now 'Umar could not contain himself and cried, "We are all alive and, with God's grace, ready to fight you and break your heads." Abū Sufyān raised the national cry, "Glory to Hubal. Glory to Hubal. For Hubal has put an end to Islam." (Hubal was the Meccans' national idol.) The Prophet could not bear this boast against the One and Only God, Allah, for Whom he and the Muslims were prepared to sacrifice their all. He had refused to correct a declaration of his own death. He had refused to correct a declaration of the death of Abū Bakr and of 'Umar for strategic reasons. Only the remnants of his small force had been left. The enemy forces were large and buoyant. But now the enemy had insulted Allah. The Prophet could not stand such an insult. His spirit was fired. He looked angrily at the Muslims who surrounded him and said, "Why stand silent and make no reply to this insult to Allah, the Only God ?"

The Muslims asked, "What shall we say, O Prophet ?"

"Say, 'Allah alone is Great and Mighty. Allah alone is Great and Mighty. He alone is High and Honoured. He alone is High and Honoured.' "

The Muslims shouted accordingly. This cry stupefied the enemy. They stood chagrined at the thought that the Prophet after all had not died. Before them stood a handful of Muslims, wounded and exhausted. To finish them was easy enough. But they dared not attack again. Content with the sort of victory they had won, they returned making a great show of rejoicing.

In the Battle of Uḥud, Muslim victory became converted into a defeat. Nevertheless, the battle affords evidence of the truth of the Prophet. For in this battle were fulfilled the prophecies the Prophet had made before going into battle. Muslims were victorious in the beginning. The Prophet's beloved uncle, Ḥamza, died fighting. The commander of the enemy was killed early in the action. The Prophet himself was wounded and many Muslims were killed. All this happened as it had been foretold in the Prophet's vision.

Besides the fulfilment of the incidents told beforehand this battle afforded many proofs of the sincerity and devotion of Muslims. So exemplary was their behaviour that history fails to provide a parallel to it. Some incidents in proof of this we have already narrated. One more seems worth narrating. It shows the certainty of conviction and devotion displayed by the Prophet's Companions. When the Prophet retired to the foot of the hill with a handful of Muslims, he sent out some of his Companions to look after the wounded lying on the field. A Companion after long search found a wounded Muslim of Medina. He was near death. The Companion bent over him and said, "Peace on you." The wounded Muslim raised a trembling hand, and holding the visitor's hand in his own, said, "I was waiting for someone to come."

"You are in a critical state," said the visitor to the soldier. "Have you anything to communicate to your relations ?"

"Yes, yes," said the dying Muslim. "Say peace to my relations and tell them that while I die here, I leave behind a precious trust to be taken care of by them. That trust is the Prophet of God. I hope my relations will guard his person with their lives and remember this my only dying wish" (Mu'aṭṭā and Zurqānī).

Dying persons have much to say to their relations, but these early Muslims, even in their dying moments, thought not of their relations, sons, daughters or wives, nor of their property, but only of the Prophet. They faced death in the certainty that the Prophet was the saviour of the world. Their children if they survived, would achieve but little. If they died guarding the Prophet's person, they would have served both God and man. They believed that in sacrificing their families they served mankind and they served their God. In inviting death for them they secured life everlasting for mankind at large.

The Prophet collected the wounded and the dead. The wounded were given first-aid and the dead were buried. The Prophet then learnt that the enemy had treated the Muslims most savagely, that they had mutilated the bodies of the dead Muslims and cut off a nose here and an ear there. One of the mutilated bodies was that of Ḥamza, the Prophet's uncle. The Prophet was moved, and said, "The actions of disbelievers now justify the treatment which we so far thought was unjustified." As he said this, he was commanded by God to let the disbelievers alone and to continue to show them compassion.

RUMOUR OF PROPHET'S DEATH REACHES MEDINA

The rumour of the Prophet's death and the news of the dispersal of the Muslim army reached Medina, before the remnants of the Muslim force could return to the town. Women and children ran madly towards Uḥud. Many of them learnt the truth from the returning soldiers and went back. One woman of the tribe of Banū Dīnār went on until she reached Uḥud. This woman had lost her husband, father and brother in the battle. According to some narrators, she had also lost a son. A returning soldier met her and told her that her father had died. She said in reply, "I do not care for my father; tell me about the Prophet." The soldier knew the Prophet was alive, so he did not answer her query at once, but went on to tell her of her brother and husband who had also died. At each report she remained unmoved and asked again and again, "What has the Prophet of God done?" It was a strange expression to use, but when we remember it was a woman who used it, it no longer seems so strange. A woman's emotions are strong. She often addresses a dead person as though he were alive. If that person is nearly related, she tends to make a complaint to him and ask why he is abandoning her and leaving her behind uncared for and unlooked after. It is common for women to mourn the loss of their dear ones in this way. The expression used by this woman, therefore, is appropriate to a woman grieving over the Prophet's death. This woman held the Prophet dear and refused to believe he was dead even after she had heard that he was. At the same time she did not deny the news but continued to say in true womanly grief, "What has the Prophet of God done?" By saying this she pretended the Prophet was alive, and complained that a loyal leader like him had chosen to give them all the pain of separation.

When the returning soldier found that this woman did not care about the death of her father, brother and husband, he understood the depth of her love for the Prophet and told her, "As for the Prophet, he is as you wish, fully alive." The woman asked the soldier to show her the Prophet. He pointed to one part of the field. The woman rushed to that part and reaching the Prophet, held his mantle in her hand, kissed it and said, "My father and mother be sacrificed to thee, O Prophet of God, if thou livest, I care not who else dies" (Hishām).

We can see, therefore, what fortitude and devotion did Muslims—both men and women—display in this battle. Christian writers narrate proudly the story of Mary Magdalene and her companions and tell us of their devotion and bravery. It is said that in the small hours of the morning they stole through the Jews and made for the tomb of Jesus. But what is this compared with the devotion of this Muslim woman of the tribe of Dinār ?

One more example is recorded in history. After the dead had been buried and the Prophet was returning to Medina, he saw women and children who had come out of Medina to receive him. The cord of his dromedary was held by Sa'd bin Mu'ādh, a chief of Medina. Sa'd was leading the dromedary pompously. He seemed to proclaim to the world that Muslims had after all succeeded in leading the Prophet back to Medina hale and hearty. As he was advancing he saw his own aged mother advancing to meet the returning party of Muslims. This aged woman was very weak-sighted. Sa'd recognized her and, turning to the Prophet, said, "Here, O Prophet, is my mother."

"Let her come forward," replied the Prophet.

The woman came forward and with a vacant look tried to spot the Prophet's face. At last she was able to spot it and was glad. The Prophet seeing her said, "Woman, I grieve over the loss of thy son."

"But," replied the devoted woman, "after I have seen you alive, I have swallowed all my misfortunes." The Arabic expression she used was "I have roasted my misfortune and swallowed it" (Ḥalbiyya, Vol. 2, p. 210). What depth of emotion does this expression indicate. Normally, grief eats up a human being, and here was an aged woman who had lost her son, a staff for her old age. But she said that, instead of letting her grief eat her up, she had eaten up her grief. The fact that her son had died for the Prophet would sustain her during the rest of her days.

The Prophet reached Medina. In this battle, many Muslims were killed and many wounded. Still the battle cannot be said to have ended in defeat for Muslims. The incidents which we have related above prove the reverse. They prove that Uḥud was as great a victory for Muslims as any other. Muslims who turn to the pages of their early history can derive sustenance and inspiration from Uḥud.

Back in Medina, the Prophet returned to his mission. He engaged himself again in training and teaching his followers. But as before, his work did not go on uninterruptedly. After Uḥud, the Jews became more daring, and the hypocrites began to raise their heads again. They began to think that the extirpation of Islam was within their means and their competence. Only, they had to make a concerted effort. Accordingly, the Jews put to use new methods of vexation. They would publish foul abuse in verse, and in this way they would insult the Prophet and his family. Once the Prophet was called to decide a dispute and he had to go to a Jewish fortress. The Jews planned to drop a stone slab on him and thus put an end to his life. The Prophet had a forewarning of this from God. It was his wont to receive such timely warnings. The Prophet left his seat without saying anything. The Jews later admitted their foul intrigue. Muslim women were insulted in the streets. In one such incident a Muslim lost his life. On another occasion the Jews stoned a Muslim girl and she died in great pain. This behaviour of the Jews strained their relations with Muslims and forced them to fight against the Jews. But Muslims only turned them out of Medina. One of the two Jewish tribes migrated to Syria. Of the other, some went to Syria and some settled in Khaibar, a well-fortified Jewish stronghold, to the north of Medina.

In the interval of peace between Uḥud and the next battle, the world witnessed an outstanding example of the influence of Islam on its followers. We refer to the prohibition of drink. In describing the condition of Arab society before Islam, we pointed out that the Arabs were confirmed drunkards. To drink five times a day was in fashion in every Arab home. To lose oneself under the effect of drink was a common practice and of this the Arabs were not in the least ashamed. Rather they thought it was a virtue. When a guest arrived, it was the duty of the house-wife to send drinks round. To wean such a people from this deadly habit was no easy matter. But in the fourth year after the Hijra the Prophet received the command that drinking had been forbidden. With the promulgation of this command, drinking disappeared from Muslim society. It is recorded that when the revelation making drink unlawful was received, the Prophet sent for a Companion and ordered him to proclaim the new command in the streets of Medina. In the house of an Anṣārī (a Muslim of Medina) a drinking party was going on. Many persons had been invited and cups of wine were being served. One large pot had been drunk and a second one was going to be broached. Many had lost their senses, and many more were on the way to lose them. In this condition they heard some one proclaim that drinking had been forbidden by the Prophet under a command of God. One of the party stood up and said, "It looks like a proclamation against drinking ; let us find out if this is so." Another stood up, struck the earthen pot full of wine with his staff, broke it to pieces and said, "First obey, then inquire. It is enough that we have heard of such a proclamation. It is not meet that we should go on drinking while we make inquiries. It is rather our duty to let the wine flow in the street and then inquire about the proclamation" (Būkharī and Muslim, *Kitāb al-Ashriba*). This Muslim was right. For, if drinking had been forbidden, they would have been guilty of an offence, had they gone on drinking ; on the other hand, if drinking had not been forbidden, they would not lose much if for once they should let the wine in their pots flow into the streets. Drinking disappeared from the entire Muslim society after this proclamation. No special effort or campaign was needed to bring about this revolutionary change. Muslims who heard this command and witnessed the ready response with which it was received lived up to seventy or eighty years. No case is known of any Muslim who, having heard of this prohibition, showed the weakness of offending against it. If there was any such case, it must have been of one who did not have the chance to come under the direct influence of the Prophet. Compare with this the prohibition movement of America and of the efforts to promote temperance which have been made for so many years in Europe. In the one case a simple proclamation by the Prophet was enough to obliterate a social evil rooted deep in Arab society. In the other, prohibition was enacted by special laws. Police and the army, custom officials and excise inspectors, all exerted themselves as a team and tried to put down the evil of drink but failed and had to confess their failure. The drunkards won and the drink evil could not be defeated. Ours is said to be an age of social progress. But when we compare our age with the age of early Islam, we wonder which of the two deserves this title—this age of ours or the age in which Islam brought about this great social revolution ?

What happened at Uḥud was not liable to be easily forgotten. The Meccans thought Uḥud was their first victory against Islam. They published the news all over Arabia and used it to excite the Arab tribes against Islam and to persuade them that Muslims were not invincible. If they continued to prosper, it was not because of any strength of their own but because of the weakness of Arab orthodoxy. It was due to the weakness of Arab idolaters. If the Arab idolaters made a concerted effort, to overpower the Muslims was not a difficult business. The result of this propaganda was that hostility against Muslims began to gather strength. The other Arab tribes began to outstrip the Meccans in harassing the Muslims. Some began to attack them openly. Some began to inflict losses upon them surreptitiously. In the fourth year after the Hijra, two Arab tribes, the 'Aḍl and the Qāra, sent their representatives to the Holy Prophet to submit that many of their men were inclined towards Islam. They requested the Prophet to send to them some Muslims well-versed in the teaching of Islam, to live among them and teach them the New Religion. Actually this was an intrigue hatched by the Banū Liḥyān, arch-enemy of Islam. They sent these delegates to the Prophet under promise of a rich reward. The Prophet received the request unsuspectingly and sent ten Muslims to teach the tribes the tenets and principles of Islam. When this party reached the territory of the Banū Liḥyān, their escorts had the news delivered to the tribesmen and invited them to arrest the party or to put them to death. On this vicious suggestion, two hundred armed men of the Banū Liḥyān set out in pursuit of the Muslim party and overtook them at last at a spot called Rajī'. An encounter took place between ten Muslims and two hundred of the enemy. The Muslims were full of faith. The enemy was without any. The ten Muslims climbed up an eminence and challenged the two hundred. The enemy tried to overpower the Muslims by vile intrigue. They offered to spare them if only they would come down. But the party chief replied that they had seen enough of the promises made by disbelievers. So saying, they turned to God and prayed. God was well aware of their plight. Was it not meet that He should inform their Prophet of this ? When the disbelievers found the small party of Muslims adamant, they launched their attack upon them. The party fought without thought of defeat. Seven of the ten fell fighting. To the three who remained the disbelievers renewed their promise to spare their lives, on condition that they should come down from the eminence. These three believed the disbelievers and surrendered. As soon as they did so, the disbelievers tied them up. One of the three said, "This is the first breach of your plighted word. God only knows what you will do next." Saying this, he refused to go with them. The disbelievers started belabouring the victim and dragging him down the way. But they were so overawed by the resistance and determination shown by this one man that they murdered him on the spot. The other two they took with them and sold them as slaves to the Quraish of Mecca. One of the two was Khubaib, the other Zaid. The purchaser of Khubaib wanted to murder him so as to avenge his own father, who had been killed at Badr. One day, Khubaib asked for a razor to complete his toilet. Khubaib was holding the razor when a child of the household approached him out of curiosity. Khubaib took the child and put him on his knee. The child's mother saw this and became terrified. Her mind was full of guilty feelings, and here was a man whom they were going to murder in a few days holding a razor so dangerously near their child. She was convinced that Khubaib was going to murder the child. Khubaib saw the consternation on the face of the woman and said, "Do you imagine I am going to murder your child. Do not think so for a moment. I cannot do such a foul thing. Muslims do not play false." The woman was impressed by the honest and straightforward bearing and behaviour of Khubaib. She remembered this ever afterwards and used to say she had never seen a prisoner like Khubaib. At last the Meccans led Khubaib to an open field to celebrate his murder in public. When the appointed moment came, Khubaib asked for leave to say two *rak'ats* of prayer. The Quraish agreed and Khubaib addressed in public view his last prayers to God in this world. When he had finished praying, he said he wanted to continue, but did not do so lest they should think he was afraid of dying. Then he quietly submitted his neck to the executioner. As he did so, he hummed the verses :

> While I die a Muslim, I care not whether my headless body drops to the right or to the left. And why should I ? My death is in the way of God ; if He wills, He can bless every part of my dismembered body (Bukhāri).

Khubaib had hardly finished murmuring these verses when the executioner's sword fell on his neck and his head fell to one side. Those who had assembled to celebrate this public murder included one Sa'īd bin 'Āmir who later became a Muslim. It is said that whenever the murder of Khubaib was related in Sa'īd's presence, he would go into a fit (Hishām).

The second prisoner, Zaid, was also taken out to be murdered. Among the spectators was Abū Sufyān, chief of Mecca. Abū Sufyān turned to Zaid and asked, "Would you not rather have Muhammad in your place? Would you not prefer to be safe at home, while Muhammad was in our hands ?"

Zaid replied proudly, "What, Abū Sufyān ? What do you say ? By God, I would rather die, than that the Prophet should tread on a thorn in a street in Medina." Abū Sufyān could not help being impressed by such devotion. He looked at Zaid in amazement and declared unhesitatingly, but in measured tones, "God is my witness, I have not known any one love another as much as the Companions of Muhammad love Muhammad" (Hishām, Vol. 2).

About this time some people of Najd also approached the Prophet for Muslims to teach them Islam. The Prophet did not trust them. But Abū Barā', chief of the 'Āmir tribe, happened to be in Medina at the time. He offered to act as surety for the tribe and assured the Prophet that they would commit no mischief. The Prophet selected seventy Muslims who knew the Quran by heart. When this party reached Bi'r Ma'ūna one of them, Ḥarām bin Malḥān went to the chief of the 'Āmir tribe (a nephew of Barā') to give him the message of Islam. Apparently Ḥarām was well received by the tribesmen. But while he was addressing the chief, a man stole up from behind and attacked Ḥarām with a lance. Ḥarām died on the spot. As the lance pierced through Ḥarām's neck, he was heard saying, "God is great. The Lord of the Ka'ba is my witness, I have attained my goal" (Bukhārī). Having murdered Ḥarām in this foul manner, the tribal leaders provoked the tribe into an attack upon the rest of this party of Muslim teachers. "But," said the tribesmen, "Our chief, Abū Barā, offered to act as surety ; we cannot attack this party." Then the tribal chiefs, with the assistance of the two tribes who had gone to the Prophet to ask for Muslim teachers and some other tribes, attacked the Muslim party. The simple appeal, "We have come to preach and to teach, not to fight," had no effect. They started murdering the party. All but three of the seventy were murdered. One of the survivors was lame and had climbed a hill before the encounter began. Two others had gone to a wood to feed their camels. On returning from the wood they found sixty-six of their companions lying dead on the field. The two counselled together. Said one, "We should go and make a report of this to the Holy Prophet."

Said the other, "I cannot leave a spot where the chief of our party, whom our Prophet appointed our leader, has been murdered." So saying, he sprang single-handed upon the disbelievers and died fighting. The other was taken prisoner but was later released in fulfilment of a vow which the tribal chief had taken. The murdered party included 'Āmir bin Fuhaira, a freedman of Abū Bakr. His murderer was one Jabbār who later became a Muslim. Jabbār attributed his conversion to this mass massacre of Muslims.

"When I started murdering 'Āmir," says Jabbār, "I heard 'Āmir say, 'By God I have met my goal.' I asked 'Āmir why a Muslim said this sort of thing when he was meeting his death. 'Āmir explained that Muslims regarded death in the path of God as a blessing and a victory." Jabbār was so impressed by this reply, that he started making a systematic study of Islam, and ultimately became a Muslim (Hishām and Usud al-Ghāba).

The news of the two sad events, in which about eighty Muslims lost their lives as the result of a mischievous intrigue, reached Medina simultaneously. These were no ordinary men who were murdered. They were bearers of the Quran. They had committed no crime and had harmed nobody. They were taking part in no battle. They had been decoyed into enemy hands by a lie told in the name of God and religion. These facts proved conclusively that enmity to Islam was determined and deep. On the other hand the zeal of Muslims for Islam was equally determined and deep.

ENCOUNTER WITH BANŪ MUṢṬALIQ

After the Battle of Uḥud, there was a severe famine at Mecca. Disregarding all enmity which the Meccans bore against him, and disregarding all machinations which they had been employing to spread disaffection against him throughout the country, the Prophet raised a fund to help the poor of Mecca in their dire need. The Meccans remained unimpressed even by this expression of goodwill. Their hostility went on unabated. In fact it became worse. Tribes which had so far been sympathetic towards Muslims also became hostile. One such tribe was Banū Muṣṭaliq. They had good relations with Muslims. But now they had started preparing for an attack on Medina. When the Prophet heard of their preparations he sent men to find out the truth. The men returned and confirmed the reports. The Prophet decided to go and meet this new attack. Accordingly, he raised a force and led it to the territory of Banū Muṣṭaliq. When the Muslim force met the enemy, the Prophet tried to persuade the enemy to withdraw without fighting. They refused. Battle was joined and in a few hours the enemy was defeated.

Because the Meccan disbelievers were bent upon mischief and friendly tribes were turning hostile, the hypocrites among

Muslims had also ventured on this occasion to take part in the battle on the Muslim side. They probably thought they might have a chance to do some mischief. The encounter with Banū Muṣṭaliq was over in a few hours. The hypocrites, therefore, did not have any chance to do any mischief during the battle. The Holy Prophet, however, decided to stay in the town of Banū Muṣṭaliq for a few days. During his stay a quarrel arose between a Meccan and a Medinite Muslim over drawing water from a well. The Meccan happened to be an ex-slave. He struck the Medinite, who raised an alarm, crying out for fellow-Medinites—known as the Anṣār or Helpers. The Meccan also raised an alarm and cried out for fellow-Meccans—known as the Muhājirīn or Refugees. Excitement prevailed. Nobody inquired what had happened. Young men on both sides drew their swords. 'Abdullah bin Ubayy ibn Salūl thought it a God-send. He decided to add fuel to the fire. "You have gone too far in your indulgence to the Refugees. Your good treatment of them has turned their heads, and now they are trying to dominate you in every way." The speech might have had the effect which 'Abdullah desired. The quarrel might have assumed serious proportions. But it did not. 'Abdullah was wrong in assessing the effect of his mischievous speech. Believing, however, that the Anṣār were being persuaded, he went so far as to say :

> Let us return to Medina. Then will the most honoured among its citizens turn out the most despised (Bukhāri).

By the most honoured citizen, he meant himself and by the most despised he meant the Prophet. As soon as he said this, believing Muslims were able to see through the mischief. It was not an innocent speech they had listened to, they said, but the speech of Satan who had come to lead them astray. A young man stood up and reported to the Prophet through his uncle. The Prophet sent for 'Abdullah bin Ubayy ibn Salūl and his friends and asked them what had happened. 'Abdullah and his friends denied that they had taken any such part as had been attributed to them in this incident. The Prophet said nothing. But the truth began to spread. In the course of time 'Abdullah bin Ubayy ibn Salūl's own son, 'Abdullah, also heard about it. Young 'Abdullah at once saw the Prophet, and said, "O Prophet, my father has insulted you. Death is his punishment. If you decide so, I would rather have you command me to kill my father. If you command someone else, and my father dies at his hands, I may be led to avenge my father by killing that man. Maybe I incur the displeasure of God in this way."

"But," said the Prophet, "I have no such intention. I will treat your father with compassion and consideration." When young 'Abdullah compared the disloyalty and discourtesy of his father with the compassion and kindness of the Prophet, he made for Medina full of suppressed anger against his father. He stopped his father on the way and said he would not let him go any farther on the road to Medina until he had withdrawn the words he had used against the Prophet. "The lips which said, 'The Prophet is despised and you are honoured,' must now say, 'The Prophet is honoured and you are despised.' Until you say this I will not let you go." 'Abdullah bin Ubayy ibn Salūl was astonished and frightened and said, "I agree, my son, that Muhammad is honoured and that I am despised." Young 'Abdullah then let his father go (Hishām, Vol. 2).

We have mentioned before two Jewish tribes who had to be banished out of Medina on account of their mischievous machinations and murderous intrigues. Banū Naḍīr, one of the two, migrated partly to Syria, partly to a town called Khaibar in the north of Medina. Khaibar was a well-fortified Jewish centre in Arabia. The Jews, who had migrated there, began to excite the Arabs against Muslims. The Meccans were already sworn enemies of Islam. No fresh provocation was needed to excite the Meccans against Muslims. Similarly the Ghaṭafān of Najd, because of their friendly relations with the Meccans, were hostile to Muslims. The Jews settled in Khaibar already counted on the Quraish of Mecca and the Ghaṭafān of Najd. Besides these, they planned to turn Banū Sulaim and Banū Asad against Islam. They also persuaded Banū Sa'd, a tribe in alliance with the Jews, to join the Meccans in an alliance against Islam. After a long intrigue a confederacy of Arab tribes was organized to fight the Muslims. This included the Meccans, the tribes living in territories around Mecca, the tribes of Najd, and those living in territories to the north of Medina.

BATTLE OF THE DITCH

A large army was raised in the fifth year of the Hijra. The strength of this army has been estimated by historians as between ten and twenty-four thousand men. But a confederated army raised out of the different tribes of Arabia could not be an army of ten thousand. Twenty-four thousand seems nearer the truth. It could easily have been eighteen or twenty thousand. The town of Medina which this horde wished to attack was a modest one, quite unable to resist a concerted attack by all Arabia. Its population at this time was little more than three thousand males (including old men, young men and children). Against this population the enemy had raised an army of twenty to twenty-four thousand able-bodied men, experienced in warfare ; and (having been assembled from different parts of the country) they were an army with a well-selected personnel. The population of Medina, on the other hand, which could be called upon to resist this huge army included males of all ages. One can judge the odds against which the Muslim population of Medina had to contend. It was a most unequal encounter. The enemy was twenty to twenty-four thousand strong, and Muslims hardly three thousand including, as we have said, all the males of the town, the old and the young. When the Prophet heard of the huge enemy preparations, he held a council and asked for advice. Among those who were consulted was Salmān the Persian, being the first Muslim convert from Persia. The Prophet asked Salmān what they did in Persia if they had to defend a town against a huge army. "If a town is unfortified, and the home force very small," said Salmān, "the custom in our country is to dig a ditch round the town and to defend from inside." The Prophet approved of the idea. Medina has hills on one side. These provided a natural protection on that side. Another side with a concentration of lanes had a compact population. On this side the town could not be attacked unawares. The third side had houses and palm-groves and, at some distance, the fortresses of the Jewish tribe, Banū Quraiẓa. The Banū Quraiẓa had signed a pact of peace with the Muslims. Therefore, this side was also considered safe from enemy attack. The fourth side was an open plain and it was from this side that the enemy attack was most likely and most feared. The Prophet, therefore, decided to dig a ditch on this open side so as to prevent the enemy from attacking unawares. The task was shared among Muslims—ten men were to dig ten yards of the ditch. Altogether a mile long ditch, of sufficient width and depth, had to be dug.

When the digging was going on, they came upon a rock which Muslim sappers found hard to tackle. A report was sent to the Prophet who made for the spot at once. Taking a pickaxe he struck the rock hard. Sparks came out and the Prophet cried aloud "Allāhu Akbar". He struck again. Again a light came out and again the Prophet cried out, "Allāhu Akbar". He struck a third time. Light came out again, the Prophet said, "Allāhu Akbar" and the rock was in fragments. The Companions asked the Prophet about all this. Why did he say, "Allāhu Akbar" again and again?

"I struck this rock three times with this pickaxe, and three times did I see scenes of the future glory of Islam revealed to me. In the first sparks I saw the Syrian palaces of the Roman Empire. I had the keys of those palaces given to me. The second time I saw the illumined palaces of Persia at Madā'in, and had the keys of the Persian Empire given to me. The third time, I saw the gates of Ṣan'ā and I had the keys of the Kingdom of Yemen given to me. These are the promises of God and I trust you will put reliance in them. The enemy can do you no harm" (Zurqānī, Vol. 2 and Bārī, Vol. 7). With their limited man-power, the ditch which the Muslims were able to dig could not be a perfect one from the point of view of military strategy, but it at least seemed to ensure against the sudden entry of the enemy into the town. That it was not impassable, subsequent events in the battle amply proved. No other side suited the enemy from which to attack the town.

From the side of the ditch, therefore, the huge army of Arabian tribesmen began to approach Medina. As soon as the Prophet got to know of this, he came out to defend it with twelve hundred men, having posted other men to defend other parts of the town.

Historians estimate differently the number which defended the ditch. Some put it at three thousand, others at twelve to thirteen hundred, still others at seven hundred. These estimates are very difficult and apparently difficult to reconcile. But, after weighing the evidence, we have come to the conclusion that all the three estimates of the Muslim numbers engaged in defending the ditch are correct. They relate to different stages of the battle.

FIGHT AGAINST HEAVY ODDS

We have already agreed that, after the withdrawal of the hypocrites at Uḥud, the number of Muslims left in the field was seven hundred. The Battle of the Ditch took place only two years after the Battle of Uḥud. During these two years, no large accessions to Islam are recorded in history. An increase during this time in the number of combatant Muslims from seven hundred to three thousand is not to be expected. At the same time, it does not stand to reason that between Uḥud and the Ditch there was no rise in the number of combatant Muslims. Islam continued to add to its numbers and we should expect some increase between the Battle of Uḥud and the Battle of the Ditch. From these two considerations, it seems to follow that the estimate which puts the number of Muslim combatants in the Battle of the Ditch at one thousand two hundred is correct. The only question to be answered is, why some authorities put the number at three thousand and some at seven hundred. Our answer to this question is that the two figures relate to two different stages of the battle. The Battle of the Ditch was fought in three stages. We had the first stage before the enemy had come near to Medina, and Muslims were engaged in digging the ditch. During this time, we may well assume that in removing the excavated earth to a distance, children and, to some extent even women must have come in to assist. In the digging of the trench we may, therefore, assume that there were altogether three thousands souls employed on the Muslim side. The number included children and some women. The children were able to help in carrying the earth, and women who always vied with the men in helping all Muslim campaigns, must have been useful in doing many ancillary jobs connected with the digging. There is evidence to support this assumption. When the digging started, even children were asked to come. Practically the whole population took part in the digging. But as soon as the enemy arrived and the battle began, the Prophet ordered boys under fifteen to withdraw from the scene of operations. Those above fifteen were allowed to take part if they were so minded (Ḥalbiyya, Vol. 2). From this it appears that at the time of digging, Muslim numbers were much larger than when the battle began. At the time of the battle the very young boys had all withdrawn. Estimates which put the Muslim numbers in the battle at three thousand relate only to the digging, and those which put the figure at one thousand two hundred relate to the actual battle in which only grown-up males took part. The only estimate we have not accounted for is that which puts the figure at seven hundred. Even this estimate, according to us, is correct. It has been proposed by as reliable an authority as Ibn Isḥāq, who is supported in this estimate by no less a person than Ibn Ḥazm. It is difficult to question this estimate. Fortunately, when we turn to the other details of the battle, even this estimate turns out to be correct. There is evidence to show that when the Banū Quraiẓa, against their plighted word, joined the enemy, and decided to attack Medina in the rear, the Holy Prophet, having been apprised of their evil intention, decided to post guards in the part of the town exposed to the attack of Banū Quraiẓa. This part of Medina had originally been left undefended because the Banū Quraiẓa were in alliance with Muslims. And it was assumed that they would not let the enemy attack the town from their side. It is known that when the defection of the Banū Quraiẓa was reported to the Prophet and it became evident that Muslim women, considered safe in this part of the town because of the alliance, were no longer safe, the Prophet decided to send two forces, of two and three hundred men, to guard two different parts of the now exposed town. The Prophet ordered them to raise occasional cries of "Allāhu Akbar", so that the main

Muslim forces should know that the Muslim women were safe. The estimate of Ibn Isḥāq, therefore, which puts the number of combatants in the Battle of the Ditch at seven hundred, is also correct. If five hundred men out of one thousand two hundred were sent to guard the rear of the town, only seven hundred could remain. Thus all the three estimates of the number of the muslim army in the Battle of the Ditch turn out to be correct.

To defend the ditch, therefore, the Holy Prophet had only seven hundred men. True, the ditch had been dug. But to face and to repel an army as large as the enemy had, even with the help of the ditch seemed well-nigh impossible. But as usual Muslims trusted their God and relied on His help. Their small force waited for the enemy host, while the women and children had been sent to two apparently safe parts of the town. When the enemy reached the ditch, they were amazed because this stratagem had never been used before in any Arab battle. So they decided to camp on their side of the ditch and to deliberate over methods of attacking and entering Medina. One side was protected by the ditch. A second side had hills with their natural protection. A third side had stone houses and groves of trees. It was impossible for the enemy to make any sudden attack on any part of the town. The enemy commanders took counsel together and decided that it was necessary to try to wean the Banū Quraiẓa, the Jewish tribe, still living in Medina, from their alliance with the Muslims and ask them to join the Arab confederates in this critical onslaught against Medina. Only the Banū Quraiẓa could give them a way to the town. At last Abū Sufyān selected Ḥuyai bin Akhṭab, chief of the banished tribe of Banū Naḍīr and principal instigator of Arab tribes against Medina, and appointed him to negotiate with the Banū Quraiẓa for facilities to attack the town from the rear. Ḥuyai bin Akhṭab went to the Jewish fortress to see the leader of the Banū Quraiẓa. At first they refused to see him. But when he explained that this was a very opportune moment to defeat the Muslims, he succeeded in winning over one of the Quraiẓites, Ka'b. He explained that all Arabia had turned out to attack and destroy the Muslims. The army which stood at the other side of the ditch was not an army, but an ocean of able-bodied men whom the Muslims could not possibly resist. Ultimately it was agreed that as soon as the army of disbelievers succeeded in forcing the ditch the Banū Quraiẓa would attack that part of Medina to which the Holy Prophet had sent all the women and children for safety. This plan, it was believed, would smash the Muslim resistance, and prove a death-trap for their entire population—men, women and children. If this plan had met with even partial success, it would have cost the Muslims dear and made things very difficult for them. They would have had no escape from this death-trap.

TREACHERY OF BANŪ QURAIẒA

The Banū Quraiẓa,as we have said, were in alliance with the Muslims. Even if they had not joined the battle on the Muslim side, it was expected that they would at least bar the way of the enemy on their side. The Prophet, therefore, had left that part of the town entirely unguarded. The Banū Quraiẓa knew that the Muslims trusted their good faith. So when they decided to join the Arabs, it was agreed that they would not join them openly lest the Muslims should become alert and take steps to guard the part of the town on the side of the Banū Quraiẓa. It was a very dangerous plot.

When it was agreed that Muslims were to be attacked from two sides, the Arab army started assailing the ditch. A few days passed, however, and nothing happened. Then they hit upon the idea of posting their archers on an eminence and ordering them to attack parties of Muslims defending the ditch. These stood on the edge separated by short intervals. As soon as the Muslim defence showed any signs of breaking, the disbelievers would try to cross the ditch with the help of their first-rate horsemen. They believed that when such attacks were repeated, they would obtain possession of a point on the Muslim side of the ditch at which they would be able to land their forces for a full-fledged attack on the town. Attack after attack was therefore made. Muslim defenders had to fight ceaselessly. One day they were kept so engaged in repelling these attacks that some of the daily prayers could not be said at the appointed time. The Prophet was grieved over this and said, "God punish the infidels, they have upset our prayers." The incident shows the intensity of the enemy attack. But it also shows that the Prophet's first and last concern was the worship of God. Medina had been beleaguered on all sides. Not only men, but also women and children were faced with certain death. The whole of the town was in the grip of anxiety. But the Prophet still thought of holding the daily prayers at their appointed hours. Muslims do not worship God only once a week, as do Christians and Hindus. Muslims are required to worship five times a day. During a battle, to hold even one public prayer is difficult, not to speak of holding five prayers a day in congregation. But the Prophet convened the five daily prayers even during battle. If one of these prayers was upset by enemy attack, it pained him.

To return to the battle, the enemy was attacking from the front, the Banū Quraiẓa were planning to attack from the rear but not in such a way as to make the Muslim population alert. They wanted to enter the town from behind and to kill the women and children sheltered there. One day the Banū Quraiẓa sent a spy to find out whether guards had been posted for the protection of women and children and, if so, in what strength. There was a special enclosure for families which the enemy regarded as their special target. The spy came and began to hover round this enclosure and to look about suspiciously. While he was doing so, Ṣafiyya, an aunt of the Prophet, spotted him. Only one male adult happened to be on guard duty at the time and even he was ill. Ṣafiyya reported to him what she had seen and suggested he should lay hand on this spy before he was able to inform the enemy how unprotected the women and children were in that part of the town. The sick Muslim refused to do anything upon which Ṣafiyya herself picked up a staff and began to fight this undesirable visitor. With the help of other women she succeeded in overpowering and killing him. Later it was proved that this man was really an agent of the Banū Quraiẓa. Muslims became nervous and began to apprehend other attacks from this side which they had so far thought quite safe. But the attack from the front was so heavy that the whole of the Muslim force was needed to resist it. Nevertheless, the Prophet decided to spare a part of the force for the protection of women and children. As we have said in our discussion of the Muslim numbers in this battle, out of twelve hundred men, the Prophet sent five hundred for the protection of women in the town. For the defence of the ditch, therefore, only seven hundred men were left to fight an army of between eighteen and twenty thousand. Many Muslims were unnerved at the odds which they had to face. They went to the Prophet and said how critical the situation was, and how impossible it seemed to save the town. They requested the Prophet to pray. They also requested him to teach them a special prayer for this occasion. The Prophet replied, "Have no fear. Only pray to God that He should protect you from your weaknesses, strengthen your hearts, and relieve your anxiety." The Prophet prayed himself in the following words:

> God, Thou hast sent to me the Quran. Thou waitest not to call anyone to account. These hordes which have come to attack us, give them defeat. God, I beseech thee again: Defeat them, make us dominate over them, and upset all their evil intentions (Bukhari).

And again:

> God, Thou hearest those who cry to Thee in misery and in affliction. Thou repliest to those who are stricken with anxiety. Relieve me of my pain, my anxiety, and my fear. Thou knowest what odds I and my Companions are up against (Zurqānī).

The hypocrites became more nervous than others in the Muslim force. All regard for the honour of their side and the safety of their town, their women and children, disappeared from their hearts. But they did not want to be disgraced in the presence of their own side. Therefore, they began to desert the Muslims one by one on slender excuses. The Quran refers to this in 33:14:

> And a section of them even asked leave of the Prophet, saying, 'Our houses are exposed and defenceless.' And they were not exposed. They only sought to flee away.

The state of battle at the moment, and the condition in which the Muslims stood at the time is described in the Quran in the following verses:

> When they came upon you from above you and from below you, and when your eyes became distracted, and the hearts reached to the throats, and you thought diverse thoughts about Allah. Then were the believers sorely tried, and they were shaken with a violent shaking. And when the hypocrites, and those in whose hearts was a disease said, 'Allah and His Messenger promised us nothing but delusion'. And when a party of them said, 'O people of Yathrib, you have possibly no stand against the enemy, therefore turn back' (33 : 11–14).

Here Muslims are reminded how they were attacked from the front by a confederacy of Arab tribes, and in the rear by the Jews. They are reminded how miserable they were at that time. Their eyes flinched and their hearts were in their mouths. They even began to entertain doubts about God. The believers were then on trial. They were all given a shaking. The hypocrites and the spiritually diseased began to say, 'We have all been fooled by false promises made to us by God and His Prophet !' A party of them even began to unnerve the Muslim force saying, 'There is no fighting now. There is nothing to do but to go back.'

How true believers behaved on this occasion is also described in the Quran :

> And when the believers saw the confederates, they said, 'This is what Allah and His Messenger promised us ; and Allah and His Messenger spoke the truth.' And it only increased them in faith and submission. Among the believers are men who have been true to the covenant they had made with Allah. There are some of them who have fulfilled their vow, and some who still wait, and they have not changed their condition in the least (33 : 23, 24).

The true believers, that is to say, were unlike the hypocrites and the weak. When they saw the huge numbers of the enemy, they were reminded of what God and His Prophet had told them already. This concerted attack by the tribes of Arabia was proof only of the truth of God and the Prophet. The true believers remained unshaken. Rather they increased in the spirit of obedience and in the fervour of faith. The true believers stood by their compact with God. Some of them had already attained to the goal of their lives by meeting their death. Some were only waiting to die in the path of God and reach their goal.

The enemy attacked the ditch fiercely and uninterruptedly. Sometimes he succeeded in clearing it. One day, important generals of the enemy succeeded in going across. But they were attacked so bravely by the Muslims that they had to fall back. In this encounter, Naufal, a big leader of the disbelievers, lost his life. So big was this leader that the disbelievers thought they would not be able to stand any insult to his dead body. They, therefore, sent word to the Prophet, that if he would return the body of this chief, they would pay ten thousand *dirhams*. It was a high price for the return of the dead body. The offer was made out of a sense of guilt. The disbelievers had mutilated the Muslim dead at Uḥud and were afraid that Muslims would do the same. But the teaching of Islam was different. Islam forbade outright the mutilation of the dead. When the Prophet received the message and the offer, he said, "What use have we for this body ? We want nothing in return for this. If it please you, take away the body" (Zurqānī, Vol. 2, p. 114).

A passage in Muir's *Life of Mohammad* (London—1878, p.322) describes eloquently the fierceness of the attack on Muslims. We need not apologize for quoting it here :

> Next morning, Mahomed found the whole force of the Allies drawn out against him. It required the utmost activity and an unceasing vigilance on his side to frustrate the manoeuvres of the enemy. Now they would threaten a general assault ; then breaking up into divisions they would attack various posts in rapid and distracting succession ; and at last, watching their opportunity, they would mass their troops on the least protected point, and, under cover of a sustained and galling discharge of arrows, attempt to force the trench. Over and again a gallant dash was made at the city, and at the tent of Mahomed, by such leaders of renown as Khālid and 'Amru ; and these were only repelled by constant counter-marches and unremitting archery. This continued throughout the day ; and, as the army of Mahomed was but just sufficient to guard the long line, there could be no relief. Even at night Khālid, with a strong party of horses, kept up the alarm, and still threatening the line of defence, rendered outposts at frequent intervals necessary. But all the endeavours of the enemy were without effect. The trench was not crossed.

The battle had gone on for two days. Still there had been no hand-to-hand fighting, no great bloodshed. Twenty-four hours of fighting had resulted in only three deaths on the enemy side and five on the Muslim side. Sa'd bin Mu'ādh, a chief of the Aus tribe and a devotee of the Prophet, was wounded. Repeated attacks on the ditch, however, resulted in some damage, and this made further attack easier. Great scenes of valour and of loyalty were witnessed. It was a cold night, perhaps the coldest in Arabia. We have on the authority of 'Ā'isha, the Prophet's holy consort, that the Prophet rose from his sleep again and again to guard the damaged part of the ditch. He became exhausted. He returned to bed but then, having warmed himself a little, went again to guard the ditch. One day he was so exhausted that he seemed quite unable to move. Then he said he wished some devoted Muslim would come and relieve him of the physical labour of guarding the ditch in the cold of the night. Soon he heard a voice. It was Sa'd bin Waqqāṣ. The Prophet asked him why he had come.

"To guard your person," said Sa'd.

"There is no need to guard my person," said the Prophet "A part of the ditch is damaged. Go and guard it that Muslims may be safe." Sa'd went, and the Prophet was able to sleep. (There was some coincidence. For when the Prophet arrived at Medina and danger to his person was very great, even then it was Sa'd who offered himself for a guard.) On another occasion during these difficult days, the Prophet heard the sound of arms. "Who is it ?" asked the Prophet. " 'Ibād bin Bishr," was the reply.

"Have you anyone else with you ?" asked the Prophet.

"Yes," said 'Ibād, "A party of Companions. We will guard your tent."

"Leave my tent alone. The disbelievers are trying to cross the ditch. Go and fight them" (Ḥalbiyya, Vol. 2).

As we said before, the Jews tried to enter the town surreptitiously. A Jewish spy lost his life in the effort. When they found that their intrigue had become known, they began to help the Arab confederates more openly. A concerted attack in the rear, however, was not attempted, because the field on this side was narrow and with the posting of the Muslim guards a large-scale attack had become impossible. But a few days later, the Jews and pagan confederates decided to make a simultaneous and sudden attack upon the Muslims.

THE CONFEDERATES DISPERSE

This dangerous plan, however, was foiled by God in a miraculous manner. It happened in this way. One Nu'aim, who belonged to the tribe of Ghaṭafān, became inclined towards Islam. He had come with the pagan armies but looked for an opportunity to help the Muslims. Alone, he could not do much. But when he saw that Jews had made common cause with the Arabs and Muslims seemed faced with certain death and destruction, Nu'aim made up his mind to do what he could to save the Muslims. He went to the Banū Quraiẓa, and talked to their chiefs. If the Arab armies ran away, what did they expect Muslims would do? The Jews being in compact with the Muslims, should they not be ready for punishment due to those who prove false to a compact? The interrogation frightened the Jewish leaders. They asked him what they should do. Nu'aim advised them to ask for seventy pagans as hostages. If the pagans were honest about a concerted attack they would not refuse the request. They should say that these seventy would guard their strategic points, while they themselves attacked the Muslims from the rear. After his talks with the Jews he went to the pagan leaders. He asked them what they would do if the Jews went back on their compact; if, to conciliate the Muslims they asked for pagan hostages and then handed them over to the Muslims. Was it not important for them to test the honesty of the Jews and ask them to participate in the common attack at once? The pagan chiefs were impressed by this advice. Acting upon it, they sent word to the Jews asking them whether they would not attack the town from the rear now that they (the confederates) were ready for the planned attack. The Jews replied that the following day was their sabbath and they could not fight on that day. Secondly, they said, they belonged to Medina, and the Arab confederates were all outsiders. Should the Arabs flee from the battle, what were the Jews going to do? The Arabs should, therefore, give seventy men as hostages. The Jews would then be ready to carry out their part of the attack. Suspicion was already at work. The Arabs refused to entertain the Jewish request. If the Jews were honest in their compact with the Arabs, there was no meaning in the sort of proposal which they had made. Suspicion being subversive of courage, the Arab armies lost their zeal, and when night came, went to sleep burdened with doubts and difficulties. Both officers and men repaired to their tents in depressed mood. Then a miracle happened, help coming from heaven to the Muslims. A keen wind began to blow. Tent walls were swept away. Cooking pots toppled over fires. Some fires were extinguished. The pagans believed in keeping alive a fire throughout the night. A blazing camp-fire was a good omen, an extinguished one a bad omen. When a fire in front of a tent became extinguished, the occupants thinking it a bad augury, would withdraw from the battle for the day, and join again. The pagan leaders were already stricken with doubts. When some campers packed away, others thought that the Muslims had made a night attack. The suggestion became contagious. They all started packing and withdrawing from the field. It is said that Abū Sufyān was asleep in his tent. News of the sudden withdrawal of the pagan divisions reached his ears. He got up agitated and, in excitement, mounted a tethered camel. He spurred the animal, but the animal would not move. His friends pointed to what he was doing, untied the animal, and Abū Sufyān with his friends was able to leave the field.

Two-thirds of the night had passed. The battle-field had cleared already. An army of between twenty and twenty-five thousand soldiers and followers disappeared, leaving a complete wilderness behind. Just at that time the Prophet had a revelation that the enemy had fled as the result of an act of God. To find out what had happened the Prophet wanted to send one of his followers to scan the battlefield and make a report. The weather was icy cold. Little wonder, the ill-clad Muslims were freezing. Some heard the Prophet's voice when he called out in the night. They wanted to reply, but could not. The cold was forbidding. Only Ḥudhaifa was able to say aloud, "Yes, Prophet of God, what do you want us to do ?"

The Prophet called out again. Again nobody could answer because of the cold. Only Ḥudhaifa answered again. The Prophet asked Ḥudhaifa to go and survey the battle-field, for God had informed him that the enemy had fled. Ḥudhaifa went near the ditch, and from there saw that the enemy had vacated the field. There were no soldiers and no men. Ḥudhaifa returned to the Prophet, recited the *Kalima* and said the enemy had fled. On the morrow Muslims also unpegged their tents and started packing for the city. A severe trial lasting for about twenty days had ended.

BANŪ QURAIẒA PUNISHED

Muslims were able to breathe again in peace. But they still had the Banū Quraiẓa to settle with. The Banū Quraiẓa had dishonoured their pact with the Muslims and this could not be passed over. The Prophet collected his exhausted force and told them that there was no rest for them yet. Before the sun went down, they must fall upon the Banū Quraiẓa in their fortifications. Then he sent 'Alī to the Banū Quraiẓa to ask them why they had gone back on their solemn word. The Banū Quraiẓa showed no regret and no inclination to ask for forgiveness. Instead, they insulted 'Alī and the other Muslim delegates and started hurling vile abuse at the Prophet and the women of his family. They said they did not care for Muhammad and had never had any kind of pact with him. When 'Alī returned to report the reply of the Jews, he found the Prophet and the Companions advancing towards the Jewish fortifications. The Jews had been abusing the Prophet, his wives and daughters. Fearing lest this should pain the Prophet, 'Alī suggested there was no need for the Prophet to take part as the Muslims themselves could deal with the Jews. The Prophet understood 'Alī and said, "You want me not to hear their abuse, Alī ?"

"Exactly," said 'Alī.

"But why ?" said the Prophet. "Moses was of their kith and kin. Yet they inflicted more suffering on him than they have on me." The Prophet continued to advance. The Jews put up their defences and started fighting. Their women also joined them. Some Muslims were sitting at the foot of a wall. A Jewish woman, seeing this, dropped a stone on them, killing one named Khallād. The siege went on for some days. At the end of this period, the Jews felt they would not be able to hold out for long. Then their chiefs sent word to the Prophet requesting him to send Abū Lubāba, an Anṣārī chief of the Aus, a tribe friendly to the Jews. They wanted to consult him about a possible settlement. The Prophet sent Abū Lubāba to the Jews, who asked him if they should lay down their arms and accept the award of the Prophet. Abū Lubāba said they should. But at the same time he passed a finger over his neck, making the sign of death. The Prophet had said nothing on this subject to anybody. But Abū Lubāba, fearing that the crime of the Jews merited nothing but death, unwittingly made this sign, which proved fateful for the Jews. The latter declined Abū Lubāba's advice and refused to accept the Prophet's award. Had they accepted it, the utmost punishment they would have had was expulsion from Medina. But as ill-luck would have it, they refused to accept the Prophet's award. Instead of the Prophet's, they said, they would accept the award of Sa'd bin Mu'ādh, chief of their allies, the Aus. They would agree to any punishment proposed by him. A dispute also arose among the Jews. Some of them began to say that their people had really gone back on their agreement with the Muslims. The behaviour of the Muslims, on the other hand, showed that they were true and honest and that their religion also was true. Those who thought in this way joined Islam. 'Amr bin Sa'dī, one of the Jewish chiefs, reproved his people and said, "You have committed a breach of faith and gone back on your plighted word. The only course now open to you is either to join Islam or give *jizya*."

They said, "We will neither join Islam nor give *jizya*, for dying is better than giving *jizya*." 'Amr replied that in that case he stood absolved, and saying this left the fort. He was sighted by Muhammad bin Maslama, commander of a Muslim column, who asked him who he was. On learning of his identity he told him to depart in peace and himself prayed loudly :

> "God, give me ever the power to screen the mistakes of the decent."

What he meant was that this Jew had shown remorse and regret over the conduct of his people. It was the moral duty of Muslims, therefore, to forgive men like him. In letting him go he had done a good thing, and he prayed that God should give him the chance to do such good deeds again and again. When the Prophet got to know of what Muhammad bin Maslama had done, he did not reprove him for letting go this Jewish leader. Rather, he approved of what had been done.

The disposition to make peace and to accept the award of the Prophet had been expressed only by individual Jews. As a people, they remained adamant and refused to accept the award of the Prophet and asked, instead, for the award of Sa'd bin Mu'ādh (Bukhārī, Ṭabarī and Khamīs). The Prophet accepted their demand and sent word to Sa'd, who was lying wounded, to come and give his award on the Jewish breach of faith. As soon as the Prophet's decision was announced, the Ausites who had been allies of the Banū Quraiẓa for a long time ran to Sa'd and began to press him to give his award in favour of the Banū Quraiẓa. The Khazraj, they said, had always tried to save Jews allied to them. It was up to Sa'd to save the Jews allied to his tribe. Sa'd went mounted to the Banū Quraiẓa. Men of his tribe ran with him on both sides, pressing him not to punish the Banū Quraiẓa. All that Sa'd said in reply was that the person who had to make an award held a trust. He had to discharge the trust with integrity. "I will therefore give my award, taking everything into consideration, and without fear or favour," he said. When Sa'd reached the Jewish fortress, he saw the Banū Quraiẓa lined up against the wall of the fort, waiting for him. On the other side were Muslims. When Sa'd got near them he asked, "Will you accept my award ?" They said, "Yes."

SA'D'S AWARD IN HARMONY WITH THE BIBLE

Turning to the Banū Quraiẓa he asked the same question,

and they also agreed. Then shyly he pointed to the side where the Prophet was sitting and asked if the people on that side also agreed to abide by his award. On hearing this, the Prophet replied, "Yes" (Ṭabarī and Hishām). Then Sa'd gave his award in accordance with the following commandment of the Bible. Says the Bible :

> When thou comest nigh unto a city to fight against it, then proclaim peace unto it. And it shall be, if it make thee answer of peace, and open unto thee, then it shall be, that all the people that is found therein shall be tributaries unto thee, and they shall serve thee. And if it will make no peace with thee, but will make war against thee, then thou shalt besiege it : And when the Lord thy God hath delivered it into thine hands, thou shalt smite every male thereof with the edge of the sword : But the women, and the little ones, and the cattle, and all that is in the city, even all the spoil thereof, shalt thou take unto thyself ; and thou shalt eat the spoil of thine enemies, which the Lord thy God hath given thee. Thus shalt thou do unto all the cities which the Lord thy God doth give thee for an inheritance, thou shalt save alive nothing that breatheth : But thou shalt utterly destroy them ; namely, the Hittites, and the Amorites, the Canaanites, and the Perizzites, the Hivites, and the Jebusites ; as the Lord thy God hath commanded thee : That they teach you not to do after all their abominations, which they have done unto their gods ; so should ye sin against the Lord your God (Deut. 20 : 10–18).

According to the teaching of the Bible, if the Jews had won and the Prophet had lost, all Muslims—men, women and children—would have been put to death. We know from history that this was the very intention of the Jews. The least the Jews would have done was to put to death the men, to enslave the women and children and make away with the belongings of the Muslims, this being the treatment laid down in Deuteronomy for enemy nations living in distant parts of the world. Sa'd was friendly to the Banū Quraiẓa. His tribe was in alliance with theirs. When he saw that the Jews had refused to accept the award of the Prophet and refused thus to have the lighter punishment prescribed for such an offence in Islam, he decided to award to the Jews the punishment which Moses had laid down. The responsibility for this award does not rest with the Prophet or the Muslims, but with Moses and his teaching and with the Jews who had treated the Muslims so cruelly. They were offered what would have been a compassionate award. But, instead of accepting this, they insisted on an award by Sa'd. Sa'd decided to punish the Jews in accordance with the Law of Moses. Yet Christians to this day continue to defame the Prophet of Islam and say that he was cruel to the Jews. If the Prophet was cruel to the Jews, why was he not cruel to other people or on other occasions? There were many occasions on which the Prophet's enemies threw themselves at his mercy, and never did they ask in vain for his forgiveness. On this occasion the enemy insisted on a person other than the Prophet making the award. This nominee of the Jews, acting as umpire between them and the Muslims, asked the Prophet and the Jews in public whether they would accept his award. It was after the parties had agreed, that he proceeded to announce it. And what was his award? It was nothing but the application of the Law of Moses to the offence of the Jews. Why then should they not have accepted it? Did they not count themselves among the followers of Moses? If any cruelty was perpetrated, it was by the Jews on the Jews. The Jews refused to accept the Prophet's award and invited instead the application of their own religious law to their offence. If any cruelty was perpetrated it was by Moses, who laid down this penalty for a beleaguered enemy and laid this down in his book under the command of God. Christian writers should not pour out the vials of their wrath on the Prophet of Islam. They should condemn Moses who prescribed this cruel penalty or the God of Moses, Who commanded him to do so.

The Battle of the Ditch over, the Prophet declared that from that day onwards pagans would not attack Muslims; instead, Muslims would now attack pagans. The tide was going to turn. Muslims were going to take the offensive against tribes and parties which had so far been gratuitously attacking and harassing them. What the Prophet said was no empty threat. In the Battle of the Ditch the Arab confederates had not suffered any considerable losses. They had lost only a few men. In less than a year's time they could have come and attacked Medina again and with even better preparations. Instead of any army of twenty thousand they could have raised for a new attack an army of forty, or even fifty, thousand. An army numbering a hundred or a hundred and fifty thousand was not beyond their capacity. But now for twenty-one years, the enemies of Islam had done their utmost to extirpate Islam and Muslims. Continued failure of their plans had shaken their confidence. They had begun to fear that what the Prophet taught was true, and that their national idols and gods were false, that the Creator was the One Invisible God taught by the Prophet. The fear that the Prophet was right and they wrong had begun to creep upon them. There was no outward sign of this fear, however. Physically, the disbelievers went about as they had always done. They went to their idols and prayed to them as national custom required. But their spirit was broken. Outwardly they lived the lives of pagans and disbelievers ; inwardly their hearts seemed to echo the Muslim slogan, 'There is no God but Allah.'

After the Battle of the Ditch the Prophet, as we have observed already, declared that henceforward disbelievers would not attack Muslims but that, instead, Muslims would attack disbelievers. Muslim endurance had reached its limit. The tide was going to turn (Bukhārī, *Kitāb al-Maghāzī*).

DID THE PROPHET SEEK TO CONTINUE WARFARE ?

In the battles which had so far been fought, Muslims had either remained in Medina or gone some distance out of it to fight the aggression of disbelievers. Muslims did not initiate these encounters, and showed no disposition to continue them after they had started. Normally hostilities once begun, can be ended in only two ways—an agreed peace or the submission of one side to the other. In the encounters between Muslims and disbelievers so far there had been no hint of a peace nor had either side offered to submit. True, there had been pauses in the fighting, but nobody could say that war between Muslims and disbelievers had ended. According to ordinary canons, Muslims could have attacked the enemy tribes and compelled them to surrender. But Muslims did not do this. When the enemy stopped fighting, Muslims stopped also. They stopped because they believed there might be a talk of peace. But when it became evident that there was no talk of peace by the disbelievers, nor was there any disposition on their part to surrender, the Prophet thought that the time had come to end the war either by a peace or by the surrender of one side to the other. War had to be ended if there was to be peace. After the Battle of the Ditch, therefore, the Prophet seemed determined to secure one of two things ; peace or surrender. That Muslims should surrender to disbelievers was out of question. The victory of Islam over its persecutors had been promised by God. Declarations to this effect had been made by the Prophet during his stay at Mecca. Could Muslims then have sued for peace ? A movement for peace can be initiated either by the stronger or by the weaker side. When the weaker side sues for peace it has to surrender, temporarily or permanently, a part of its territory or part of its revenues ; or it has to accept other conditions imposed upon it by the enemy. When the stronger side proposes peace it is understood that it does not aim at the total destruction of the weaker side but is willing to let it retain complete or partial independence in return for certain conditions. In the battles which had so far been fought between Muslims and disbelievers the latter had suffered defeat after defeat. Yet their power had not been broken. They had only failed in their attempts to destroy Muslims. Failure to destroy another does not mean defeat. It only means that aggression has not yet succeeded ; attacks which have failed may be repeated. The Meccans, therefore, had not been beaten ; only their aggression against Muslims had failed. Militarily speaking, Muslims were decidedly the weaker side. True, their defence was still maintained, but they constituted a miserable minority and a minority which, though it had been able to resist the aggression of the majority, had been unable to take the offensive. Muslims, therefore, had not yet established their independence. If they had sued for peace, it would have meant that their defence had broken, and that they were now ready to accept the terms of the disbelievers. An offer of peace by them would have been disastrous for Islam. It would have meant self-annihilation. It would have brought new life to an enemy demoralized by repeated defeats. A growing sense of defeat would have given place to renewed hope and ambition. Disbelievers would have thought that though Muslims had saved Medina they were still pessimistic about their ultimate victory over disbelievers. A suggestion of peace, therefore, could not have proceeded from the Muslim side. It could have proceeded from the Meccan side, or from a third side, if a third side could have been found. No third side could, however, be found. In the conflict which had arisen Medina was set against all Arabia. It was the disbelievers, therefore, who could have sued the Muslims for peace, and there was no sign of this. Thus warfare between Muslims and Arabs might have gone on for ever. The Muslims *could* not, and the Arabs *would* not, sue for peace. Civil strife in Arabia, therefore, seemed to have no end, at least not for another hundred years.

There was only one way open to Muslims if they wanted to put an end to this strife. They were not prepared to surrender their conscience to the Arabs, to renounce, that is to say, their right to profess, practise and preach what they liked ; and there was no movement for peace from the side of disbelievers. Muslims had been able to repel repeated aggression. It was for them, therefore, to force the Arabs either to surrender or to accept peace. The Prophet decided to do so.

Was it war which the Prophet sought ? No, it was not war but peace that he wanted to bring about. If he had done nothing at this time, Arabia would have remained in the grip of civil warfare. The step which he took was the only way to peace. There have been some long wars in history. Some have lasted for a hundred, some for thirty years or so. Long wars have always resulted from lack of decisive action by either side. Decisive action, as we have said, can take only one of two forms—complete surrender or a negotiated peace.

Could the Prophet have remained passive ? Could he have withdrawn himself and his small force of Muslims behind the walls of Medina and left everything else to take care of itself ? This was impossible. The disbelievers had started the aggression. Passivity would not have meant the end of war but, rather, its continuation. It would have meant that the disbelievers could attack Medina whenever they liked. They could stop when they liked and attack when they liked. A pause in warfare did not mean the end of war. It meant only a strategic move.

TEACHINGS OF JUDAISM AND CHRISTIANITY ABOUT WAR

But the question now arises—Can it ever be right to fight for a faith ? Let us, therefore, turn to this question.

The teaching of religion on the subject of war takes different forms. The teaching of the Old Testament, we have cited above. Moses is commanded to enter the land of Canaan by force, to defeat its population and to settle his own people in it (Deut. 20 : 10–18). In spite of this teaching in the Book of Moses, and in spite of its reinforcement by practical example of the Prophets Joshua, David and others, Jews and Christians continue to hold their Prophets in reverence and to regard their books as the Books of God.

At the end of the Mosaic tradition, we had Jesus who taught;

> But I say unto you, That ye resist not evil : but whosoever shall smite thee on thy right cheek, turn to him the other also (Matthew 5 : 39).

Christians have often cited this teaching of Jesus and argued that Jesus preached against war. But in the New Testament, we have passages which purport to teach quite the opposite. One passage, for instance, says :

> Think not that I am come to send peace on earth : I came not to send peace, but a sword (Matthew 10 : 34).

And another passage says :

> Then said he unto them. But now, he that hath a purse, let him take it, and likewise his scrip : and he that hath no sword, let him sell his garment, and buy one (Luke 22 : 36).

Of the three verses the last two contradict the first. If Jesus came for war, why did he teach about turning the other cheek ? It seems we have either to admit a contradiction in the New Testament, or we have to explain one of the contradictory teachings in a suitable manner. We are not concerned here with the question whether turning the other cheek can ever be practicable. We are concerned only to point out that, throughout their long history, no Christian people have ever hesitated to make war. When Christians first attained to power in Rome, they took part in wars both defensive and aggressive. They are dominant powers in the world today, and they continue to take part in wars both defensive and aggressive. Only now the side which wins is canonized by the rest of the Christian world. Their victory is said to be the victory of Christian civilization. Christian civilization has come to mean whatever tends to be dominant and successful. When two Christian powers go to war, each claims to be the protector of Christian ideals. The power which wins is canonized as the true Christian power. It is true, however, that from the time of Jesus to our time, Christendom has been involved—and indications are that it will continue to remain involved—in war. The practical verdict of the Christian peoples, therefore, is that war is the real teaching of the New Testament, and that turning the other cheek was either an opportunist teaching dictated by the helplessness of early Christians, or it is meant to apply only to individuals, not to States and peoples.

Secondly, even if we assume that Jesus taught peace and not war, it does not follow that those who do not act upon this teaching are not holy and honoured. For Christendom has ever revered exponents of war such as Moses, Joshua and David. Not only this, the Church itself has canonized national heroes who suffered in wars. They were made saints by the Popes.

THE QURAN ON WAR AND PEACE

The teaching of Islam is different from both these teachings. It strikes a mean between the two. Islam does not teach aggression as did Moses. Nor does it, like present-day (and presumably corrupt) Christianity, preach a contradiction. It does not ask us to turn the other cheek and at the same time to sell our clothes to buy a sword. The teaching of Islam fits into the natural instincts of man, and promotes peace in the only possible way.

Islam forbids aggression, but it urges us to fight if failure to fight jeopardizes peace and promotes war. If failure to fight means the extirpation of free belief and of the search of truth, it is our duty to fight. This is the teaching on which peace can ultimately be built, and this is the teaching on which the Prophet based his own policies and his practice. The Prophet suffered continuously and consistently at Mecca but did not fight the aggression of which he was an innocent victim. When he escaped to Medina, the enemy was out to extirpate Islam; it was, therefore, necessary to fight the enemy in defence of truth and freedom of belief.

We quote below the passages in the Quran which bear on the subject of war.

(1) In 22 : 40–42 we have :

> Permission to fight is given to those against whom war is made, because they have been wronged—and Allah indeed has power to help them—Those who have been driven out from their homes unjustly only because they said, "Our Lord is Allah"—And if Allah did not repel some men by means of others, there would surely have been pulled down cloisters and churches and synagogues and mosques, wherein the name of Allah is oft commemorated. And Allah will surely help one who helps Him. Allah is indeed Powerful, Mighty.—Those who, if We establish them in the earth, will observe Prayer and pay the Zakāt and enjoin good and forbid evil. And with Allah rests the final issue of all affairs.

The verse purports to say that permission to fight is given to the victims of aggression. God is well able to help the victims—those who have been driven out of their homes because of their beliefs. The permission is wise because, if God were not to repel the cruel with the help of the righteous, there would be no freedom of faith and worship in the world. God must help those who help to establish freedom and worship. It follows that fighting is permitted when a people have suffered long from wanton aggression—when the aggressor has had no cause for aggression and he seeks to interfere with the religion of his victim. The duty of the victim, if and when he attains to power, is to establish religious freedom and to protect all religions and all religious places. His power is to be used not for his own glorification, but for the care of the poor, the progress of the country and the general promotion of peace. This teaching is as unexceptionable as it is clear and precise. It proclaims the fact that early Muslims took to war because they were constrained to do so. Aggressive wars were forbidden by Islam. Muslims are promised political power, but are warned that this power must be used not for self-aggrandizement, but for the amelioration of the poor and the promotion of peace and progress.

(2) In (2 : 191–194) we have :

> And fight in the cause of Allah against those who fight against you, but do not transgress. Surely, Allah loves not transgressors. And kill them wherever you meet them and drive them out from where they have driven you out ; for persecution is worse than killing. And fight them not in, and near, the Sacred Mosque until they fight you, then fight them : such is the requital for the disbelievers. But if they desist, then surely Allah is Most Forgiving, Merciful. And fight them until there is no persecution, and religion is professed for Allah. But if they desist, then remember that no hostility is allowed except against the aggressors.

Fighting is to be for the sake of God, not for our own sake or out of anger or aggrandizement, and even fighting is to be free from excesses, for excesses are displeasing to God. Fighting is between parties of combatants. Assaults on individuals are forbidden. Aggression against a religion is to be met by active resistance, for such aggression is worse than bloodshed. Muslims are not to fight near the Sacred Mosque, unless an attack is first made by the enemy. Fighting near the Sacred Mosque interferes with the public right of pilgrimage. But if the enemy attacks, Muslims are free to reply, this being the just reward of aggression. But if the enemy desists, Muslims must desist also, and forgive and forget the past. Fighting is to continue so long as religious persecution lasts and religious freedom is not established. Religion is for God. The use of force or pressure in religion is wrong. If the *Kafirs* desist from it and make religion free, Muslims are to desist from fighting the *Kafirs*. Arms are to be taken up against those who commit excesses. When excesses cease, fighting must cease also.

Categorically, we may say, the verses teach the following rules :

(*i*) War is to be resorted to only for the sake of God and not for the sake of any selfish motives, not for aggrandizement or for the advancement of any other interests.

(*ii*) We can go to war only against one who attacks us first.

(*iii*) We can fight only those who fight against us. We cannot fight against those who take no part in warfare.

(*iv*) Even after the enemy has initiated the attack, it is our duty to keep warfare within limits. To extend the war, either territorially or in respect of weapons used, is wrong.

(*v*) We are to fight only a regular army charged by the enemy to fight on his side. We are not to fight others on the enemy side.

(*vi*) In warfare immunity is to be afforded to all religious rites and observances. If the enemy spares the places where religious ceremonies are held, then Muslims also must desist from fighting in such places.

(*vii*) If the enemy uses a place of worship as a base for attack, then Muslims may return the attack. No blame will attach to them if they do so. No fighting is allowed even in the neighbourhood of religious places. To attack religious places and to destroy them or to do any kind of harm to them is absolutely forbidden. A religious place used as a base of operations may invite a counter-attack. The responsibility for any harm done to the place will then rest with the enemy, not with Muslims.

(*viii*) If the enemy realizes the danger and the mistake of using a religious place as a base, and changes the battle-front, then Muslims must conform to the change. The fact that the enemy started the attack from a religious place is not to be used as an excuse for attacking that place. Out of reverence Muslims must change their battle-front as soon as the enemy does so.

(*ix*) Fighting is to continue only so long as interference with religion and religious freedom lasts. When religion becomes free and interference with it is no longer permitted and the enemy declares and begins to act accordingly, then there is to be no war, even if it is the enemy who starts it.

(3) In 8 : 39–41 we have :

> Say to those who disbelieve, if they desist, that which is past will be forgiven them ; and if they return thereto, then verily the example of the former people has already gone before them.

> And fight them until there is no persecution and relgion is wholly for Allah. But if they desist, then surely Allah is Watchful of what they do. And if they turn their backs, then know that Allah is your Protector. What an excellent Protector and what an excellent Helper.

That is to say, wars have been forced upon Muslims. But if the enemy desists, it is the duty of Muslims to desist also, and forgive the past. But if the enemy does not desist and attacks Muslims again and again, then he should remember the fate of the enemies of earlier Prophets. Muslims are to fight, while religious persecution lasts, and so long as religion is not for God and interference in religious matters is not abandoned. When the aggressor desists, Muslims are to desist also. They are not to continue the war because the enemy believes in a false religion. The value of beliefs and actions is well known to God and He will reward them as He pleases. Muslims have no right to meddle with another people's religion even if that religion seems to them to be false. If after an offer of peace the enemy continues to make war, then Muslims may be sure of victory even though their numbers are small. For God will help them and who can help better than God ?

These verses were revealed in connection with the Battle of Badr. This battle was the first regular fight between Muslims and disbelievers. In it Muslims were the victims of unprovoked aggression. The enemy had chosen to disturb the peace of Medina and of the territory around. In spite of this, victory went to the Muslims and important leaders of the enemy were killed. To retaliate against such unprovoked aggression seems natural, just and necessary. Yet Muslims are taught to stop fighting as soon as the enemy ceases it. All that the enemy is required to concede is freedom of belief and worship.

(4) In 8 : 62–63 we have :

> And if they incline towards peace, incline thou also towards it, and put thy trust in Allah. Surely, it is He Who is All-Hearing, All-Knowing. And if they intend to deceive thee, then surely Allah is sufficient for thee. He it is Who has strengthened thee with His help and with the believers.

That is to say, if in the course of a battle the disbelievers at any time incline towards peace, Muslims are to accept the offer at once and to make peace. Muslims are to do so even at the risk of being deceived. They are to put their trust in God. Cheating will not avail against Muslims, who rely on the help of God. Their victories are due not to themselves but to God. In the darkest and most difficult times, God has stood by the Prophet and his followers. So will He stand by them against cheats. An offer of peace is to be accepted. It is not to be rejected on the plea that it may only be a ruse with which the enemy seeks to gain time for a fresh attack.

The stress on peace in the verses is not without significance. It anticipates the peace which the Prophet signed at Ḥudaibiya. The Prophet is warned that a time will come when the enemy will sue for peace. The offer is not to be turned down on the ground that the enemy was the aggressor and had committed excesses, or that he cannot be trusted. The straight path inculcated by Islam requires a Muslim to accept an offer of peace. Both piety and policy make the acceptance desirable.

(5) In 4 : 95 we have :

> O ye who believe ! when you go forth in the cause of Allah, make proper investigation and say not to anyone who greets you with the greeting of peace, "Thou art not a believer." You seek the goods of this life, but with Allah are good things in plenty. Such were you before this, but Allah conferred His favour on you ; so do make proper investigation. Surely, Allah is well aware of what you do.

That is to say, when Muslims go out for war, they are to make sure that the unreasonableness of war has been explained to the enemy and that he still wants war. Even so, if a proposal of peace is received from an individual or a group, Muslims are not to turn it down on the plea that it is not honest. If Muslims turn down proposals of peace, they will not be fighting for God, but for self-aggrandizement and worldly gain. Just as religion comes from God, worldly gain and glory also come from Him. Killing is not to be the aim. One whom we wish to kill today may be guided tomorrow. Could Muslims have become Muslims if they had not been spared ? Muslims are to abstain from killing because lives spared may turn out to be lives guided. God is well aware of what men do and to what ends and with what motives they do it.

The verse teaches that even after war has begun, it is the duty of Muslims to satisfy themselves that the enemy is bent upon aggression. It often happens that no aggression is intended but that out of excitement and fear the enemy has started preparations for war. Unless Muslims are satisfied that an aggressive attack has been planned by the enemy, they are not to go to war. If it turns out, or if the enemy claims, that his preparations are for self-defence, Muslims are to accept the claim and desist from war. They are not to argue that the enemy preparations point to nothing but aggression; maybe he intended aggression, but his intention has changed. Are not intentions and motives continually changing? Did not enemies of Islam become friends?

(6) On the inviolability of treaties the Quran says clearly:

> Excepting those of the idolaters with whom you have entered into a treaty and who have not subsequently failed you in anything nor aided anyone against you. So fulfil to these the treaty you have made with them till their term. Surely, Allah loves those who are righteous (9 : 4).

Pagans, who enter into a pact with Muslims, keep the pact and do not help the enemy against Muslims, are to have reciprocal treatment from Muslims. Piety requires that Muslims should fulfil their part of a pact in the letter as well as the spirit.

(7) Of an enemy at war with Muslims who wishes to study the Message of Islam, the Quran orders:

> And if anyone of the idolaters ask protection of thee, grant him protection, so that he may hear the word of Allah: then convey him to his place of security. That is because they are a people who have no knowledge (9 : 6).

That is to say, if any of those at war with Muslims seek refuge with Muslims in order to study Islam and ponder over its Message, they are to have refuge with Muslims for such time as may be reasonably necessary for such a purpose.

(8) Of prisoners of war, the Quran teaches:

> It does not behove a Prophet that he should have captives until he engages in a regular fighting in the land. You desire the goods of the world, while Allah desires for you the Hereafter. And Allah is Mighty, Wise (8 : 68).

That is to say, it does not become a Prophet to make prisoners of his enemy save as a result of regular war involving much bloodshed. The system of making prisoners of enemy tribes without war and bloodshed practised until—and even after—the advent of Islam, is here made unlawful. Prisoners can be taken only from combatants and after a battle.

(9) Rules for the release of prisoners are also laid down. Thus we have:

> Then afterwards either release them as a favour or by taking ransom—until the war lays down its burdens (47 : 5).

The best thing, according to Islam, is to let off prisoners without asking for ransom. As this is not always possible, release by ransom is also provided for.

(10) There is provision for prisoners of war who are unable themselves to pay, and who have none who can or will pay, for their release. Often, relations are able to pay, but do not, because they prefer to let their relations remain prisoners—possibly with the intention of misappropriating their property in their absence. This provision is contained in the Quran:

> And such as desire a deed of manumission from among those whom your right hands possess, write it for them, if you know any good in them; and give them out of the wealth of Allah which He has bestowed upon you (24 : 34).

That is, those who do not deserve to be released without ransom but who have no one to pay ransom for them—if they still ask for their freedom—can obtain it by signing an undertaking that, if allowed to work and earn, they will pay their ransom. They are to be allowed to do so, however, only if their competence to work and earn is reasonably certain. If their competence is proved, they should even have financial help from Muslims in their effort to work and earn. Individual Muslims who can afford to do so should pay; or, public subscription should be raised to put these unfortunates on their feet.

The passages from the Quran which we have quoted above contain the teaching of Islam on the subject of war and peace. They tell us in what circumstances, according to Islam, is it right to go to war and what limits have to be observed by Muslims when they make war.

THE PROPHET'S PRECEPTS ABOUT WAR

Muslim teaching, however, does not consist only of precepts laid down in the Quran. It also includes the precepts and example of the Prophet. What he did or what he taught in concrete situations is also an essential part of the Islamic teaching. We append here some sayings of the Prophet on the subject of war and peace.

(*i*) Muslims are forbidden altogether to mutilate the dead (Muslim).

(*ii*) Muslims are forbidden to resort to cheating (Muslim).

(*iii*) Children are not to be killed, nor women (Muslim).

(*iv*) Priests and religious functionaries and religious leaders are not to be interfered with (Ṭaḥāvī).

(*v*) The old and decrepit and women and children are not to be killed. The possibility of peace should always be kept in view (Abū Dāwūd).

(*vi*) When Muslims enter enemy territory, they should not strike terror into the general population. They should permit no ill-treatment of common folk (Muslim).

(*vii*) A Muslim army should not camp in a place where it causes inconvenience to the general public. When it marches it should take care not to block the road nor cause discomfort to other wayfarers.

(*viii*) No disfigurement of face is to be permitted (Bukhārī and Muslim).

(*ix*) The least possible losses should be inflicted upon the enemy (Abū Dāwūd).

(*x*) When prisoners of war are put under guard, those closely related should be placed together (Abū Dāwūd).

(*xi*) Prisoners should live in comfort. Muslims should care more for the comfort of their prisoners than for their own (Tirmidhī).

(*xii*) Emissaries and delegates from other countries should be held in great respect. Any mistakes or discourtesies they commit should be ignored (Abū Dāwūd, *Kitāb al-Jihād*).

(*xiii*) If a Muslim commits the sin of ill-treating a prisoner of war, atonement is to be made by releasing the prisoner without ransom.

(*xiv*) When a Muslim takes charge of a prisoner of war, the latter is to be fed and clothed in the same way as the Muslim himself (Bukhārī).

The Holy Prophet was so insistent on these rules for a fighting army that he declared that whoever did not observe these rules, would fight not for God but for his own mean self (Abū Dāwūd).

Abū Bakr, the First Khalīfa of Islam, supplemented these commands of the Prophet by some of his own. One of these commands appended here also constitutes part of the Muslim teaching :

(*xv*) Public buildings and fruit-bearing trees (and food crops) are not to be damaged (Mu'aṭṭā).

From the sayings of the Prophet and the commands of the First Khalīfa of Islam it is evident that Islam has instituted steps which have the effect of preventing or stopping a war or reducing its evil. As we have said before, the principles which Islam teaches are not pious precepts only ;. they have their practical illustration in the example of the Prophet and the early Khalīfās of Islam. As all the world knows, the Prophet not only taught these principles ; he practised them and insisted on their observance.

Turning to our own time we must say that no other teaching seems able to solve the problem of war and peace. The teaching of Moses is far from our conceptions of justice and fair-play. Nor is it possible to act upon that teaching today. The teaching of Jesus is impracticable and has ever been so. Never in their history have Christians tried to put this teaching into practice. Only the teaching of Islam is practicable ; one which has been both preached and practised by its exponents, and the practice of which can create and maintain peace in the world.

In our time, Mr. Gandhi apparently taught that even when war is forced on us we should not go to war. We should not fight. But this teaching has not been put into practice at any time in the history of the world. It has never been put in the crucible and tested. It is impossible, therefore, to say what value this teaching may have in terms of war and peace. Mr. Gandhi lived long enough to see the Indian Congress attain to political independence. Yet the Congress Government has not disbanded either the army or the other armed forces of India. It is only making plans for their Indianization. It also has plans for the reinstatement of those Indian officers who constituted themselves into the Indian National Army (and who were dismissed by the British authorities) during the Japanese attack on Burma and India in the last stages of the recent World War. Mr. Gandhi has himself, on many occasions, raised his voice in extenuation of crimes of violence, and urged the release of those who committed such crimes. This shows at least that Mr. Gandhi's teaching cannot be put into practice and that Mr. Gandhi knows it as well as all his followers. No practical example at least has been offered to show the world how non-violence can be applied when armed disputes arise between nation and nation and State and State, or how non-violence can prevent or stop a war. To preach a method of stopping wars, but never to be able to afford a practical illustration of that method indicates that the method is impracticable. It would, therefore, seem that human experience and human wisdom point to only one method of preventing or stopping war; and that method was taught and practised by the Prophet of Islam.

SPORADIC ATTACKS BY DISBELIEVERS

The Arab confederates returned from the Battle of the Ditch defeated and depressed, but far from realizing that their power to harass the Muslims was over. Though defeated, they knew they were still a dominant majority. They could easily maltreat individual Muslims, beat and even kill them. By assaults on individuals they hoped to wipe away their feeling of defeat. Not long after the battle, therefore, they began to attack Muslims around Medina. Some men of the Fazāra tribe mounted on camels attacked Muslims near Medina. They made away with the camels found in that part, took a woman as prisoner and escaped with the loot. The woman made good her escape, but the party of Fazāra succeeded in taking away a number of animals. A month later, a party of the Ghatafān tribe attacked from the north in an attempt to dispossess Muslims of their herds of camels. The Prophet sent Muhammad bin Maslama with ten mounted Companions for a reconnaissance, and for the protection of the Muslim herds. But the enemy waylaid the Muslim party and murderously attacking them, left them all for dead. Muhammad bin Maslama, however, was only lying unconscious. Recovering consciousness he pulled himself together, returned to Medina and made a report. A few days later, an envoy of the Prophet on his way to the Roman capital was attacked and robbed by men of the Judhām tribe. A month later, the Banū Fazāra attacked a Muslim caravan and made away with much loot. It is possible that this attack was not prompted by religious antagonism. The Banū Fazāra were a tribe of marauders given to looting and killing. The Jews of Khaibar, the main factor in the Battle of the Ditch, were also determined to avenge the crushing defeat which they suffered in that battle. They went about inciting tribal settlements and officers of State on the Roman frontier. Arab leaders, therefore, unable to make a straightforward attack on Medina, were intriguing with the Jews to make life impossible for Muslims. The Prophet, however, had yet to make up his mind for a decisive fight. Arab leaders might make an offer of peace, he thought, and civil strife might end.

THE PROPHET LEAVES FOR MECCA WITH ONE THOUSAND FIVE HUNDRED COMPANIONS

During this time the Prophet saw a vision which is mentioned thus in the Quran :

> You will certainly enter the Sacred Mosque, if God will, in security, some having their heads shaven, and others having their hair cut short ; and you will not fear. But He knew what you knew not. He has in fact ordained for you, besides that, a victory near at hand (48 : 28).

That is to say, God had decided to let Muslims enter the precincts of the Ka'ba in peace, with heads shaven and hair cut (these being the external signs of pilgrims to the Ka'ba), and without fear. But Muslims did not know exactly how God was to let this happen. Moreover, before Muslims performed their pilgrimage in peace, they were to have another victory, a precursor of the victory promised in the vision.

In this vision God foretold the ultimate victory of Muslims, their peaceful march into Mecca and the conquest of Mecca without the use of arms. But the Prophet understood it to mean that Muslims had been commanded by God immediately to attempt a circuit of the Ka'ba. The Prophet's error in interpreting the vision was to become the occasion of the victory 'near at hand' promised in the vision. In error, therefore, the Prophet planned a march towards the Ka'ba. He announced his vision and his interpretation of it to Muslims and asked them to prepare. "You will go," he said, "only to perform a circuit of the Ka'ba. There were, therefore, to be no demonstrations against the enemy." Late in February 628, fifteen hundred* pilgrims, headed by the Prophet, set out on their journey to Mecca. A mounted guard of twenty went some distance ahead to warn the Muslims in case the enemy showed signs of attacking.

The Meccans soon had reports of this caravan. Tradition had established the circuit of the Ka'ba as a universal right. It could not very well be denied to Muslims. They had announced in unambiguous terms that the purpose of their march was to perform the circuit, nothing else. The Prophet had forbidden demonstrations of every kind. There were to be no disputes, no questionings or claims. In spite of this, the Meccans started preparing as for an armed conflict. They put up defences on all sides, called the surrounding tribes to their aid and seemed determined to fight. When the Prophet reached near Mecca, he was informed that the Quraish were ready to fight. They were clad in tiger skins, had their wives and children with them and had sworn solemnly not to let the Muslims pass. The tiger skins were a sign of a savage determination to fight. Soon after, a column of Meccans marching in the van of their army confronted the Muslims. Muslims could not now advance except by drawing the sword. The

*In this pilgrimage planned a year after the Battle of the Ditch, only one thousand five hundred men accompanied the Prophet. The number of Muslim combatants in the Battle of the Ditch could have been less but not more than this number. Historians who put the number of the Muslim combatants in the Battle of the Ditch at three thousand, therefore, are wrong. The number can quite reasonably be put at one thousand two hundred.

Prophet, however, was determined to do nothing of the kind. He employed a guide to show the Muslim caravan an alternative route through the desert. Led by this guide, the Prophet and his Companions reached Ḥudaibiya, a spot very near Mecca. The Prophet's dromedary stopped and refused to go any farther.

"The animal seems tired, O Prophet of God. Better change your mount," said a Companion.

"No, no," said the Prophet. "the animal is not tired. It seems rather that God wants us to stop here and to go no further. I propose, therefore, to camp here and to ask the Meccans if they would let us perform the Pilgrimage. I, for one, will accept any conditions they may choose to impose" (Ḥalbiyya, Vol. 2, p. 13).

The Meccan army at this time was not in Mecca. It had gone out some distance to meet the Muslims on the main road to Medina. If the Prophet wanted, he could have led his fifteen hundred men into Mecca and taken the town without resistance. But he was determined to attempt only the circuit of the Ka'ba, and that only if the Meccans permitted. He would have resisted and fought the Meccans only if the Meccans had chosen to strike first. Therefore, he abandoned the main road and camped at Ḥudaibiya. Soon the news reached the Meccan commander, who ordered his men to withdraw and post themselves near Mecca. Then the Meccans sent a chief, Budail by name, to parley with the Prophet. The Prophet explained to Budail that he and the Muslims wanted only to perform the circuit of the Ka'ba ; but if the Meccans wished to fight, the Muslims were ready. Then 'Urwa, son-in-law of Abū Sufyān, the Meccan commander, came to the Prophet. He behaved most discourteously. He called the Muslims tramps and dregs of society and said the Meccans would not let them enter Mecca. More and more Meccans came to have talks and the last thing they said was that at least that year they would not let Muslims perform even the circuit of the Ka'ba. The Meccans would be humiliated if they permitted the circuit this year. The following year, they might do so.

Some tribes allied with the Meccans urged upon the Meccan leaders to let the Muslims perform the circuit. After all, it was only the right of circuit they wanted. Why should they be stopped even from this? But the Meccans remained adamant. Thereupon the tribal leaders said, the Meccans did not want peace and threatened to dissociate themselves from them. Out of fear, the Meccans were persuaded to try to reach a settlement with the Muslims. As soon as the Prophet got to know of this, he sent 'Uthmān (later the Third Khalīfa of Islam) to the Meccans. 'Uthmān had many relatives in Mecca. They came out and surrounded him, and offered to let him perform the circuit, but declared that they would not let the Prophet do so until the following year. "But," said 'Uthmān, "I will not perform the circuit unless it is in the company of my Master." 'Uthmān's talks with the chiefs of Mecca became prolonged. A rumour was mischievously spread that he had been murdered. It reached the ears of the Prophet. Upon this the Prophet assembled the Companions and said, "The life of an envoy is held sacred among all nations. I have heard that the Meccans have murdered 'Uthmān. If this is true, we have to enter Mecca, whatever the consequences." The Prophet's earlier intention to enter Mecca peacefully had to be changed, under the changed circumstances. The Prophet went on, "Those who promise solemnly that if they have to go further, they will not turn back save as victors, should come forward and take the oath on my hand." The Prophet had hardly finished speaking, when all the fifteen hundred Companions stood up and jumped over one another to hold the Prophet's hand and take the oath. This oath possesses a special importance in the history of early Islam. It is called the "Pledge of the Tree". When the oath was taken, the Prophet was sitting under a tree. Everyone of those who took the oath remained proud of it to the end of his days. Of the fifteen hundred present on the occasion, not one held back. They all promised that if the Muslim envoy had been murdered, they would not go back. Either they would take Mecca before dusk, or they would all die fighting. The taking of the oath was not over when 'Uthmān returned. He reported that the Meccans did not agree to let the Muslims perform the circuit until the following year. They had appointed their delegates to sign a settlement with the Muslims. Soon after, Suhail, a chief of Mecca, came to the Prophet. A settlement was reached and recorded.

TREATY OF ḤUDAIBIYA

It ran as follows:

> In the name of Allah. These are the conditions of peace between Muhammad, son of 'Abdullah, and Suhail ibn 'Amr, the envoy of Mecca. There will be no fighting for ten years. Anyone who wishes to join Muhammad and to enter into any agreement with him is free to do so. Anyone who wishes to join the Quraish and to enter into an agreement with them is also free to do so. A young man, or one whose father is alive, if he goes to Muhammad without permission from his father or guardian, will be returned to his father or guardian. But should anyone go to the Quraish, he will not be returned. This year Muhammad will go back without entering Mecca. But next year he and his followers can enter Mecca, spend three days and perform the circuit. During these three days the Quraish will withdraw to the surrounding hills. When Muhammad and his followers enter into Mecca, they will be unarmed except for the sheathed swords which wayfarers in Arabia always have with them (Bukhāri).

Two interesting things happened during the signing of this peace. After the terms had been settled the Prophet started to dictate the agreement and said, "In the name of Allah, the Gracious, the Merciful."

Suhail objected and said, "Allah we know and believe in, but what is this 'the Gracious and the Merciful ?' This agreement is between two parties. Therefore the religious beliefs of both parties will have to be respected."

The Prophet agreed at once and said to his scribe, "Only write, 'In the name of Allah'." The Prophet then proceeded to dictate the terms of the agreement. The opening sentence was, 'These are the conditions of peace between the people of Mecca and Muhammad, the Prophet of God'. Suhail objected again, and said, "If we thought you a Prophet of God, we would not have fought you." The Prophet accepted this objection also. Instead of Muhammad, the Prophet of God, he proposed Muhammad son of 'Abdullah. As the Prophet was agreeing to everything the Meccans proposed, the Companions felt agitated over the humiliation. Their blood began to boil, and 'Umar, the most excited of them all, went to the Prophet and asked, "O Prophet of God, are we not in the right ?"

"Yes," said the Prophet, "we are in the right." "And were we not told by God that we would perform the circuit of the Ka'ba ?" asked 'Umar.

" Yes," said the Prophet.

"Then why this agreement and why these humiliating terms ?"

"True," said the Prophet, "God did foretell that we would perform the circuit in peace but He did not say when. I did judge as though it was going to be this year. But I could be wrong. Must it be this year ?"

'Umar was silenced.

Then other Companions raised their objections. Some of them asked why they had agreed to restore to his father or guardian a young man who should turn Muslim, without obtaining the same condition for a Muslim who should turn over or happen to go to the Meccans. The Prophet explained there was no harm in this. "Everybody who becomes a Muslim," he said, "does so because he accepts the beliefs and practices inculcated by Islam. He does not become a Muslim in order to join a party and to adopt its customs. Such a man will propagate the Message of Islam wherever he goes, and serve as an instrument for the spread of Islam. But a man who gives up Islam is no use to us. If he no longer believes at heart what we believe, he is no longer one of us. It is better he should go elsewhere." This reply of the Prophet satisfied those who had doubted the wisdom of the course adopted by the Prophet. It should satisfy today all those who think that in Islam the punishment of apostasy is death. Had this been so, the Prophet would have insisted on the return and punishment of those who gave up Islam.

When the agreement had been written down and the signatures of the parties affixed, there soon arose an occasion which tested the good faith of the parties. A son of Suhail, the Meccan plenipotentiary, appeared before the Prophet, bound, wounded and exhausted. He fell at the Prophet's feet and said, "O Prophet of God, I am a Muslim at heart, and because of my faith I have to suffer these troubles at the hands of my father. My father was here with you. So I escaped and managed to come to you." The Prophet had not spoken when Suhail intervened and said that the agreement had been signed and he would have to go with him. Abū Jandal—this being the young man's name—stood before the Muslims, a brother of brothers, driven to desperation by the ill-treatment of his father. To have to send him back was an obligation they could not endure. They unsheathed their swords and seemed determined to die or save this brother. Abū Jandal himself entreated the Prophet to let him remain. Would he send him back to the tyrants from whose clutches he had managed to escape? But the Prophet was determined. He said to Abū Jandal, "Prophets do not eat their words. We have signed this agreement now. It is for you to bear with patience and to put your trust in God. He will certainly provide for your freedom and for the freedom of other young persons like you." After the peace had been signed, the Prophet returned to Medina. Soon after, another young convert from Mecca, Abū Baṣīr by name, reached Medina. But in accord with the terms of the agreement, he also was sent back by the Prophet. On the way back, he and his guards had a fight in the course of which he killed one of the guards and thus managed to escape. The Meccans went to the Prophet again and complained. "But," said the Prophet, "we handed over your man to you. He has now escaped out of your hands. It is no longer our duty to find him and hand him over to you again. A few days later, a woman escaped to Medina. Some of her relations went after her and demanded her return. The Prophet explained that the agreement had laid down an exception about men, not about women; so he refused to return this woman.

PROPHET'S LETTERS TO VARIOUS KINGS

After settling down in Medina on return from Ḥudaibiya, the Prophet instituted another plan for the spread of his Message. When he mentioned this to the Companions, some of them who were acquainted with the customs and forms observed in the courts of kings told the Prophet that kings did not entertain letters which did not bear the seals of the senders. Accordingly the Prophet had a seal made on which were engraved the words, *Muhammad Rasūl Allah.*

Out of reverence, *Allah* was put at the top, beneath it *Rasūl* and lastly *Muhammad.*

In Muḥarram 628, envoys went to different capitals, each with a letter from the Prophet, inviting the rulers to accept Islam. Envoys went to Heraclius, the Roman Emperor, the Kings of Iran, Egypt (the King of Egypt was then a vassal of the Kaiser) and Abyssinia. They went to other kings and rulers also. The letter addressed to the Kaiser was taken by Diḥya Kalbi who was instructed to call first on the Governor of Buṣra. When Diḥya saw the Governor, the great Kaiser himself was in Syria on a tour of the Empire. The Governor readily passed Diḥya on to the Kaiser. When Diḥya entered the court, he was told that whoever was received in audience by the Kaiser must prostrate himself before him. Diḥya refused to do this, saying that Muslims did not bow before any human being. Diḥya, therefore, sat before the Kaiser without making the prescribed obeisances. The Kaiser had the letter read by an interpreter and asked if an Arab caravan was in the town. He said he desired to interrogate an Arab about this Arabian Prophet who had sent him an invitation to accept Islam. It so happened that Abū Sufyān was in the town with a commercial caravan. The court officials took him to the Kaiser. Abū Sufyān was ordered to stand in front of the other Arabs, who were told to correct him if he should tell a lie or make a wrong statement. Then Heraclius proceeded to interrogate Abū Sufyān. The conversation is thus recorded in history :

H : Do you know this man who claims to be a Prophet and who has sent me a letter ? Can you say what sort of family he comes from ?

A–S : He comes of a noble family and is one of my relations.

H : Have there been Arabs before him who have made claims similar to his ?

A–S : No.

H : Did your people ever charge him with lying before he announced his claim ?

A–S : No.

H: Has there been a king or a ruler among his forefathers?

A-S: No.

H: How do you judge his general ability and his capacity for judgement?

A-S: We have never found any fault in his ability and his capacity for judgement.

H: What are his followers like? Are they big and powerful persons or are they poor and humble?

A-S: Mostly poor and humble and young.

H: Do their numbers tend to increase or decrease?

A-S: To increase.

H: Do his followers ever go back to their old beliefs?

A-S: No.

H: Has he ever broken a pledge?

A-S: Not so far. But we have recently entered into a new pact with him. Let us see what he does about it.

H: Have you had any fight with him yet?

A-S: Yes.

H: With what result?

A-S: Like buckets on a wheel, victory and defeat alternate between us and him. In the Battle of Badr, for instance, in which I was not present, he was able to overpower our side. In the Battle of Uḥud, in which I commanded our side, we took his side to task. We tore their stomachs, their ears and their noses.

H: But what does he teach?

A-S: That we should worship the One God and not set up equals with Him. He preaches against the idols our forefathers worshipped. He wants us, instead, to worship the Only God, to speak the truth only and always to abjure all vicious and corrupt practices. He exhorts us to be good to one another and to keep our covenants and discharge our trusts.

This interesting conversation came to an end and then the Kaiser said:

> I first asked you about his family and you said he belonged to a noble family. In truth, Prophets always come of noble families. I then asked you if anyone before him had made a similar claim and you said, No. I asked you this question because I thought that if in the recent past some one had made such a claim, then one could say that this Prophet was imitating that claim. I then asked you whether he had ever been charged with lying before his claim had been announced and you said, No. I inferred from this that a person who does not lie about men will not lie about God. I next asked you if there had been

a king among his forefathers and you said, No. From this I understood that his claim could not be a subtle plan for the recovery of the kingdom. I then asked you whether the entrants into his fold were mostly big, prosperous and powerful individuals or poor and weak. And you said in reply, that they were generally poor and weak, not proud and big, and so are the early followers of a Prophet. I then asked you whether his numbers were increasing or decreasing and you said they were increasing. At this I remembered that the followers of a Prophet go on increasing until the Prophet attains his goal. I then asked you if his followers left him out of disgust or disappointment, and you said, No. At this I remembered that the followers of Prophets are usually steadfast. They may fall away for other reasons, but not out of disgust for the faith. I then asked you if there had been fights between you and him and, if so, with what results. And you said that you and his followers were like buckets on a wheel and the Prophets are like that. In the beginning their followers suffer reverses and meet with misfortunes, but in the end they win. I then asked you about what he teaches and you said he teaches the worship of One God, truth-speaking, virtue and the importance of keeping covenants and discharging trusts. I asked you also whether he ever played false, and you said, No. And this is the way of virtuous men. It seems to me, therefore, that his claim to being a Prophet is true. I was half expecting his appearance in our time, but I did not know he was going to be an Arab. If what you have told me is true, then I think his influence and his dominion will certainly spread over these lands (Bukhārī).

The speech unsettled the courtiers who began to blame the King for applauding a Teacher of another community. Protests were raised. The court officials then sent away Abū Sufyān and his friends. The text of the letter which the Prophet wrote to the Kaiser is to be found in historical records. It runs as follows :

From Muhammad, the Servant of God and His Messenger. To the Chief of Rome, Heraclius. Whoever treads the path of divine guidance, on him be peace. After this, O King, I invite you to Islam. Become a Muslim. God will protect you from all afflictions, and reward you twice over. But if you deny and refuse to accept this Message, then the sin not only of your own denial, but of the denial of your subjects, will be on your head. "Say, 'O People of the Book ! come to a word equal between us and you that we worship none but Allah, and that we associate no partner with Him, and that some of us take not others for lords beside Allah.' But if they turn away, then say, 'Bear witness that we have submitted to God'" (Zurqānī).

The invitation to Islam was an invitation to believe that God is One and that Muhammad is His Messenger. Where the letter says that if Heraclius becomes a Muslim, he will be rewarded twice over, the reference is to the fact that Islam teaches belief in both Jesus and Muhammad.

It is said that when the letter was presented to the Emperor, some courtiers suggested it should be torn up and thrown away. The letter, they said, was an insult to the Emperor. It did not describe the Emperor as Emperor but only as Ṣāḥib al-Rūm, *i.e.*, the Chief of Rome. The Emperor, however, said that it was unwise to tear up the letter without reading it. He also said that the address, 'Chief of Rome', was not wrong. After all, the Master of everything was God. An Emperor was only a chief.

When the Prophet was told how his letter had been received by Heraclius, he seemed satisfied and pleased and said that because of the reception which the Roman Emperor had given his letter, his Empire would be saved. The descendants of the Emperor would continue long to rule over the Empire. That is in fact what happened. In the wars which took place later, a large part of the Roman Empire, in accordance with another prophecy of the Prophet of Islam, passed out of the possession of Rome ; yet for six hundred years after this, the dynasty of Heraclius remained established in Constantinople. The Prophet's letter remained preserved in the State archives for a long time. Ambassadors of the Muslim King, Manṣūr Qalāwūn, visited the court of Rome, and were shown the letter deposited in a case. The then Roman Emperor showing the letter said it had been received by a forefather of his from their Prophet and had been carefully preserved.

LETTER TO THE KING OF IRAN

The letter to the King of Iran was sent through 'Abdullah bin Ḥudhāfa. The text of this letter was as follows :

In the name of Allah, the Gracious, the Merciful. This letter is fiom Muhammad, the Messenger of God, to Chosroes, the Chief of Iran. Whoever submits to a perfect guidance, and believes in Allah, and bears witness that Allah is One, and has no equal or partner, and that Muhammad is His Servant and Messenger, on him be peace. O King, under the command of God, I invite you to Islam. For I have been sent by God as His Messenger to all mankind, so that I may warn all living men and complete my Message for all unbelievers. Accept Islam and protect yourself from all afflictions. If you reject this invitation, then the sin of the denial of all your people will rest on your head (Zurqānī and Khamīs).

'Abdullah bin Ḥudhāfa says that when he reached the court of Chosroes he applied for admission to the royal presence. He handed over the letter to the Emperor and the Emperor ordered an interpreter to read it and explain its contents. On listening to the contents, the Chosroes was enraged. He took back the letter and tore it to pieces. 'Abdullah bin Ḥudhāfa reported the incident to the Prophet. On hearing the report, the Prophet said :

What the Chosroes has done to our letter even that will God do to his Empire (*i.e.*, rend it to pieces).

The fit of temper which the Chosroes showed on this occasion was the result of the pernicious propaganda carried on against Islam by Jews who had migrated from Roman territory to Iran. These Jewish refugees took a leading part in anti-Roman intrigues sponsored in Iran, and had, therefore, become favourites at the Iranian court. The Chosroes was full of rage against the Prophet. The reports about the Prophet which the Jews had taken to Iran, it seemed to him, were confirmed by this letter. He thought the Prophet was an aggressive adventurer with designs on Iran. Soon after, the Chosroes wrote to the Governor of Yemen, saying that one of the Quraish in Arabia had announced himself a Prophet. His claims were becoming excessive. The Governor was asked to send two men charged with the duty of arresting this Quraishite and bringing him to the court of Iran. Bādhān, the Governor of Yemen under the Chosroes, sent an army chief with a mounted companion to the Prophet. He also gave them a letter addressed to the Prophet, in which he said that on receipt of the letter the Prophet should at once accompany the two messengers to the court of Iran. The two planned to go first to Mecca. When somewhere near Ṭā'if, they were told that the Prophet lived in Medina. So they went to Medina. On arrival this army chief told the Prophet that Bādhān, the Governor of Yemen, had been ordered by the Chosroes to arrange for the Prophet's arrest and despatch to Iran. If the Prophet refused to obey, he and his people were to be destroyed and their country made desolate. Out of compassion for the Prophet, this delegate from Yemen insisted that the Prophet should obey and agree to be led to Iran. Having listened to this, the Prophet suggested that the delegates should see him again the following day. Overnight the Prophet prayed to God Who informed him that the insolence of the Chosroes had cost him his life. "We have set his own son against him, and this son will murder his father on Monday the 10th Jumād al-'Ūlā of this year." According to some reports, the revelation said, "The son has murdered the father this very night." It is possible that that very night was the 10th of Jumād al-'Ūlā. In the morning, the Prophet sent for the Yemen delegates and told them of what had been revealed to him overnight. Then he prepared a letter for Bādhān saying that the Chosroes was due to be murdered on a certain day of a certain month. When the Governor of Yemen received the letter he said, "If this man be a true Prophet, it will be even as he says. If he be not true, then God help him and his country." Soon after, a boat from Iran anchored at the port of Yemen. It brought a letter from the Emperor of Iran to the Governor of Yemen. The letter bore a new seal, from which the Governor concluded that the prophecy of the Arabian Prophet had proved true. A new seal meant a new king. He opened the letter. It said :

> From Chosroes Siroes to Bādhān, the Governor of Yemen. I have murdered my father because his rule had become corrupt and unjust. He murdered the nobles and treated his subjects with cruelty. As soon as you receive this letter, collect all officers and ask them to affirm their loyalty to me. As for my father's orders for the arrest of an Arabian Prophet, you should regard those orders as cancelled (Ṭabarī, Vol. 3, pp. 1572–1574 and Hishām p. 46).

Bādhān was so impressed by these events that he and many of his friends at once declared their faith in Islam and informed the Prophet accordingly.

THE LETTER TO THE NEGUS

The letter to the Negus, King of Abyssinia, was carried by 'Amr bin Umayya Ḍamrī. It ran as follows :

> In the name of Allah, the Gracious, the Merciful, Muhammad, the Messenger of God, writes to the Negus, King of Abyssinia. O King, peace of God be upon you. I praise before you the One and Only God. None else is worthy of worship. He is the King of kings, the source of all excellences, free from all defects, He provides peace to all His servants and protects His creatures. I bear witness that Jesus, son of Mary was a Messenger of God, who came in fulfilment of promises made to Mary by God. Mary had consecrated her life to God. I invite you to join with me in attaching ourselves to the One and Only God and in obeying Him. I invite you also to follow me and believe in the God Who hath sent me. I am His Messenger. I invite you and your armies to join the Faith of the Almighty God. I discharge my duty hereby. I have delivered to you the Message of God, and made clear to you the meaning of this Message. I have done so in all sincerity and I trust you will value the sincerity which has prompted this message. He who obeys the guidance of God becomes heir to the blessings of God (Zurqānī).

When this letter reached the Negus, he showed very great regard and respect for it. He held it up to his eyes, descended from the throne and ordered an ivory box for it. Then he deposited it in the box and said, "While this letter is safe, my kingdom is safe." What he said proved true. For one thousand years Muslim armies were out on their career of conquest. They went in all directions, and passed by Abyssinia on all sides, but they did not touch this small kingdom of the Negus ; and this, out of regard for two memorable acts of the Negus—the protection he afforded the refugees of early Islam and the reverence he showed to the Prophet's letter. The Empire of Rome became dismembered. The Chosroes lost his dominions. The kingdoms of China and India disappeared but this small kingdom of the Negus remained inviolate, because its ruler received and protected the first Muslim refugees and showed respect and reverence for the Prophet's letter.

Muslims returned the magnanimity of the Negus in this way. Compare with this the treatment which a Christian people, in this age of civilization meted out to this Christian kingdom of the Negus. They bombarded from the air the open cities of Abyssinia and destroyed them. The royal family had to take refuge elsewhere and to stay away from their country for several years. The same people have been treated in two different ways by two different peoples. Muslims held Abyssinia sacred and inviolate because of the magnanimity of one of its rulers. A Christian nation attacked and plundered it in the name of civilization. It shows how wholesome and lasting in their effects are the Prophet's teaching and example. Muslim gratitude to a Christian kingdom made the kingdom sacred to Muslims. Christian greed attacked the same kingdom, not caring it was Christian.

LETTER TO THE RULER OF EGYPT

The letter to Muqauqis was carried by Ḥāṭib ibn Abī Balta'a. The text of this letter was exactly the same as that to the Roman Emperor. The letter to the Roman Emperor said that the sin of the denial of the Roman subjects would be on his head. The letter to the Muqauqis said that the sin of the denial of the Copts would be on the head of the ruler. It ran as follows:

> In the name of Allah, the Gracious, the Merciful. This letter is from Muhammad, the Messenger of Allah, to Muqauqis, the Chief of the Copts. Peace be upon him who follows the path of rectitude. I invite you to accept the Message of Islam. Believe and you will be saved and your reward will be twofold. If you disbelieved, the sin of the denial of the Copts will also be on your head. Say, "O People of the Book ! come to a word equal between us and you that we worship none but Allah, and that we associate no partner with Him, and that some of us take not others for lords beside Allah. But if they turn away, then say, 'Bear witness that we have submitted to God' " (Ḥalbiyya, Vol. 3, p. 275).

When Ḥāṭib reached Egypt, he did not find the Muqauqis

in the capital. Ḥāṭib followed him to Alexandria, where he was holding court near the sea. Ḥāṭib went by boat. The court was strongly guarded. Therefore Ḥāṭib showed the letter from a distance and began to speak aloud. The Muqauqis ordered Ḥāṭib to be brought to him. The Muqauqis read the letter and said, "If this man be a true Prophet, why does he not pray for the destruction of his enemies?" Ḥāṭib replied, "You believe in Jesus. He was ill-treated by his people, yet he did not pray for their destruction." The King paid a tribute to Ḥāṭib and said he was a wise envoy of a wise man. He had answered well the questions put to him. Upon this Ḥāṭib spoke again. "Before you," he said, "there was a king who was proud, arrogant and cruel. He was the Pharaoh who persecuted Moses. At last he was overtaken by divine punishment. Show no pride therefore. Believe in this Prophet of God. By God Moses did not foretell about Jesus as clearly as did Jesus foretell about Muhammad We invite you to Muhammad the Prophet, just as you Christians invite the Jews to Jesus. Every Prophet has his followers. The followers must obey their Prophet. Now that a Prophet has appeared in your time it is your duty to believe in him and follow him. And remember our religion does not ask you to deny or disobey Jesus. Our religion requires everyone to believe in Jesus."

Hearing this, Muqauqis revealed that he had heard of the teaching of this Prophet and he felt that he did not teach anything evil nor forbid anything good. He had also made inquiries and found that he was no sorcerer or soothsayer. He had heard of some of his prophecies which had come true. Then he sent for an ivory box and placed the letter of the Prophet in it, sealed it and handed it over to a servant girl for safe deposit. He also wrote a letter in reply to the Prophet. The text of this letter is recorded in history. It runs as follows :

> In the name of Allah, the Gracious, the Merciful. From Muqauqis, King of the Copts, to Muhammad, son of Abdullah. Peace be on you. After this, I say that I have read your letter and pondered over its contents and over the beliefs to which you invite me. I am aware that the Hebrew Prophets have foretold the advent of a Prophet in our time. But I thought he was going to appear in Syria. I have received your envoy, and made

> a present of one thousand *dīnārs* and five *khil'ats* to him and I send two Egyptian girls as a present to you. My people, the Copts, hold these girls in great esteem. One of them is Mary and the other Sīrīn. I also send you twenty garments made of Egyptian linen of high quality. I also send you a mule for riding. In the end I pray again that you may have peace from God (Zurqānī and Ṭabarī).

From this letter it is clear that, though Muqauqis treated the letter with respect he did not accept Islam.

LETTER TO CHIEF OF BAḤRAIN

The Prophet also sent a letter to Mundhir Taimī, Chief of Baḥrain. This letter was carried by 'Alā ibn Ḥaḍramī. The text of this letter has been lost. When it reached this Chief, he believed, and wrote back to the Prophet saying that he and many of his friends and followers had decided to join Islam. Some, however, had decided to stay outside. He also said that there were some Jews and Magians living under him. What was he to do about them ?

The Prophet wrote again to this Chief thus :

> I am glad at your acceptance of Islam. Your duty is to obey the delegates and messengers whom I should send to you. Whoever obeys them, obeys me. The messenger who took my letter to you praised you to me, and assured me of the sincerity of your belief. I have prayed to God for your people. Try, therefore, to teach them the ways and practices of Islam. Protect their property. Do not let anyone have more than four wives. The sins of the past are forgiven. As long as you are good and virtuous you will continue to rule over your people. As for Jews and Magians, they have only to pay a tax. Do not, therefore, make any other demands on them. As for the general population, those who do not have land enough to maintain them should have four *dirhams* each, and some cloth to wear (Zurqānī and Khamīs).

The Prophet also wrote to the King of 'Umān, the Chief of Yamāma, the King of Ghassān, the Chief of Banī Nahd, a tribe of Yemen, the Chief of Hamdān, another tribe of Yemen, the Chief of Banī 'Alīm and the Chief of the Ḥaḍramī tribe. Most of them became Muslims.

These letters show how perfect was the Prophet's faith in

God. They also show that from the very beginning the Prophet believed that he had been sent by God not to any one people or territory, but to all the peoples of the world. It is true that these letters were received by their addressees in different ways. Some of them accepted Islam at once. Others treated the letters with consideration, but did not accept Islam. Still others treated them with ordinary courtesy. Still others showed contempt and pride. But it is true also—and history is witness to the fact—that the recipients of these letters or their peoples met with a fate in accordance with their treatment of these letters.

FALL OF KHAIBAR

As we have said above, the Jews and other opponents of Islam were now busy inflaming the tribes against the Muslims. They were now convinced that Arabia was unable to withstand the rising influence of Islam and that Arab tribes were unable to attack Medina. The Jews, therefore, began to intrigue with the Christian tribes settled on the southern frontier of the Roman Empire. At the same time they started writing against the Prophet to their co-religionists in Iraq. By malicious propaganda carried on through correspondence they sought to excite the Chosroes of Iran against Islam. As a result of Jewish machinations the Chosroes turned against Islam, and even sent orders to the Governor of Yemen to arrest the Prophet. It was by special divine intervention and divine grace that the Prophet remained safe, and the foul plan of the Emperor of Iran was brought to nought. It should be obvious that, but for the divine help which attended the Prophet throughout his career, the tender movement of early Islam would have been nipped in the bud under the hostility and opposition of the Emperors of Rome and Iran. When the Chosroes ordered the arrest of the Prophet, it so happened that before the orders could be carried out the Emperor was deposed and put to death by his own son and his orders for the arrest of the Prophet cancelled by the new ruler. The officials of Yemen were impressed by this miracle; so the province of Yemen readily became part of the Muslim Empire. The intrigues which the Jews kept on hatching against Muslims and their town of Medina made it necessary that they should be driven farther away from Medina. If they had been allowed to continue to live nearby their intrigues were almost certain to give rise to more and more bloodshed and violence. On returning from Ḥudaibiya the Prophet waited for five months and then decided to banish them from Khaibar. Khaibar was only a little distance from Medina and from here the Jews found it very easy to carry on their intrigues. With this intent, the Prophet (some time in August 628 A.D.) marched to Khaibar. He had one thousand six hundred men with him. Khaibar, as we have said, was a well-fortified town. It was surrounded on all sides by rocks on which were perched little fortresses. To conquer such a place with so small a force was no easy task. The small posts lying on the outskirts of Khaibar fell after a little fighting. But when the Jews collected themselves into the central fort of the town, all attacks on it and all forms of strategy employed against it seemed to fail. One day the Prophet had a revelation that Khaibar would fall at the hands of 'Alī. The following morning the Prophet announced this to his followers and said, "Today, I will hand over the black flag of Islam to him who is dear to God, His Prophet and all the Muslims. God has ordained that our victory at Khaibar should take place at his hands." The following day he sent for 'Alī and handed to him the flag. 'Alī did not wait. He took his men and attacked the central fort. In spite of the fact that the Jews had collected in force inside this fort, 'Alī and his division were able to conquer it before dark. A peace was signed. The conditions were that all Jews, their wives and their children would quit Khaibar and settle in some place far away from Medina. Their property and their belongings would pass into the hands of Muslims. Anyone who tried to conceal any of his property or stores, or made a wrong statement, would not be protected by the peace. He would have to pay the penalty laid down for breach of faith.

Three interesting incidents took place in this siege of Khaibar. One of them constitutes a Sign of God and two afford insight into the high moral character of the Prophet.

A widow of Kināna, a chief of Khaibar, was married to the

Prophet. The Prophet saw that her face bore some marks, the impression of a hand. "What is this on your face, Ṣafiyya ?" asked the Prophet.

"It was like this," replied Ṣafiyya. "I saw the moon fall in my lap in a dream. I related the dream to my husband. No sooner had I related the dream than my husband gave a heavy slap on my face and said, 'You desire to marry the King of Arabia' " (Hishām). The moon was the national emblem of Arabia. The moon in the lap denoted some intimate connection with the King of Arabia. A split moon or a dropping moon meant dissensions in the Arab State or its destruction.

The dream of Ṣafiyya is a sign of the truth of the Holy Prophet. It is also a sign of the fact that God reveals the future to His servants through dreams. Believers have more of this grace than unbelievers. Safiyya was a Jewess when she saw this dream. It so happened that her husband was killed in the siege of Khaibar. This siege was a punishment for the Jewish breach of faith. Ṣafiyya was made a prisoner and, in the distribution of prisoners, was given to a Companion. It was then found that she was the widow of a chief. It was, therefore, felt that it would be more in accord with her rank if she were to live with the Prophet. The Prophet, however, chose to give her the status of a wife and she agreed. In this way was her dream fulfilled.

There were two other incidents. One relates to a shepherd who looked after the sheep of a Jewish chief. This shepherd became a Muslim. After his conversion he said to the Prophet, "I cannot go back to my people now, O Prophet of God. What shall I do with the sheep and goats of my old master ?"

"Set the faces of the animals towards Khaibar and give them a push. God will lead them back to their master" said the Prophet. The shepherd did as he was told, and the herd reached the Jewish fort. The guards at the fort received them (Hishām, Vol. 2, p. 191). The incident shows how seriously the Prophet regarded the question of individual rights and how important in his view it was for a trustee to discharge his trust. In war the property and belongings of the losers are rightfully appropriated by the victors. Ours is an age of civilization and culture, but can we show anything equal to this ? Has it ever happened that a retreating enemy left behind stores which the victors sent back to their owners ? In the present case the goats belonged to one of the combatants of the enemy side. The return of the goats meant making over to the enemy food which would last them for several months. With it the enemy could resist the siege for a long time. Yet the Prophet had the goats returned, and this in order to impress upon a new convert the importance of discharging a trust.

The third incident relates to a Jewish woman who tried to poison the Prophet. She asked the Companions what part of an animal the Prophet relished for a dish. She was told that he preferred the shoulder of lamb or goat. The woman slaughtered a goat and made cutlets on hot stones. Then she mixed with them a deadly poison, especially in pieces cut from the shoulder, believing the Prophet would prefer them.

The Prophet was returning to his tent, having said the evening prayers in congregation. He saw this woman waiting for him near his tent and asked, "Is there anything I can do for you, woman ?"

"Yes, Abu'l Qāsim, you can accept a present from me." The Prophet asked a Companion to take whatever the woman had brought. When the Prophet sat down to his meal this present of roasted meat was also laid before him. The Prophet took a morsel. A Companion Bishr ibn al-Barā' ibn al-Ma'rūr also took a morsel. The other Companions present at the meal stretched their hands to eat the meat. But the Prophet stopped them saying, he thought the meat was poisoned. Upon this Bishr said that he also thought the same. He wanted to throw away the meat but was afraid it might disturb the Prophet. "Seeing you take a morsel," he said, "I also took one, but I soon began to wish you had not taken yours at all." Soon afterwards Bishr became ill and, according to some reports, died there and then. According to other reports he died after remaining ill for some time. The Prophet then sent for the woman and asked her if she had poisoned the meat. The woman asked the Prophet how he ever got to know about it. The Prophet was holding a piece in his hand, and said,

"My hand told me this," meaning he was able to judge from its taste. The woman admitted what she had done.

"What made you do this ?" asked the Prophet.

"My people were at war with you and my relations were killed in this battle, I decided to poison you, believing that if you were an impostor you would die and we should be safe, but if you were a Prophet, God would save you."

Hearing this explanation the Prophet forgave the woman, although she had earned the penalty of death (Muslim). The Prophet was ever ready to forgive, and punished only when punishment was necessary, when it was feared the guilty one would continue to commit mischief.

THE PROPHET'S VISION FULFILLED

In the seventh year after the Hijra, in February 629 to be exact, the Prophet was due to go to Mecca for the circuit of the Ka'ba. This had been agreed to by the Meccan leaders. When the time came for the Prophet to depart, he collected two thousand followers and set out in the direction of Mecca. When he reached Marr al-Ẓahrān, a halting place near Mecca, he ordered his followers to shed their armours. These were collected in one place. In strict conformity with the terms of the agreement signed at Ḥudaibiya, the Prophet and his followers entered the Sacred Enclosure, wearing only sheathed swords. Returning to Mecca after seven years' externment, it was no ordinary thing for two thousand persons to enter Mecca. They remembered the tortures to which they had been subjected during their days at Mecca. At the same time, they saw how gracious God had been to them in letting them come back and make a circuit of the Ka'ba in peace. Their anger was only equal to their joy. The people of Mecca had come out of their houses and perched themselves on the hill-tops to see the Muslims. The Muslims were full of zeal and enthusiasm and pride. They wanted to tell the Meccans that the promises which God had made to them had all come true. 'Abdullah bin Rawāḥa started singing songs of war, but the Prophet stopped him saying, "No war songs. Only say, There is none to be worshipped except the One God. It is God Who helped the Prophet and raised the believers from degradation to dignity and Who drove off the enemy" (Ḥalbiyya, Vol. 3, p. 73).

After circuiting the Ka'ba and running between the hills of Ṣafā and Marwa, the Prophet and his Companions stopped in Mecca for three days. 'Abbās had a widowed sister-in-law, Maimūna, and he proposed that the Prophet should marry her. The Prophet agreed. On the fourth day the Meccans demanded the withdrawal of the Muslims. The Prophet ordered the withdrawal and asked his followers to start back for Medina. So religiously did he carry out the agreement and so careful was he to respect Meccan sentiments that he left his newly-wed wife behind in Mecca. He arranged that she should join him with the part of the caravan carrying the personal effects of the pilgrims. The Prophet mounted his camel and was soon out of the limits of the sacred precincts. For the night the Prophet camped at a place called Sarif, and there in his tent Maimūna joined him.

We might have omitted this insignificant detail from a short account of the Life of the Prophet, but the incident has one important interest, and it is this. The Prophet has been attacked by European writers because he had several wives. They think a plurality of wives is evidence of personal laxity and love of pleasure. This impression of the Prophet's marriages, however, is belied by the devotion and self-consuming love which the Prophet's wives had for him. Their devotion and love proved that the Prophet's married life was pure, unselfish and spiritual. It was so singular in this respect that no man can be said to have treated his one wife so well as the Prophet treated his many. If the Prophet's married life had been motivated by pleasure, it would most certainly have resulted in making his wives indifferent and even antagonistic to him. But the facts are quite otherwise. All the Prophet's wives were devoted to him, and their devotion was due to his unselfish and high-minded example. To his unselfish example they reacted by unsparing devotion. This is proved by many incidents recorded in history. One relates to Maimūna herself. She met the Prophet for the first time in a tent in the desert. If their marital relations had been coarse, if the Prophet had preferred some wives to others because of their physical charms, Maimūna would not have cherished her first meeting with the Prophet as a great memory. If her marriage with the Prophet had been associated with unpleasant or indifferent memories, she would have forgotten everything about it. Maimūna lived long after the Prophet's death. She died full of years but could not forget what her marriage with the Prophet had meant for her. On the eve of her death at eighty, when the delights of the flesh are forgotten, when things only of lasting value and virtue move the heart, she asked to be buried at one day's journey from Mecca, at the very spot where the Prophet had camped on his return to Medina, and where after his marriage she had first met him. The world knows of many stories of love both real and imaginary, but not of many which are more moving than this.

Soon after this historic circuit of the Ka'ba, two renowned generals of the enemy joined Islam. They proved renowned generals of Islam. One was Khālid bin Walīd whose genius and courage shook the Roman Empire to its foundations and under whose generalship country after country was added by Muslims to their Empire. The other was 'Amr bin al-'Āṣ, the conqueror of Egypt.

BATTLE OF MŪTA

On return from the Ka'ba, the Prophet began to receive reports that Christian tribes on the Syrian border, instigated by Jews and pagans, were preparing for an attack upon Medina. He, therefore, despatched a party of fifteen to find out the truth. They saw an army massing on the Syrian border. Instead of returning at once with the report they tarried. Their zeal for expounding Islam got the better of them, but the effect of their well-meaning zeal proved to be the very opposite of what they had wished and expected.

Reviewing events now, we can see that those who, under enemy provocation, were planning to attack the Prophet's homeland could be expected to behave in no other way. Instead of listening to the exposition, they took out their bows and started raining arrows on this party of fifteen. The party, however, remained unmoved. They received arrows in reply to arguments, but they did not turn back. They stood firm, fifteen against thousands, and fell fighting.

The Prophet planned an expedition to punish the Syrians for this wanton cruelty, but in the meantime he had reports that the forces which had been concentrating on the border had dispersed. He, therefore, postponed his plans.

The Prophet, however, wrote a letter to the Emperor of Rome (or to the Chief of the Ghassān tribe who ruled Buṣra in the name of Rome). In this letter, we may presume, the Prophet complained of the preparations which had been visible on the Syrian border and of the foul and entirely unjust murder of the fifteen Muslims whom he had sent to report on the border situation. This letter was carried by al-Ḥarth, a Companion of the Prophet. He stopped *en route* at Mūta where he met Shuraḥbīl, a Ghassān chief acting as a Roman official. "Are you a messenger of Muhammad ?" asked this chief. On being told "Yes," he arrested him, tied him up and belaboured him to death. It may quite reasonably be assumed that this Ghassān chief was a leader of the army which had engaged and put to death the fifteen Muslims who had tried only to preach. The fact that he said to al-Ḥarth, "Perhaps you are carrying a message from Muhammad" shows he was afraid lest the Prophet's complaint that tribesmen under the Kaiser had attacked the Muslims should reach the Kaiser. He was afraid lest he should have to account for what had happened. There was safety, he thought, in murdering the Prophet's envoy. The expectation was not realized. The Prophet got to know of the murder. To avenge this and the earlier murders, he raised a force of three thousand and despatched it to Syria under the command of Zaid bin Ḥāritha, freed slave of the Prophet, whom we mentioned in our account of his life in Mecca. The Prophet nominated Ja'far ibn Abī Ṭālib as the successor of Zaid, should Zaid die, and 'Abdullah bin Rawāḥa, should Ja'far die. Should 'Abdullah bin Rawāḥa also die, Muslims were to choose their own commander. A Jew who heard this exclaimed, "O Abu'l Qāsim, if thou art a true Prophet, these three officers whom thou hast named are sure to die ; for God fulfils the words of a Prophet." Turning to Zaid, he said,

"Take it from me, if Muhammad is true you will not return alive." Zaid, a true believer that he was, said in reply, "I may return alive or not, but Muhammad is a true Prophet of God" (Ḥalbiyya, Vol. 3, p. 75).

The following morning the Muslim army set out on its long march. The Prophet and the Companions went some distance with it. A large and important expedition such as this had never before gone without the Prophet commanding in person. As the Prophet walked along to bid the expedition farewell, he counselled and instructed. When they reached the spot where the people of Medina generally bade farewell to friends and relations going to Syria, the Prophet stopped and said :

> I urge you to fear God and to deal justly with Muslims who go with you. Go to war in the name of Allah and fight the enemy in Syria, who is your enemy, as well as Allah's. When you are in Syria, you will meet those who remember God much in their houses of worship. You should have no dispute with them, and give no trouble to them. In the enemy country do not kill any women or children, nor the blind or the old ; do not cut down any tree, nor pull down any building (Ḥalbiyya, Vol. 3).

Having said this, the Prophet returned and the Muslim army marched forward. It was the first Muslim army sent to fight the Christians. When Muslims reached the Syrian border, they heard that the Kaiser himself had taken the field with one hundred thousand of his own soldiers and another hundred thousand recruited from the Christian tribes of Arabia. Confronted by such large enemy numbers, the Muslims half wanted to stop on the way and send word to the Prophet at Medina. For he might be able to reinforce their numbers or wish to send fresh instructions. When the army leaders took counsel, 'Abdullah bin Rawāḥa stood up, full of fire, and said, "My people, you set out from your homes to die as martyrs in the way of God, and now when martyrdom is in sight you seem to flinch. We have not fought so far because we were better equipped than the enemy in men or material. Our mainstay was our faith. If the enemy is so many times superior to us in numbers or equipment, what does it matter ? One reward out of two we must have. We either win, or die as martyrs in the way of God." The army heard ibn Rawāḥa and was much impressed. He was right, they said, with one voice. The army marched on. As they marched, they saw the Roman army advancing towards them. So at Mūta the Muslims took up their positions and the battle began. Soon Zaid, the Muslim commander, was killed and the Prophet's cousin Ja'far ibn Abī Ṭālib received the standard and the command of the army. When he saw that enemy pressure was increasing and Muslims, because of utter physical inferiority, were not holding their own. he dismounted from his horse and cut its legs. The action meant that at least he was not going to flee ; he would prefer death to flight.

To cut the legs of one's mount was an Arab custom to prevent stampede and panic. Ja'far lost his right hand, but held the standard in his left. He lost his left hand also and then held the standard between the two stumps pressed to his chest. True to his promise, he fell down fighting. Then 'Abdullah bin Rawāḥa, as the Prophet had ordered, grasped the standard and took over the command. He also fell fighting. The order of the Prophet now was for Muslims to take counsel together and elect a commander. But there was no time to hold an election. The Muslims might well have yielded to the vastly superior numbers of the enemy. But Khālid bin Walīd, accepting the suggestion of a friend, took the standard and went on fighting until evening came. The following day Khālid took the field again with his crippled and tired force but employed a stratagem. He changed the positions of his men—those in front changed with those in the rear and those on the right flank changed with those on the left. They also raised some slogans. The enemy thought Muslims had received reinforcements overnight and withdrew in fear. Khālid saved his remnants and returned. The Prophet had been informed of these events through a revelation. He collected the Muslims in the mosque. As he rose to address them his eyes were wet with tears. He said :

> I wish to tell you about the army which left here for the Syrian border. It stood against the enemy and fought. First Zaid, then Ja'far and then 'Abdullah bin Rawāḥa held the standard. All three fell, one after the other, fighting bravely. Pray for them all. After them the standard was held by

> Khālid bin Walīd. He appointed himself. He is a sword among the swords of God. So he saved the Muslim army and returned (Zād al-Ma'ād, Vol. 1, and Zurqānī).

The Prophet's description of Khālid became popular. Khālid came to be known as 'the sword of God'.

Being one of the later converts, Khālid was often taunted by other Muslims. Once he and 'Abd al-Raḥmān bin 'Auf quarrelled over something. 'Abd al-Raḥmān bin 'Auf reported against Khālid to the Prophet. The Prophet chid Khālid and said, "Khālid, you annoy one who has been serving Islam from the time of Badr. I say to you that even if you give away gold of the weight of Uḥud in the service of Islam, you will not become as deserving of divine reward as 'Abd al-Raḥmān."

"But they taunt me," said Khālid, "and I have to reply."

Upon this the Prophet turned to others and said, "You must not taunt Khālid. He is a sword among the swords of God which remains drawn against disbelievers."

The Prophet's description came to literal fulfilment a few years later.

On Khālid's return with the Muslim army, some Muslims of Medina described the returning soldiers as defeatist and lacking in spirit. The general criticism was that they should all have died fighting. The Prophet chid the critics. Khālid and his soldiers were not defeatist or lacking in spirit, he said. They were soldiers who returned again and again to the attack. The words meant more than appeared on the surface. They foretold battles which Muslims were to fight with Syria.

THE PROPHET MARCHES ON MECCA WITH TEN THOUSAND FOLLOWERS

In the eighth year of the Hijra in the month of Ramaḍān (December, 629 A.D.) the Prophet set out on that last expedition which definitely established Islam in Arabia.

At Ḥudaibiya it was agreed between Muslims and disbelievers that Arab tribes should be allowed to join the disbelievers as well as the Prophet. It was also agreed that for ten years the parties would not go to war against each other unless one party should violate the pact by attacking the other. Under this agreement, the Banū Bakr joined the Meccans, while the Khuzā'a entered into an alliance with Muslims. The Arab disbelievers had scant regard for treaties, especially for treaties with Muslims. It so happened that the Banū Bakr and the Khuzā'a had some outstanding differences. The Banū Bakr consulted the Meccans about settling their old scores with the Khuzā'a. They argued that the Ḥudaibiya treaty had been signed. The Khuzā'a felt secure because of their pact with the Prophet. Now, therefore, was the time for them to attack the Khuzā'a. The Meccans agreed. They and the Banū Bakr, accordingly, joined in a night attack on the Khuzā'a and put to death many of their men. The Khuzā'a sent forty of their men mounted on fleet camels to Medina to report this breach of agreement to the Prophet. They said it was up to Muslims now to march on Mecca to avenge this attack. The delegation met the Prophet and the Prophet told them unambiguously that he regarded their misfortunes as his own. He pointed to a rising cloud in the sky and said, "Like the rain drops which you see yonder, Muslim soldiers will drop down to your aid." The Meccans were perturbed over the news of the Khuzā'a delegation to Medina. They sent Abū Sufyān post-haste to Medina to restrain Muslims from the attack. Abū Sufyān reached Medina and began to urge that, as he was not present at Ḥudaibiya, a new peace will have to be signed by Muslims. The Prophet thought it unwise to answer this plea. Abū Sufyān became excited, went to the mosque and announced :

> "O People, I renew, on behalf of the Meccans, our assurance of peace to you" (Zurqānī).

The people of Medina did not understand this speech. So, they only laughed. The Prophet said to Abū Sufyān, "Your statement is one-sided and we cannot agree to it." In the meantime, the Prophet had sent word to all the tribes. Assured that they were ready and on the march, he asked the Muslims of Medina to arm themselves and prepare. On the 1st January, the Muslim army set out on its march. At different points on their way, they were joined by other Muslim tribes. Only a few days' journey had been covered, when the army entered the wilderness of Fārān. Its number—exactly as the Prophet Solomon had foretold long before—had now swelled to ten thousand. As this army marched towards Mecca, the silence all around seemed more and more ominous to the Meccans. They persuaded Abū Sufyān to move out again and find out what the Muslim design was. He was less than one day's journey out of Mecca when he saw at night the entire wilderness lit up with camp-fires. The Prophet had ordered a fire in front of every camp. The effect of these roaring fires in the silence and darkness of the night was awful. "What could this be ?" Abū Sufyān asked his companions, "Has an army dropped from the heavens ? I know of no Arab army so large." They named some tribes and at every name Abū Sufyān said, "No Arab tribe or people could have an army as large." Abū Sufyān and his friends were still speculating when a voice from the dark shouted, "Abū Ḥanẓala" ! (Ḥanẓala was a son of Abū Sufyān.)

" 'Abbās, are you here ?" said Abū Sufyān.

"Yes, the Prophet's army is near. Act quickly or humility and defeat await you," replied 'Abbās.

'Abbās and Abū Sufyān were old friends. 'Abbās insisted that Abū Sufyān should accompany him on the same mule and go to the Prophet. He gripped Abū Sufyān's hand, pulled him up and made him mount. Spurring the mule, they soon reached the Prophet's camp. 'Abbās was afraid lest 'Umar, who was guarding the Prophet's tent, should fall upon Abū Sufyān and kill him. But the Prophet had taken precautions, announcing that if anybody should meet Abū Sufyān he should make no attempt to kill him. The meeting impressed Abū Sufyān deeply. He was struck by the rise which had taken place in the fortunes of Islam. Here was the Prophet whom Meccans had banished from Mecca with but one friend in his company. Hardly seven years had passed since then, and now he was knocking at the gates of Mecca with ten thousand devotees. The tables had been completely turned. The fugitive Prophet who, seven years before, had escaped from Mecca for fear of life, had now returned to Mecca, and Mecca was unable to resist him.

FALL OF MECCA

Abū Sufyān must have been thinking furiously. Had not an incredibly great change taken place in seven years ? And now as leader of the Meccans, what was he going to do ? Was he going to resist, or was he going to submit ? Troubled by such thoughts, he appeared stupefied to outside observers. The Prophet saw this agitated Meccan leader. He told 'Abbās to take him away and entertain him for the night, promising to see him in the morning. Abū Sufyān spent the night with 'Abbās. In the morning they called on the Prophet. It was time for the early morning prayers. The bustle and activity which Abū Sufyān saw at this early hour was quite unusual in his experience. He had not known—no Meccan had known—such early risers as Muslims had become under the discipline of Islam. He saw all the Muslim campers turned out for their morning prayers. Some went to and fro in quest of water for ablutions, others to supervise the lining up of worshippers for the service. Abū Sufyān could not understand this activity early in the morning. He was frightened. Was a new plan afoot to overawe him ?

"What can they all be doing ?" he asked in sheer consternation.

"Nothing to be afraid of," replied 'Abbās. "They are only preparing for the morning prayers."

Abū Sufyān then saw thousands of Muslims lined up behind the Prophet, making the prescribed movements and devotions at the bidding of the Prophet—half prostrations, full prostrations, standing up again, and so on. 'Abbās was on guard duty, so he was free to engage Abū Sufyān in conversation.

"What could they be doing now ?" asked Abū Sufyān. "Everything the Prophet does, is done by the rest."

"What are you thinking about ? It is only the Muslim prayer, Abū Sufyān. Muslims would do anything at the bidding of the Prophet—give up food and drink for instance."

"True," said Abū Sufyān, "I have seen great courts. I have seen the court of the Chosroes and the court of the Kaiser, but I have never seen any people as devoted to their leader as Muslims are to their Prophet" (Ḥalbiyya, Vol. 2, p. 90).

Filled with fear and guilt, Abū Sufyān went on to ask 'Abbās if he would not request the Prophet to forgive his own people —meaning the Meccans.

The morning prayers over, 'Abbās led Abū Sufyān to the Prophet.

Said the Prophet to Abū Sufyān. "Has it not yet dawned upon you that there is no one worthy of worship except Allah ?"

"My father and my mother be a sacrifice to you. You have ever been kind, gentle and considerate to your kith and kin. I am certain now that if there were anyone else worthy of worship, we might have had some help against you from him."

"Has it not also dawned upon you that I am a Messenger of Allah ?"

"My father and my mother be a sacrifice to you, on this I still have some doubts."

While Abū Sufyān hesitated to acknowledge the Prophet as Messenger of God, two of his companions who had marched out of Mecca with him to do reconnoitring duty for the Meccans, became Muslims. One of them was Ḥakīm bin Ḥizām. A little later, Abū Sufyān also joined, but his inner conversion seems to have been deferred until after the conquest of Mecca. Ḥakīm bin Ḥizām asked the Prophet if the Muslims would destroy their own kith and kin.

"These people," said the Prophet, "have been very cruel. They have committed excesses and proved themselves of bad faith. They have gone back on the peace they signed at Ḥudaibiya and attacked the Khuzā'a savagely. They have made war in a place which had been made inviolate by God."

"It is quite true, O Prophet of God, our people have done exactly as you say, but instead of marching upon Mecca you should have attacked the Hawāzin," suggested Ḥakīm.

"The Hawāzin also have been cruel and savage. I hope God will enable me to realize all the three ends : the conquest of Mecca, the ascendancy of Islam and the defeat of the Hawāzin."

Abū Sufyān, who had been listening, now asked the Prophet : "If the Meccans draw not the sword, will they have peace ?"

"Yes," replied the Prophet, "everyone who stays indoors will have peace."

"But O Prophet," intervened 'Abbās, "Abū Sufyān is much

concerned about himself. He wishes to know if his rank and position among the Meccans will be respected."

"Very good," said the Prophet: "Whoever take shelter in the house of Abū Sufyān will have peace. Whoever enters the Sacred Mosque will have peace. Those who lay down their arms will have peace. Those who close their doors and stay in will have peace. Those who stay in the house of Ḥakīm bin Ḥizām will have peace."

Saying this, he called Abū Ruwaiḥa and handed over to him the standard of Islam. Abū Ruwaiḥa had entered into a pact of brotherhood with Bilāl, the negro slave. Handing over the standard, the Prophet said, "Whoever stands under this standard will have peace." At the same time, he ordered Bilāl to march in front of Abū Ruwaiḥa and announce to all concerned that there was peace under the standard held by Abū Ruwaiḥa.

THE PROPHET ENTERS MECCA

The arrangement was full of wisdom. When Muslims were persecuted in Mecca, Bilāl, one of their targets, was dragged about the streets by ropes tied to his legs. Mecca gave no peace to Bilāl, but only physical pain, humiliation and disgrace. How revengeful Bilāl must have felt on this day of his deliverance. To let him avenge the savage cruelties suffered by him in Mecca was necessary, but it had to be within the limits laid down by Islam. Accordingly, the Prophet did not let Bilāl draw the sword and smite the necks of his former persecutors. That would have been un-Islamic. Instead, the Prophet handed to Bilāl's brother the standard of Islam, and charged Bilāl with the duty of offering peace to all his former persecutors under the standard borne by his brother. There was beauty and appeal in this revenge. We have to picture Bilāl marching in front of his brother and inviting his enemies to peace. His passion for revenge could not have lasted. It must have dissolved as he advanced inviting Meccans to peace under a standard held aloft by his brother.

While the Muslims marched towards Mecca, the Prophet had ordered 'Abbās to take Abū Sufyān and his friends to a spot from where they could easily view the Muslim army, its behaviour and bearing. 'Abbās did so and from a vantage-point Abū Sufyān and his friends watched go past the Arab tribes on whose power the Meccans had banked all these years for their plots against Islam. They marched that day not as soldiers of disbelief but as soldiers of belief. They raised now the slogans of Islam, not the slogans of their pagan days. They marched in formation, not to put an end to the Prophet's life, but to lay down their lives to save his ; not to shed his blood, but their own for his sake. Their ambition that day was not to resist the Prophet's Message and save the superficial solidarity of their own people. It was to carry to all parts of the world the very Message they had so far resisted. It was to establish the unity and solidarity of man. Column after column marched past until the Ashja' tribe came in Abū Sufyān's view. Their devotion to Islam and their self-sacrificing zeal could be seen in their faces, and heard in their songs and slogans.

"Who can they be ?" asked Abū Sufyān.

"They are the Ashja' tribe."

Abū Sufyān looked astonished and said, "In all Arabia, no one bore greater enmity to Muhammad."

"We owe it to the grace of God. He changed the hearts of the enemy of Islam as soon as He deemed fit," said 'Abbās.

Last of all came the Prophet, surrounded by the columns of Anṣār and Muhājirīn. They must have been about two thousand strong, dressed in suits of armour. The valiant 'Umar directed their marching. The sight proved the most impressive of all. The devotion of these Muslims, their determination and their zeal seemed overflowing. When Abū Sufyān's eyes fell on them, he was completely overpowered.

"Who can they be ?" he asked.

"They are the Anṣār and the Muhājirīn surrounding the Prophet," replied 'Abbās.

"No power on earth could resist this army," said Abū Sufyān, and then, addressing 'Abbās more specifically, " 'Abbās, your nephew has become the most powerful king in the world."

"You are still far from the truth, Abū Sufyān. He is no king ; he is a Prophet, a Messenger of God," replied 'Abbās.

"Yes, yes, let it be as you say, a Prophet, not a king," added Abū Sufyān.

As the Muslim army marched past Abū Sufyān, the commander of the Anṣār, Sa'd bin 'Ubāda happened to eye Abū Sufyān and could not resist saying that God that day had made it lawful for them to enter Mecca by force and that the Quraish would be humiliated.

As the Prophet was passing, Abū Sufyān raised his voice and addressing the Prophet said, "Have you allowed the massacre of your own kith and kin ? I heard the commander of the Anṣār, Sa'd and his companions say so. They said it was a day of slaughter. The sacredness of Mecca will not avert bloodshed and the Quraish will be humiliated. Prophet of God, you are the best, the most forgiving, the most considerate of men. Will you not forgive and forget whatever was done by your own people ?"

Abū Sufyān's appeal went home. Those very Muslims who used to be insulted and beaten in the streets of Mecca, who had been dispossessed and driven out of their homes, began to entertain feelings of mercy for their old persecutors. "Prophet of God," they said, "the accounts which the Anṣār have heard of the excesses and cruelties committed by Meccans against us, may lead them to seek revenge. We know not what they may do."

The Prophet understood this. Turning to Abū Sufyān, he said, "What Sa'd has said is quite wrong. It is not the day of slaughter. It is the day of forgiveness. The Quraish and the Ka'ba will be honoured by God."

Then he sent for Sa'd, and ordered him to hand over the Anṣār flag to his son, Qais (Hishām, Vol. 2). The command of the Anṣār thus passed from Sa'd to Qais. It was a wise step. It placated the Meccans and saved the Anṣār disappointment. Qais, a pious young man, was fully trusted by the Prophet. An incident of his last days illustrates the piety of his character. Lying on his death-bed, Qais received his friends. Some came and some did not. He could not understand this and asked why some of his friends had not come to see him. "Your charity is abundant," explained one. 'You have been helping the needy by your loans. There are many in the town who are in debt to you. Some may have hesitated to come lest you should ask them for the return of the loans."

"Then I have been the cause of keeping my friends away. Please announce that no one now owes anything to Qais." After this announcement Qais had so many visitors during his last days that the steps to his house gave way.

When the Muslim army had marched past, 'Abbās told Abū Sufyān to hasten for Mecca and announce to the Meccans that the Prophet had come and explain to them how they could all have peace. Abū Sufyān reached Mecca with this message of peace for his town, but his wife, Hind, notorious for her hostility towards Muslims, met him. A confirmed disbeliever, she was yet a brave woman. She caught Abū Sufyān by the beard and called on Meccans to come and kill her cowardly husband. Instead of moving his townsmen to sacrifice their lives for the defence and honour of their town, he was inviting them to peace.

But Abū Sufyān could see that Hind was behaving foolishly "That time is gone," said he. "You had better go home and sit behind closed doors. I have seen the Muslim army. Not all Arabia could withstand it now."

He then explained the conditions under which the Prophet had promised peace to the Meccans. On hearing these conditions the people of Mecca ran for protection to the places which had been named in the Prophet's proclamation. From this proclamation eleven men and four women had been excepted. The offences which they had committed were very grave. Their guilt was not that they had not believed nor that they had taken part in wars against Islam; it was that they had committed inhumanities which could not be passed over. Actually, however, only four persons were put to death.

The Prophet had ordered Khālid bin Walīd not to permit any fighting unless they were fought against and unless the Meccans first started fighting. The part of the town which Khālid entered had not heard the conditions of peace. The Meccans posted in that part challenged Khālid and invited him to fight. An encounter ensued in which twelve or thirteen men were killed (Hishām, Vol. 2, p. 217). Khālid was a man of fiery temper. Somebody, warned by this incident, ran to the

Prophet to request him to stop Khālid from fighting. If Khālid did not stop, said this man, all Mecca would be massacred.

The Prophet sent for Khālid at once and said, "Did I not stop you from fighting ?"

"Yes, you did, O Prophet of God, but these people attacked us first and began to shoot arrows at us. For a time I did nothing and told them we did not want to fight. But they did not listen, and did not stop. So I replied to them, and dispersed them."

This was the only untoward incident which took place on this occasion. The conquest of Mecca was thus brought about practically without bloodshed.

The Prophet entered Mecca. They asked him where he would stop.

"Has 'Aqīl left any house for me to live in ?" asked the Prophet. 'Aqīl was the Prophet's cousin, a son of his uncle. During the years of the Prophet's refuge at Medina, his relations had sold all his property. There was no house left which the Prophet could call his own. Accordingly the Prophet said, "I will stop at Khīf Banī Kināna." This was an open space. The Quraish and the Kināna once assembled there and swore that unless the Banū Hāshim and the Banū 'Abdal Muṭṭalib handed over the Prophet to them to deal with him as they liked, they would have no dealings with the two tribes. They would neither sell anything to them nor buy anything from them. It was after this solemn declaration that the Prophet, his uncle Abū Ṭālib, his family and followers, had to take refuge in the valley of Abū Ṭālib and suffer a severe blockade and boycott lasting for three years.

The place which the Prophet chose for his stay was, therefore, full of significance. The Meccans had once assembled there and taken the oath that unless the Prophet was made over to them, they would not be at peace with his tribe. Now the Prophet had come to the same spot. It was as though he had come to tell the Meccans : "You wanted me here. So, here am I. But not in the way you wanted. You wanted me as your victim, one completely at your mercy. But I am here in power. Not only my own people, but the whole of Arabia is now with me. You wanted my people to hand me over to you. Instead of that, they have handed you over to me." This day of victory was a Monday. The day on which the Prophet and Abū Bakr left the cave of Thaur for their journey to Medina was also a Monday. On that day, standing on the hill of Thaur, the Prophet turned to Mecca and said, 'Mecca ! you are dearer to me than any other place but your people would not let me live here.'

When the Prophet entered Mecca, mounted on his camel, Abū Bakr walked with him holding a stirrup. As he walked along, Abū Bakr recited verses from the Sūra, Al Fatḥ in which the conquest of Mecca had been foretold years before.

KA'BA CLEARED OF IDOLS

The Prophet made straight for the Ka'ba and performed the circuit of the holy precincts seven times, mounted on his camel. Staff in hand, he went round the house which had been built by the Patriarch Abraham and his son Ishmael for the worship of the One and Only God, but which by their misguided children had been allowed to degenerate into a sanctuary for idols. The Prophet smote one by one the three hundred and sixty idols in the house. As an idol fell, the Prophet would recite the verse, "Truth has come and falsehood has vanished away. Falsehood does indeed vanish away fast." This verse was revealed before the Prophet left Mecca for Medina and is part of the Chapter, Banī Isra'īl. In this Chapter was foretold the flight of the Prophet and the conquest of Mecca. The Chapter is a Meccan Chapter, a fact admitted even by European writers. The verses which contain the prophecy of the Prophet's flight from Mecca, and the subsequent conquest of Mecca are as follows :

> And say 'O my Lord, make my entry a good entry, and make my going out a good outgoing. And grant me from Thyself a power that may help me.' And, 'Truth has come and falsehood has vanished away. Falsehood does indeed vanish away fast !' (17 : 81–82).

The conquest of Mecca is foretold here in the form of a prayer taught to the Prophet. The Prophet is taught to pray for entering Mecca and for departing from it under good auspices; and for the help of God in assuring an ultimate victory of truth over falsehood. The prophecy had literally come true. The recitation of these verses by Abū Bakr was appropriate. It braced up the Muslims, and reminded the Meccans of the futility of their fight against God and of the truth of the promises made by God to the Prophet.

With the conquest of Mecca, the Ka'ba was restored to the functions for which it had been consecrated many thousands of years before by the Patriarch Abraham. The Ka'ba was again devoted to the worship of the One and Only God. The idols were broken. One of these was Hubal. When the Prophet smote it with his staff, and it fell down in fragments, Zubair looked at Abū Sufyān and with a half-suppressed smile reminded him of Uḥud. "Do you remember the day when Muslims wounded and exhausted stood by and you wounded them further by shouting, 'Glory to Hubal, Glory to Hubal'? Was it Hubal who gave you victory on that day? If it was Hubal, you can see the end it has come to today."

Abū Sufyān was impressed, and admitted it was quite true that if there had been a God other than the God of Muhammad, they might have been spared the disgrace and defeat they had met with that day.

The Prophet then ordered the wiping out of the pictures which had been drawn on the walls of the Ka'ba. Having ordered this the Prophet said two *rak'ats* of prayer as thanksgiving to God. He then withdrew to the open court and said another two *rak'ats* of prayer. The duty of wiping out the pictures had been entrusted to 'Umar. He had all the pictures obliterated except that of Abraham. When the Prophet returned to inspect and found this picture intact, he asked 'Umar why he had spared this one. Did he not remember the testimony of the Quran that Abraham was neither Jew nor Christian, but a single-minded and obedient Muslim? (3 : 68).

It was an insult to the memory of Abraham, a great exponent of the Oneness of God to have his picture on the walls of the Ka'ba. It was as though Abraham could be worshipped equally with God.

It was a memorable day, a day full of the Signs of God.

Promises made by God to the Prophet, at a time when their fulfilment seemed impossible, had been fulfilled at last. The Prophet was the centre of devotion and faith. In and through his person, God had manifested Himself, and shown His face, as it were, again. The Prophet sent for water of the Zamzam. He drank some of it and with the rest performed ablutions. So devoted were Muslims to the Prophet's person, that they would not let a drop of this water fall on the ground. They received the water in the hollows of their hands to wet their bodies with it ; in such reverence did they hold it. The pagans who witnessed these scenes of devotion said again and again that they had never seen an earthly king to whom his people were so devoted (Ḥalbiyya, Vol. 3, p. 99).

THE PROPHET FORGIVES HIS ENEMIES

All rites and duties over, the Prophet addressed the Meccans and said : "You have seen how true the promises of God have proved. Now tell me what punishment you should have for the cruelties and enormities you committed against those whose only fault was that they invited you to the worship of the One and Only God."

To this the Meccans replied, "We expect you to treat us as Joseph treated his erring brothers."

By significant coincidence, the Meccans used in their plea for forgiveness the very words which God had used in the Sūra Yūsuf, revealed ten years before the conquest of Mecca. In this the Prophet was told that he would treat his Meccan persecutors as Joseph had treated his brothers. By asking for the treatment which Joseph had meted out to his brothers, the Meccans admitted that the Prophet of Islam was the like of Joseph and as Joseph was granted victory over his brothers the Prophet had been granted victory over the Meccans. Hearing the Meccans' plea, the Prophet declared at once : "By God, you will have no punishment today and no reproof" (Hishām).

While the Prophet was engaged in expressing his gratitude to God and in carrying out other devotions at the Ka'ba, and while he was addressing the Meccans announcing his decision to forgive and forget, misgivings arose in the minds of the Anṣār, the Medinite Muslims. Some of them were upset over the scenes of home-coming and of reconciliation which they witnessed on the return of Meccan Muslims to Mecca. Was the Prophet parting company with them, his friends in adversity who provided the first home to Islam ? Was the Prophet going to settle down at Mecca, the town from which he had to flee for his life ? Such fears did not seem too remote now that Mecca had been conquered and his own tribe had joined Islam. The Prophet might want to settle down in it. God informed the Prophet of these misgivings of the Anṣār. He raised his head, looked at the Anṣār and said "You seem to think Muhammad is perturbed by the love of his town, and by the ties which bind him to his tribe." "It is true," said the Anṣār, "we did think of this."

"Do you know," said the Prophet, "who I am ? I am a Servant of God and His Messenger. How can I give you up ? You stood by me, and sacrificed your lives when the Faith of God had no earthly help. How can I give you up and settle elsewhere ? No, Anṣār, this is impossible. I left Mecca for the sake of God and I cannot return to it. I will live and die with you."

The Anṣār were moved by this singular expression of love and loyalty. They regretted their distrust of God and His Prophet, wept and asked to be forgiven. They explained that they would not have any peace if the Prophet left their town and went elsewhere. The Prophet replied that their fear was understandable and that, after their explanation, God and His Prophet were satisfied about their innocence and acknowledge their sincerity and loyalty.

How must the Meccans have felt at this time ? True they did not shed the tears of devotion but their hearts must have been full of regret and remorse. For, had they not cast away with their own hands the gem which had been found in their own town ? They had all the more reason to regret this because the Prophet, having come back to Mecca, had decided to leave it again for Medina.

‘IKRIMA BECOMES MUSLIM

Of those who had been excepted from the general amnesty, some were forgiven on the recommendation of the Companions. Among those who were thus forgiven was ‘Ikrima, a son of Abū Jahl. ‘Ikrima’s wife was a Muslim at heart. She requested the Prophet to forgive him. The Prophet forgave. At the time ‘Ikrima was trying to escape to Abyssinia. His wife pursued him and found that he was about to embark. She reproved him. "Are you running way from a man as gentle and soft as the Prophet ?" she said.

‘Ikrima was astonished and asked whether she really thought the Prophet would forgive him. ‘Ikrima’s wife assured him that even he would be forgiven by the Prophet. In fact she had had word from him already. ‘Ikrima gave up his plan of escaping to Abyssinia and returned to see the Prophet. "I understand from my wife that you have forgiven even one like me," he said.

"Your wife is right. I have really forgiven you," said the Prophet.

‘Ikrima decided that a person capable of forgiving his deadliest enemies could not be false. He, therefore, declared his faith in Islam. "I bear witness that God is One and has no equal and I bear witness that you are His Servant and His Messenger." So saying, ‘Ikrima bent his head in shame. The Prophet consoled him. " ‘Ikrima," said he, "I have not only forgiven you, but as proof of my regard for you, I have decided to invite you to ask me for anything I can give."

‘Ikrima replied, "There is nothing more or better I can ask you for than that you should pray for me to God and ask for His forgiveness and whatever excesses and enormities I have committed against you."

Hearing this entreaty, the Prophet prayed to God at once and said : "My God, forgive the enmity which ‘Ikrima has born against me. Forgive him the abuse which has issued from his lips."

The Prophet then stood up and put his mantle over ‘Ikrima and said, "Whoever comes to me, believing in God, is one with me. My house is as much his as mine."

The conversion of 'Ikrima fulfilled a prophecy which the Holy Prophet had made many years before. The Prophet, addressing his Companions, once had said : "I have had a vision in which I saw that I was in Paradise. I saw there a bunch of grapes. When I asked for whom the bunch was meant, someone replied saying, 'For Abū Jahl'." Referring to this vision on this occasion of the conversion of 'Ikrima, the Prophet said he did not understand the vision at first. How could Abū Jahl, an enemy of believers, enter Paradise and how could he have a bunch of grapes provided for him. "But now," said the Prophet, "I understand my vision ; the bunch of grapes was meant for 'Ikrima. Only, instead of the son I was shown the father, a substitution common in visions and dreams" (Ḥalbiyya, Vol. 3, p. 104).

Of the persons who had been ordered to be executed as exceptions to the general amnesty was one who had been responsible for the cruel murder of Zainab, a daughter of the Prophet. This man was Habbār. He had cut the girths of Zainab's camel, on which Zainab fell to the ground and, being with child, suffered abortion. A little later she died. This was one of the inhumanities which he had committed and for which he deserved the penalty of death. This man now came to the Prophet and said, "Prophet of God, I ran away from you and went to Iran, but the thought came to me that God had rid us of our pagan beliefs and saved us from spiritual death. Instead of going to others and seeking shelter with them why not go to the Prophet himself, acknowledge my faults and my sins and ask for his forgiveness ?"

The Prophet was moved and said, "Habbār, if God has planted in your heart the love of Islam, how can I refuse to forgive you ? I forgive everything you have done before this."

One cannot describe in detail the enormities these men had committed against Islam and Muslims. Yet how easily the Prophet forgave them ! This spirit of forgiveness converted the most stone-hearted adversaries into devotees of the Prophet.

BATTLE OF ḤUNAIN

The Prophet's entry into Mecca was sudden. Tribes in the

vicinity of Mecca, especially those in the south, remained unaware of the event until sometime later. On hearing of it, they began to assemble their forces and to prepare for a fight with the Muslims. There were two Arab tribes, the Hawāzin and the Thaqīf, unusually proud of their valiant traditions. They took counsel together and after some deliberation elected Mālik ibn 'Auf as their leader. They then invited the tribes round about to join them. Among the tribes invited was the Banū Sa'd. The Prophet's wet-nurse, Ḥalīma, belonged to this tribe and the Prophet as a child had lived among them. Men of this tribe collected in force and set out towards Mecca taking with them their families and their effects. Asked why they had done so, they replied it was in order that the soldiers might be reminded that, if they turned back and fled, their wives and children would be taken prisoners and their effects looted —so strong was their determination to fight and destroy the Muslims. This force descended in the valley of Auṭās— a most suitable base for a battle, with its natural shelters, abundance of fodder and water, and facilities for cavalry movements. When the Prophet got to know of this, he sent 'Abdullah bin Abī Ḥadrad to report on the situation. 'Abdullah reported that there were military concentrations in the place and there was determination to kill and be killed. The tribe was renowned for its skill in archery, and the base they had selected afforded a very great advantage to them. The Prophet approached Ṣafwān, a prosperous chief of Mecca for the loan of suits of armour and weapons. Ṣafwān replied, "You seem to put pressure on me and think I will be overawed by your growing power and make over to you whatever you ask ?"

The Prophet replied, "We wish to seize nothing. We only want a loan of these things, and are ready to give a suitable surety."

Ṣafwān was satisfied and agreed to lend the material. Altogether he supplied one hundred suits of armour and a suitable number of weapons. The Prophet borrowed three thousand lances from his cousin, Naufal bin Ḥārith and about thirty thousand *dirhams* from 'Abdullah bin Rabī'a (Mu'aṭṭa, Musnad and Ḥalbiyya). When the Muslim army set out towards the

Hawāzin, the Meccans expressed a wish to join the Muslim side. They were not Muslims, but they had agreed to live under a Muslim regime. Accordingly, two thousand Meccans joined the Muslims. On the way, they came to the noted Arab shrine, Dhāt Anwāṭ. Here was an old jujube tree, sacred to the Arabs. When Arabs bought arms they first went to Dhāt Anwāṭ and hung them in the shrine to receive its blessings for their arms. When the Muslim army passed by this shrine some of the soldiers said, "Prophet of God, there should be a Dhāt Anwāṭ for us also."

The Prophet disapproved and said, "You talk like the followers of Moses. When Moses was going to Canaan, his followers saw on the way people worshipping idols, and said to Moses, 'O Moses, make for us a god just as they have gods' " (7 : 139).

"THE PROPHET OF GOD CALLS YOU"

The Prophet urged Muslims ever to remember that Allah was Great and to pray to Him to save them from the superstitions of earlier peoples. Before the Muslim army reached Ḥunain, the Hawāzin and their allies had already prepared a number of ambuscades from which to attack the Muslims, like the fox-holes and camouflaged artillery positions of modern warfare. They had built walls around them. Behind the walls were soldiers lying in wait for the Muslims. A narrow gorge was left for Muslims to pass through. Much the larger part of the army was posted to these ambuscades, while a small number was made to line up in front of their camels. Muslims thought enemy numbers to be no more than they could see. So they went forward and attacked. When they had advanced far and the hiding enemy was satisfied that they could be attacked very easily, the soldiers lined up in front of the camels and attacked the centre of the Muslim army while the hiding archers rained their arrows on the flanks. The Meccans, who had joined for a chance to display their valour, could not stand this double attack by the enemy. They ran back to Mecca. Muslims were accustomed to difficult situations, but when two thousand soldiers mounted on horses and camels pierced their way through the Muslim army, the animals of the Muslims also took fright. There was panic in the army. Pressure came from three sides, resulting in a general rout. In this, only the Prophet, with twelve Companions, stood unmoved. Not that all the Companions had fled from the field. About a hundred of them still remained, but they were at some distance from the Prophet. Only twelve remained to surround the Prophet. One Companion reports that he and his friends did all they could to steer their animals towards the battlefield. But the animals had been put to fright by the stampede of the Meccan animals. No effort seemed to avail. They pulled at the reins but the animals refused to turn. Sometimes they would pull the heads of the animals so as almost to make them touch their tails. But when they spurred the animals towards the battlefield, they would not go. Instead, they moved back all the more. "Our hearts beat in fear—fear for the safety of the Prophet," says this Companion, "but there was nothing we could do." This was how the Companions were placed. The Prophet himself stood with a handful of men, exposed on three sides to volleys of arrows. There was only one narrow pass behind them through which only a few men could pass at a time. At that moment Abū Bakr dismounted and holding the reins of the Prophet's mule said, "Prophet of God, let us withdraw for a while and let the Muslim army collect itself."

"Release the reins of my mule, Abū Bakr," said the Prophet. Saying this, he spurred the animal forward into the gorge on both sides of which were enemy ambuscades from where the archers were shooting. As the Prophet spurred his mount, he said, "I am a Prophet. I am no pretender. I am a son of 'Abd al-Muṭṭalib" (Bukhārī). These words spoken at a time of extreme danger to his person are full of significance. They stressed the fact that the Prophet was really a Prophet, a true Messenger of God. By stressing this, he meant that he was not afraid of death or of the failure of his cause. But if, in spite of being overwhelmed by archers he remained safe, Muslims should not attribute any divine qualities to him. For he was but a human being, a son of 'Abd al-Muṭṭalib. How careful was the Prophet ever to impress upon his followers the difference between faith and superstition. After uttering these memorable words, the Prophet called for 'Abbās. 'Abbās had a powerful voice. The Prophet said to him, " 'Abbās, raise your voice and remind the Muslims of the oath they took under the tree at Ḥudaibiya, and of what they were taught at the time of the revelation of the Sūra Baqara. Tell them, the Prophet of God calls them." 'Abbās raised his powerful voice. The message of the Prophet fell like thunder, not on deaf ears but on ears agog. It had an electric effect. The very Companions who had found themselves powerless to urge their mounts towards the battlefield, began to feel they were no longer in this world but in the next, facing God on the Judgement Day. The voice of 'Abbās did not sound like his own voice but the voice of the angel beckoning them to render an account of their deeds. There was nothing then to stop them from turning to the battlefield again. Many of them dismounted and with only sword and shield rushed to the battlefield, leaving their animals to go where they liked. Others dismounted, cut off the heads of their animals and rushed back on foot to the Prophet. It is said that the Anṣār on that day ran towards the Prophet with the speed with which a mother-camel or a mother-cow runs to her young on hearing its cries. Before long the Prophet was surrounded by a large number of Companions, mostly Anṣār. The enemy again suffered a defeat.

The presence of Abū Sufyān on the side of the Prophet on this day was a mighty divine Sign, a Sign of the power of God on the one hand and of the purifying example of the Prophet on the other. Only a few days before, Abū Sufyān was a blood-thirsty enemy of the Prophet, commander of a blood-thirsty army determined to destroy the Muslims. But here, on this day the same Abū Sufyān stood by the side of the Prophet, a friend, follower and Companion. When the enemy camels stampeded, Abū Sufyān, a wise and seasoned general, saw that his own horse was likely to run wild. Quickly he dismounted and, holding the stirrup of the Prophet's mule, started going on foot. Sword in hand, he walked by the side of the Prophet determined not to let anyone come near the Prophet's person without first attacking and killing him. The Prophet watched this change in Abū Sufyān with delight and astonishment.

He reflected on this fresh evidence of the power of God. Only ten or fifteen days before, this man was raising an army to put an end to the Movement of Islam. But a change had come. An erstwhile enemy commander now stood by the Prophet's side, as an ordinary foot-soldier, holding the stirrup of his Master's mule, and determined to die for his sake. 'Abbās saw the astonishment in the Prophet's look and said, "Prophet of God, this is Abū Sufyān, son of your uncle, and so your brother. Aren't you pleased with him ?"

"I am," said the Prophet, "and I pray, God may forgive him all the wrongs he has done." Then turning to Abū Sufyān himself, he said, "Brother !" Abū Sufyān could not restrain the affection welling up in his heart. He bent and kissed the Prophet's foot in the stirrup he was holding (Ḥalbiyya).

After the battle of Ḥunain, the Prophet returned the war material he had received on loan. While returning it he compensated the lenders many times over. Those who had made the loan were touched by the care and consideration which the Prophet had shown in returning the material and in compensating the lenders. They felt the Prophet was no ordinary man, but one whose moral example stood high above others. No wonder, Ṣafwān joined Islam at once.

A SWORN ENEMY BECOMES A DEVOTED FOLLOWER

The battle of Ḥunain ever reminds historians of another interesting incident which took place while it was in progress. Shaiba, a resident of Mecca and in the service of the Ka'ba, took part in the encounter on the side of the enemy. He says that he had only one aim before him in this battle—that when the two armies met, he would find an opportunity to kill the Prophet. He was determined that even if the whole world joined the Prophet (let alone the whole of Arabia), he would stand out and continue to oppose Islam. When fighting became brisk, Shaiba drew his sword and started advancing towards the Prophet. As he came very near, he became unnerved. His determination began to shake. "When I got very near the Prophet," says Shaiba, "I seemed to see a flame threatening to consume me. I then heard the voice of the Prophet saying, 'Shaiba, come near me.' When I got near, the Prophet moved his hand over my chest in great affection. As he did so, he said, 'God, relieve Shaiba of all satanic thought'." With this little touch of affection Shaiba changed. His hostility and enmity evaporated, and from that moment Shaiba held the Prophet dearer than anything else in the world. As Shaiba changed, the Prophet invited him to come forward and fight. "At that moment," says Shaiba, "I had but one thought, and that was to die for the sake of the Prophet. Even if my father had come my way, I would have hesitated not a moment to thrust my sword in his chest" (Ḥalbiyya).

The Prophet then marched towards Ṭā'if, the town which had stoned him and driven him out. The Prophet besieged the town, but accepting the suggestion of some friends abandoned the siege. Later, the people of Ṭā'if joined Islam voluntarily.

THE PROPHET DISTRIBUTES BOOTY

After the conquest of Mecca and the victory of Ḥunain, the Prophet was faced with the task of distributing the money and property paid as ransom or abandoned in the battlefield by the enemy. If custom had been followed, this money and property should have been distributed among the Muslim soldiers who took part in these encounters. But on this occasion, instead of distributing it among the Muslims, the Prophet distributed it among the Meccans and the people who lived round about Mecca. These people had yet to show an inclination towards the Faith. Many were professed deniers. Those who had declared their faith were yet new to it. They had no idea how self-denying a people could become after they had accepted Islam. But, instead of benefiting by the example of self-denial and self-sacrifice which they saw, instead of reciprocating the good treatment they received from the Muslims, they became more avaricious and greedier than ever. Their demands began to mount. They mobbed the Prophet, and pushed him to a spot under a tree with his mantle having been torn from his shoulders. At last the Prophet said to the crowd, "I have nothing else to give. If I had, I would have made it over to you. I am no miser, nor am I mean" (Bukhārī, chap. on *Faraḍ al-Khums*).

Then going near his dromedary and pulling out a hair, he said to the crowd, "Out of this money and property I want nothing at all, not even as much as a hair. Only, I must have a fifth, and that for the State. That is the share which Arab custom has ever admitted as just and right. That fifth will not be spent on me. It will be spent on you and your needs. Remember that one who misappropriates or misuses public money will be humiliated in the sight of God on the Judgement Day."

It has been said by malicious critics that the Prophet longed to become a king and to have a kingdom. But imagine him confronted by a mean crowd, while he is already a king. If he had longed to become a king and to have a kingdom, would he have treated a beggarly mob as he treated this Meccan mob ? Would he have agreed to be mobbed at all in the way he was ? Would he have argued and explained ? It is only Prophets and Messengers of God who can set such an example. All the booty, the money, and the valuable material that there was to distribute had been distributed among the deserving and the poor. Still there were those who remained unsatisfied, who mobbed the Prophet, protested against the distribution charging the Prophet with injustice.

One Dhu'l Khuwaiṣira came near the Prophet and said, "Muhammad, I am a witness to what you are doing."

"And what am I doing ? " asked the Prophet.

"You are committing an injustice," said he.

"Woe to you," said the Prophet. "If I can be unjust, then there is no one on the face of the earth who can be just" (Muslim, *Kitāb al-Zakāt*).

True believers were full of rage. When this man left the assembly some of them said, "This man deserves death. Will you let us kill him ?"

"No," said the Prophet. "If he observes our laws and commits no visible offence, how can we kill him ?"

"But," said the believers, "when a person says and does one thing but believes and desires quite another, would he not deserve to be treated accordingly ?"

"I cannot deal with people according to what they have in their hearts. God has not charged me with this. I can deal with them according to what they say and do."

The Prophet went on to tell the believers that one day this man and others of his kin would stage a rebellion in Islam. The Prophet's words came true. In the time of 'Alī, the Fourth Khalīfa of Islam, this man and his friends led the rebellion against him and became the leaders of a universally condemned division of Islam, the Khawārij.

After dealing with the Hawāzin, the Prophet returned to Medina. It was another great day for its people. One great day was when the Prophet arrived at Medina a refugee from the ill-treatment of the Meccans. On this great day, the Prophet re-entered Medina, full of joy and aware of his determination and promise to make Medina his home.

MACHINATIONS OF ABŪ 'ĀMIR

We must now turn to the activities of one Abū 'Āmir Madanī. He belonged to the Khazraj tribe. Through long association with Jews and Christians he had acquired the habit of silent meditation and of repeating the names of God. Because of this habit, he was generally known as Abū 'Āmir, the Hermit. He was, however, not a Christian by faith. When the Prophet went to Medina after the Hijra, Abū 'Āmir escaped from Medina to Mecca. When at last Mecca also submitted to the growing influence of Islam, he began to hatch a new intrigue against Islam. He changed his name and his habitual mode of dress and settled down in Qubā, a village near Medina. As he had been away for a long time and had altered his appearance and his dress, the people of Medina did not recognize him. Only those hypocrites recognized him with whom he had relations in secret. He took the hypocrites of Medina into his confidence and with their concurrence planned to go to Syria and excite and provoke the Christian rulers and Christian Arabs into attacking Medina. While he was engaged in his sinister mission in the north, he had planned for the spread of disaffection in Medina. His colleagues, the hypocrites, were to spread rumours that Medina was going to be attacked by Syrian forces. As a result of this dual plot Abū 'Āmir hoped that Muslims and Syrian Christians would go to war. If his plot did not succeed, he hoped that Muslims would themselves be provoked into attacking Syria. Even thus a war might start between Muslims and Syrians and Abū 'Āmir would have something to rejoice over. Completing his plans, he went to Syria. While he was away the hypocrites at Medina—according to plan—began to spread rumours that caravans had been sighted which were coming to attack Medina. When no caravan appeared, they issued some kind of explanation.

THE EXPEDITION OF TABŪK

These rumours became so persistent, that the Prophet thought it worth while to lead in person a Muslim army against Syria. These were difficult times. Arabia was in the grip of a famine. The harvest in the previous year had been poor and both grain and fruit were in short supply. The time for the new harvest had not yet come. It was the end of September or the beginning of October when the Prophet set out on this mission. The hypocrites knew that the rumours were their own inventions. They knew also that their design was to provoke Muslims into an attack on the Syrians if the Syrians did not attack Muslims. In either case, a conflict with the great Roman Empire was to result in the destruction of Muslims. The lesson of Mūta was before them. At Mūta Muslims had to face such a huge army that it was with great difficulty that they were able to effect a retreat. The hypocrites were hoping to stage a second Mūta in which the Prophet himself might lose his life. While the hypocrites were busy spreading rumours about the Syrian attack on Muslims, they also made every effort to strike fear in the minds of Muslims. The Syrians could raise very large armies which Muslims could not hope to stand against. They urged Muslims not to take part in the conflict with Syria. Their plan was, on the one hand, to provoke Muslims into attacking Syria and, on the other, to discourage them from going in large numbers. They wanted Muslims to go to war against Syria and meet with certain defeat. But as soon as the Prophet announced his intention of leading this new expedition, enthusiasm ran high among Muslims. They went forward with offers of sacrifice for the sake of their faith. Muslims were ill-equipped for a war on such a scale. Their treasury was empty. Only the more prosperous Muslims had means to pay for the war. Individual Muslims vied with one another in the spirit of sacrifice for the sake of their faith. It is said that when the expedition was under way and the Prophet appealed for funds, 'Uthmān gave away the greater part of his wealth. His contribution is said to have amounted to about one thousand gold *dinārs*, equivalent to about twenty-five thousand rupees. Other Muslims also made contributions according to their capacity. The poor Muslims were also provided with riding animals, swords and lances. Enthusiasm prevailed. There was at Medina at the time a party of Muslims who had migrated from Yemen. They were very poor. Some of them went to the Prophet and offered their services for this expedition. They said, "O Prophet of God, take us with you. We want nothing beyond the means of going." The Quran makes a reference to these Muslims and their offers in the following words :

> Nor against those to whom, when they came to thee that thou shouldst mount them, thou didst say, 'I cannot find whereon I can mount you' ; they turned back, their eyes overflowing with tears, out of grief that they could not find what they might spend (9 : 92).

That is to say, they are not to blame who did not take part in the war because they were without means and who applied to the Prophet to provide them with the means of transport to the battlefield. The Prophet was unable to provide the transport, so they left disappointed feeling they were poor, and were unable to contribute to the war between Muslims and Syrians. Abū Mūsā was the leader of this group. When asked what they had asked for, he said, "We did not ask for camels or horses. We only said we did not have shoes and could not cover the long journey bare-footed. If we only had shoes, we would have gone on foot and taken part in the war alongside of our Muslim brethren." As this army was going to Syria and Muslims had not yet forgotten what they had suffered at Mūta, every Muslim was full of anxiety with regard to the personal safety of the Prophet. The women of Medina played their part. They were busy inducing their husbands and sons to join the war. One Companion who had gone out of Medina returned when the Prophet had already set out with the army. This Companion entered his house and was expecting his wife to greet him with the affection and emotion of a woman who meets her husband after a long time. He found his wife sitting in the courtyard and went forward to embrace and kiss her. But the wife raised her hands and pushed him back. The astonished husband looked at his wife and said, "Is this the treatment for one who comes home after a long time ?"

"Are you not ashamed ?" said the wife. "The Prophet of God should go on dangerous expeditions, and you should be making love to your wife ? Your first duty is to go to the battle-field. We shall see about the rest." It is said the Companion went out of the house at once, tightened the girths of his mount and galloped after the Prophet. At a distance of about three days' journey he overtook the Muslim army. The disbelievers and the hypocrites had probably thought that the Prophet acting upon rumours, invented and spread by them, would spring upon the Syrian armies without a thought. They forgot that the Prophet was concerned to set an example to generations of followers for all time to come. When the Prophet neared Syria, he stopped and sent his men in different directions to report on the state of affairs. The men returned and reported there were no Syrian concentrations anywhere. The Prophet decided to return, but stayed for a few days during which he signed agreements with some of the tribes on the border. There was no war and no fighting. The journey took the Prophet about two months and a half. When the hypocrites at Medina found that their scheme for inciting war between Muslims and Syrians had failed and that the Prophet was returning safe and sound, they began to fear that their intrigue had been exposed. They were afraid of the punishment which was now their due. But they did not halt their sinister plans. They equipped a party and posted it on the two sides of a narrow pass some distance from Medina. The pass was so narrow that only a single file could go through it. When the Prophet and the Muslim army approached the spot, he had a warning by revelation that the enemy was in ambush on both sides of the narrow pass. The Prophet ordered his Companions to reconnoitre. When they reached the spot they saw men in hiding with the obvious intent to attack. These men, however, fled as soon as they saw this reconnoitring party. The Prophet decided not to pursue them.

When the Prophet reached Medina, the hypocrites who had kept out of this battle began to make lame excuses. But the Prophet accepted them. At the same time he felt that the time had come when their hypocrisy should be exposed. He had a command from God that the mosque at Qubā, which the hypocrites had built in order to be able to hold their meetings in secret, should be demolished. The hypocrites were compelled to say their prayers with other Muslims. No other penalty was proposed.

Returning from Tabūk, the Prophet found that the people of Ṭā'if also had submitted. After this the other tribes of Arabia applied for admission to Islam. In a short time the whole of Arabia was under the flag of Islam.

THE LAST PILGRIMAGE

In the ninth year of the Hijra the Prophet went on a pilgrimage to Mecca. On the day of the Pilgrimage, he received the revelation containing the famed verse of the Quran which says :

> This day have I perfected your religion for you and completed My favour upon you and have chosen for you Islam as religion (5 : 4).

This verse said in effect that the Message which the Holy Prophet had brought from God and which by word and deed he had been expounding all these years, had been completed. Every part of this Message was a blessing. The Message now completed embodied the highest blessings which man could receive from God. The Message is epitomized in the name 'al-Islam', which means submission. Submission was to be the religion of Muslims, the religion of mankind. The Holy Prophet recited this verse in the valley of Muzdalifa, where the pilgrims had assembled. Returning from Muzdalifa, the

Prophet stopped at Minā. It was the eleventh day of the month of Dhu'l-Ḥijja. The Prophet stood before a large gathering of Muslims and delivered an address, famed in history as the farewell address of the Prophet. In the course of this address he said:

> O men, lend me an attentive ear. For I know not whether I will stand before you again in this valley and address you as I address you now. Your lives and your possessions have been made immune by God to attacks by one another until the Day of Judgement. God has appointed for every one a share in the inheritance. No 'will' shall now be admitted which is prejudicial to the interests of a rightful heir. A child born in any house will be regarded as the child of the father in that house. Whoever contests the parentage of this child will be liable to punishment under the Law of Islam. Anyone who attributes his birth to some one else's father, or falsely claims someone to be his master, God, His angels and the whole of mankind will curse him.
>
> O men, you have some rights against your wives, but your wives also have some rights against you. Your right against them is that they should live chaste lives, and not adopt ways which may bring disgrace to the husband in the sight of his people. If your wives do not live up to this, then you have the right to punish them. You can punish them after due inquiry has been made by a competent authority, and your right to punish has been established. Even so, punishment in such a case must not be very severe. But if your wives do no such thing, and their behaviour is not such as would bring disgrace to their husbands, then your duty is to provide for them food and garments and shelter, according to your own standard of living. Remember you must always treat your wives well. God has charged you with the duty of looking after them. Woman is weak and cannot protect her own rights. When you married, God appointed you the trustees of those rights. You brought your wives to your homes under the Law of God. You must not, therefore, insult the trust which God has placed in your hands.
>
> O men, you still have in your possession some prisoners of war. I advise you, therefore, to feed them and to clothe them in the same way and style as you feed and clothe yourselves. If they do anything wrong which you are unable to forgive, then pass them on to someone else. They are part of God's creation. To give them pain or trouble can never be right.
>
> O men, what I say to you, you must hear and remember. All Muslims are as brethren to one another. All of you are equal. All men, whatever nation or tribe they may belong to, and whatever station in life they may hold, are equal.

While he was saying this the Prophet raised his hands and joined the fingers of the one hand with the fingers of the other and then said :

> Even as the fingers of the two hands are equal, so are human beings equal to one another. No one has any right, any superiority to claim over another. You are as brothers.

Proceeding the Prophet said :

> Do you know what month this is ? What territory we are in ? What day of the year it is today ?

The Muslims said in reply, they knew it was the sacred month, the sacred land and the day of the Ḥajj.

Then the Prophet said :

> Even as this month is sacred, this land inviolate, and this day holy, so has God made the lives, property and honour of every man sacred. To take any man's life or his property, or attack his honour, is as unjust and wrong as to violate the sacredness of this day, this month, and this territory. What I command you today is not meant only for today. It is meant for all time. You are expected to remember it and to act upon it until you leave this world and go to the next to meet your Maker.

In conclusion, he said :

> What I have said to you, you should communicate to the ends of the earth. Maybe those who have not heard me may benefit by it more than those who have heard (Ṣiḥāḥ Sitta, Ṭabarī, Hishām and Khamīs).

The Prophet's address is an epitome of the entire teaching and spirit of Islam. It shows how deep was the Prophet's concern for the welfare of man and the peace of the world ; also how deep was his regard for the rights of women and other weak creatures. The Prophet knew his end was near. He had had hints from God about his death. Among the cares and anxieties to which he gave expression were his care and anxiety about the treatment women received at the hands of men. He took care that he should not pass away from this world to the next without assuring to women the status which was theirs by right. Since the birth of man, woman had been regarded as the slave and handmaid of man. This was the Prophet's one care. His other care was for prisoners of war.

They were wrongly looked on and treated as slaves and were subjected to cruelties and excesses of all kinds. The Prophet felt he should not leave this world without assuring to prisoners of war the rights which were theirs in the sight of God. Inequality between man and man also oppressed the Prophet. Occasionally differences were stressed to a degree which could not be endured. Some men were raised to the skies and others were degraded to the depths. The conditions which made for this inequality were conditions which made for antagonism and war between nation and nation and country and country. The Prophet thought of these difficulties also. Unless the spirit of inequality was killed and conditions which induced one people to usurp the rights of another and to attack their lives and their possessions—unless these conditions which become rampant at times of moral decay were removed, the peace and progress of the world could not be assured. He taught that human life and human possessions had the same sacredness which belonged to sacred days, sacred months and sacred places. No man ever showed such concern and such care for the welfare of women, the rights of the weak, and for peace between nations as did the Prophet of Islam. No man ever did as much as the Prophet to promote equality among mankind. No man pined as much as he for the good of man. No wonder, Islam has ever upheld the right of women to hold and to inherit property. European nations did not conceive of this right until about one thousand three hundred years after the advent of Islam. Every person who enters Islam becomes the equal of everyone else, no matter how low the society from which he comes. Freedom and equality are characteristic contributions of Islam to the culture of the world. The conceptions which other religions hold of freedom and equality are far behind those which Islam has preached and practised. In a Muslim mosque, a king, a religious leader and a common man have the same status ; there is no difference between them. In the places of worship of other religions and other nations these differences exist to this day, although those religions and nations claim to have done more than Islam for freedom and equality.

THE PROPHET GIVES HINTS OF HIS DEATH

On the way back, the Prophet again informed his Companions of his approaching death. He said, "O men I am but one like you. I may receive the Call any day and I may have to go. My Kind and Vigilant Master has informed me that a Prophet lives up to half the years of the Prophet before him.* I think I shall soon receive the Call and I shall depart. O my Companions, I shall have to answer God, and you will have to answer also. What will you then say?"

Upon this the Companions said, "We will say that you delivered well the Message of Islam and devoted all your life to the service of the Faith. You had the most perfect passion for the good of man. We will say : Allah, give him the best of rewards."

Then the Prophet asked, "Do you bear witness that God is One, that Muhammad is His Servant and Prophet, that Heaven and Hell are true, that death is certain, that there is life after death, that the Judgement Day must come, and that all the dead will one day be raised from their graves, restored to life and assembled ?"

"Yes," said the Companions. "We bear witness to all these truths."

Turning to God, the Prophet said, "Be Thou also a witness to this—that I have explained Islam to them."

After this Pilgrimage, the Prophet was very busy teaching and training his followers, trying to raise their moral standard and to reform and refine their conduct. His own death became his frequent theme and he prepared the Muslims for it.

One day, rising for an address to the Faithful, he said, "Today I have had the revelation :

> When the help of Allah comes, and victory, and thou seest men entering into the religion of Allah in troops, extol thou the glory of thy Lord, with His praise, and seek forgiveness of Him. Verily He is Oft-Returning with compassion" (110 : 2–4).

*This was not meant as a general law. It referred only to the Holy Prophet. A tradition puts down the age of Jesus at one hundred and twenty or so. As he had already attained to sixty-two or sixty-three, he thought his death must be near.—Ed.

That is to say, the time was coming when, with the help of God, multitudes were to join the Faith of Islam. It was then to be the duty of the Prophet—and of his followers—to praise God and pray to Him to remove all obstacles in the way of the establishment of the Faith.

The Prophet made use of a parable on this occasion : God said to a man, 'If it please you, you may return to Me, or you may work a little longer at reforming the world.' The man said that he preferred to return to his Lord.

Abū Bakr was among the audience. He had been listening to this last address of the Prophet, with fervour and anxiety —the fervour of a great believer and the anxiety of a friend and follower who could see in this address the portents of the Prophet's death. On hearing the parable Abū Bakr could contain himself no longer. He broke down. The other Companions, who had taken a surface view of what they had been listening to, were amazed when Abū Bakr burst into tears. What could be the matter with Abū Bakr ? they asked. The Prophet was relating the coming victories of Islam, yet he was weeping. 'Umar, particularly, felt annoyed at Abū Bakr. The Prophet was giving glad news, yet this old man was crying. But only the Prophet understood what was happening. Only Abū Bakr, he thought had understood him. Only he had perceived that the verses which promised victories also portended the Prophet's approaching death.

The Prophet went on to say, "Abū Bakr is very dear to me. If it were permissible to love anyone more than others, I would so have loved Abū Bakr. But that degree of love is only for God. O my people, all the doors which open to the mosque should be closed from today except the door of Abū Bakr."

There was no doubt that this last instruction implied a prophecy that after the Prophet Abū Bakr would be the First Khalīfa. To lead the Faithful in prayers he would have to come to the mosque five times a day and, for this, he would have to keep open the door of his house into the mosque. Years afterwards, when 'Umar was Khalīfa, he asked some of those present the meaning of the verse, "When the help of God and victory come." Evidently he remembered the circumstances in which the Prophet taught Muslims this and the verses which follow. He must have remembered also that then only Abū Bakr understood the meaning of these verses. 'Umar was trying to test Muslims for their knowledge of these verses. They had failed to understand them at the time of their revelation : did they know the meaning now ? Ibn 'Abbās, who must have been ten or eleven years of age at the time of their revelation and who was now seventeen or eighteen, volunteered to answer. He said, "Leader of the Faithful, these verses contained a prophecy about the death of the Holy Prophet. When a Prophet's work is done, he wishes no longer to live in the world. The verses spoke of the imminent victory of Islam. This victory had a sad side and that was the impending departure of the Prophet from this world." 'Umar complimented Ibn 'Abbās and said that when the verses were revealed only Abū Bakr understood their meaning.

LAST DAYS OF THE PROPHET

At last the day drew near which every human being must face. The Prophet's work was done. All that God had to reveal to him for the benefit of man had been revealed. The spirit of Muhammad had infused new life into his people. A new nation had arisen, a new outlook on life and new institutions ; in short, a new heaven and a new earth. The foundations of a new order had been laid. The land had been ploughed and watered and the seed scattered for a new harvest. And now the harvest itself had begun to show. It was not, however, for him to reap it. It was for him only to plough, to sow and to water. He came as a labourer, remained a labourer and was now due to depart as a labourer. He found his reward not in the things of this world but in the pleasure and the approval of his God, his Maker and Master. When the time came for reaping the harvest, he preferred to go to Him, leaving others to reap.

The Holy Prophet fell ill. For some days he continued to visit the mosque and lead the prayers. Then he became too weak to do this. The Companions were so used to his daily company that they could hardly believe he would die. But he had been telling them of his death again and again. One day, touching upon this very theme, he said, "If a man make a mistake, it is better he should make amends for it in this very world so that he should have no regrets in the next. Therefore I say, if I have done any wrong to any of you, it may be only unwittingly, let him come forward and ask me to make amends. If even unknowingly I have injured any one of you, let him come forward and take his revenge. I do not wish to be put to shame when I face my God in the next world. The Companions were moved. Tears sprang to their eyes. What pains had he not taken and what sufferings had he not endured for their sake ? He put up with hunger and thirst in order that others might have enough to eat and to drink. He mended his own clothes and cobbled his own shoes in order that others might dress well. And yet here he was, eager to right even fancied wrongs he might have done to others ; so much did he respect the rights of others.

All the Companions received the Prophet's offer in solemn silence. But one came forward and said, "O Prophet of God, I once received an injury from you. We were lining up for battle when you passed by our line and while passing you dug your elbow in my side. It was all done unwittingly, but you said we could avenge even unintentional wrongs. I want to avenge this wrong." The Companions, who had received the Prophet's offer in solemn silence, were full of wrath. They became enraged at the insolence and stupidity of this man who had failed completely to understand the spirit of the Prophet's offer and the solemnity of the occasion. But the Companion seemed adamant—determined to take the Prophet at his word.

The Prophet said, "You are welcome to take your revenge."

He turned his back to him and said, "Come and hit me as I hit you."

"But," explained this Companion, "when you hit me my side was bare, because I was wearing no shirt at the time."

"Raise my shirt," said the Prophet, "and let him hit my side with his elbow." They did so but, instead of hitting the bare side of the Prophet, this Companion bent forward with bedewed eyes and kissed the Prophet's bare body.

"What is this ?" asked the Prophet.

"Didn't you say that your days with us were numbered ? How many more occasions can we then have of touching you, in the flesh and expressing our love and affection for you? True, you did hit me with your elbow, but who could think of avenging it. I had this idea here and now. You offered to let us take revenge. I said to myself—let me kiss you under cover of revenge."

The Companions full of wrath until then began to wish the thought had occurred to them.

THE PROPHET PASSES AWAY

But the Prophet was ill and the ailment seemed to advance. Death seemed to draw nearer and nearer, and depression and gloom descended over the hearts of the Companions. The sun shone over Medina as brightly as ever, but to the Companions it seemed paler and paler. The day dawned as before but it seemed to bring darkness, not light. At last came the time when the soul of the Prophet was to depart from its physical frame and meet its Maker. His breathing became more and more difficult. The Prophet, who was spending his last days in 'Ā'isha's chamber, said to her, "Raise my head a little and bring it near to your side. I cannot breathe well." 'Ā'isha did so. She sat up and held his head. The death-pangs were visible. Greatly agitated, the Prophet looked now to this side and now to that. Again and again he said, "Woe to the Jews and the Christians. They encouraged the worship of the graves of their Prophets." This, we might say, was his dying message for his followers. While he lay on his death-bed, he seemed to say to his followers, "You will learn to hold me above all other Prophets, and more successful than any of them. But take care, do not turn my grave into an object of worship. Let my grave remain only a grave. Others may worship the graves of their Prophets and turn them into centres of pilgrimage, places where they may repair and perform austerities, make their offerings, and do their thanksgiving. Others may do this, but not you. You must remember your one and only objective—that is, the worship of the One and Only God."

After he had thus warned Muslims about their duty to guard the hard-won idea of One God and the distinction between God and Man, his eyelids began to droop. His eyes began to close. All he then said was, "To my Friend the Highest of the High—to my Friend the Highest of the High," meaning evidently that he was heading towards God. As he said this he gave up the ghost.

The news reached the mosque. There many Companions had assembled, having given up their private tasks. They were expecting to hear better news but instead heard of the Prophet's death. It came like a bolt from the blue. Abū Bakr was out. 'Umar was in the mosque, but he was utterly stupefied with grief. It angered him if he heard anyone say the Prophet was dead. He even drew his sword and threatened to kill those who should say the Prophet had died. There was much the Prophet had yet to do, so the Prophet could not die. True, his soul had departed from his body, but it had gone only to meet its Maker. Just as Moses had gone for a time to meet his Maker only to return, the Prophet must return to do what had been left undone. There were the hypocrites, for instance, with whom they had yet to deal. 'Umar walked about sword in hand almost as a mad man. As he walked he said: "Whosoever says the Prophet has died will himself die at 'Umar's hands." The Companions felt braced and they half-believed what 'Umar said. The Prophet could not die. There must have been a mistake. In the meantime some Companions went in search of Abū Bakr, found him and told him what had happened. Abū Bakr made straight for the mosque at Medina and speaking not a word to anyone, entered 'Ā'isha's room and asked her, "Has the Prophet died ?"

"Yes," replied 'Ā'isha. Then he went straight to where the Prophet's body was lying, uncovered the face, bent down and kissed the forehead. Tears laden with love and grief fell from his eyes and he said, "God is our witness. Death will not come upon you twice over."

It was a sentence full of meaning. It was Abū Bakr's reply to what 'Umar had been saying out of his mad grief. The Prophet had died once. That was his physical death—the death everyone must die. But he was not to have a second death. There was to be no spiritual death—no death to the beliefs which he had established in his followers and for the establishment of which he had taken such pains. One of those beliefs—one of the more important beliefs—he had taught was that even Prophets were human and even they must die. Muslims were not going to forget this so soon after the Prophet's own death. Having said this great sentence over the dead body of the Prophet, Abū Bakr came out and, piercing through the lines of the Faithful, advanced silently to the pulpit. As he stood, 'Umar stood by him, his sword drawn as before, determined that if Abū Bakr said the Prophet had died Abū Bakr must lose his head. As Abū Bakr started to speak, 'Umar pulled at his shirt, wanting to stop him from speaking but Abū Bakr snatched back his shirt and refused to stop.

He then recited the verse of the Quran :

> And Muhammad is only a Messenger. Verily, all Messengers have passed away before him. If then he die or be slain, will you turn back on your heels ? (3 : 145).

That is to say, Muhammad was a man with a Message from God. There had been other men with Messages from God, and all of them had died. If Muhammad should die, would they turn back upon everything which they had been taught and which they had learnt ? This verse was revealed at the time of Uḥud. Rumour had then gone round that the Prophet had been killed by the enemy. Many Muslims lost heart and withdrew from the battle. The verse came from heaven to brace them. It had the same effect on this occasion. Having recited the verse, Abū Bakr added to it a word of his own. He said, "Those amongst you who worship God, let them know that God is still alive, and will ever remain alive. But those amongst you who worshipped Muhammad, let them know it from me that Muhammad is dead." The Companions recovered their balance on hearing this timely speech. 'Umar himself was changed when he heard Abū Bakr recite the verse quoted above. He began to return to his senses, and to recover his lost judgement. By the time Abū Bakr had finished the recitation of the verse 'Umar's spiritual eye was fully opened. He understood that the Prophet had really died. But no sooner had he realized it, than his legs began to tremble and give way. He fell down exhausted. The man who wanted to terrorize Abū Bakr with his bare sword had been converted by Abū Bakr's speech. The Companions felt the verse had been revealed for the first time on that day, so strong and so new was its appeal. In a paroxysm of grief, they forgot that the verse was in the Quran.

Many expressed the grief which overtook Muslims on the death of the Prophet, but the pithy and profound expression which Ḥassān, the poet of early Islam, gave to it in his couplet remains to this day the best and the most enduring. He said :

'Thou wast the pupil of my eye. Now that thou hast died my eye hath become blind. I care not who dies now. For I feared only thy death.'

This couplet voiced the feeling of every Muslim. For months in the streets of Medina men, women and children went about reciting this couplet of Ḥassān bin Thābit.

THE PROPHET'S PERSONALITY AND CHARACTER

HAVING briefly described the outstanding events in the life of the Holy Prophet we would now attempt a short sketch of his character. In this connection we have available the collective testimony of his own people which they bore to his character before he claimed to be a Prophet. At that stage he was known among his people as "The Trusty" and "The True" (Hishām). There are living at all times large numbers of people against whom no charge of dishonesty is preferred. There are also large numbers who are never exposed to a severe trial or temptation and in the ordinary affairs and concerns of life they behave with honesty and integrity, yet they are not regarded as worthy of any special distinction on that account. Special distinctions are conferred only when the life of a person illustrates in a conspicuous degree some high moral quality. Every soldier that goes into battle puts his life in jeopardy but not every such British soldier has been regarded as worthy of the award of the Victoria Cross, nor every such German soldier of the Iron Cross. There are hundreds of thousands of people in France who occupy themselves with intellectual pursuits but not every one of them is decorated with the Legion of Honour. The mere fact, therefore, that a man is trustworthy and true does not indicate that he possesses eminence in these respects, but when a whole people combines to confer upon an individual the titles of "The Trusty" and "The True", that is evidence of the possession of exceptional qualities. Had it been the practice of the people of Mecca to confer such a distinction upon some individual in each generation, even then the recipient would have been looked upon as occupying a high position. But the history of Mecca and of Arabia furnishes no indication that it was customary for the Arabs to confer these or similar titles upon eminent individuals in each generation. On the contrary, through centuries of Arab history we find that it was only in the case of the Holy Prophet of Islam that his people conferred the titles of "The Trusty" and "The True". This is proof of the fact that the Holy Prophet possessed these qualities in so eminent a degree that within the knowledge and the memory of his people no other individual could be regarded as his equal in these respects. The Arabs were well known for their keenness of mind and what they chose to regard as rare must in truth have been rare and unique.

When the Holy Prophet was summoned by God to assume the burden and responsibilities of prophethood, his wife, Khadīja, testified to his high moral qualities—an incident which has been related in the biographical portion of this General Introduction. We shall now proceed to illustrate some of his high moral qualities so that the reader may be able to appreciate even those aspects of his character which are not generally well known.

THE PROPHET'S PURITY OF MIND AND CLEANLINESS OF BODY

It is related of the Holy Prophet that his speech was always pure and that he was (unlike most of his contemporaries) not given to the use of oaths (Tirmidhī). This was something exceptional for an Arab. We do not imply that the Arabs at the time of the Holy Prophet habitually indulged in foul language, but there is no doubt that they were in the habit of punctuating their speech with a generous measure of oaths, a habit that persists among them even to this day. The Holy Prophet, however, held the name of God in such reverence that he never uttered it without full justification.

He was very particular, even punctilious, with regard to physical cleanliness. He used to brush his teeth several times a day and was so keen on the practice that he used to say that were he not afraid that the ordinance might prove onerous, he would make it obligatory upon every Muslim to brush his teeth before every one of the five daily prayers. He always washed his hands before and after each meal and, after eating anything that had been cooked, he always rinsed his mouth and considered it desirable that every person who had eaten anything cooked should rinse his mouth before joining in any of the prayers (Bukhārī).

In the polity of Islam a mosque is the only place of gathering prescribed for the Muslims. The Holy Prophet, therefore, laid particular stress upon the cleanliness of mosques, especially on occasions when people were expected to collect in them. He had directed that on such occasions incense should be burnt in the mosques to purify the air (Abū Dāwūd). He also gave directions that nobody should go to a mosque on the occasion of a congregation or gathering after eating anything that was likely to exhale an offensive odour (Bukhārī).

He insisted upon streets being kept clean and clear of twigs, stones, and all articles or matter which was likely either to obstruct or to prove offensive. Whenever he himself found any such matter or article lying in a street he would remove it, and he used to say that a person who helps to keep streets and roads clean and clear, earns spiritual merit in the sight of God. He is also reported to have enjoined that public thoroughfares should not be so used as to cause obstruction nor should any unclean or undesirable matter or article be thrown on to a public street, nor should a street be defiled in any other way, as all such acts are displeasing to God. He was very keen that all supply of water conserved for human use should be kept clean and pure. For instance, he prohibited anything being thrown into standing water which might befoul it and any reservoir of water being used in a manner which would render it impure (Bukhārī and Muslim, *Kitāb al-Birr wa'l-Ṣila*).

THE PROPHET'S SIMPLE LIFE

The Prophet was extremely simple in the matter of food and drink. He never expressed displeasure with ill-prepared or ill-cooked food. If he could eat such food he would do so to save the person who had prepared it from disappointment. If, however, a dish was uneatable, he merely refrained from partaking of it and never expressed his disapproval of it. When he sat down to a meal he paid attention to the food placed before him and used to say that he did not like an attitude of indifference towards food as if the person eating was above paying attention to mere matters of food and drink. When any eatable was presented to him he always shared it with those present. On one occasion somebody presented him with some dates. He looked round and after making an estimate of the number of people present divided the dates equally among them, each of them receiving seven. Abū Huraira relates that the Holy Prophet never ate his fill even of barley bread (Bukhārī).

On one occasion while he was passing along a road he noticed some people gathered round a roast kid ready to enjoy the feast. When they saw the Holy Prophet they invited him to join them, but he declined. This was not due to his not having a liking for roast meat but to the fact that he did not approve of people indulging in a feast in the open where they could be observed by poor people who had themselves not enough to eat. It is related of him that on other occasions he did partake of roast meat. 'Ā'isha has related that the Holy Prophet did not, till the day of his death, on any occasion, eat his fill on three consecutive days. He was very particular that a person should not go to a meal in another person's house uninvited. On one occasion somebody invited him to a meal and requested that he might bring four other persons with him. When he arrived at the house of his host he found that a sixth person had also joined his party. The host came to the door to receive him and his party and the Holy Prophet drew his attention to the fact that there were now six of them and that it was for the host to decide whether he would permit the sixth person to join them in the meal or whether the latter should depart. The host, of course, readily invited the sixth person also (Bukhārī, *Kitāb al-Aṭ'ima*).

Whenever the Holy Prophet sat down to a meal he always began to eat by invoking the name and blessings of Allah, and as soon as he concluded he rendered thanks in these words : "All praise is due to Allah, Who has given us to eat : Praise, abundant and sincere and ever-increasing : Praise, which does not leave an impression upon one's mind that one has rendered enough praise but which creates in one's mind the feeling that enough has not been said and the praise which ought never to be terminated and which makes one think that every divine act is worthy of praise and should be praised. Oh Allah ! do Thou fill our hearts with these sentiments." Sometimes he used these words : "All praise is due to God Who has satisfied our hunger and thirst. May our hearts ever yearn after His praise and never be ungrateful to Him." He always admonished his Companions to stop before they had eaten their fill and used to say that one man's food should always suffice for two. Whenever any special food was prepared in his house he used to suggest that a portion of it should be sent as a present to his neighbours ; and presents of food and other articles used constantly to be sent from his house to his neighbours' houses (Muslim and Bukhārī, *Kitāb al-Adab*).

He always tried to ascertain from the faces of those who were in his company whether any of them was in need of sustenance. Abū Huraira relates the following incident : On one occasion he had been without food for over three days. He stood at the entrance to the mosque and observed Abū Bakr passing near. He asked Abū Bakr the meaning of a verse of the Quran which enjoins the feeding of the poor. Abū Bakr explained its meaning and passed on. Abū Huraira when relating this incident used to say with indignation that he too understood the Quran as well as Abū Bakr did. His object in asking the latter to explain the meaning of the verse had been that Abū Bakr might guess that he was hungry and might arrange to get food for him. Shortly after, 'Umar passed by and Abū Huraira asked him also to explain the meaning of the verse. 'Umar also explained its meaning and passed on. Abū Huraira, like all Companions of the Holy Prophet, was loath to make a direct request and when he perceived that his indirect attempts to draw attention to his condition had failed, he began to feel very faint. Thereupon he heard his name being called in a very soft and tender voice. Looking to the side from which the voice came he saw that the Holy Prophet was looking out from the window of his house and was smiling. He inquired of Abū Huraira : "Are you hungry ?" to which Abū Huraira replied : "Verily, O Messenger of Allah ! I am hungry." The Holy Prophet said : "There is no food in our house either, but somebody has just sent us a cup of milk. Go to the mosque and see whether there are any other persons there who may be hungry like you." Abū Huraira goes on to relate : "I thought to myself, I am hungry enough to consume the whole of the milk in the cup, yet the Prophet has asked me to invite any other persons that may be in similar case, which means that I shall get very little of the milk. But I had to carry out the Prophet's orders, so I went into the mosque and found six persons sitting there whom I brought with me to the Prophet's door. He gave the cup of milk into the hands of one of them and asked him to drink. When he had finished and put away the cup from his mouth the Prophet insisted upon his drinking a second time and a third time till he had had his fill. In the same way he insisted upon every one of the six drinking his fill of the milk. Each time he asked anyone to drink I was afraid that little would be left for me. After all the six had drunk of the milk the Prophet gave the cup to me and I saw that there was still plenty of milk in it. In my case also he insisted that I should drink my fill and made me drink a second and a third time and at the end he drank what was left in the cup himself and rendered thanks to God and shut the door" (Bukhārī, *Kitāb al-Riqāq*). The Holy Prophet's object in offering the milk to Abū Huraira last of all may have been to indicate to him that he should have continued to endure the pangs of hunger, trusting in God, and should not have drawn attention to his condition even indirectly.

He always ate and drank with his right hand and always stopped three times to take breath in the middle of a drink. One reason for this may be that if a person who is thirsty drinks water at one stretch he is apt to drink too much and thus upset his digestion. In the matter of eating the rule that he followed was that he partook of all things that are pure and permissible but not in a manner which would savour of indulgence or would deprive other people of their due share. As has been stated, his normal food was always very simple but if anybody presented him with something specially prepared he did not decline it. He did not, however, hanker after good food, though he had a particular liking for honey and for dates. As regards dates, he used to say that there was a special relationship between a Muslim and the date tree whose leaves and bark and fruit, both ripe and unripe, and even the stones of whose fruit could all be put to some use or the other and no part of which was without its proper use. The same was the case with a true Muslim. No act of his was without its beneficence and all that he did promoted the welfare of mankind (Bukhārī and Muslim).

The Holy Prophet preferred simplicity in dress. His own dress normally consisted of a shirt and an *izār** or a shirt and a pair of trousers. He always wore his *izār* or his trousers so that the garment covered his body up to a point above his ankles. He did not approve of the knee or any portion of the body above the knee being exposed without extreme necessity. He did not approve of the use, whether as part of dress or in the way of curtains, etc., of cloth which had figures embroidered or painted on it, especially if the figures were large and might be interpreted as representing gods or goddesses or other objects of worship. On one occasion he found a curtain hanging in his house bearing large figures and he directed it to be removed. He, however, saw no harm in the use of cloth bearing small figures which could not be so interpreted. He never wore silk himself and did not consider it permissible for Muslim men to wear it. For the purpose of authenticating the letters that he wrote to certain sovereigns inviting them to accept Islam he caused to be prepared a signet-ring, but directed that it should be made of silver and not of gold, for he said that the wearing of gold had been prohibited to Muslim men (Bukhārī and Muslim). Muslim women are permitted to wear silk and gold but in their case also the Holy Prophet's direction was that excess should be avoided. On one occasion he called for subscriptions for the relief of the poor and a lady took off one of her bracelets and placed it before him as her contribution. Addressing her, he said : "Does not your other hand deserve to be saved from the Fire ?" The lady thereupon removed her bracelet from the other hand also and offered it for the purpose that he had in view. None of his wives possessed ornaments of any considerable value and other Muslim women also very seldom possessed any ornaments. In accordance with the teachings of the Quran he deprecated the hoarding of money or bullion, as he held that this was harmful to the interests of the poorer sections of the community and resulted in upsetting the economy of a community and was thus a sin.

* A piece of cloth wrapped round the waist and hanging to the ankles—Ed.

'Umar suggested to the Holy Prophet on one occasion that as he had to receive Embassies from great monarchs, he should have a rich cloak prepared for himself which he could wear on such ceremonial occasions. The Prophet did not approve of the suggestion and said : "It would not be pleasing to God for me to adopt ways like this. I shall meet everybody in the clothes that I normally wear." On one occasion silk garments were presented to him and of these he sent one to 'Umar. Upon this 'Umar said, "How can I wear it when you have yourself disapproved of wearing silk garments." The Holy Prophet observed : "Every present is not meant for personal use." His meaning was that since the garment was of silk 'Umar should have presented it to his wife or to his daughter or should have put it to some other use (Bukhārī, *Kitāb al-Libās*).

The Prophet's bed was also very simple. He never used a bedstead or a couch but always slept on the ground, the bedding consisting of a piece of leather or of a piece of camelhair cloth. 'Ā'isha relates : "Our bedding was so small that when the Holy Prophet used to get up at night for prayers I used to lie on one side of the bedding and stretched out my legs while he was in the standing posture and folded them back when he had to prostrate himself (Muslim, Tirmidhī and Bukhārī, *Kitāb al-At'ima*).

He adopted the same simplicity with regard to his residential arrangements. His house consisted normally of one room and a small courtyard. A rope used to be strung half way across the room so that when he had visitors a piece of cloth could be hung from the rope to convert a part of the room into an audience chamber separated from the portion occupied by his wife. His life was so simple that 'Ā'isha related that during the life-time of the Prophet they often had to sustain themselves on dates and water and that on the day of his death there was no food in the house except a few dates (Bukhārī).

RELATIONSHIP WITH GOD

Every aspect of the Holy Prophet's life appears to have been governed and coloured by his love for and devotion to God.

In spite of the very heavy responsibilities that had been laid upon his shoulders the greater portion of his time during the day as well as during the night was spent in the worship and praise of God. He would leave his bed at midnight and devote himself to the worship of God till it was time to go to the mosque for the morning prayers. He sometimes stood so long in prayer during the latter part of the night that his feet would get swollen, and those who saw him in that condition were always much affected. On one occasion 'Ā'isha said to him: "God has honoured you with His love and nearness. Why then do you subject yourself to so much discomfort and inconvenience?" He replied: "If God has by His Grace and Mercy conferred His love and nearness upon me, is it not my duty in return to be always rendering thanks to Him? Gratitude should increase in proportion to the favours received" (Bukhārī, *Kitāb al-Kusūf*).

He never entered upon any undertaking without divine command or permission. It has already been related in the biographical portion that, in spite of the very severe persecution to which he was subjected by the people of Mecca, he did not leave the town till he received the divine command to do so. When persecution became very severe and he gave permission to his Companions to migrate to Abyssinia, some of them expressed a desire that he should accompany them. He declined to do so on the ground that he had not received divine permission to that effect. Thus, during a period of hardships and persecution when people usually like to keep their friends and relations close to themselves, he directed his Companions to seek refuge in Abyssinia and himself stayed behind in Mecca, for God had not yet directed him to leave it.

Whenever he heard the word of God being recited, he was overcome by emotion and tears would start from his eyes, especially if he was listening to verses which emphasized his own responsibilities. 'Abdullah bin Mas'ūd relates that he was on one occasion asked by the Holy Prophet to recite some verses of the Quran to him. He said: "O Messenger of Allah! The Quran has been revealed to you (*i.e.*, you know it best of all). How then shall I recite it to you?" But the Holy Prophet said: "I love to hear it recited by other people also."

Thereupon 'Abdullah bin Mas'ūd began to recite from Sūra Al-Nisā. When he recited the verse : "And how will it fare with them when We shall bring a witness from every people, and shall bring thee as a witness against them" (4 : 42), the Holy Prophet exclaimed : 'Enough ! Enough !' 'Abdullah bin Mas'ūd looked up and saw that tears were streaming from the Holy Prophet's eyes (Bukhārī, *Kitāb Faḍā'il al-Qur'ān*).

He was so particular about joining the congregational prayers that, even during severe illness when it is permissible not only to say one's prayers in one's room but even to say them lying in bed, he would go to the mosque to lead the prayers himself. On one occasion when he was unable to proceed to the mosque he directed that Abū Bakr should lead the prayers. Presently however, he felt some improvement in his condition and asked to be supported into the mosque. He rested his weight on the shoulders of two men but was in so feeble a condition that, according to 'Ā'isha, his feet trailed along the ground (Bukhārī).

It is a common practice to give expression to one's pleasure or to draw attention to any particular matter by the clapping of hands and the Arabs used to follow the same practice. The Holy Prophet, however, so loved the remembrance of God that for these purposes also he substituted the praise and remembrance of God in place of the clapping of hands. On one occasion while he was occupied with some important matter, the time of the next service drew near and he directed that Abū Bakr should lead the prayers. Shortly thereafter he was able to conclude the business upon which he was engaged and proceeded at once to the mosque. Abū Bakr was leading the prayers but when the congregation perceived that the Holy Prophet had arrived, they began to clap their hands for the purpose both of giving expression to their joy at his arrival and also to draw Abū Bakr's attention to the fact that the Prophet himself had arrived. Thereupon Abū Bakr stepped back and made room for the Holy Prophet to lead the prayers. When the prayers were over, the Prophet addressed Abū Bakr and said : "Why did you step back after I had directed you to lead the prayers ?" Abū Bakr replied : "O Messenger of Allah ! How would it befit the son of Abū Quḥāfa to lead the prayers in the presence of the Messenger of Allah ?" Then addressing the congregation the Prophet said: "Why did you clap your hands? It is not seemly that while you are engaged in the remembrance of God you should clap your hands. If it should so happen that during the course of prayers attention has to be drawn to some matter, instead of clapping your hands you should utter the name of God aloud. This would draw attention to whatever may have to be taken note of" (Bukhārī).

The Prophet did not approve of prayers or worship being carried on as a penance or imposition. On one occasion he came home and observed a rope dangling between two pillars. He inquired what its purpose was, and was informed that his wife Zainab was in the habit of supporting herself by means of the rope when she became tired in the course of her prayers. He directed the rope to be removed and said that prayers should be continued only so long as one felt easy and cheerful and that if a person became tired he should sit down. Prayers were not an imposition, and if carried on after the body became fatigued they failed of their purpose (Bukhārī, *Kitāb al-Kusūf*).

He abhorred every action and practice which savoured even remotely of idolatry. When his end was approaching and he was in the grip of the death agony he turned from side to side exclaiming: "May the curse of God descend upon those Jews and Christians who have converted the graves of their Prophets into places of worship" (Bukhārī). He had in mind those Jews and Christians who prostrated themselves at the graves of their Prophets and saints and addressed their prayers to them, and he meant that if Muslims fell into similar practices they would not be deserving of his prayers but would, on the contrary, cut themselves asunder from him.

His extreme sense of jealousy for the honour of God has already been referred to in the biographical portion. The people of Mecca sought to place all sorts of temptations in his way to persuade him to give up his opposition to idol-worship (Ṭabarī). His uncle Abū Ṭālib also tried to dissuade him and expressed his fear that if he persisted in his denunciation of idol-worship, Abū Ṭālib would have to choose between ceasing to give him his protection and the bitter opposition of his people. The only reply that the Prophet made to his uncle on that occasion was: "If these people were to place the sun on my right hand and the moon on my left, I would not desist from proclaiming and preaching the Unity of God" (Zurqānī). Again, during the Battle of Uḥud when a remnant of wounded Muslims were grouped round him at the foot of a hill and their enemies were giving vent to their feeling of jubilation at having broken the Muslim ranks in shouts of victory and their leader Abū Sufyān called out: "May Hubal (one of the idols worshipped by the Meccans) be exalted! May Hubal be exalted!" the Holy Prophet, in spite of realizing that his own safety and that of the small band of Muslims who were gathered round him lay in keeping silent could restrain himself no longer and directed his Companions to shout in reply, "To Allah alone belongs victory and glory! To Allah alone belongs victory and glory!" (Bukhārī).

It was a common misconception among the followers of different religions before the advent of Islam that heavenly and terrestrial manifestations took place to mark occasions of joy and sorrow for Prophets, saints and other great men and that even the movements of the heavenly bodies could be controlled by them. For instance, it is related of some of them that they caused the sun to become stationary in its course or stopped the progress of the moon or caused running water to become still. Islam taught that such notions were baseless and that references to phenomena of this kind in religious Scriptures were only by way of metaphor which, instead of being interpreted in accordance with its correct significance, had given rise to superstitions. Nevertheless, some among Muslims were prone to attribute these phenomena to events in the lives of the great Prophets. In the closing years of the Holy Prophet's life his son Ibrāhīm died at the age of two and a half years. An eclipse of the sun occurred on the same day. Some Muslims in Medina gave currency to the idea that the sun had been darkened on the occasion of the death of the Prophet's son as a mark of divine condolence. When this was mentioned to the Holy Prophet he expressed great displeasure and severely condemned the notion. He explained that the sun and the moon and other heavenly bodies were all governed by divine laws and that their movements and the phenomena connected with them had no relation to the life or death of any person (Bukhārī).

Arabia is a very dry country and rain is always welcome and is eagerly waited for. The Arabs used to imagine that the coming of rain was controlled by the movements of stars. Whenever anybody gave expression to that idea, the Holy Prophet used to be very upset and admonished his people not to attribute favours bestowed upon them by Providence to other sources. He explained that rain and other natural phenomena were all governed by divine laws and that they were not controlled by the pleasure or displeasure of any god or goddess or of any other power (Muslim, *Kitāb al-Īmān*).

He had perfect trust in God which no combination of adverse circumstances could shake. On one occasion an enemy of his, finding him asleep and unguarded, stood over his head with drawn sword and threatened to despatch him at once. Before doing so he asked : "Who can rescue you from this predicament ?" The Holy Prophet calmly replied : "Allah." He uttered this word with such perfect assurance that even the heart of his disbelieving enemy was forced to acknowledge the loftiness of his faith and trust in God. The sword fell from his hand, and he, who a moment before was bent upon his destruction, stood before him like a convicted criminal awaiting sentence (Muslim, *Kitāb al'Faḍā'il* and Bukhārī, *Kitāb al-Jihād*).

At the other end of the scale was his sense of perfect humility *vis-à-vis* the Divine. Abū Huraira relates : "One day I heard the Holy Prophet say that no man would attain salvation through his own good deeds. Thereupon I said : 'O Messenger of Allah ! Surely you will enter Paradise through your own good actions,' to which he replied : 'No, I too cannot enter Paradise through my own actions save only that God's Grace and Mercy should envelop me' " (Bukhārī, *Kitāb al-Riqāq*).

He always exhorted people to choose and follow the right path and to be diligent in their search for means whereby they could attain nearness to God. He taught that no man should desire death for himself, for if he is good he will, by living longer, be able to achieve greater good ; and if he is evil, he may, if given time, be able to repent of his evil ways and start on a good way. His love for, and devotion to, God found expression in many ways. For instance, whenever after a dry season the first rain-drops began to descend, he would put out his tongue to catch a rain-drop and would exclaim : "Here is the latest favour from my Lord." He was constantly occupied in praying for God's forgiveness and beneficence, more particularly when he was sitting among people so that those who were in his company or were connected with him and Muslims generally should save themselves from divine wrath and should become deserving of divine forgiveness. The consciousness that he was always in the presence of God never deserted him. When he used to lie down to sleep, he would say : "O Allah ! let me die (go to sleep) with Thy name on my lips and with Thy name on my lips let me rise." When he woke up, he would say : "All praise is due to God who has brought me to life after death (sleep) and one day we shall all be gathered unto Him" (Bukhārī).

He constantly yearned for nearness to God and one of his oft-repeated prayers was "O Allah ! Do Thou fill my heart with Thy light and fill my eyes with Thy light and fill my ears with Thy light and put Thy light on my right and put Thy light on my left and put Thy light above me and put Thy light below me and put Thy light in front of me and put Thy light behind me and do Thou, O Allah, convert the whole of me into light" (Bukhārī).

Ibn 'Abbās relates : "Shortly before the Holy Prophet's death, Musailima (the false prophet) came to Medina and proclaimed that if Muhammad would appoint him his successor he would be prepared to accept him. Musailima was accompanied by a very large retinue and the tribe with which he was connected was the largest among the tribes of Arabia. When the Holy Prophet was informed of his advent he went to meet him, accompanied by Thābit bin Qais bin Shams. He had in his hand a dried palm twig. When he arrived at Musailima's camp he went and stood in front of him. In the meantime some more of his Companions had come up and ranged themselves round him. Addressing Musailima he said, "It has been conveyed to me that you have said that if I were to appoint you my successor you would be ready to follow me, but I am not willing to bestow even this dried palm twig upon you contrary to God's commands. Your end will be as God has appointed. If you turn your back on me God will bring you to naught. I perceive very clearly that God will deal out to you what He has revealed to me." He then added: "I will now retire. If you have anything further to say, you may talk to Thābit bin Qais bin Shams, who will act as my representative." He then returned. Abū Huraira was also with him. Somebody inquired of the Prophet what he meant by saying that God would deal out to Musailima what had been revealed to him. The Holy Prophet replied: "I saw in a dream two bracelets round my wrists which I disliked. While still in my dream I was directed by God to blow upon the bracelets. When I blew upon them, both of them disappeared. I interpreted this to mean that two false claimants (to prophethood) would appear after me" (Bukhārī, *Kitāb al-Maghāzī*). This incident occurred towards the end of the Holy Prophet's life. The last and the largest of the Arab tribes who had not yet accepted him was prepared to make its submission and the only condition put forward by it was that the Holy Prophet should appoint its chief as his successor. Had the Prophet been actuated even remotely by any personal motives, nothing stood in the way of his securing the unity of the whole of Arabia by promising his succession to the chief of the largest tribe of Arabia. The Holy Prophet had no son of his own and no dynastic ambition could have stood in the way of such an arrangement, but he never regarded even the smallest thing as belonging to him and as being at his absolute disposal. He could, therefore, not deal with the leadership of Muslims as if it were in his gift. He regarded it as a sacred divine trust and believed that God would bestow it upon whomsoever He thought fit. He therefore rejected Musailima's offer with contempt, and told him that, let alone the leadership of Muslims, he was not prepared to bestow upon him even a dry palm twig.

Whenever he referred to or discoursed about God, it appeared to onlookers as if his whole being was in the grip of a passion of love for and devotion to God.

He always insisted upon simplicity in divine worship. The mosque, that he built in Medina and in which he always led prayers, had only a mud floor which was innocent of all covering or matting and the roof, which was made of dried palm branches and leaves, leaked whenever it rained. On such occasions the Holy Prophet and members of the congregation would be drenched with rain and mud but he would continue with the prayers till the end and on no occasion did he give any indication that he would postpone the service or remove to more weather-tight shelter (Bukhārī, *Kitāb al-Ṣaum*).

He was also watchful regarding his Companions. 'Abdullah bin 'Umar was a man of extreme piety and purity of life. Concerning him the Holy Prophet once said : " 'Abdullah bin 'Umar would be an even better man if he were to be more regular with regard to his *Tahajjud* prayers."* When this was communicated to 'Abdullah bin 'Umar he never thereafter missed these prayers. It is recorded that the Holy Prophet, happening to be in the house of his daughter Fāṭima, inquired of her and his son-in-law, 'Alī, whether they were regular with regard to their *Tahajjud* prayers. 'Alī replied : "O Messenger of Allah ! We try to get up for *Tahajjud* prayers but on occasion when God so wills that we are unable to wake up in time we miss them." He went back and, on the way, repeated several times a verse of the Quran which means that a man is often reluctant to admit his fault and tries to cover it up with excuses (Bukhārī, *Kitāb al-Kusuf*). The Prophet meant that 'Alī should not have attributed his default to God by saying that when God willed that they should not wake up they were unable to wake up in time, but should have admitted his own weakness in the matter.

DISAPPROVAL OF PENANCE

The Holy Prophet, however, strongly disapproved of formality in the matter of worship and condemned the imposition of any penance upon oneself as a form of worship. He taught that true worship consists in the beneficent use of the faculties with which God has endowed man. God having bestowed eyes upon man to see with, it would not be worship but imper-

* This a prayer which is said in the latter part of the night and is not one of the daily prayers.—Ed.

tinence to keep them shut or to have them removed. It is not the proper use of the faculty of sight which can be regarded as sinful, it is the improper use of the faculty that would be a sin. It would be ingratitude on the part of a man to have himself deprived of the faculty of hearing, though it would be sinful of him to use that faculty for the purpose of listening to slander and backbiting. Abstention from food (except on occasions when it is prescribed or is otherwise desirable) may amount to suicide and thus constitute an unforgivable sin, though it would also be sinful on the part of a man to devote himself entirely to food and drink or to indulge in the eating or drinking of prohibited or undesirable articles. This is a golden principle which was taught and emphasized by the Holy Prophet of Islam and which had not been inculcated by any previous Prophet.

The correct use of natural faculties constitutes high moral qualities ; the frustration or stultification of those qualities is folly. It is their improper use that is evil or sinful. Their proper use is true virtue. This is the essence of the moral teachings inculcated by the Holy Prophet of Islam. And this, in brief, was also a picture of his own life and actions. 'Ā'isha relates : "Whenever the Holy Prophet had a choice of two courses of action he always chose the easier of the two, provided it was free from all suspicion of error or sin. Where a course of action was open to such suspicion, the Holy Prophet of all men gave it the widest berth" (Muslim, *Kitāb al-Faḍā'il*). This is indeed the highest and the most admirable course open to man. Many men voluntarily court pain and privations, not for the purpose of winning God's pleasure, for God's pleasure is not to be won by inflicting purposeless pain and privations upon oneself, but with the object of deceiving mankind. Such people possess little inherent virtue and wish to cover up their faults and to acquire merit in the eyes of others by assuming false virtues. The object of the Holy Prophet of Islam, however, was to attain to real virtue and to win the pleasure of God. He was, therefore, completely free from pretence and make-believe. That the world should regard him as bad or should appraise him as good was a matter of complete indifference to him. All that mattered to him was how he found himself and how God would judge him. If in addition to the testimony of his conscience and the approval of God he also won the true testimony of mankind he was grateful, but if men looked upon him with jaundiced eyes he was sorry for them and attached no value to their opinion.

ATTITUDE TOWARDS HIS WIVES

He was extremely kind and fair towards his wives. If on occasion any one of them failed to comport herself with due deference towards him he merely smiled and passed the matter over. He said to 'Ā'isha one day : " 'Ā'isha, whenever you are upset with me I always get to know it." 'Ā'isha enquired : "How is that ?" He said : "I have noticed that when you are pleased with me and in the course of conversation you have to refer to God, you refer to Him as the Lord of Muhammad. But if you are not pleased with me, you refer to Him as the Lord of Ibrāhīm." At this 'Ā'isha laughed and said he was right (Bukhārī, *Kitāb al-Nikāḥ*). Khadīja was his first wife and had made great sacrifices in his cause. She was much older than the Prophet. After her death he married younger women but never permitted the memory of Khadīja to become dim. Whenever any of Khadīja's friends visited him he would stand up to receive her (Muslim). If he chanced to see any article that had belonged to or had been connected with Khadīja, he was always overcome by emotion. Among the prisoners taken by the Muslims in the Battle of Badr was a son-in-law of the Prophet. He possessed nothing which he could offer as ransom. His wife Zainab (the Prophet's daughter) sent to Medina a necklace which had belonged to her mother (Khadīja) and offered it as ransom for her husband. When the Prophet saw the necklace he recognized it and was much affected. He said to his Companions : "I have no authority to give any direction in this matter, but I know that this necklace is cherished by Zainab as a last memento of her deceased mother and, provided it commends itself to you, I would suggest that she should not be deprived of it and it may be returned to her." They intimated that nothing would give them greater pleasure and readily adopted his suggestion (Ḥalbiyya, Vol. 2). He often praised Khadīja to his other wives and stressed her virtues and the sacrifices that she had made in the cause of Islam. On one such occasion 'Ā'isha was piqued and said : "O Messenger of Allah, why go on talking of the old lady ? God has bestowed better, younger and more attractive wives upon you." The Holy Prophet was overcome by emotion at hearing this and protested : "O no, 'Ā'isha ! You have no idea how good Khadīja was to me" (Bukhārī).

HIGH MORAL QUALITIES

He was always very patient in adversity. He was never discouraged by adverse circumstances nor did he permit any personal desire to get a hold over him. It has been related already that his father had died before his birth and his mother died while he was still a little child. Up to the age of eight, he was in the guardianship of his grandfather and after the latter's death he was taken care of by his uncle, Abū Ṭālib. Both on account of natural affection and also because he had been specially admonished in that behalf by his father, Abū Ṭālib always watched over his nephew with care and indulgence but his wife was not affected by these considerations to the same degree. It often happened that she would distribute something among her own children, leaving out their little cousin. If Abū Ṭālib chanced to come into the house on such an occasion he would find his little nephew sitting apart, a perfect picture of dignity and without a trace of sulkiness or grievance on his face. The uncle, yielding to the claims of affection and recognizing his responsibility, would run to the nephew, clasp him to his bosom and cry out : "Do pay attention to this child of mine also ! Do pay attention to this child of mine also !" Such incidents were not uncommon and those who were witnesses to them were unanimous in their testimony that the young Muhammad never gave any indication that he was in any way affected by them or that he was in any sense jealous of his cousins. Later in life when he was in a position to do so, he took upon himself the care and upbringing of two of his uncle's sons, 'Alī and Ja'far, and discharged this responsibility in the most excellent manner.

The Holy Prophet, throughout his life, had to encounter a succession of bitter experiences. He was born an orphan, his mother died while he was still a small child and he lost his grandfather at the age of eight years. After marriage he had to bear the loss of several children, one after the other, and then his beloved and devoted wife Khadīja died. Some of the wives he married after Khadīja's death, died during his lifetime and towards the close of his life he had to bear the loss of his son Ibrāhīm. He bore all these losses and calamities cheerfully, and none of them affected in the least degree either his high resolve or the urbanity of his disposition. His private sorrows never found vent in public and he always met everybody with a benign countenance and treated all alike with uniform benevolence. On one occasion he observed a woman who had lost a child occupied in loud mourning over her child's grave. He admonished her to be patient and to accept God's will as supreme. The woman did not know that she was being addressed by the Holy Prophet and replied : "If you had ever suffered the loss of a child as I have, you would have realized how difficult it is to be patient under such an affliction." The Prophet observed : "I have suffered the loss not of one but of seven children," and passed on. Except when he referred to his own losses or misfortunes in this indirect manner, he never cared to dwell upon them nor did he permit them in any manner to interfere with his unceasing service to mankind and his cheerful sharing of their burdens.

HIS SELF-CONTROL

He always held himself under complete control. Even when he became a Sovereign he always listened to everybody with patience, and if a person treated him with impertinence he bore with him and never attempted any retaliation. In the East, one way of showing respect for a person whom one is addressing is not to address him by his personal name. The Muslims used to address the Holy Prophet as : "O Messenger of Allah", and non-Muslims used to address him as "Abu'l Qāsim" (*i.e.*, Qāsim's father : Qāsim being the name of one of his sons). On one occasion a Jew came to him in Medina and started a discussion with him. In the course of the discussion he repeatedly addressed him as "O Muhammad, O Muhammad". The Prophet paid no attention to his form of address and went on patiently expounding the matter under discussion to him. His Companions, however, were getting irritated at the discourteous form of address adopted by his interlocutor till one of them, not being able to restrain himself any longer, admonished the Jew not to address the Prophet by his personal name but to address him as Abu'l Qāsim. The Jew said that he would address him only by the name which his parents had given him. The Prophet smiled and said to his Companions : "He is right. I was named Muhammad at the time of my birth and there is no reason to be upset at his addressing me by that name."

Sometimes people stopped him in the way and engaged him in conversation, explaining their needs and preferring their requests to him. He always stood patiently and let them go on and proceeded only after they had done. On occasion people when shaking hands with him kept hold of his hand for some time and, though he found this inconvenient and it occasioned a loss of precious time also, he was never the first to withdraw his hand. People went freely to him and laid their troubles and difficulties before him and asked him for help. If he was able to help he never declined to do so. Sometimes he was pestered with requests and they were unreasonably pressed but he went on complying with them as far as he was able. On occasion, after complying with a request, he would admonish the person concerned to have greater trust in God and to avoid asking others for relief. On one occasion a devout Muslim asked him several times for money and each time he complied with his request but in the end said : "It is best for a man to put his trust in God and to avoid making requests." The person concerned was a sincere man. Out of regard for the feelings of the Prophet, he did not offer to return what he had already received but he declared that in future he would never make a request to anybody under any circumstances. Years later, he was taking part in a battle, mounted on a charger, and in the thick of it when the din and confusion and the clash of arms were at their highest and he was surrounded by his enemies, his whip fell from his hand. A Muslim soldier who was on foot, perceiving his predicament, bent down to pick up the whip for him but the mounted man begged him to desist and jumped from his horse and picked up the whip himself, explaining to the soldier that he had long since promised the Holy Prophet that he would never make any request to anybody and that if he had permitted the soldier to pick up the whip for him it would have amounted to his having made an indirect request and would thus have rendered him guilty of breaking his promise to the Holy Prophet.

JUSTICE AND FAIR DEALING

The Arabs were greatly given to favouritism and applied different standards to different persons. Even among the so-called civilized nations of today one observes a reluctance to bring prominent persons or persons occupying high positions or offices to account for their doings, though the law is enforced rigorously against the common citizen. The Holy Prophet was, however, unique in enforcing uniform standards of justice and fair dealing. On one occasion a case came before him in which a young woman belonging to a highly respectable family was found to have committed theft. This caused great consternation as, if the normal penalty were imposed upon the young woman, a leading family would be humiliated and disgraced. Many were anxious to intercede with the Prophet on behalf of the offender but were afraid to do so. Eventually Usāma was prevailed upon to undertake the mission. Usāma went to the Holy Prophet but the moment the latter perceived the trend of his submission he was much upset and said: "You had better desist. Nations have come to a bad end for showing favours to highly placed persons while pressing hard on the common people. Islam does not permit this and I will certainly not do it. Verily, if my own daughter, Fāṭima, were to commit an offence I would not hesitate to impose the appropriate penalty" (Bukhārī, *Kitāb al-Ḥudūd*).

It has already been related that when the Prophet's uncle 'Abbās became a prisoner in the Battle of Badr, he was, like other prisoners, tied up with a rope to prevent his escape. The rope was so tightly secured that he groaned with pain during the night. The Prophet heard his groans and was unable to sleep. The Companions of the Prophet, perceiving this, loosened the rope that bound 'Abbās. When the Prophet got to learn of this, he directed that all prisoners should be treated alike, saying that there was no reason for showing favour to his own relative. He insisted that either they must loosen the bonds of all the prisoners or must tighten the bonds of 'Abbās like those of the others. As the Companions of the Prophet did not wish him to be subjected to uneasiness on account of his uncle they undertook to guard the prisoners carefully and loosened the bonds of all of them (Zurqānī, Vol. 3, p. 279).

Even during the exigencies of war he was most particular in observing all accepted rules and conventions. On one occasion he despatched a party of his Companions on a scouting expedition. They encountered some men of the enemy on the last day of the Sacred Month, Rajab. Thinking that it would be dangerous to let them escape and carry to Mecca the tidings of the scouting party being so near, they attacked them and in the course of the skirmish one of them was killed. After the scouting party had returned to Medina the Meccans began to protest that the Muslim scouts had killed one of their men in the Sacred Month. The Meccans had often been guilty of violating the sanctity of the Sacred Months *vis-à-vis* the Muslims whenever it suited them, and it would have been a suitable reply to their protest to say that as the Meccans had themselves set at naught the convention relating to the Sacred Months, so they were not entitled to insist upon their observance by Muslims. But the Prophet did not make this reply. He severely reprimanded the members of the party, refused to accept the booty and according to some reports even paid the blood-money for the person killed, till the revelation of 2 : 218 cleared the whole position (Ṭabarī and Ḥalbiyya).

People are generally careful not to hurt the feelings of their friends and relations but the Holy Prophet was very particular in this respect even regarding people who were opposed to him. On one occasion a Jew came to him and complained that Abū Bakr had hurt his feelings by saying that God had exalted Muhammad above Moses. The Prophet summoned Abū

Bakr and asked him what had transpired. Abū Bakr explained that the Jew had started by saying that he swore by Moses whom God, he said, had exalted above the whole of mankind, and that he (Abū Bakr) had thereupon retorted by swearing by Muhammad, whom God had exalted above Moses. The Prophet said: "You should not have said this as the feelings of other people should be respected. Nobody should exalt me above Moses" (Bukhārī, *Kitāb al-Tauḥīd*). This did not mean that the Holy Prophet did not in fact occupy a higher position than Moses but that an affirmation like this addressed to a Jew was likely to hurt his feelings and should have been avoided.

REGARD FOR THE POOR

The Holy Prophet was ever concerned to ameliorate the condition of the poorer sections of the community and to raise their status in society. On one occasion while he was sitting with his Companions, a rich man happened to pass by. The The Prophet inquired of one of his Companions what he thought of him. He replied: "He is a well-to-do and well-connected man. If he were to ask for the hand of a girl in marriage the request would be favourably considered and if he were to intercede on behalf of anybody the intercession would be accepted." Shortly after, another man passed by who appeared to be poor and of no substance. The Prophet inquired of the same Companion what he thought of him. He replied: "O Messenger of Allah! He is a poor man. If he were to request the hand of a girl in marriage the request would not be favourably received and if he were to intercede on behalf of any person the intercession would be rejected and if he were to seek to engage anybody in conversation no attention would be paid to him." On hearing this the Prophet observed: "The worth of this poor man is much greater than the value of a quantity of gold sufficient to fill the whole universe" (Bukhārī, *Kitāb al-Riqāq*).

A poor Muslim woman used to clean out the Holy Prophet's mosque in Medina. The Prophet did not see her in the mosque for some days and made inquiries concerning her. He was told that she had died. He said: "Why was I not informed when she died ? I would have wished to join her funeral prayers," and added, "perchance you did not consider her worthy of consideration as she was poor. This was not right. Direct me to her grave." He then proceeded to her grave and prayed for her (Bukhārī, *Kitāb al-Ṣālāt*). He used to say that there were people with tangled hair whose bodies were covered with dust and who were not welcomed by those who were well-to-do but who were so highly valued by God that if, trusting in God's beneficence, they swore in His name that a certain matter would take a certain turn He would support them." (Muslim, *Kitāb al-Birr wa'l-Ṣila*). On one occasion some Companions of the Holy Prophet who were freed slaves were sitting together when Abū Sufyān (who was a chieftain among the Quraish and had fought the Muslims up to the surrender of Mecca and had accepted Islam only on that occasion) happened to pass by. These Companions, addressing him, recalled the victory that God had bestowed upon Islam. Abū Bakr also heard this and did not approve of a chieftain of the Quraish being reminded of their humiliation and he reprimanded the group of Companions. He then went to the Holy Prophet and related the incident to him. The Prophet said : "O Abū Bakr ! I fear you may have hurt the feelings of these servants of God. If that should be so, God would be offended with you." Abū Bakr at once returned to those people and inquired : "Brothers of mine ! Did you feel hurt over what I said ?" To which they replied : "We felt no offence at what you said. May God forgive you !" (Muslim, *Kitāb al-Faḍā'il*).

While, however, the Prophet insisted that poor people should be respected and their feelings should not be injured and strove to fulfil their needs, he also sought to instil the sentiment of self-respect into them and taught them not to beg for favours. He used to say that it behoved a poor man not to seek to be content with a date or two or with a mouthful or two of food but to restrain himself from making a request, however severely he might be tried (Bukhārī, *Kitāb al-Kusūf*). On the other hand he used to say that no entertainment would be blessed unless some poor people were also invited to it. 'Ā'isha relates that a poor woman came to visit her on one occasion accompanied by her two little daughters. 'Ā'isha had nothing with her at the time except one date which she gave to the woman. The woman divided it between her little daughters and then they all departed. When the Prophet came home 'Ā'isha related this to him and he said : "If a poor man has daughters and he treats them with consideration, God will save him from the torments of Hell," and added : "God will bestow Paradise upon this woman on account of the consideration she showed towards her daughters" (Muslim). On one occasion he was told that one of his Companions, Sa'd, who was a well-to-do person, was boasting of his enterprise to others. When the Prophet heard this, he said : "Let no man imagine that his wealth or standing or power is the result merely of his own efforts or enterprise. That is not so. Your power and your position and your wealth are all earned through the poor." One of his prayers was : "O God ! Keep me humble while I am alive and keep me humble when I die and let my resurrection on the Day of Judgement be with the humble" (Tirmidhī, *Abwāb al-Zuhd*).

On one occasion during the hot weather when he was passing through a street, he observed a very poor Muslim carrying heavy loads from one place to another. He was very plain of features which were rendered still more unattractive by a heavy coating of perspiration and dust. He bore a melancholy look. The Holy Prophet approached him stealthily from the back and, as children sometimes do in fun, he put forward his hands and covered the labourer's eyes with them, expecting him to guess who he was. The man put back his own hands and feeling over the body of the Prophet realized that it was the Holy Prophet himself. He probably guessed also that nobody else would show such intimate affection for a man in his condition. Being pleased and encouraged, he pressed against the Holy Prophet's body and clasped him to himself from the back rubbing his dust and sweat-covered body against the clothes of the Prophet, desiring perhaps to ascertain how far the Prophet would be willing to indulge him. The Prophet went on smiling and did not ask him to desist. When the man had been put in a thoroughly happy mood the Prophet said to him : "I possess a slave ; do you think anybody will be willing to buy him ?" The man realized that probably there was nobody in the whole world, save the Holy Prophet himself who would be ready to see any worth in him, and with a melancholy sigh he replied : "O Messenger of Allah ! there is nobody in this world who would be prepared to purchase me." The Prophet said : "No ! No ! You must not say that. You are of great worth in the eyes of God" (Sharḥ al-Sunna).

Not only was he himself watchful of the welfare of the poor but he constantly exhorted others to be the same. Abū Mūsā Ash'arī relates that if a needy person approached the Holy Prophet and made a request, he would say to those around him, "You should also support his request so that you may acquire merit by becoming sharers in promoting a good deed" (Bukhārī and Muslim), his object being to create on the one side in the minds of his Companions a feeling of eagerness to help the poor and on the other in the minds of the needy a realization of the affection and sympathy felt for them by their better-off brethren.

SAFE-GUARDING THE INTERESTS OF THE POOR

When Islam began to be generally accepted over the greater part of Arabia, the Holy Prophet often received large quantities of goods and money which he immediately distributed amongst those who were in need. On one occasion his daughter Fāṭima came to him and, showing him her hands which had become calloused by the labour involved in crushing grain with stones, requested that a slave might be allotted to her to lighten her labour. The Prophet replied : "I shall tell you something which will prove to be of far greater worth than a slave. When you go to bed at night you should utter the praise of God thirty-three times, and affirm His perfection an equal number of times and affirm His greatness thirty-four times. This will help you a great deal more than could the possession of a slave" (Bukhārī).

While distributing money on one occasion a coin fell from his hands and rolled out of sight. Having finished with the distribution he went to the mosque and led the prayers. It was his practice to remain sitting for a short while after the conclusion of the prayers, occupied in the remembrance of God and thereafter to let people approach him and put questions to him or prefer requests. On this occasion, as soon as the prayers were concluded, he got up and proceeded quickly to his house. He looked for the missing coin and, having recovered it, came back and bestowed it upon a needy person, explaining that the coin had fallen from his hands during the distribution of money and the matter had gone out of his mind but he suddenly recollected it while leading the prayers and he was made uneasy by the thought that if he were to die before he could recover the coin and give it away to some person in need, he would be held responsible for it before God ; that was the reason why he had left the mosque in such a hurry to recover the coin (Bukhārī, *Kitāb al-Kusūf*).

In his anxiety fully to safe-guard the interests of the poor and the needy he went so far as to lay down that no charity should ever be bestowed upon his descendants, fearing lest Muslims out of their love for and devotion towards himself should in course of time make his descendants the principal objects of their charity and thus deprive the poor and needy of their due share. On one occasion somebody brought to him a quantity of dates and offered them as charity. His grandson Imām Ḥasan, who was then only two and a half years of age, happened to be sitting with the Prophet. He picked up one of the dates and put it into his mouth. The Prophet immediately put his finger into the child's mouth and forced the date out of it saying : "We have no right in this. This belongs to the poor among God's creatures" (Bukhārī, *Kitāb al-Kusūf*).

TREATMENT OF SLAVES

He constantly exhorted those who owned slaves to treat them kindly and well. He had laid down that if the owner of a slave beat his slave or abused him, the only reparation that he could make was to set the slave free (Muslim, *Kitāb al-Īmān*). He devised means for, and encouraged, the freeing of slaves on every pretext. He said : "If a person owning a slave sets him free, God will in recompense save every part of his body corresponding to every part of the slave's body from the torment of Hell." Again, he laid down that a slave should be asked to perform only such tasks as he could easily accomplish and that when he was set to do a task, his master should help him in performing it so that the slave should experience no feeling of humiliation or degradation (Muslim). If a master went on a journey accompanied by a slave, it was his duty to share his mount with the slave either by both riding together or each riding in turn. Abū Huraira, who used to spend the whole of his time after becoming a Muslim in the company of the Prophet and who had repeatedly heard the Prophet's injunctions regarding the treatment of slaves, has said: "I call God to witness in Whose hands is my life that were it not for the opportunities that I get of joining in holy war and of performing the Pilgrimage and were it not that I have opportunities of serving my old mother, I would have desired to die a slave, for the Holy Prophet constantly insisted upon slaves being well and kindly treated" (Muslim). Ma'rūr bin Suwaid relates: "I saw Abū Dharr Ghaffārī (a Companion of the Holy Prophet) wearing clothes exactly similar to those worn by his slave. I inquired of him the reason of this and he said: 'During the lifetime of the Holy Prophet I once taunted a man with his mother having been a slave. Upon this the Holy Prophet rebuked me and said: "You still seem to entertain pre-Islamic notions. What are slaves? They are your brethren and the source of your power. God in His wisdom confers temporary authority upon you over them. He who has such authority over his brother should feed him with the kind of food he himself eats; clothe him with the kind of clothes he himself wears and should not set him a task beyond his strength and should himself help him in whatever he is asked to do".' " On another occasion the Prophet said: "When your servant cooks food for you and sets it out before you, you should ask him to sit down with you to eat or at least to partake of a portion of it in your company, for he has established a right in it by working on it' (Muslim).

TREATMENT OF WOMEN

The Holy Prophet was very keen on improving the condition of women in society and on securing for them a position of dignity and fair and equitable treatment. Islam was the first religion which conferred upon women the right of inheritance. The Quran makes daughters along with sons heirs to the property left by their parents. In the same way a mother is made an heir to her son's or daughter's property and a wife is made an heir to her husband's property. When a brother becomes an heir of his deceased brother's property a sister is also an heir to that property. No religion before Islam had so clearly and firmly established a woman's right of inheritance and her right to possess property. In Islam a woman is the absolute owner of her own property and her husband cannot obtain any control over it by virtue merely of their relationship. A woman is at full liberty to deal with her property as she chooses.

The Holy Prophet was so careful with regard to the kind treatment of women that those around him who had not previously been accustomed to looking upon women in the light of helpmates and partners found it difficult to accommodate themselves to the standards that the Prophet was anxious to see set up and maintained. 'Umar relates: "My wife occasionally sought to intervene in my affairs with her counsel and I would rebuke her, saying that the Arabs had never permitted their women to intervene in their affairs. She would retort: 'That is all past. The Holy Prophet lets his wives counsel him in his affairs and he does not stop them. Why don't you follow his example?' My reply used to be: 'As regards 'Ā'isha the Prophet is particularly fond of her but as regards your daughter (Ḥafṣa), if she does this she will one day have to suffer the consequences of her impertinence.' It so happened that thereafter on one occasion the Holy Prophet, being upset over something, decided to spend a period of time apart from his wives. When I learnt of this I said to my wife, What I had feared had come to pass. Then I went to the house of my daughter Ḥafṣa and found her crying. I inquired of her what the matter was and whether the Prophet had divorced her. She said: 'I don't know about divorce, but the Prophet has decided to remain away from us for some time.' I said to her: 'Did I not often tell you not to take the same liberties with him as 'Ā'isha does, for the Holy Prophet is particularly fond of 'Ā'isha, but you seem to have brought upon yourself what I had feared.' I then went to the Holy Prophet and found him lying down on a rough matting. He was at that time wearing no shirt and his body bore the marks of the pattern of the matting. I sat down near him and said: 'O Messenger of Allah ! the Kaiser and the Chosroes do not deserve any of God's favours and yet they pass their lives in great comfort and you who are His Messenger pass your days in such discomfort.' The Prophet replied: 'That is not so. The Messengers of Allah are not expected to spend their time in comfort. That kind of life befits only secular monarchs.' I then related to the Prophet all that had passed between me and my wife and daughter. Hearing me, the Prophet laughed and said: 'It is not true that I have divorced my wives. I have merely thought it advisable to spend a little time away from them' " (Bukhārī, *Kitāb al-Nikāḥ*).

He was so careful concerning the sentiments of women that on one occasion when he was leading the prayers he heard the cry of a child and concluded the service quickly, explaining thereafter that as he had heard the cry of the child he imagined that the child's mother would be distressed at its cry and he had therefore concluded the service quickly so that the mother could go to the child and look after it.

When during any of his journeys women were also among the party he always gave directions that the caravan should move slowly and by easy stages. One one such occasion when the men were eager to push forward, he said: "Take care of glass ! Take care of glass !" meaning thereby that women were of the party and that if camels and horses were put to the gallop they would suffer from the joltings of the animals (Bukhārī, *Kitāb al-Adab*). During a battle confusion arose among the ranks of the mounted soldiers and the animals became unmanageable. The Holy Prophet fell from his horse and some of the women also fell from their mounts. One of his Companions, who was riding a camel immediately behind the Prophet jumped down and ran towards him crying: "May I be your sacrifice, O Messenger of Allah." The Prophet's foot was still in the stirrup. He released it hastily and said to his Companion: "Don't bother about me, go and help the women." Just before his death one of the injunctions he addressed to Muslims and laid stress upon was that they should always treat women with kindness and consideration. It was an oft-repeated saying of his that if a man had daughters and he arranged to have them educated and took pains with their upbringing, God would save him from the torment of Hell (Tirmidhī).

It was a common practice with the Arabs to inflict physical chastisement upon women for every little fault. The Holy Prophet taught that women were equally with men the creatures of God and were not the slaves of men and should not be beaten. When women got to know of this they went to the other extreme and began to oppose men in everything, with the result that in many homes domestic peace was continually disturbed. ‘Umar complained of this to the Holy Prophet and said that unless women could on occasion be chastised they would become unruly and there would be no holding them in check. As detailed Islamic teachings with regard to the treatment of women had not yet been revealed, the Prophet said that if a woman was guilty of serious transgression she might be chastised. This in its turn led the men in many cases to revert to the old Arab practice. It was now the turn of the women to complain and they laid their grievances before the Prophet's wives. Thereupon, the Prophet admonished men and told them that those who treated women with unkindness could never win the favour of God. Thereafter the rights of women were established, and for the first time women began to be treated as free individuals in their own right (Abū Dāwūd, *Kitāb al-Nikāḥ*).

Mu‘āwiya al-Qushairī relates: "I inquired of the Holy Prophet what claim my wife had upon me," and he replied: "Feed her with that which God bestows upon you in the way of food, and clothe her with that which God bestows upon you in the way of clothes and do not chastise her nor abuse her nor put her out of your house." He was so careful of the feelings and sentiments of women that he always exhorted those who had to go upon a journey to finish their errands quickly and return home as soon as possible so that their wives and children should not suffer separation longer than was necessary. Whenever he returned from a journey he always came home during the day-time. If he found night approaching towards the end of his journey, he would camp outside Medina for the night and enter it next morning. He also told his Companions that when they returned from a journey they should not come home suddenly without notice of their return (Bukhārī and Muslim). In giving this direction he had in mind the fact that the relations between the sexes are largely governed by sentiment. In the absence of the husband a wife may often neglect the care of her body and of her dress and if the husband were to return home unexpectedly the finer sentiments of the wife or the husband might be upset. By giving the direction that when a man returns from a journey he should contrive to arrive home during the day-time and after intimation to the members of his family of his return, he ensured that the members of his family would be ready to receive the returning member in a befitting manner.

ATTITUDE TOWARDS THE DEAD

He enjoined that every person should make a will concerning the regulation of his affairs after his death so that those connected with him should suffer the minimum of inconvenience after his demise.

He laid down that no man should speak ill of a person who was dead but that whatever of good he had possessed should be emphasized, for no benefit could result to anybody from mentioning the weaknesses or vices of the deceased but by emphasizing his virtues people would be inclined to pray for him (Bukhārī). He insisted upon a deceased person's debts being paid before he was buried. He very often satisfied the liabilities of a deceased person himself, but if he was not able to do this, he exhorted the heirs and relatives of the deceased or other persons to discharge his liabilities and would not say the funeral prayers over a deceased person till his liabilities had been discharged.

TREATMENT OF NEIGHBOURS

He always treated his neighbours with extreme kindness and consideration. He used to say that the angel Gabriel had emphasized consideration towards one's neighbours so often that he sometimes began to think that a neighbour would perhaps be included among the prescribed heirs. Abū Dharr relates that the Holy Prophet said to him : "Abū Dharr, while broth is being cooked for your family, add a little more water to it so that your neighbour might also share in it." This does not mean that the neighbour should not be invited to share in other things but, as the Arabs were mostly a migratory people and their favourite dish was broth, the Holy Prophet referred to this dish as a typical one and taught that one should not think so much of the taste of the food as of the obligation to share it with one's neighbour.

Abū Huraira relates : "On one occasion the Holy Prophet exclaimed : 'I call God to witness that he is not a believer ! I call God to witness that he is not a believer ! I call God to witness that he is not a believer !' The Companions inquired : 'Who is not a believer, O Messenger of Allah ?' and he replied : 'He whose neighbour is not secure against injury and ill-treatment at his hands.' On one occasion when he was addressing women, he said : 'If anybody finds only the foot of a goat to cook, that person should share it with his or her neighbour.' He asked people not to object to their neighbours driving pegs into their walls or putting them to any other use which occasioned no injury." Abū Huraira relates : "The Prophet said : 'He who believes in God and in the Day of Judgement should occasion no inconvenience to his neighbour : he who believes in God and in the Day of Judgement should occasion no inconvenience to his guest, and he who believes in God and in the Day of Judgement should utter only words of virtue or should keep quiet' " (Muslim).

TREATMENT OF RELATIVES

Most people suffer from the failing that when they marry and set up house for themselves, they begin to neglect their parents. The Holy Prophet, therefore, laid great stress upon the meritoriousness of serving one's parents and treating them with kindness and consideration. Abū Huraira relates : "A man came to the Holy Prophet and asked to be told who was most deserving of kind treatment at his hands. The Prophet replied: 'Your mother'. The man asked 'And next to her?' The Prophet repeated, 'Again thy mother'. The man asked a third time, 'And after my mother?' and the Prophet again replied, 'Still thy mother', and when the man asked him a fourth time, he said: 'After her thy father and after him thy nearest relatives and after them thy more remote relatives.'" The Prophet's own parents and grand parents had died while he was still a child. The parents of some of his wives were, however, alive and he always treated them with great consideration and deference. On the occasion of the surrender of Mecca when the Holy Prophet entered the town as a victorious general, Abū Bakr brought his father to meet him. He said to Abū Bakr: "Why did you trouble your father to come to me? I would gladly have gone to him myself" (Ḥalbiyya, Vol. 3, p. 99). One of his sayings was: "Unlucky is the man whose parents live to old age and he fails to earn Paradise even then," meaning that the service of one's parents particularly when they reach old age attracts the grace and favour of God and, therefore, a person to whom is afforded the opportunity of serving his aged parents and who avails himself of the opportunity to the full is bound to become confirmed in righteous ways and a recipient of the grace of God.

A man once complained to the Holy Prophet that the more benevolence he exercised towards his relations the more hostile they became towards him, and that the more he treated them with kindness the more they persecuted him, and the more he demonstrated affection towards them the more they frowned upon him. The Prophet said: "If what you say is true you are very fortunate, for you will ever be the recipient of God's succour" (Muslim, *Kitāb al-Birr wa'l Ṣila*). On one occasion when the Holy Prophet was exhorting people to alms and charity one of his Companions, Abū Ṭalḥa Anṣārī, came to him and offered to dedicate an orchard for charitable purposes. The Prophet was very pleased and exclaimed, "What an excellent charity! What an excellent charity! What an excellent charity!" and added: "Having dedicated this orchard to the service of the poor, I want you now to divide it among your poor relatives" (Bukhārī, *Kitāb al-Tafsīr*). A man came to him on one occasion and said : "O Messenger of Allah ! I am prepared to make a covenant of Hijrat and I am prepared to make a covenant to take part in the holy war, for I am anxious to win the pleasure of God." The Holy Prophet inquired whether either of his parents was alive and the man told him that both were alive. He then asked : "Are you indeed anxious to win the pleasure of God ?" and on the man replying in the affirmative the Prophet said : "Then go back to your parents and serve them and serve them well." He pointed out that one's non-Muslim relations were equally entitled to be treated kindly and with consideration along with one's Muslim relations. One of Abū Bakr's wives, who was a non-Muslim, visited her daughter Asmā' and the latter inquired of the Holy Prophet whether she might serve her and make presents to her, to which the Holy Prophet replied : "Certainly, for she is thy mother" (Bukhārī, *Kitāb al-Adab*).

He treated not only his near relatives but even remote ones and anybody connected with them with great consideration. Whenever he sacrificed an animal he would send a portion of the meat to the friends of Khadīja (his deceased wife) and told his wives never to overlook them on such occasions. Many years after Khadīja's death when he was sitting with some of his Companions, Khadīja's sister, Hālah, came to see him and asked permission to enter. Her voice sounded in the Prophet's ears very much like that of Khadīja and when he heard it he said : "Oh Lord ! This is Hālah, Khadīja's sister." Indeed, true affection always manifests itself thus that one becomes fond of and considerate towards all those who may be connected with a person whom one loves or holds in high esteem.

Anas bin Mālik relates that during the course of a journey he found himself in the company of Jarīr bin 'Abdullah and observed that the latter busied himself in looking after him as a servant looks after his master. As Jarīr bin 'Abdullah was older than Anas, the latter was embarrassed and protested that Jarīr should not put himself out on his account. Jarīr replied : "I used to observe how devotedly the Anṣār served the Holy Prophet and, being impressed with their devotion to and love for the Holy Prophet, I had resolved in my mind that if I ever happened to be in the company of an Anṣārī, I would serve him like a servant. I am, therefore, only carrying out my resolve and you should not seek to dissuade me" (Muslim). This incident affirms that where one person truly loves another, his affection extends also to those who sincerely serve the object of his attachment. In the same way those who truly honour their parents are always deferential and considerate towards those who may be connected with their parents through bonds of affection or relationship. On one occasion the Holy Prophet stressed it as the highest virtue for a man to honour the friends of his father. Among the persons addressed was 'Abdullah bin 'Umar. Many years after, while proceeding on Pilgrimage, he met a Bedouin and he made over to him his own mount and also presented him with his turban. One of his companions observed that he had been over-generous as a Bedouin would be pleased with very little. 'Abdullah bin 'Umar said : "This man's father was a friend of my father's and I have heard the Holy Prophet say that it is one of the highest virtues for a man to honour his father's friends."

KEEPING GOOD COMPANY

He always preferred to keep company with the virtuous and if he observed any weakness in any of his Companions he admonished him gently and in private. Abū Mūsā Ash'arī relates : "The Holy Prophet illustrated the benefit to be derived from good friends and virtuous companions and the injury to be apprehended from evil friends and vicious companions by saying : 'A man who keeps company with virtuous people is like a person who carries about musk with him. If he partakes of it he derives benefit from it ; if he sells it he makes a profit out of it and if he merely keeps it he enjoys its perfume. A man who keeps company with evil persons is like one who blows into a charcoal furnace ; all that he can expect is that a spark may alight upon his clothes and set them on fire or that the gas emitted by the charcoal may upset his brain'." He used to say that a man's character takes on the colour of the company he keeps and that therefore one should be careful to spend one's time in the company of the good (Bukhārī and Muslim).

SAFE-GUARDING PEOPLE'S FAITH

The Holy Prophet was very careful to safe-guard against possible misunderstandings. On one occasion his wife Ṣafiyya came to see him in the mosque. When the time came for her to return home it had become dark and the Prophet decided to escort her to her house. On the way he passed by two men and, wishing to avoid any speculation on their part as to his companion, he stopped them and lifting the veil from the face of his wife said : "See, this is Ṣafiyya my wife." They protested saying : "O Messenger of Allah ! why did you imagine that we should fall into any misconception regarding you ?" The Prophet replied : "Satan (*i.e.*, evil thoughts) often courses through a man's blood. I was afraid lest your faith be affected" (Bukhārī, *Abwāb al-I'tikāf*).

OVERLOOKING FAULTS OF OTHERS

He never gave publicity to the faults and shortcomings of others and admonished people not to proclaim their own faults. He used to say : "If a person covers up the faults of another, God will cover up his faults on the Day of Judgement." And, "Every one of my followers can escape the consequences of his errors (*i.e.*, by true repentance and reform) except those who go on proclaiming their wrongdoing" and illustrated this by saying : "A man commits a sin at night and God covers it up ; in the morning he meets his friends and boasts before them : 'I did this last night, I did that last night,' and thus he himself lays bare that which God had covered up" (Bukhārī and Muslim).

Some people foolishly imagine that a confession of sin helps towards repentance ; the truth is that it only fosters immodesty. Sin is an evil and he who slips into it and becomes a prey to shame and remorse has a chance of climbing back into the path of purity and righteousness through repentance. His case is like that of a person who has been seduced by evil but is pursued by righteousness and as soon as a chance offers, the evil is vanquished and the sinner is claimed back by righteouness. Those, however, who proclaim their sins and take pride in them lose all sense of good and evil and become incapable of repentance.

On one occasion a man came to the Holy Prophet and said: "I have been guilty of adultery" (this when established by proper evidence being a punishable offence under Islamic Law). Hearing the man's confession, the Holy Prophet turned away from him and became occupied with something else. He meant to indicate that the proper remedy in such a case was repentance and not public confession. But the man did not realize this and imagining that the Prophet had not heard him, went and stood in front of him and, addressing him, repeated his confession. The Holy Prophet again turned away from him but the man again went and stood in front of him and repeated his confession. When he had done this four times the Prophet said: "I had wished that this man should not have proclaimed his sin till God should have indicated His will with regard to him but, as he has repeated his confession four times, I am compelled to take action" (Tirmidhī). He then added: "This man has himself confessed and has not been charged by the woman concerning whom he makes the confession. The woman should be questioned and, if she denies her guilt, she should not be molested and only this man should be punished in accordance with his confession but, if she confesses she should also be punished." It was the practice of the Holy Prophet to follow the Law of the Torah in matters regarding which the Quran was silent, and as the Torah prescribes that an adulterer should be stoned to death he pronounced the sentence upon this man accordingly. When the sentence was being carried out the man tried to run away but the people pursued him and carried out the sentence. When the Prophet came to know of this he disapproved of it. He said that the man had been sentenced in accordance with his own confession. His attempt to run away was in effect a retraction of his confession and thereafter he should not have been subjected to a penalty which had been imposed upon him solely on account of his confession.

The Prophet laid down that the Law was concerned only with overt acts. During the course of a war, a party of Muslims came upon a non-Muslim who used to lie in wait in lonely places and whenever he found a solitary Muslim he would attack and kill him. On this occasion Usāma bin Zaid pursued him and, having overtaken and caught him, drew his sword to kill him. When the man found that no way of escape was left open to him he repeated the first portion of the Muslim confession of faith, viz., "There is no being worthy of worship save Allah," thereby indicating that he had accepted Islam. Usāma paid no heed to this and killed him. When this, among the other incidents of the campaign, was related to the Holy Prophet he sent for Usāma and questioned him. On his confirming the account of the incident the Prophet said : "How will it be with you on the Day of Judgement when his confession of faith will bear witness in his favour ?" Usāma replied, "O Messenger of Allah ! that man was a murderer of Muslims and his declaring himself to be a Muslim was merely a ruse to escape just retribution." But the Prophet went on repeating : "Usāma, how will it be with you when the man's confession of faith will bear witness against you on the Day of Judgement ?" —meaning that God would hold Usāma to account for the man's death, for though he had been guilty of the murder of Muslims, his reciting the confession was an indication that he had repented of his misdeeds. Usāma protested that the man's reciting of confession of faith was due to his fear of death and was not an indication of repentance. Thereupon the Holy Prophet said : "Did you peep into his heart to see whether he was telling the truth or not ?" and went on repeating : "How will you answer on the Day of Judgement when his confession of faith will be cited in evidence against you ?" Usāma says : "On hearing the Prophet repeat this so often I wished that I had become a convert to Islam only that moment and had not been guilty of what was charged against me" (Muslim, *Kitāb al-Īmān*).

The Holy Prophet was ever ready to forgive people their faults and trespasses. One of the persons concerned in the affair of the slander against his wife, 'Ā'isha, was dependent for his living upon the charity of Abū Bakr ('Ā'isha's father). When the falsehood of the allegation against 'Ā'isha was clearly established, Abū Bakr stopped his support of this man. Even this is evidence of Abū Bakr's commendable moderation and restraint. An average person would have proceeded to extreme lengths against a dependent who had been guilty of defaming his daughter. When the Prophet came to know of what Abū Bakr had done, he spoke to him and pointed out that though the man had been at fault, it did not behove a person like Abū Bakr to deprive him of his means of sustenance on account of his wrongdoing. Thereupon Abū Bakr resumed his patronage of the man (Bukhārī, *Kitāb al-Tafsīr*).

PATIENCE IN ADVERSITY

The Holy Prophet used to say : "For a Muslim, life is all full of good and nobody but a true believer finds himself in that position ; for, if he meets with success he is grateful to God and becomes the recipient of greater favours from Him. On the other hand, if he suffers pain or tribulation he endures it with patience and thus again makes himself deserving of God's favours." When his end drew near and he gave vent to a groan in the extremity of his condition, his daughter Fāṭima exclaimed that she could not bear to see him in that state. Thereupon he said : "Have patience ! Your father will suffer no pain after this day," meaning that all his troubles were confined to this world and from the moment that he was released from this life and entered the presence of his Maker he would be subject to no further pain. During the prevalence of an epidemic he would not approve of people moving out of an afflicted town into another, for this serves to enlarge the area of the pestilence. He used to say that in times of epidemic if a person stayed on in his own town and refrained from carrying infection into unaffected areas and died of the epidemic, he would be regarded as a martyr (Bukhārī, *Kitāb al-Tibb*).

MUTUAL CO-OPERATION

He used to teach that one of the best Islamic characteristics was that a man should not interfere in matters with which he was not concerned and that people should not go about criticizing others and interfering in matters that were not their concern. This is a principle which if generally adopted and enforced would go a long way towards securing peace and orderliness in the world. A large part of our troubles is due to the tendency of the majority of people to indulge in undue interference and to hold back their co-operation when it may be needed in providing relief for those in distress.

The Holy Prophet laid great stress upon mutual co-operation. He had made it a rule that if any person was called upon to pay a sum of money by way of penalty and was unable to put up the whole amount, his neighbours or his fellow-citizens or his fellow-tribesmen should make up the amount by raising a subscription. People sometimes came and took up their residence near the Prophet, devoting their time to the service of Islam in various ways. He always counselled their relatives to assume the responsibility of providing for their modest requirements. It is reported by Anas that during the time of the Holy Prophet two brothers accepted Islam and one of them stayed on with the Holy Prophet while the other continued with his normal occupation. The latter, later on, complained to the Holy Prophet that his brother was spending his time in idleness. The Holy Prophet said : "God provides for you also on account of your brother and it behoves you therefore to make provision for him and leave him free to serve the Faith" (Tirmidhī).

During the course of a journey, when the Prophet's party arrived at their camping place, his Companions immediately occupied themselves with their respective tasks in setting up camp for the night. The Holy Prophet said : "You have allotted no task to me. I shall go and collect fuel for çooking." His Companions protested and said : "O Messenger of Allah ! why should you occupy yourself in that way when all of us are here to do whatever may be necessary ?" He said : "No, No. It is my duty to do my share of whatever may have to be done," and he collected fire-wood from the jungle for cooking the food (Zurqānī, Vol. 4, p. 306).

TRUTHFULNESS

As has been related the Holy Prophet was himself so rigid in his standards of truthfulness that he was known among his people as "The Trusty" and "The True". He was equally anxious that Muslims should adopt the same standards of truth as were observed by himself. He regarded truth as the basis of all virtue, goodness and right conduct. He taught that a truthful person is one who is so confirmed in truth that he is counted truthful by God.

On one occasion a prisoner was brought to the Holy Prophet who had been guilty of the murder of many Muslims. 'Umar, who was also present, believed that the man richly deserved the imposition of the death penalty and he looked repeatedly at the Prophet expecting that the Prophet would at any moment indicate that the man should be put to death. After the Holy Prophet had dismissed the man 'Umar submitted that he should have been put to death as that was the only appropriate penalty. The Prophet replied: "If that is so, why did you not kill him?" 'Umar replied: "O Messenger of Allah! if you had but given me an indication even by a flicker of your eyelids, I would have done so." To this the Prophet rejoined: "A Prophet does not act equivocally. How could I have employed my eye to indicate the imposition of a death penalty upon the man while my tongue was employed in talking amicably to him?" (Hishām, Vol. 2, p. 217).

A man once came to the Holy Prophet and said: "O Messenger of Allah! I suffer from three evils: falsehood, indulgence in strong drinks and fornication. I have tried my utmost to get rid of them but have not succeeded. Will you tell me what to do?" The Prophet replied: "If you make a firm promise to me to give up one of them I guarantee that you will be rid of the other two." The man promised and asked the Prophet to tell him which of the three he should give up. The Prophet said: "Give up falsehood." Some time later the man came back and told the Holy Prophet that, having followed his advice, he was now free from all three vices. The Prophet asked him for the details of his struggle and the man said: "One day I wanted to indulge in liquor and was about to do so when I bethought myself of my promise to you and realized that if any of my friends asked me whether I had taken liquor, I would have to admit it as I could no longer utter a falsehood. This would mean that I would acquire an evil reputation among my friends and they would in future avoid me. Thinking thus, I persuaded myself to postpone drinking to some later occasion and was able to withstand the temptation at the time. In the same way when I found myself inclined towards fornication I argued with myself that indulgence in the vice would expose me to the loss of the esteem of my friends as I would either have to tell a falsehood if questioned by them, thus breaking my promise to you, or I would have to admit my sin. In this way I continued to struggle between my resolve to fulfil my promise to you and my desire to indulge in liquor and in adultery. When some time had passed I began to lose the inclination to indulge in these vices and the resolve to keep away from falsehood has now saved me from the other two also."

INQUISITIVENESS

The Holy Prophet always exhorted people against inquisitiveness and to think well of each other. Abū Huraira relates: "The Prophet said: 'Save yourselves from thinking ill of others for this is the greatest falsehood, and do not be inquisitive or apply epithets to each other out of contempt nor be envious of each other and do not entertain ill feelings towards each other; let each of you regard himself as the servant of God and treat others as his brothers as God has commanded,' and also 'Remember that every Muslim is a brother to every other Muslim. No Muslim should trespass against another or desert another in times of distress or look down upon another on account of his lack of substance or learning or any other thing. Purity springs from the heart and it is enough to defile a man's heart that he should look down upon his brother. Every Muslim must regard another Muslim's life, honour and property as sacred and inviolate. God does not regard your bodies nor your countenances nor your external actions but looks into your hearts" (Muslim, *Kitāb al-Birr wa'l Ṣila*).

FRANK AND STRAIGHTFORWARD DEALING

He was anxious to safe-guard Muslims against indulgence in any form of unfairness in their transactions. Passing through the market-place on one occasion, he observed a heap of corn which was being put to auction. He thrust his arm into the heap and found that though the outer layer of the corn was dry the corn inside was wet. He inquired from the owner the cause of this. The man explained that a sudden shower of rain had made part of the corn wet. The Prophet said that in that case he should have allowed the wet layer of corn to remain on the outside so that prospective purchasers could have appraised its real condition. He observed: "He who deals unfairly with others can never become a useful member of society" (Muslim). He insisted upon trade and commerce being entirely free from every suspicion of sharp practice. He exhorted purchasers always to inspect the goods and articles they proposed to purchase, and forbade any person to open negotiations for a transaction while negotiations about it were in progress with any other person. He also forbade the hoarding of commodities against a rise in the market and insisted that the market should be regularly supplied.

PESSIMISM

He was an enemy of pessimism. He used to say that whoever was guilty of spreading pessimism among the people was responsible for the downfall of the people, for pessimistic ideas have a tendency to discourage people and arrest progress (Muslim, Part II, Vol. 2). He warned his people against pride and boastfulness on the one hand and against pessimism on the other. He exhorted them to tread the middle path between these extremes. Muslims must work diligently in the trust that God would bless their efforts with the best results. Each should strive to go forward and should seek to promote the welfare and progress of the community, but everyone should be free from any feeling of pride or any tendency towards boastfulness.

CRUELTY TO ANIMALS

He warned people against cruelty to animals and enjoined kind treatment to them. He used to relate the instance of a Jewish woman who was punished by God for having starved her cat to death. He also used to relate the story of a woman who found a dog suffering from thirst near a deep well. She took off her shoe and lowered it into the well and thus drew up some water. She gave the water to the thirsty dog to drink. This good deed earned her God's forgiveness for all her previous sins.

'Abdullah bin Mas'ūd relates: "While we were in the course of a journey along with the Holy Prophet we saw two young doves in a nest and we caught them. They were still very small. When their mother returned to the nest, not finding her little ones in it, she began to fly wildly round and round. When the Holy Prophet arrived at the spot he observed the dove and said, 'If any one of you has caught its young ones he must release them at once to comfort it' " (Abū Dāwūd). 'Abdullah bin Mas'ūd also relates that on one occasion they observed an ant-hill and, placing some straw on top of it, they set fire to it; whereupon they were rebuked by the Holy Prophet. On one occasion the Prophet observed a donkey being branded on the face. He inquired the reason for this and was told that the Romans had recourse to this practice for the purpose of identifying high-bred animals. The Prophet said that as the face was a very sensitive part of the body, an animal should not be branded on the face and that if it had to be done the branding should be done on its haunches (Abū Dāwūd and Tirmidhī). Since then Muslims always brand animals on their haunches and, following this Muslim practice, Europeans also do the same.

TOLERANCE IN RELIGIOUS MATTERS

The Holy Prophet not only emphasized the desirability of tolerance in religious matters but set a very high standard in this respect. A deputation from a Christian tribe of Najrān visited him in Medina to exchange views on religious matters. It included several Church dignitaries. The conversation was held in the mosque and extended over several hours. At one stage the leader of the deputation asked permission to depart from the mosque and to hold their religious service at some convenient spot. The Holy Prophet said that there was no need for them to go out of the mosque, which was itself a place consecrated to the worship of God, and they could hold their service in it (Zurqānī).

BRAVERY

Several instances of his courage and bravery have been set out in the biographical portion. It suffices to relate one here. At one time Medina was full of rumours that the Romans were preparing a large army for its invasion. During that time Muslims were always on the *qui vive* at night. One night sounds of an uproar came from the desert. Muslims hurried out of their homes and some of them collected in the mosque and waited for the Holy Prophet to appear and to give them directions to meet the contingency. Presently they saw the Holy Prophet on a horse coming back from the direction of the sounds. They then discovered that at the very first sound of alarm the Prophet had mounted a horse and gone in the direction from which the sounds had come to find out whether there was any reason for alarm and had not waited for people to collect together so that he could proceed in company. When he came back he assured his Companions that there was no cause for alarm and that they could return to their homes and go to sleep (Bukhārī, chap. on *Shujā'at fi'l Ḥard*).

CONSIDERATION TOWARDS THE UNCULTURED

He was particularly considerate towards those who from lack of cultural training did not know how to behave. On one occasion a dweller of the desert who had only recently accepted Islam and who was sitting in the company of the Holy Prophet in the mosque got up and walking away a few paces sat down in a corner of the mosque to pass water. Some of the Companions of the Prophet got up to stop him from doing so. The Prophet restrained them, pointing out that any interference with the man was bound to cause inconvenience to him and might possibly cause him injury. He told his Companions to let the man alone and to clean the spot later.

THE FULFILLING OF COVENANTS

The Holy Prophet was very particular with regard to the fulfilling of covenants. On one occasion an envoy came to him on a special mission and, after he had remained in his company for some days, he was convinced of the truth of Islam and suggested that he might declare his adherence to it. The Prophet told him that this would not be proper as he was there in a representative capacity and it was incumbent upon him to return to the headquarters of his Government without acquiring a fresh allegiance. If, after he had returned home, he still felt convinced of the truth of Islam he could return as a free individual and declare his acceptance of it (Abū Dāwūd, chap. on *Wafa bi'l 'Ahd*).

DEFERENCE TOWARDS SERVANTS OF HUMANITY

He paid special deference to those who devoted their time and substance to the service of mankind. The Arab tribe, the Banū Ṭai' started hostilities against the Prophet and in the ensuing battle their forces were defeated and some were taken prisoner. One of these was the daughter of Ḥātim Ṭā'ī, whose generosity had become a proverb amongst the Arabs. When Ḥātim's daughter informed the Holy Prophet of her parentage he treated her with great consideration and as the result of her intercession he remitted all the penalties imposed upon her people on account of their aggression (Ḥalbiyya, Vol. 3, p. 227).

The character of the Holy Prophet is so many-sided that it is not possible to deal adequately with it within the space of a few pages, but as this is not a work dealing primarily with his character we must, having regard to the limitations of this General Introduction, content ourselves with what has already been set down.

THE COMPILATION OF THE QURAN

It has been demonstrated in the opening portion of this Introduction that the text of none of the sacred Scriptures, claimed to have been revealed before the Quran, has been preserved intact. They have all been interfered with to such an extent that an earnest seeker after truth finds it impossible to adopt any of them as a practical guide for right conduct. In contrast with this, the text of the Quran has been preserved intact and every word of it has come down to us as free from interference and interpolation as when it was revealed to the Holy Prophet one thousand three hundred and fifty years ago.

The Quran began to be revealed at the outset of the Mission of the Holy Prophet. The first revelation, comprising only a few verses, was received by him in the Ḥirā Cave. Thereafter the revelation continued till his death. Thus the total period during which the entire Quran was revealed extended to twenty-three years. We know, on the basis of the testimony of his contemporaries, that in the beginning revelation came to the Prophet at intervals and in small bits, but as time passed it grew both in volume and in frequency till in the last years of his life it swelled into an almost continuous stream. One reason for this, among others, was that the teachings contained in this revelation were altogether novel and it was not easy for people to grasp their full significance. Therefore the Quran was revealed in small portions in the beginning. But after the basic principles of Islam had been fully grasped and it became comparatively easy for people to understand the teachings and the topics dealt with in the Quran the revelation began to arrive faster and in larger volume. The object was that all Muslims should be enabled fully to grasp the teachings of the Quran. Another reason was that the number of Muslims was very small in the beginning and, as God intended that the text of the Quran should be scrupulously preserved and that it should not become the subject of any doubt, only small portions were revealed at a time in the beginning and there was always an interval, sometimes extending to several months, between the revelation of one group of verses and the next. In this manner the few Muslims were enabled to commit the whole revelation to memory, so as to place the matter of the preservation of the text beyond doubt. When the number of Muslims began to increase and the safe-guarding and preservation of the text of the Quran became easier, the revelation began to arrive faster. Towards the close of the Holy Prophet's life the number of Muslims exceeded a hundred thousand and the memorizing of the Quran became very easy. At that time the revelation came faster still. By this divine plan the purity of the text of the Quran was placed beyond doubt.

During the Caliphate of 'Uthmān seven copies of the Quran were despatched to different parts of the Muslim world and they in turn became the standard texts from which other copies were made and thereafter in each generation hundreds of thousands of people have been in the habit of committing the entire text of the Quran to memory. Even the bitterest enemies of Islam do not allege that any interference with the text of the Quran has taken place since the time of 'Uthmān. Those who seek to raise doubts regarding the purity of the text of the Quran direct their criticism to the period between the death of the Holy Prophet and the Caliphate of 'Uthmān.

Whenever any portion of the Quran was revealed to the Holy Prophet, he used to commit it to memory and, as he continuously recited the Quran from one end to the other, he always carried the whole of the revealed Quran at all times in his memory. In addition to this the following devices were adopted for safe-guarding and preserving intact the text of the Quran :

DEVICES ADOPTED TO SAFE-GUARD TEXT OF THE QURAN

(1) As soon as a revelation was received by the Holy Prophet it was recorded in writing from his dictation. A number of persons are known to have been employed by the Holy Prophet for this purpose. Of these the names of the following fifteen have been mentioned in the traditions (Fatḥ al-Bārī, Vol. 9, p. 19) :

1. Zaid bin Thābit.
2. Ubayy ibn Ka'b.
3. 'Abdullah bin Sa'd bin Abī Sarḥ.
4. Zubair bin al-'Awwām.
5. Khālid bin Sa'īd bin al-'Āṣ.
6. Abān bin Sa'īd bin al-'Āṣ.
7. Hanẓalā bin al-Rabī' al-Asadī.
8. Mu'aiqīb bin Abī Fāṭima.
9. 'Abdullah bin Arqam al-Zuhrī.
10. Shuraḥbīl bin Ḥasana.
11. 'Abdullah bin Rawāḥa.
12. Abū Bakr.
13. 'Umar.
14. 'Uthmān.
15. 'Alī.

Whenever the Holy Prophet received a revelation, he would send for one of these persons and dictate to him the text of the revelation he had received.

(2) As is well known, the five daily congregational prayers are obligatory upon every Muslim and a portion of the Quran must be recited in each of them so that every Muslim knows some portion of the Quran by heart. If every hundred out of the Prophet's Companions who numbered more than one hundred thousand had between them learnt the whole of the Quran by heart the entire Quran must have been preserved in the memory of his Companions a thousand times over.

(3) The whole of the Law, doctrine, philosophy, moral precepts and other teachings of Islam are contained in the Quran. The building up and the fostering of a nation require the aid of all these. The Holy Prophet used to train Muslims for the discharge of the multifarious duties and functions involved in the building up and direction of a civilized and cultured community. For instance, there were needed judges, jurists, expounders of doctrine and those who explained the legal and moral injunctions of Islam and these people could not adequately discharge their functions unless they had learnt the Quran by heart. All such people, therefore, were under the necessity of committing the entire Quran to memory.

(4) The Holy Prophet used always to stress the meritoriousness of committing the Quran to memory, so much so that he is reported as having said that if a person commits the Quran to memory he would be saved from the torment of Hell. God had blessed the Holy Prophet with Companions who were always eager to acquire merit in every way so that when he made this announcement very large numbers from among them began to commit the Quran to memory, including those whose enunciation was not very clear and who were not men of any learning at all. Imām Ahmad Ḥanbal has related on the authority of 'Abdullah bin 'Umar that a man came to the Holy Prophet and said to him : "O Messenger of Allah ! I memorize the Quran but my mind does not grasp its full meaning." This shows that not only men of learning but even the common people were in the habit of committing the Quran to memory. Another tradition, related by Imān Ahmad Ḥanbal on the same authority, states that a man brought his son to the Holy Prophet and said : "O Messenger of Allah ! this son of mine goes on reciting the Quran the whole day and spends his night in sleep." The Holy Prophet observed : "Then where is the occasion for you to worry ? Your son spends the day in the remembrance of God and instead of committing any transgression at night spends it in restful sleep." This shows that even the common people living at a distance from the Holy Prophet had started the practice of committing the Quran to memory.

INSTRUCTORS OF THE QURAN

(5) As the eagerness of the people for memorizing the Quran increased, the Holy Prophet appointed four principal teachers of the Quran who used to memorize it under the supervision of the Holy Prophet and then taught other people to commit it to memory. These four in turn trained a number of other people who became competent to teach the Quran. These four were :

1. 'Abdullah bin Mas'ūd.
2. Sālim Maulā Abī Ḥudhaifa.
3. Mu'ādh bin Jabal.
4. Ubayy ibn Ka'b.

The first two of these were Meccans who had migrated to Medina and the last two were Anṣārīs. 'Abdullah bin Mas'ūd used to occupy himself as a labourer, Sālim was a freed slave, and Mu'ādh and Ubayy were two of the leading men of Medina. Thus the Holy Prophet appointed teachers of the Quran from among different sections so that nobody should have any difficulty in approaching them and learning from them. The Holy Prophet used to say: "Those of you who wish to learn the Quran should learn it from 'Abdullah bin Mas'ūd, Sālim Maulā Abī Ḥudhaifa, Mu'ādh bin Jabal or Ubayy ibn Ka'b" (Muslim). These four had learnt the whole of the Quran under the supervision of the Holy Prophet. But many other Companions of the Holy Prophet had also learnt portions of it directly from him. It is related that on one occasion when 'Abdullah bin Mas'ūd was reciting the Quran 'Umar pointed out that a certain word should be pronounced in a particular way. 'Abdullah bin Mas'ūd protested that he had been taught by the Holy Prophet to pronounce it in the manner in which he had pronounced it. 'Umar took him to the Holy Prophet and complained that he did not recite the Quran correctly. The Holy Prophet asked him to recite the portion concerning which there was a difference of opinion between the two and when he recited it the Prophet said he was quite right. Thereupon 'Umar submitted that he had been taught by the Prophet to pronounce the word differently. The Prophet then asked him to recite the verse and when he did so, told him that that was also correct.

This shows that in addition to the four Companions whom the Holy Prophet used to teach the whole of the Quran there were others who used to learn portions of it from him. 'Umar's submission that he had been taught to pronounce a certain word in a particular way shows that he, too, used to learn portions of the Quran from the Holy Prophet himself.

The difference that arose between 'Umar and 'Abdullah bin Mas'ūd had no reference to any variation in the text of the Quran. It related only to a vowel point. Vowel points are a peculiarity of the Arabic language and in the case of certain verbs a variation in respect of vowel points is permissible and does not affect the meaning. For instance, in some cases a reading both with an 'a' and with an 'i' is permissible either as a general alternative reading or as a tribal or family practice. But the meaning in each case is the same. The Holy Prophet, recognizing such practices, gave permission under divine dispensation for the adoption of alternative enunciations, as this had not the effect of altering the meaning or sense of the words. As non-Arabic-speaking peoples are not familiar with this peculiarity of the Arabic language, they are apt to fall into the misconception that such alternative enunciations amounted to variations in the text and that the Holy Prophet was in the habit of teaching certain verses of the Quran in one way to one person and in a different way to another. In fact nothing of the kind ever took place. The variations which have become the subject-matter of discussion were not variations either of the text of a verse or even variations of a word. They were all cases of enunciation of vowel points which did not in any way alter the meaning or significance of a word. The only difference was that some tribes or families, being accustomed to pronounce certain verbs in particular declensions in a certain manner, were permitted to do so.

RECITERS OF THE QURAN

In addition to the four principal teachers of the Quran who had been trained by the Holy Prophet himself there were certain other well-known reciters who had committed the whole of the Quran to memory. Among these were:

(1) Zaid bin Thābit, who was also one of the recorders of the revelation.

(2) Abū Zaid Qais bin Al-Sakan, an Anṣārī, who belonged to the Banū Najjār, which was the tribe of the Prophet's mother (Fatḥ al-Bārī, Vol. 9, p. 49).

(3) Abū al-Dardā' Anṣārī (Bukhārī).

(4) Abū Bakr, concerning whom also it is related that from the very beginning he was in the habit of committing the Quran to memory.

(5) 'Alī not only knew the Quran by heart but shortly after the Holy Prophet's death undertook to arrange the Quran in the order in which it had been revealed.

(6) Nasa'ī relates that 'Abdullah bin 'Umar also knew the Quran by heart and used to recite the whole of it in the course of one night. When the Holy Prophet got to know of this he told him to complete the recitation in the course of a month and not to attempt to recite the whole of the Quran in one night as this might prove burdensome for him.

(7) Abū 'Ubaid relates that out of the Muhājirīn the following had committed the Quran to memory: Abū Bakr, 'Umar, 'Uthmān, 'Alī, Ṭalḥa, Sa'd, Ibn Mas'ūd, Ḥudhaifa, Sālim, A bū Huraira, 'Abdullah 'bin Sā'ib, 'Abdullah bin 'Umar and 'Abdullah bin 'Abbās.

And out of the women:

'Ā'isha, Ḥafṣa and Umm Salma.

Most of these had committed the Quran to memory during the Prophet's lifetime and some of them after his death. Ibn Abī Dāwūd relates in his book, the Al-Sharī'ah, that Tamīm bin Aus al-Dārī and 'Uqba bin 'Āmir from among the Muhājirīn had also committed the Quran to memory. Other historians include in this list 'Amr bin al-'Āṣ and Abū Mūsā Ash'arī.

From among the Anṣār those who were well known to have committed the Quran to memory were:

'Ubāda bin Ṣāmit, Mu'ādh, Majma' bin Ḥaritha, Fuḍāla bin 'Ubaid, Maslama bin Mukhallad, Abū Dardā', Abū Zaid, Zaid bin Thābit, Ubayy bin Ka'b, Sa'd bin 'Ubāda, and Umm Waraqa.

THE QURAN COMMITTED TO MEMORY

In actual fact it is well known that a very large number of the Companions of the Holy Prophet had committed the Quran to memory. As has been related in the biographical portion with reference to the incident of Bi'r Ma'ūna, the Holy Prophet in the fourth year of the Hijra despatched seventy of his Companions as instructors for certain tribes and every one of them knew the Quran by heart.

Those who had committed the Quran to memory spent the greater part of their time in reciting it to others at all hours of the day and night. Ḥāfiẓ Abū Ya'lā relates that the Holy Prophet was informed on one occasion that Abū Mūsā was instructing the people in the recitation of the Quran in his house. The Prophet asked to be led to some part of the house where he could listen to Abū Mūsā without his presence becoming known to the assembled company. He was led to such a place and having heard Abū Mūsā recite the Quran he approved of his recitation and was much pleased with it and observed: "He recites the Quran in the beautiful manner of the Prophet David" (Muslim, *Kitāb al-Ṣalāt*). This shows that the Holy Prophet took pains to supervise the recitation of the Quran by people other than the four whom he had appointed as the principal teachers of the Quran and was anxious to see that no error should creep into their recitation.

Imām Ahmad Ḥanbal relates on the authority of Jābir bin 'Abdullah that on one occasion when the Holy Prophet came to the mosque he found people reciting the Quran and he said: "Recite the Quran and recite it well and strive to win the pleasure of God through it, before the time comes when people will recite the Quran correctly, but with the object of making it a means of earning their livelihood rather than a means of the purification of their hearts" (Musnad, Vol. 3). Jābir bin 'Abdullah relates that the company that was engaged in the recitation of the Quran on this occasion comprised not only the Muhājirīn and the Anṣār but also desert-dwellers and non-Arabs.

Those who had become competent to recite the Quran during the lifetime of the Holy Prophet could be numbered in thousands. Immediately after the death of the Holy Prophet, when Musailima declared war and marched against Medina at the head of a hundred thousand warriors, Abū Bakr sent Khālid bin Walīd in command of thirteen thousand soldiers to oppose him. As this number included many who had only recently accepted Islam and had not yet become imbued with its spirit or traditions, the Muslim forces were pressed back at several points. At this juncture some of the Companions of the Holy Prophet who knew the Quran by heart put forward the suggestion that all those in the army who had the Quran by heart should be formed into a separate force and should be sent forward to oppose Musailima's men. It was thought that as these people appreciated the true value of Islam and the need of safe-guarding it with their lives, their zeal and devotion would prevail against the much larger numbers of the enemy. Khālid bin Walīd accepted this suggestion and formed a special force of those who knew the Quran by heart. These numbered three thousand. This force attacked Musailima's army with such vehemence that it was forced to retreat and was eventually beleaguered and destroyed. On that occasion these three thousand chose as their motto: "O ye that know the Sūra al-Baqara by heart" (Sūra al-Baqara was mentioned as it is the longest Chapter of the Quran). Five hundred of this special force of three thousand were killed in this battle. Says Sir William Muir: "The carnage amongst the 'Readers' (those who had the Koran by heart) was so great as to give Omar the first idea of collecting the Sacred Text lest any part of it should be lost" (The Caliphate).

Thus we find that in the time of the Holy Prophet himself the Quran used to be recorded in writing, was committed to memory and was constantly recited and thousands of people knew the whole of it by heart, though it had not yet been collected in one volume.

THE QURAN COLLECTED IN ONE VOLUME

When it was found that five hundred of the reciters of the Quran had been killed in the battle with Musailima's army, 'Umar suggested to Abū Bakr (who was then the Khalīfa) that if those who had the Quran by heart began to be lost in battles in such large numbers, the safe-guarding of the purity of its text would become difficult and that the time had therefore arrived when the whole of the Quran should be collected in one volume. Abū Bakr at first demurred but eventually accepted the suggestion and appointed Zaid bin Thābit, being one of those who used to record the Quran at the dictation of the Holy Prophet, to collect the text of the Quran in one volume and appointed prominent Companions of the Holy Prophet to assist him in the task. Abū Bakr directed that the text of the Quran should be collected from its recorded fragments and that the accuracy of the text should be certified by two persons who knew the whole of the Quran by heart. This task was soon accomplished and a written text of the whole of the Quran was got together in one volume, which was certified as accurate by those who knew it by heart. On the basis of these facts can there be the slightest ground for suggesting that variations in the text of the Quran had crept in between the death of the Holy Prophet and the compilation of the Quran into one volume under the directions of Abū Bakr and the supervision of Zaid bin Thābit ? Can it be reasonably suggested that any difficulty could arise in the compilation into one volume of a Book which was being continuously recited every day by large numbers of persons, the whole text of which used to be recited from beginning to end in the course of the month of Ramaḍān by persons who had committed it to memory to the Muslims assembled in congregational prayers, the congregation itself containing large numbers of people who knew the whole of it by heart, and which had been reduced to writing at the dictation of the Holy Prophet himself as the revelation was received from time to time ; more specially when the task of compilation was committed to the care of a person who was himself one of the recorders of the Quran and had committed the whole of it to memory ? Had the compiled volume contained a single variation from the text as dictated by the Holy Prophet and as committed to memory under his supervision by a large number of people, it would at once have been detected and set right. The authenticity and accuracy of the text of the Quran are thus established on the surest and most irrefutable evidence. The accuracy of the text of no other writing in the world is so far above the possibility of doubt as that of the Quran.

STANDARDIZED COPIES OF THE QURAN

During the time of 'Uthmān complaints began to be received that different tribes enunciated certain words of the Quran in their own peculiar manner and that as a result of this non-Muslims who heard these words differently enunciated fell into the misconception that there were variations in the text of the Quran. It has already been explained that these variations were the result of tribal or family practice and had nothing whatsoever to do with any variation in the text nor did they affect the meaning of any word. Nevertheless, 'Uthmān thought it wise to forbid all variations even of enunciation of vowel points. He had copies prepared of the text which had been collected in the time of Abū Bakr and despatched these copies into different parts of the Muslim dominions and issued a direction that no variation in the recitation of the Quran from the standard text, even if it was only in the matter of enunciation of vowel points, should be permitted. In the time of the Holy Prophet the social life of the Arabs was based upon their tribal divisions; each tribe led an existence separate from and independent of the others. In their speech they were accustomed to pronounce certain words in accordance with their own practice. When they accepted Islam they were welded into one cultured society and Arabic at once became the vehicle of that culture. Literacy spread very rapidly among the Arabs and it became quite easy for every one of them to adopt the correct literary enunciation of every Arabic word. The language of Mecca became the standard for this purpose. By the time of 'Uthmān, therefore, no justification had been left for variations in the enunciation of vowel points in accordance with tribal practices in the recitation of the Quran, particularly when such variations were likely to lead to misconception in the minds of non-Arabs. 'Uthmān's very prudent and timely action has been made the basis of the charge by non-Muslim writers that he made changes in the Quran or that the copies of the Quran promulgated by him were in some manner different from the standard text or the text as revealed to the Holy Prophet. These authors imagine that they have discovered a potent weapon of attack against the accuracy of the text of the Quran, but those who are acquainted with the Arabic language and with the history of the compilation of the Quran merely smile at the lack of intelligence betrayed by them.

There can thus be no room for doubt that the text of the Quran promulgated by 'Uthmān was exactly the same as that revealed to the Holy Prophet. There is still less room for doubt that the text of the Quran has continued absolutely pure and uncorrupted since 'Uthmān had despatched copies of the standard text to different parts of the Muslim dominions. These copies were in turn multiplied so extensively and rapidly that very soon almost every literate Muslim possessed his own copy of the Quran. It is recorded that a few years later during the struggle between 'Alī and Mu'āwiya the soldiers of the latter's army on one occasion tied copies of the Quran to thc points of their lances and proclaimed that the Quran should decide between the two opposing factions (The Caliphate). This shows that by that time it was usual for every Muslim to possess his own copy.

PRACTICE OF COMMITTING THE QURAN TO MEMORY CONTINUED

The reciting, copying and publication of the Quran have always been regarded as acts of great spiritual merit in Islam. History tells us that great Muslim divines and even Muslim monarchs used to occupy themselves in copying out the text of the Quran. Even in a non-Arab country like India, centuries after the time of the Holy Prophet, when Muslims had in many respects adopted Hindu customs and practices, the great Mughal Emperor Aurangzeb used to devote his leisure hours to the copying out of the text of the Quran. It is recorded that he had written out with his own hand seven complete copies.

The practice of committing the Quran to memory was not confined to the time of the Holy Prophet or the early Caliphs. Even after written copies of the Quran began to be multiplied and became easily available, the Quran was in each age committed to memory by large numbers of Muslims. A modest estimate is that between one hundred and two hundred thousand Muslims have learnt the Quran by heart during all periods of Muslim history and sometimes the number of such persons was very much in excess of this estimate. European writers, not being conversant with the sentiments of Muslims and the degree of love and devotion inspired by the Quran in their hearts, are reluctant to believe that the purity and accuracy of the text of the Quran should have been safe-guarded by Muslims in this manner. They find that history does not record the instance of a single person who had learnt the whole of the Bible by heart and it therefore seems to them incredible that the entire text of the Quran should have been committed to memory by large numbers of people in each generation. It must be remembered, however, that it is one of the outstanding characteristics of the Quran that its language is very rhythmic and that it lends itself very easily to memorization. The eldest son of the writer, Mirzā Nāṣir Ahmad, who is a B.A. (Hons.) of the Punjab University and M.A. of Oxford University, had under his direction committed the whole of the Quran to memory before he started on the course of his secular studies. In a small place like Qadian two doctors and several graduates know the Quran by heart. One of these two doctors committed the whole of the Quran to memory within the space of four or five months. The father of Sir Ẓafrulla Khān, Judge of the Federal Court of India, committed the Quran to memory within the space of a few months after he had attained the age of fifty years. Ḥāfiẓ Ghulām Muhammad, who was at one time the Missionary of our Movement in Mauritius, committed the Quran to memory in the space of three months. When the writer was on pilgrimage to Mecca, he met the grandson of Munshī Muhammad Jamāl 'ud-Dīn Khān (who had for a number of years been Minister in Bhopal State) and he told the writer that he had succeeded in committing the Quran to memory within one month. These instances show that the text of the Quran is couched in language which lends itself easily to memorization. It has been related to the writer by very aged persons that Mirzā Gul Muhammad, great grandfather of the Founder of the Ahmadiyya Movement, who lived in the time of the Mughal Emperor, 'Ālamgīr II, used to maintain five hundred people at his court who knew the whole of the Quran by heart. Mirzā Gul Muhammad was a chieftain who exercised authority over only two hundred and fifty square miles of territory. In some parts of India, which is a country where the Arabic language is not widely understood, it has been the practice of a majority of Muslims through the centuries to commit the Quran to memory.

One of the devices adopted by Muslims for safe-guarding the purity of the text of the Quran and one which has been acted upon for centuries is that children who are born blind or who lose their sight during infancy are encouraged to commit the Quran to memory. This is done out of a feeling that as a blind person is not competent to adopt a normal occupation he can turn his handicap to account by becoming a guardian of the text of the Quran. This practice is so common that in India a blind Muslim is indiscriminately given the courtesy-title of *Ḥafiẓ* (*i.e.*, the guardian) meaning a person who has become the guardian of the text of the Quran by committing it to memory.

During the month of Ramaḍān the whole of the Quran is recited aloud in the course of congregational prayers in all the principal mosques throughout the world. The Imām recites the Quran and another Ḥāfiẓ stands immediately behind him and keeps watch over the accuracy of the recitation, prompting the Imām when necessary. In this manner the whole of the Quran is recited from memory during the month of Ramaḍān in hundreds and thousands of mosques all over the world.

These are the various devices and precautions adopted by Muslims to safe-guard the purity and accuracy of the text of the Quran, with the result that even the bitterest enemies of Islam have had to admit that the text of the Quran has been fully safe-guarded since the time of the Holy Prophet. It can, therefore, be asserted with the utmost confidence that the Quran exists today exactly as the Holy Prophet gave it to the world. We set out below the testimony of some Western writers in this behalf:

Sir William Muir in his work, "The Life of Mohammad" (p. xxviii), sums up his conclusion on this matter as follows: "What we have, though possibly corrected by himself, is still his own . . . ." "We may, upon the strongest presumption, affirm that every verse in the Quran is the genuine and unaltered composition of Mohammad himself" (p. xxviii). "There is otherwise every security, internal and external, that we possess the text which Mohammad himself gave forth and used" (p. xxvii). And again, ". . . and conclude with at least a close approximation to the verdict of Von Hammer that we hold the Quran to be as surely Mohammad's word as the Mohammadans hold it to be the word of God" (p. xxviii).

Noldeke says: "Slight clerical errors there may have been, but the Quran of 'Uthmān contains none but genuine elements, though sometimes in very strange order. The efforts of European scholars to prove the existence of later interpolations in the Quran have failed" (Enc. Brit. 9th edition, under the word "Quran").

ARRANGEMENT OF CHAPTERS AND VERSES

It is sometimes asserted that the arrangement of the Chapters of the Quran is the work of 'Uthmān. This is not correct. It is well known that the Holy Prophet used to recite the whole of the Quran in Ramaḍān and some of his Companions also did so. It is also mentioned in the traditions that the Holy Prophet used to recite the whole of the Quran to the angel Gabriel during the month of Ramaḍān (Bukhārī). A non-Muslim may not be prepared to accept this last statement, but it is beyond doubt that the Holy Prophet used to recite the Quran and he must have done it in accordance with some arrangement.

After the Holy Prophet's death 'Alī did not call on Abū Bakr (who had been elected Caliph) for some time. Abū Bakr sent for him and asked him whether he was displeased with his election as Caliph. 'Alī replied that it was not so, but that he had been busy in copying out the Quran in the order in which it had been revealed, as he had resolved at the time of the death of the Prophet that he would undertake this duty. This also shows that in the time of the Holy Prophet the Quran used to be recited in a certain order and that that order was different from the order in which it had been revealed. That is why 'Alī decided that he should copy it out in the order in which it had been revealed so that for purposes of history that arrangement should also be preserved. There are traditions which relate that whenever a verse or group of verses was revealed to the Holy Prophet, he would send for one of the recorders and direct him to record the verse or verses indicating at the same time to which Chapter and where they belonged. This shows that at the time of receiving a revelation the Holy Prophet was also informed where the revealed verse or verses belonged.

The strongest evidence, however, in support of the arrangement adopted in the compilation of the Quran is the evidence of the subject-matter itself. A study of the Quran reveals that the subject-matter of each Chapter is connected with the subject-matter of the preceding and the following Chapters. If the current arrangement was adopted by 'Uthmān merely with reference to the length of each Chapter, how is it that the arrangement reveals a continuity of topics and subject-matter? For instance, the Sūra al-Fātiḥa was revealed in Mecca and is the opening Chapter of the Quran. The Sūra al-Baqara was revealed at Medina and follows immediately after the Sūra al-Fātiḥa, leaving out several Chapters that had been revealed during the interval. Western writers allege that the Sūra al-Baqara has been placed first as it is the longest Chapter of the Quran. To begin with, they forget that the first Chapter in the Quran is not the Sūra al-Baqara but the Sūra al-Fātiḥz, which is a very short Sūra comprising only seven verses. Further, when we read the Sūra al-Fātiḥa we find that it concludes with the prayer: "Guide us in the right path", and the Sūra al-Baqara, which is the immediately succeeding Chapter, opens with the verse: "This is a perfect Book; there is no doubt in it; it is a guidance for the righteous." If the Sūra al-Baqara was selected to follow after the Sūra al-Fātiḥa merely by reason of the fact that it is the longest Chapter of the Quran, how is it that its very opening verse furnishes an answer to the concluding verse of the immediately preceding Chapter, the Sūra al-Fātiḥa? The Sūra al-Fātiḥa concludes with a prayer for guidance and the Sūra al-Baqara opens with a verse which points to the guidance which had been prayed for at the end of the previous Chapter. This is not a mere coincidence; for, this continuity of topics and subject-matter is to be found throughout the Quran in spite of the fact that sometimes a Chapter revealed at Mecca follows one revealed at Medina and *vice versa*. This proves that the arrangement of the Chapters and the verses of the Quran was adopted under divine direction.

The question then arises why the arrangement adopted in the compilation of the Quran was different from the order in which its verses were revealed. The answer is that when the Quran was being revealed, the teachings and doctrines contained in it were entirely novel and unfamiliar to Arabs. Their minds had to be familiarized and impregnated with the background of Islamic doctrines and teachings so as to prepare them for the reception of the details of those teachings and doctrines. The earlier revelations were, therefore, cast in the form of brief Chapters containing fundamental teachings like the Unity of God, kindness and consideration towards the poor, the necessity for and the benefits to be derived from the worship of God and His remembrance, and also prophecies indicating what kind of opposition the Holy Prophet would have to encounter, how Muslims would be treated, how Islam would progress, and what the end of its enemies and opponents would be. As the number of Muslims increased and Islam began to spread, the details of the Islamic Law and teachings also began to be revealed. The order in which the Quran was revealed was, therefore, best suited to the needs of the times in which it was revealed, but once the revelation was complete and hundreds of thousands of people had accepted it and even the non-Muslims had become aware of its background, it became necessary to present its teachings and doctrines to Muslims and non-Muslims from a fresh angle. To meet this need the Holy Prophet went on giving directions under divine guidance regarding the permanent arrangement of the Quran for use in the future. It is indeed an outstanding miracle of the Quran that it was revealed in the order which was best suited for the needs of the period during which it was revealed and was arranged for permanent use in the order which was best suited for the needs of Muslims in subsequent times. For a book to be revealed in fragments over a period of twenty-three years in an order best suited to the requirements of that period and simultaneously to be cast into a shape best suited for the requirements of future ages was an achievement which could have been accomplished only under divine direction.

The connection subsisting between the subject-matter of one Chapter and that of a succeeding Chapter has been explained in the preliminary note set out in the beginning of each Chapter.

SOME PROPHECIES OF THE QURAN

It has been explained in the earlier portion of this General Introduction that Scriptures revealed before the Quran contained prophecies relating to the Quran. Western writers have alleged that the Quran itself contains no prophecies. This is not correct. The very first revelation received by the Holy Prophet in Ḥirā Cave contains the prophecy that through the Quran knowledge would be vouchsafed to man to which he had not had access before. Consequently we find several instances where the Quran points out errors which had crept into previous Scriptures and in these respects the Quran has subsequently been confirmed by events. For instance, it was revealed in the Quran that when Pharaoh was drowned his body was saved and was preserved so that it should serve as a Sign for future generations. God says in the Quran :

> And We brought the children of Israel across the sea ; and Pharaoh and his hosts pursued them wrongfully and aggressively, till, when the calamity of drowning overtook him, he said, "I believe that there is no god but He in Whom the children of Israel believe, and I am of those who submit to Him." "What ! now ! while thou wast disobedient before this and wast of those who create disorder. So this day We will save thee in thy body alone that thou mayest be a Sign to those who come after thee." And surely many of mankind are heedless of Our Signs (10 : 91–93).

That is to say : God carried the Israelites in safety across the sea and they were pursued by Pharaoh and his army out of enmity and transgression and the latter continued in their pursuit till they were overtaken by drowning. And at that moment Pharaoh said : 'I now believe that there is no god save the One in Whom the Israelites believe and I submit myself to Him.' Thereupon God decreed, 'Thou dost declare thy belief now whereas thou didst indulge in disobedience and transgression before. In return for thy last-moment declaration of belief We shall save only thy body from destruction so that it should serve as a Sign for coming generations, though in truth the majority of mankind pay little heed to Our Signs.' This incident is not described in the Bible or in any Jewish history or in any other authentic record of that period. The Quran made mention of it over thirteen and a half centuries ago. Thirteen centuries thereafter the body of this particular Pharaoh was discovered and identified which established beyond controversy the fact that after he was drowned his dead body was recovered and was embalmed and preserved. In spite of its having been embalmed it could have been destroyed during the many convulsions through which the land of Egypt has passed after the time of Moses but it escaped destruction and was preserved to serve as a Sign and a lesson to mankind and to confirm the truth of the Quran.

Again, the very early revelations contain the verse : "By the night when it spreads" (92 : 2), which means that God calls to witness the night to point to the fact that Islam would be subjected to a succession of severe trials and persecutions. This prophecy was made at a time when even the Holy Prophet himself did not apprehend that his people would put up a severe opposition to his Mission. Immediately after he had received the first revelation, Khadīja took the Holy Prophet to her cousin, Waraqa bin Naufal. After the Holy Prophet had related his recent experience to him, Waraqa said : "The angel that brought the revelation to Moses has also descended upon you. I fear, however, that your people will persecute you and expel you from Mecca." The Prophet was very much struck by this and asked in great surprise : "Will my people indeed expel me ?" (Bukhārī). He knew that he was a great favourite with his people and did not apprehend that he would be opposed by them. At that very time, however, God informed him that Islam and the Muslims would have to pass through a very dark night of opposition and persecution. That night soon commenced and lasted through ten weary years.

That this period of persecution and trial would extend over ten years was also foretold in another place in the Quran. In the opening verses of Sūra al-Fajr God calls to witness the ten nights which will precede the dawn. Sir William Muir and other Western writers agree that this Sūra was revealed towards the close of the third year of the Prophet's Ministry. Up to that time opposition by the people of Mecca had not taken on a severe complexion. At that time the Quran gave a warning that Muslims would have to pass through ten dark nights of persecution. Those who are familiar with the phraseology of sacred Scriptures are aware that a day or a night often signifies a year. The Bible contains many instances of this, though it employs the expression "a day" to indicate a year while the Quran when indicating a period of distress employs the word "night," for a period of distress is a period of darkness and is signified more properly by "night." This verse gave warning of severe trials and persecutions which would last for a period of ten years. That period commenced almost immediately after this verse was revealed and continued for ten years. A hostile critic might suggest that at the time when this verse was revealed the Holy Prophet could well have anticipated that the Meccans would soon convert their opposition into persecution ; but were there any means, apart from divine revelation, by which he could have ascertained that the period of persecution would continue for ten years and not for five or for eight or for twelve or for thirteen ? The revelation specified ten years and the Holy Prophet was permitted to remain in Mecca for only ten years after this revelation was received and was subjected to persecution throughout that period. After ten years, he was compelled to depart from Mecca which had nothing but persecution to offer to him and his followers and he arrived at Medina where God made provision for the rapid progress of Islam and of Muslims and his departure from Mecca thus became the dawn of Islam's spread and progress.

It might be suggested that the period of ten years was an intelligent guess on the part of the Holy Prophet, but was it also an intelligent guess on his part that ten years after the revelation was received a large number of the people of Medina would accept Islam and that he would migrate to that town ? Was it left to his option to convert the people of Medina to Islam and was it left to his option to accomplish the journey from Mecca to Medina in safety ?

But the revelation did not end there. It went on to say : "And the night when it passes away" (89 : 5). In this verse

God calls to witness another night with which the darkness will depart, meaning that after the dawn which would appear at the end of ten years of persecution the darkness would not disappear altogether but that the dawn would be followed by another night and that thereafter there would be no further period of darkness. This is exactly what happened. The Migration from Mecca was followed by another year of alarm and distress when Muslims in Medina were in continuous dread of being invaded by the Meccans. The Battle of Badr was fought about one year after the Prophet's Migration from Mecca and this battle, as had been foretold in the Bible and as we have already stated in the earlier part of this Introduction, laid low the glory of Kedar and brought to an end the whole series of persecutions of Muslims by Meccans. The Muslims had to fight other and greater battles later, but the Battle of Badr established them as an independent and sovereign people and swept into the common pit of ruin and destruction the leading men of the Quraish, who had been prominent persecutors of Muslims.

Again, while the Prophet was still in Mecca he received the revelation :

> Verily He Who has prescribed the teachings of the Quran for thee will bring thee back to the ordained place of return (28 : 86).

The verse means to say that God Who has revealed the Quran to the Prophet and has imposed upon him the duty of obedience to it guarantees that He will restore him once more to Mecca. This verse not only revealed that the Holy Prophet would have to migrate from Mecca but also contained the prophecy that after his Migration he would return to Mecca as a victor. Nobody passing through the circumstances which surrounded the Holy Prophet at the time when this verse was revealed could have guessed that after he had been forced to depart from Mecca he would return to it in triumph. There is another prophecy in the Quran foretelling the same event and that was also revealed while the Prophet was still in Mecca :

> And say, "O my Lord, make my entry a good entry, and then make me come forth with a good forthcoming. And grant me from Thyself a helping power" (17 : 81).

In this verse God commanded the Prophet to pray that He should make his entry (into the town to which He was sending him) a successful entry and thereafter enable him to issue forth therefrom with success to deliver his attack and be his Ally in that attack. This verse foretold that the Prophet would migrate from Mecca to Medina and that he would invade Mecca from Medina and that Mecca would eventually submit to him.

Again, while the Prophet was still in Mecca he received the revelation to the effect that the hour of the victory of Islam was approaching and that the moon would be rent (54 : 2). The moon was the symbol of Arab power and the rending of the moon meant that the Arab power was about to be shattered. This verse was revealed at a time when the Muslims had been compelled to migrate in different directions and the Holy Prophet was persecuted in Mecca and was not permitted even to say his prayers in the Ka'ba. On one occasion when he wanted to say his prayers there, he was ignominiously dragged from its precincts. At that time when the whole of Mecca was afire with opposition to him the Holy Prophet informed the Meccans that God had decreed that their power would be broken and that the victory of Islam was drawing near. Within a few years, this prophecy was fulfilled in the clearest possible manner. In the Battle of Badr the vaunted power and glory of Kedar was broken and the banner of Islam was planted firmly for ever. The moon was indeed rent. That day was the Day of Judgement for the Arabs. On that day a new heaven and a new earth were created.

While Islam and the Muslims were still the targets of Arab persecution in Mecca, news arrived that the Persians had vanquished the Romans in battle. This occasioned great rejoicing among Meccans, for the Persians were idolaters and the Romans were Christians. The Meccans took the victory of the Persians as a good omen indicating their own ultimate triumph over Muslims. On this occasion the Holy Prophet received the revelation that the Romans had been vanquished in a neighbouring land but within nine years of their defeat they would again be victorious (30 : 3–5) ; the word occurring in the verse, viz., بِضْع expresses a number from three to nine. When this revelation was announced among the

Meccans they laughed and jeered at the Muslims. Some of them laid a wager of a hundred camels with Abū Bakr that the prophecy would not be fulfilled. Events indicated that there was very little chance of the Romans defeating the Persians as their defeat in Syria was followed by further victories of the Persians and the Roman army was pushed back by stages to the shores of the Sea of Marmora. Constantinople was cut off from its Eastern dominions and the Roman Empire was reduced to the size of a small State. The word of God was, however, bound to be fulfilled and was fulfilled. The Romans, though smaller in number and not so well equipped as the Persians, won a complete victory and the Persians were put to flight. They retreated into Persia and the Romans re-occupied their Asiatic and African possessions.

The Quran contains several prophecies relating to later times, some of which have already been fulfilled. For instance, at one place it says :

> He has let loose the two bodies of water, which will meet one day. Between them is a barrier ; they encroach not one upon the other. . . . There come out from them pearls and coral. . . . And His are the lofty ships upon the sea, looking like mountains (55 : 20, 21, 23, 25).

These verses purport to say that two oceans from which pearls and coral are recovered and which are separated would meet each other and high-prowed vessels would pass through them. This prophecy was fulfilled by the construction of the Suez and the Panama Canals. The oceans that were joined together by these canals are well known for their pearl fisheries and coral.

The Sūra al-Kahf contains prophecies relating to the rise and progress of the Christian nations, their naval might and hegemony over the greater part of the earth and their mutual wars. The ultimate victory and triumph of Islam have also been foretold. The greater part of the prophecies regarding the rise and fall of the Christian nations has been fulfilled. The next stage is the fulfilment of the prophecy relating to the victory and triumph of Islam. A European Christian or a European atheist, judging only from the present condition of Muslims, would laugh at this ; but the God Who revealed these prophecies and Who has fulfilled those of them that related to the Christian nations will surely cause the prophecy relating to the triumph of Islam to be fulfilled also. The days of the victory of Islam are at hand. The rays of the sun of Islam are penetrating the thick curtains of darkness. God's angels are descending from the Heavens. The earth is no doubt in the grip of satanic powers but the days of the clear triumph of divine forces against the forces of Satan are rapidly drawing near. The Unity of God will then be firmly established and mankind will realize and admit that the Quran alone is capable of making peace between God and man and of establishing justice and fair dealing between man and man and of setting up the Kingdom of God upon earth.

CHARACTERISTICS OF QURANIC TEACHINGS

ONE special feature that distinguishes the Quran from all other Scriptures is that it deals adequately with all problems arising within the sphere of religion, and by stressing the function of religion it directs attention to its proper sphere and the benefits that may be derived from it. A reader of the Old and the New Testaments or of the Vedas or of the Zend-Avesta is left with the impression that somebody appearing at an intermediate stage in the middle of a long drawn-out phenomenon of nature had set out to describe those stages of it of which he had been a witness. That is not the case with the Quran. It expounds the philosophy of creation and all matters connected therewith. It explains why God created the universe and the object of man's creation and the means to be adopted for the achievement of that object. It sheds light on the nature of the Godhead and Its attributes and the manner in which those attributes find their manifestation. In connection with the object of man's creation it expounds the laws on which the running of the universe is based. It points out that for the physical development and evolution of man God has put into force the laws of nature which regulate the physical and mental conditions of man and that one group of angels is entrusted with the enforcement of these laws. For the development and enlightenment of the human soul God has revealed the Law of Sharī'at (*i.e.*, Sacred Law) through His Prophets. In some cases the revelation containing the Sacred Law has been limited in character, but there has also been the revelation containing the complete and perfect code of the Sacred Law. In other cases the object of the revelation has been to restore the Sacred Law to its original purity after it had suffered from human misinterpretation. In other words, God raises Prophets among mankind with different objects. Some Prophets are Law-bearers, and through them a new dispensation is revealed. The function of others is limited to the modification of an already revealed Law while still others are entrusted with the duty of sweeping away misinterpretations of the Law. The Quran also explains the need for, and the benefits to be derived from, the Law of Sharī'at and its function in relation to the evolution of man.

BELIEF IN A LIVING GOD

The Quran points out the distinction between God and His attributes, appreciation of which enables us to judge the error of those who have said, "In the beginning was the word, and the word was with God and the word was God" (John 1 : 1). The Quran teaches that an attribute cannot become the substitute of the being and that the two are entirely distinct.

The Quran explains to what extent man is left free to determine his course of action and to what extent he is subject to compulsion. It teaches that man has been left with enough choice to make him responsible for his actions to God and to enable him to embark upon a continuous course of self-improvement. On the other hand, the sphere of his activities is circumscribed and it is not possible for him to transgress its limits. Despite all effort, it is not possible for man to discard the limitations to which human life is subject. He cannot sink into a condition of static solidity nor climb to an ethereal existence. Within his own sphere, however, he possesses great faculties and large powers and is capable of continuous improvement and progress.

The Quran explains the need of belief in God and draws attention to the proofs of His existence. It emphasizes that God has always sent down His word by means of revelation in times of darkness and that He manifests His power through extraordinary Signs and thus gives irrefutable proof of His existence. The Prophets and their perfect followers are indispensable for the purpose of creating in men's minds perfect faith in God. If God were to cease to manifest His attributes through the Prophets and their followers, mankind would become a prey to doubt and uncertainty and firm faith in the existence of God would disappear. It is imperative, therefore, that so long as mankind continue to exist, divine revelation should continue to descend upon some of them. Faith in the existence of God can be maintained only through this means. From the inception of the Universe God has spoken to man through His Prophets down to Jesus and on to the Holy Prophet of Islam, just as He has throughout continued to manifest His attributes of creation, hearing and seeing. In the same manner He will continue to speak till the end of time to His chosen servants and will continue to manifest His existence by these means. Reason revolts against the suggestion that God exercised His attribute of speech up to the time of Jesus but became silent thereafter or that He exercised this attribute up to the time of the Holy Prophet and thereafter became dumb for ever. As we repudiate as blasphemous any suggestion that God possessed the attribute of seeing up to the time of Jesus or up to the time of the Holy Prophet but that thereafter He ceased to see or that He was capable of creating up to the time of Jesus or up to the time of the Holy Prophet but that thereafter He lost the attribute of creation or that He was All-Powerful up to the time of Jesus or the Holy Prophet but thereafter He ceased to have any power, so we must repudiate the suggestion that God spoke up to any particular period and thereafter ceased to speak. All His attributes are perfect and everlasting. This is a self-evident truth, yet Christians, Jews, Zoroastrians and a very large majority of those who call themselves Muslims have come to believe that revelation came to an end with Zoroaster or with the Prophets of Israel or with Jesus or with the Holy Prophet. The Quran utterly rejects such a notion. The Quran teaches belief in a living God and puts forward as proof the fact that He will continue ever to speak to His chosen and righteous servants as He has always spoken to them. The truth of this doctrine taught by the Quran has been confirmed in this age by the appearance of the Promised Messiah, the Founder of the Ahmadiyya Movement. Once more the revelation received by him and by his true followers stands out as a challenge to all those who assert, if not by word of mouth, at least by the doctrines they preach, that God has lost His attribute of speech.

The Quran teaches that divine revelation has not been confined to any particular people but that God has raised

Prophets among all peoples. It explains why it was necessary to send Prophets one after the other; why a perfect Law was not revealed in the early stages of man's history. It deals at length with the subject of the Unity of God and sets out convincing proofs in support of it. It demonstrates that a plurality of gods would offend both against reason and against fact. It explains in what manner the doctrine of the Unity of God helps man in his spiritual advance.

The Quran sheds a flood of light on the question of prophethood. The word "prophet" or its equivalents have been freely used in religious Scriptures but not one of them explains the conception underlying prophethood. Who may be called a Prophet and who may not be so called and what are the different kinds of prophethood? The Quran alone defines a Prophet and draws a distinction between different kinds of prophethood. It explains the difference between a Prophet and a non-prophet and defines the duties of a Prophet and a Prophet's relationship to God. It also explains why Prophets are raised and what should be the relationship between them and their followers and between them and those who do not believe in them. It defines the rights of a Prophet and explains whether a Prophet stands as a barrier between God and man or is only a helper and a guide.

The Quran deals in detail with the subject of angels, their functions and the purpose for which they have been created.

It also explains what Satan is and in what manner the existence of such a being is of help to man. What is the relationship between man and Satan? How can a man guard himself against satanic promptings? Has Satan power to force a man to adopt a particular course of action? It points out that angels ever prompt a man to good and Satan ever prompts him to evil and that man has the option to accept or reject the good promptings of angels and equally to accept or reject the evil promptings of Satan. These two categories of beings have been created to help man towards perfection and to invest his existence with reality. In the absence of angelic and satanic promptings man would not be entitled to any reward nor would he deserve any punishment. A man's fight against satanic suggestions makes him worthy of reward and opens the way of progress to him; his turning away from angelic suggestions and promptings makes him liable to punishment.

The Quran expounds the philosophy of prayer and points out how one ought to pray, under what circumstances prayers may be accepted and what kind of prayers may not be accepted and what is the sphere within which prayer operates.

It discusses good and evil and defines both and explains where their boundaries meet. It defines absolute good and absolute evil and relative good and relative evil. It points out the way of acquiring high moral qualities and goodness and how evil may be avoided. It sheds light on the sources of good and evil and teaches man to clean out the source of evil.

It treats of repentance and explains what true repentance means. It enumerates the benefits to be derived from repentance, explains the requisites of true repentance and when repentance may be resorted to. It also explains the principles upon which rewards and penalties are based and the factors to which regard is had in adjudging them. It explains the relationship between transgression and punishment and how they ought to be adjusted to each other.

QURANIC CONCEPTION OF SALVATION

The Quran explains what salvation is and how it is attained. It teaches that salvation is of three kinds: (1) Perfect; (2) Imperfect; and (3) Deferred. Perfect salvation is attained in this very life. A person who attains imperfect salvation in this life gradually perfects the means of attaining salvation after death. Deferred salvation is attained only after suffering for a period the punishment of Hell. The teachings of Christianity and Islam with respect to this last kind of salvation have one feature of resemblance but are at variance with each other in a fundamental respect. Christianity teaches that even this kind of salvation can be achieved only by those who believe firmly in the doctrines of Christianity but who may have failed to attain perfect salvation in this life. These are the people who, after passing for a period through the torments of Hell, would attain perfect salvation. Islam, on the other hand, teaches that every human being has been created with the purpose that he or she will ultimately attain perfect salvation. The most rabid disbeliever and wrongdoer after being subjected to certain kinds of reformatory treatment, one of which is the torment of Hell, would ultimately attain salvation and would enter Paradise. In this connection the Quran emphasizes the doctrine of weighing and balancing of actions. It teaches that the preponderance of good actions in a man's life is proof of sincere effort on his part to attain salvation and that a person who dies while making a sincere effort to attain an object is like a soldier who is killed before victory is achieved. Death is controlled entirely by God. A soldier on the field of battle has no power to postpone it till after victory is achieved. In the same way a person who is struggling sincerely to attain salvation has no power to postpone death till his struggle ends in victory. If such a person dies in the middle of this struggle, he becomes deserving of the Grace and Mercy of God and not of His wrath and punishment. No nation has ever condemned its warriors for being killed before victory was achieved. Every soldier who sincerely strives for victory is honoured. The same is the case with a person who strives to overcome Satan, and in spite of ups and downs, continues to sustain the struggle steadfastly and with courage till the end so that God's Kingdom may be established. According to the Quran such a person is certainly deserving of salvation. His weakness is not a blemish but an ornament, for he was not thereby deterred from joining the ranks of those fighting on the side of God and did not hesitate to sacrifice himself in the struggle.

The Quran describes the stages of spiritual evolution and explains their number and details. For instance, it explains the kinds and degrees of purity, chastity, charity, truthfulness, mercy, kind treatment, etc. Thus, it enables a man to plan in accordance with his moral and spiritual development. By thus placing the immediate objective within a man's reach it encourages him to set out on the path of progress, and by setting out before him a series of ever-higher objectives it incites him to greater effort at each stage. It thus carries man forward on the path of progress step by step and stage by stage.

The Quran sheds light on man's intellectual evolution also

and explains how it is carried out and teaches that divine wisdom in judging of a man's actions takes into account his intellectual development. He who was fortunate enough to be nurtured in a favourable environment and for whom the path of virtue was made easy may be judged by a standard different from that applied to a person whose intellectual development was inferior to the former and whose environment was not so favourable. Allowance would be made for the latter in respect of the handicaps against which he had to struggle.

The Quran explains what faith is ; how it may be acquired, and how it may be known. It explains the need of the Law of Sharī'at and its philosophy. It teaches that God's Law is based upon wisdom and is designed to help man forward on the path of progress. God's commandments are not devised as a burden or a penalty for His servants but each of them is designed as an aid and a prop to man in his progress and to help to improve his social environment. The Quran does not support the doctrine of the compulsory imposition of commandments and penalties. It teaches that God condemns no person without taking into full account every circumstance that might excuse or palliate his conduct. It also teaches that no man may be condemned unless he has had due warning in advance.

MIRACLES

Christian writers have asserted that, apart from the claim that it is unique in its language and its philosophy, the Quran does not prefer any claim to miracles. It is necessary to explain in a few words the attitude of the Quran towards miracles.

The Quran puts forward two fundamental doctrines. First, that there are certain divine laws which are not subject to variation. For instance, the Quran teaches that a dead person never comes back to life upon this earth, and that nobody except God possesses the power of creation. The world may produce artificers, technicians, and inventors, but the attribute of creation manifests itself only through the work of God. As regards the first of these two matters God says in the Quran :

> Until, when death comes to one of them, he says entreating, "My Lord, send me back, that I may do righteous deeds in the

> life which I have left behind." By no means, it is but a mere word that he utters. And behind them is a barrier until the day when they shall be raised again (23 : 100, 101).

Again, it says :

> And it is an inviolable law for a township which We have destroyed that they shall not return. It shall be so even when Gog and Magog are let loose and they shall hasten forth from every height (21 : 96, 97).

The verses mean to say that God has decreed that the people that have passed away shall not return to the earth till Gog and Magog are released and spread over the earth from the summit of every hill and the top of every wave. This shows clearly that the dead cannot return to the earth. The reference to Gog and Magog in the last verse does not mean that the dead would be permitted to return to the earth at that time. As the release of Gog and Magog is one of the signs of the approach of the end of days, the verse means that this law will continue to operate till the end of days. Some grammarians have interpreted this part of the verse to mean that after the rise of Gog and Magog attempts would be made to resuscitate the dead but that these attempts would not be successful, meaning that science would make unsuccessful efforts to solve the riddle of death. In short, the Quran teaches that a dead person cannot be permitted to return to the earth.

It also teaches that nobody except God possesses the power to create. It says :

> And those on whom they call beside Allah create not anything, but they are themselves created. They are dead, not living ; and they know not when they will be raised (16 : 21, 22).

The Quran also teaches that since wisdom is one of the attributes of God, nothing may be attributed to Him which is contrary to wisdom. God is referred to as The Wise at several places in the Quran. At one place it says :

> What has happened to you that you expect not wisdom and staidness from Allah (71 : 14).

In this verse God reprimands the disbelievers saying that while they claim that all their actions are based upon wisdom, they do not make the same presumption with respect to God and attribute to Him things that are contrary to wisdom.

It follows therefore that if anything contravening any of these three laws, that have been cited as instances, is alleged to have occurred at any time, the Quran would reject it whether such occurrences are described as miracles or mysteries or magic. The Quran does not admit the possibility of any such occurrence and does not attribute any such miracle to any of the Prophets, nor does it claim any such miracle on behalf of the Holy Prophet himself. It is not to be thought of any reasonable person that he would first make a law or prescribe a rule and then himself proceed to contravene it. How is it possible then to think that God, Who is perfect wisdom, would act in that manner? He who attributes things like this to the righteous Prophets of God in no way adds to the respect and honour in which they should be held but is guilty of an attack upon their intelligence and integrity. It is the duty therefore of every right-thinking person to refute allegations of this kind as they amount not to praise but to defamation of the persons concerning whom they are made.

The Quran, on the other hand, not only does not deny but positively claims that God makes His Prophets the means of certain kinds of manifestations which do not in any manner contravene His fundamental laws. This is a truth which cannot be controverted and this is the kind of miracle that the Quran claims for the Holy Prophet. Is it not a miracle that God should vouchsafe to a human being the sure knowledge of things hidden in the womb of the future? Is it not a miracle for God to bestow success and victory upon a weak and humble person not possessed of any visible means against strong, powerful and numerous opponents? The Quran claims not only that it is unique in itself but also that God bestowed upon the Holy Prophet the knowledge of things hidden and that He constantly manifested His power and glory in support of the Holy Prophet. How can it then be said that the Quran does not attribute any miracles to the Holy Prophet? In truth it makes that claim repeatedly. Was it not a miracle that the Holy Prophet was warned of severe opposition and persecution on the part of the Meccans when he himself had no reason to suspect that he would become the object of such opposition and persecution? Was it not a miracle that he was informed that he would have to migrate from Mecca and that even the time of the migration was indicated in advance ? Was it not a miracle that several years before the Battle of Badr he was informed that such a conflict would take place in which the Muslims would be victorious and their enemies would be vanquished and that even the time of the conflict was specified ? Was it not a miracle that the Holy Prophet was informed years before the event not only that he would have to migrate from Mecca but also that he would re-enter Mecca as a victor ? Was it not a miracle that after the defeat of the Romans by the Persians in Syria the Holy Prophet was informed that within nine years the Romans would vanquish the Persians ? Was it not a miracle that the Holy Prophet was told that Islam would spread throughout Arabia and would then prevail against all other Faiths ? When every one of these events came to pass at its appointed time, what doubt could there have been left that every one of them constituted a miracle ? All these matters and many others of a similar kind are narrated in the Quran. Then how can it be said that the Quran disclaims miracles on the part of the Holy Prophet ? Those who are responsible for this assertion have been misled into making it on account of their lack of knowledge of the Arabic language and idiom and the style of the Quran. Where, for instance, the Quran says : "And nothing could hinder Us from sending Signs, except that the former people rejected them" (17 : 60), it does not mean, as Christian writers appear to have apprehended, that God declines to show any further Signs. The verse means that people for whose benefit Signs were shown in previous ages did not accept them and this might have been a reason for showing no further Signs, but God would not cease to manifest His Signs on that account. The people rejected the Signs shown by the earlier Prophets and yet Signs were shown in support of later Prophets ; thus there was no reason why Signs should not have been shown in support of the Holy Prophet of Islam.

Again, when in answer to the demands of disbelievers the Holy Prophet was directed in the Quran to say that he was but a human being like unto others, it did not mean that God did not show Signs in his support. All that was meant was that

Signs were shown by God and that the Holy Prophet could not produce them at his will. This is a fundamental truth and the statement of it by the Quran enhances our appreciation of it. Which of the two persons is a follower of the truth and which of them is in error : he who affirms that God had handed over His attributes and authority to some of His creatures or he who proclaims that he is but a creature of God and that God makes His Signs manifest through His beloved servants ?

In addition to prophecies the Quran makes mention of other miracles also. For instance, it refers to the following miracle. On the occasion of the Migration the Holy Prophet, accompanied by Abū Bakr, left Mecca and took refuge in Thaur Cave, three miles from Mecca. When the Meccans discovered that the Holy Prophet had slipped through their fingers, they procured their best tracker and tracked him up to the mouth of the cave. The Quran makes mention of the fact that, perceiving that the tracking party had arrived at the mouth of the cave, Abū Bakr was afraid lest on discovering him they should do injury to the Holy Prophet. But the latter said, 'Grieve not, for Allah is with us' (9 : 40), meaning that their enemies would not succeed in capturing them. Was not what followed on that occasion a peerless miracle indeed ? Two men utterly bereft of all earthly support fly from the concerted vengeance of their enemies and take refuge in a cave. When it is discovered that they have slipped out of the town in the darkness of the night, their enemies are filled with anger and dismay. They feel that the escape of the fugitives would not only cheat them of their prey but would inflict everlasting humiliation and disgrace upon them. They proclaim a reward of one hundred camels for whomsoever should capture and produce before them the principal fugitive, dead or alive. They then procure their best tracker who leads them to the mouth of the cave in which the two have concealed themselves and confidently asserts that the tracks lead no further. The tracking party are afire with the thirst for vengeance and are determined to leave no chance of escape to the runaways. After a pursuit extending over three miles they arrive within a few feet of their quarry and have only to look down and to peep into the cave which opens at their feet to discover the whereabouts of those whom they seek, but God exercises such control over their intelligence and their eyes that nobody cares to look into the cave and they return foiled and disappointed. Has the world ever witnessed a grander miracle than this ?

Again, with reference to the Battle of Badr the Quran states that the Holy Prophet threw a handful of pebbles in the direction of the enemy and that this created confusion in their ranks (Anfāl). In the traditions this incident is described in greater detail. It appears that when the battle was at its height and the enemy was pressing the Muslims hard, the Holy Prophet took up a handful of pebbles and threw them in the direction of the enemy saying : "May their faces be deformed" (Ṭabarī and Zurqānī). Simultaneously, God caused a fierce wind to blow from the direction of the Muslims towards the Meccans which whipped up the sand and threw it into the faces and the eyes of the latter. The result was that the Meccans could not see clearly and it became difficult for them to aim their arrows accurately. The force of the opposing wind also stopped their arrows half-way. On the other hand, the Muslims had a clear view of the helpless Meccans and their arrows were carried forward by the wind with great force. This gave the small, ragged and ill-armed band of Muslims a complete victory over the very much more numerous, better mounted and better armed force of the Meccans. Was this not a miracle and does not the Quran when referring to it purport to describe it as a miracle ?

The Quran does clearly ascribe miracles to the Holy Prophet and makes mention of some of them. Only, it refrains from ascribing to him such stupidities as the bringing back to physical life of persons that were truly dead or arresting the sun and the moon in their course or causing rivers to stand still or moving mountains. Accounts of occurrences like these are but fables which serve only to amuse little babies in their cradles. The Quran does not ascribe occurrences like these either to the Holy Prophet or to any other Prophet. On the other hand the Quran furnishes explanations of passages which occur in some of the older Scriptures the literal construction of which has led people to believe that occurrences like those referred to above did actually take place. The Quran points out that such language was used only in a metaphorical sense and is not susceptible of literal construction.

WORSHIP OF GOD

The Quran deals in detail with the subject of the worship of God. It divides all worship into four categories :

(1) Worship the object of which is to strengthen man's relationship with God and to increase his love for Him.

(2) Worship which is designed to improve man's physical condition and to incite him to make sacrifices for the sake of God.

(3) Worship which is prescribed for the purpose of promoting concord and unity among men and to create attachment to a centre.

(4) Worship the object of which is to bring about equitable economic adjustments within the community.

The Quran prescribes different kinds of worship under each of these categories. It teaches that worship does not merely mean that man should concentrate upon and offer homage to God but also consists in paying attention to one's fellow-beings. It further emphasizes that worship is not merely individual but is also collective. A man's duty in respect of worship does not end with presenting himself before God ; he must also prepare his brethren to appear before God. For this reason all the ordinances of the Quran relating to worship have a collective as well as an individual aspect.

Under the first category the Quran has prescribed the five daily services. The Islamic prayer service is very different from those prescribed in other religions. It has both an individual and a collective part and is entirely devoid of all show and ceremonial. The Quran has dispensed with the necessity of consecrated buildings like churches and temples and all formalities in the matter of the worship of God. It teaches that every portion of the earth's surface is fit to be used for the worship of God. The Holy Prophet had this in mind when he said : "The whole earth has been fashioned into a mosque for me" (Bukhārī). This saying of his has multifarious significance, one meaning being that a Muslim may say his prayers where he may happen to be when the time of prayers arrives. It is not obligatory upon him to proceed to a church or a temple nor is he dependent for the performance of his worship upon the ministrations of a priest or a person in holy orders. Islam does not countenance an ordained priesthood. It regards every good man as the vicegerent of God and recognizes the competence of every such person to lead the prayers.

THE MOSQUES OF ISLAM

Muslims make use of mosques for purposes of congregational prayers but this is not due to any feeling that the sites or buildings of these mosques possess any peculiar sanctity for the purposes of divine worship. A mosque is built to enable muslims of the neighbourhood to assemble for the purpose of congregational prayers. Mosques facilitate the performance of collective worship and are used for other religious and social purposes also. No particular ceremony is required for consecrating mosques and dedicating them to the worship of God, as is the case with temples and churches. Any building that is used for the purpose of congregational prayers by the Muslims is a mosque. No structural design has been prescribed for a mosque nor is a mosque divided into naves and transepts, nor does it possess anything resembling an altar. There are no pictures or images in a mosque and no relics of saints. The Muslims gather for divine worship in the simplest possible manner and Islamic religious services are free from all artistic and emotional distractions. There is no music or singing, no temple dances, no priestly vestments, no burning of candles and no attempt to create an emotional atmosphere by the aid of organs and incense. The light inside a mosque is not dimmed artificially to create an atmosphere of awe and no images of saints divert the attention of worshippers from God. At the appointed hour the worshippers collect in the mosque and range themselves in rows to indicate that, having concluded their individual worship in their homes or in the mosque, they are now ready to offer collective worship to God. They praise God and render thanks to Him and offer prayers to Him for their own spiritual, moral and physical advancement and for that of their friends and relations and of the whole of mankind. They do this in a perfectly calm atmosphere undisturbed even by the strains of music. While so engaged no worshipper may look to the right or to the left nor speak to any other worshipper. The rich and the poor stand shoulder to shoulder with each other ; the king may find his shoeblack standing next to him ; a judge may have as his neighbour an accused person who is on trial before him and a general may be standing next to a private. No worshipper may object to another worshipper standing next to him nor may any worshipper be moved from his station to another. They all stand humble and subdued in the presence of God and bow and prostrate themselves and revert to the standing posture under the leadership of the Imām. During some of the services the Imām recites aloud a few verses from the Quran to impress their purport upon the minds of the whole congregation. In certain parts of the service each worshipper offers prescribed prayers or prayers of his own composition.

In addition to the prescribed services Muslims offer prayers and devote themselves silently to the remembrance of God and ponder over His attributes, whenever during the day or night they can find the opportunity of doing so. Mosques are used not solely for the purposes of congregational and individual worship but for all kinds of religious and intellectual pursuits. They serve as schools and for the celebration of marriages, as courts of law and places of meeting where plans are settled for the social and economic progress of the community.

THE ISLAMIC FAST

The second form of worship which has as its principal object the physical improvement of the worshipper is fasting. The Islamic Fast differs from the fasts prescribed in other religions. A Hindu while fasting is permitted to eat certain kinds of food ; the Christian Lent is also observed by abstaining from the eating of particular kinds of food, for instance, meat or leavened bread. A Muslim, however, while fasting may not eat or drink anything from dawn till after sunset. A part of the obligation attaching to the Islamic Fast is that apart from abstention from food and drink during the hours of fasting a Muslim must make special efforts throughout the month of fasting to attain to higher standards of virtue and purity. One lesson that the Fast teaches is that a man who abstains from the use of permissible things during the Fast should on no account indulge on any occasion in that which is prohibited. The period of the Fast, that is to say, from dawn till after sunset, applies to all countries where there is an alternation of day and night during twenty-four hours. At the extremities of the earth where this does not hold good the period of the Fast is to be determined with reference to the length of a normal day.

This form of worship is also both individual and collective. Muslims are expected to fast individually on different days during the year but during the month of Ramaḍān all Muslims, wherever they may be, must observe the Fast.

THE PILGRIMAGE

The third form of worship prescribed by Islam is the Pilgrimage to Mecca. The object of this is to create in the minds of Muslims a feeling of attachment to a Centre. For the performance of the Pilgrimage Muslims who are able to afford the journey collect together at Mecca during a prescribed period. Thus an opportunity is afforded to them to come together from different parts of the world, to strengthen their relationship with each other and to exchange views upon national and international problems. This form of worship is also both collective and individual. The Pilgrimage may be performed only during the prescribed days, but the *'Umra* may be performed at any time. Whenever during the year a Muslim is able to make arrangements for the journey he can proceed to Mecca and perform the *'Umra*. This form of worship teaches Muslims that for the purpose of maintaining and strengthening the Centre they ought to be ready to make both collective and individual sacrifices.

The fourth form of worship is alms and charity. This too is both collective and individual and both prescribed and voluntary. For instance, on the occasion of the 'Id al-Fiṭr (the festival of the breaking of the Fast) it is obligatory upon every

Muslim, man and woman, adult and child, before taking part in the additional service prescribed for that day, to offer three pounds of wheat or corn or its equivalent in money as a contribution towards helping the poor. Even the poorest person is not exempt from this obligation. He who is able to afford it must make this contribution out of his own substance, but he who is not able to afford it must nevertheless provide the contribution out of that which he may receive in charity on that day.

THE ZAKĀT

Another financial obligation imposed upon Muslims is Zakāt, which is leviable from every person who possesses a certain minimum quantity of cash or goods or cattle. The incidence of the assessment varies. For instance, the rate is ten per cent in respect of agricultural produce and two and a half per cent on commercial capital and profits. This at first sight appears discriminatory and unbalanced, but the assessment on commercial capital and profits is not so light as it appears. While the assessment on agricultural produce is levied only on produce, the assessment on commercial enterprises is levied on both capital and profits. The object is not only to provide means for the relief of the distressed and the promotion of the welfare of the economically less favoured sections of the community but also to discourage the hoarding of money and commodities and thus to ensure a brisk circulation of both, resulting in healthy economic adjustments.

The Quran expounds in detail the principles upon which human intercourse ought to be based. It stresses the need of co-operation and defines the limits of individual and collective rights and obligations. It explains the fundamentals of government and its obligations and the relationship that ought to subsist between Government and people. It regulates the relationship of master and servant and lays down the principles that ought to govern international relationships.

The Quran expressly enjoins that wealth should not be permitted to accumulate in a few hands and that it ought to be kept constantly in circulation. To achieve this, it prohibits the lending of money on interest by means of which a few clever people are able to monopolize the greater part of the wealth of the community and makes provision for the compulsory distribution of inheritance. It does not permit any person to leave the whole of his property to one out of several heirs or even to augment the share of one heir at the expense of another. It seeks to bring about equitable adjustments in the distribution of wealth through Zakāt, alms and charity. It imposes as a first charge upon all government revenues and resources the obligation of providing for the welfare and progress of the poorer sections of the community. Through these means it provides for the economic prosperity of all sections of the people.

The Quran stresses the need of education and intellectual development. It prescribes reflection and contemplation as religious obligations. It dissuades people from entering into conflicts and going to war with each other and prohibits aggression. It lays down detailed rules for the regulation of relations between the followers of different religions. It prohibits Muslims from saying anything derogatory to the Founders or Leaders of other religions. With regard to religious controversies it points out the unreasonableness of criticism levelled against a rival creed to which one's own beliefs and doctrines are equally open. It teaches that all great religions are based upon revelation and that their deterioration is due to subsequent corruption at human hands. It therefore prohibits the wholesale condemnation of other religions.

The Quran fully safe-guards the rights of women. It is the first Scripture which has laid down in express words that men owe duties and obligations to women as women owe duties and obligations to men. It explains the rights and duties of parents, brothers and sisters, husbands and wives, sons and daughters, neighbours, the poor, orphans, widows, friends and strangers, both those that are of one's own country and those that are foreigners who have taken up residence in one's country or are merely on a visit to it.

ISLAMIC FORM OF GOVERNMENT

The Quran introduced entirely new conceptions in the

political field. It is the first Scripture that laid down the principle that no person can acquire the right to rule over others by virtue of hereditary succession. It teaches that government is a trust which should be committed to the care of those whom the people elect. The principle of democracy so proudly proclaimed by Europe and so much abused today was first established by the Quran. The Quran enjoins organization, discipline and obedience on the one hand, and on the other it requires public servants to discharge their obligations with honesty and integrity. It is the first Scripture that has limited the power of those in authority and has subjected them to discipline. The Quran does not admit the right of any individual to assume absolute authority over the community and does not admit that beneficent rule and administration are a matter of favour shown by the ruler to the ruled. The Quran stresses the principle that sovereignty belongs to the people and that those in authority are entrusted with it on behalf of God (4 : 59). The exercise of authority on proper occasions and in a suitable manner is no favour shown to the people but is only the discharge of the trust imposed upon those in whom authority has been vested. The Quran emphasizes, therefore, that in the exercise of the franchise electors should not be influenced by party or personal considerations but that the sole criterion should be the suitability of the candidate for the discharge of the duties to be entrusted to him. It is only then that the person elected would be in the best position to discharge those duties in the most beneficent manner. He who out of party or personal considerations helps to set up in authority an unsuitable person must share with him the responsibility for his maladministration. He cannot plead that the misfeasance is not his, for he was instrumental in putting the person concerned in a position where he could misbehave with regard to public matters.

The Quran insists upon the same moral standards being observed by Governments and public authorities as are obligatory upon individuals. It does not countenance the doctrine that rigid moral standards need not be insisted upon in the case of Governments and administrations. It teaches that truth is as valuable and indispensable in the case of statesmen as in the case of private citizens and that transgression is as evil and condemnable in the case of an administration as in the case of an individual. It prescribes equitable treatment and fair dealing for a Government not only towards its own people but also, as in the case of individuals, towards its neighbouring Governments.

The Quran enjoins constant alertness upon a believer. It exhorts Muslims to be diligent and condemns cowardice, bullying and fanaticism. It encourages the exercise of reason and reflection. It prohibits suicide and all acts or conduct that may result in self-destruction. It enjoins upon Governments the obligation of safe-guarding their frontiers. It prohibits aggression but enjoins unyielding resistance to it. In a war it prohibits surprise night-attacks. It insists upon the rigid observance of treaties and enjoins that no opportunity of making peace should be missed.

THE QURAN ON SLAVERY

The Quran does not permit the enslavement of one's countrymen or foreigners. It does, however, permit the taking of prisoners of war but prescribes that every prisoner is entitled to his freedom on payment of ransom (47 : 5). No person may keep another in captivity after the latter has paid his ransom. If a person who has been taken prisoner in a war is unable to pay his ransom immediately, he is entitled to earn his freedom by means of labour. If he is not able even to do this, the Quran exhorts Muslims to help him and to find means for procuring his liberty (24 : 34). It may, however, be that a prisoner may prefer to remain with his Muslim master rather than return to his non-Muslim relations and live under a non-Muslim Government. In such a case the Quran prescribes that he should be fairly and equitably treated. The Holy Prophet has said that in such a case the master should feed his prisoner on the kind of food he himself eats and should clothe him with the kind of garments he himself wears and should provide him with a mount like his own or should share his own with him (Bukhārī).

The Quran stresses the equality of all mankind. It is the

first Scripture that teaches that mankind is one community. It recognizes the division into countries, nations and tribes but explains that this is only for the purpose of identification and that with regard to rights all mankind are equal. It deprecates all distinctions based on racial, economic or other fancied superiority. It warns people that those who arrogate any kind of superiority to themselves will be humbled and laid low and that those upon whom they look down will one day be raised above them. If this sublime doctrine taught by the Quran were universally accepted, the principal obstacles in the way of the establishment of world-peace would be removed.

The Quran prohibits everything that has a tendency to incite people to folly and frivolity. For instance, it prohibits gambling and the use of intoxicants. It disapproves of all frivolous and light conduct. It prohibits the use of ornaments and silk garments by men, but permits women to use them to a moderate extent.

THE HUMAN SOUL

The Quran is the only Scripture that deals at length with the subject of the human soul and its creation. Other Scriptures either ignore the subject altogether or merely speculate upon it. The Quran says: "And they ask thee concerning the soul. Say, the soul is by the command of my Lord; and of the knowledge thereof you have been given but a little" (17 : 86). This verse refutes the theory that human souls are self-existing and eternal and that they remain, as it were, in reserve in some other universe and descend to the earth from time to time and enter into human bodies. It points out that the human soul, like other created things, is created by God and develops under divine guidance. It also indicates that the birth of the soul is not a process distinct from the birth of the body. The series of developments that bring about the birth of the body also bring about the birth of the soul and provide for its progress and uplift. This subject is dealt with in greater detail at another place in the Quran where it is said:

> Verily, We created man from an extract of clay; then We placed him as a drop of sperm in a safe depository; then We fashioned the sperm into a clot; then We fashioned the clot

> into a shapeless lump; then We fashioned bones out of this shapeless lump; then We clothed the bones with flesh; then We developed it into another creation. So blessed be Allah, the Best of creators (23 : 13–15).

This verse explains that a human being is born as the result of the nourishment which man and woman take to sustain life and to maintain their strength. This nourishment produces in the human body matter by means of which procreation takes place. When this matter enters into the womb, a portion of it which is charged with the faculty of procreation adheres to the womb and begins to draw sustenance. Within a few days it begins to thicken and grows into a flexible substance in which bones begin to form and later on, when these bones are clothed with flesh, the stages of physical procreation are completed. Simultaneously with this development a sort of distillation takes place as the result of which this growth develops animal characteristics and ultimately results in the birth of an intelligent human being. The verse shows clearly that the soul does not enter the body from outside but is a distillation from the substance which is being developed in the mother's womb. It is no doubt distinct from the substance from which it is distilled and has the effect of bestowing upon that substance animal characteristics and of converting it into a human being endowed with reason and intelligence and the faculty of progress. To illustrate this one may as a rough comparison draw attention to certain chemical processes whereby certain substances combine to form a new substance possessing distinct qualities of its own. For instance, alcohol is distilled from beet, wheat, corn or treacle. It possesses qualities different from those of the basic substance from which it is manufactured. Whereas the raw material of alcohol is liable to rot, alcohol is a preservative. Again, while the use of the raw material does not directly affect man's intellectual powers, alcohol is very potent in that respect.

In short, the Quran puts forward an altogether new conception concerning the birth of the human soul which is not to be found in any previous Scripture. As has already been stated, some of these Scriptures are altogether silent on this subject. They confine themselves to dealing with man as they find him and do not feel the need of discussing the subject of the creation of man and of the human soul. Those that purport to deal with this subject put forward one of two theories. One of these theories is that human souls are not created by God but are eternal and self-existing like God Himself. God causes these eternal souls to enter into human bodies at the appropriate time. The second theory is that souls are created and not self-existing but God created the requisite number of them at the same time as He created the universe, and that these souls are kept in reserve and out of this reserve God causes some to enter into human bodies from time to time. The Quran is the first and only Scripture which puts forward the correct view on this matter. It teaches that the birth of the soul is the ultimate stage of the volution of the human body in the course of its creation. It does not enter the body from outside but is born as a consequence of the changes that the body goes through in the course of its development. Yet it is something distinct from the body. It is not merely the motive power of the human body but is a distinct and permanent entity distilled from the substance of the body, just as alcohol and vinegar, though distilled from corn or fruit, are nevertheless distinct from the substances from which they are manufactured. By bringing this truth to light the Quran has entirely revolutionized the attitude of man towards the relationship between the body and the soul. Those who believe that human souls are self-existing and eternal or that they were all created in a bunch at the inception of the universe and are sent down to the earth as required from time to time, repudiate any suggestion that physical conditions and physical development have any effect upon the development of the soul. On the other hand, the Quran, by revealing the truth and reality, has emphasized that the condition and development of a person bear the closest relationship to his spiritual condition and physical development. It is true that even under the Quranic teachings every human body is bound at a certain stage to develop a soul, but the teaching of the Quran draws pointed attention to the principle that if care is devoted to the development of the human body along healthy and hygienic lines, the personality resulting therefrom will be more dynamic and more intelligent than if such development is neglected. By drawing attention to this fact the Quran has opened up new avenues for man's intellectual and spiritual development.

Some people assert that the soul possesses no faculties of its own and can therefore not be affected by any changes in the body. This is not correct. To say that the soul possesses no faculties is meaningless. If it possesses no faculties it can have no independent existence. It certainly possesses faculties but is able to manifest them only through the body. There are instances even in the material universe in which we find that certain things can manifest themselves only through coarser substances. For example, we are almost every moment brought up against the phenomenon that electricity can manifest itself only through other substances. In the same way, the faculties of the soul find expression in various ways through the body.

The Quran deals with all these and similar other subjects, but for obvious reasons they cannot all be discussed within the space of this Introduction. The Quran claims that it deals with all matters which are necessary for man's physical, moral and spiritual development and progress and in every age this claim has been found to have been justified. In this twentieth century also when science and learning are supposed to have reached a high stage of advancement, we find that the Quran fulfils all real needs and that there is no matter connected with the physical, moral, intellectual or spiritual purity and advancement of man which is not adequately dealt with in the Quran. These matters can only be briefly alluded to here. The details may be gathered from the Translation and the Explanatory Notes appended to the relevant verses. The Explanatory Notes in this Commentary have of necessity been kept to the minimum but more detailed information on these matters will be found in our Urdu Commentary of the Quran.

QURANIC PLAN OF SPIRITUAL UNIVERSE

Having briefly summarized the characteristics of Quranic teachings we would next draw attention to the plan of the spiritual universe which is described by the Quran. Our observation of the material universe shows that it works on a system in which several planets revolve round the sun and the sun along with all its dependent planets travels towards a goal concerning which modern mathematicians allege that it is a centre to which several solar systems are related. Whether these speculations are based upon reality or not it is undeniable that the whole of the material universe is running on a system ; otherwise it would have ended in chaos long ago. This system is governed by a code of laws which regulate different phases of matter and as the result of which the universe is filled with a vast variety of material substances and objects. The progress and development of the material universe are dependent upon the utilization and exploitation of these material substances and objects. The Quran teaches that the spiritual universe also works under a system which revolves round an all-embracing Centre which controls the whole universe. There is nothing in the universe which is outside or independent of the control of this Centre. This Centre is a Being Self-Existent and Uncreated. He is not dependent upon anything else for the purpose of fulfilling His designs. He is neither begotten nor He begets nor has He a partner or associate who shares with Him His powers or functions. This is set out very clearly in Sūra Ikhlāṣ (Chap. 112). In that Sūra God directs the Holy Prophet to proclaim that the truth is that God is unique in all His powers and attributes. On occasion one may discover a resemblance between the attributes of a thing or person and some of the attributes of God but the resemblance is only apparent and superficial. For instance, we say that God exists and it may be said that men and animals and other things also exist. The word employed to give expression to the idea of existence is the same in both cases, but it does not signify the same reality in each case. When we say that God exists we mean that He is Self-Existing and perfect in Himself and is not dependent for His existence upon any other being or thing. But when we say that a man exists or an animal exists or some other thing exists, all that we mean is that so long as those causes and conditions continue the interaction of which resulted in the creation of the man or of the animal or of the thing, they will continue to exist ; but that if those causes and conditions are removed or are materially affected the man and the animal and the thing would also cease to exist or would be materially affected. For instance, a man is said to be alive so long as the relationship between his soul and body continues to subsist. But this relationship is temporary and terminable and when it is terminated the human body still continues to exist but it is not alive. Again, the body is composed of a multitude of atoms which assume a particular shape and enter into certain combinations under certain conditions. When these combinations are dissolved the body ceases to exist as a body. When a dead body is buried in the earth certain chemical changes take place in it and it decomposes. The atoms which had constituted the human body still remain in existence but the causes and conditions which had brought about their combination in the shape of the body having been altered, the body ceases to exist. The same happens when the body is decomposed by the action of water or of fire or of electricity. The atoms of matter which had constituted the body remain in existence but they assume new shapes and the body is no longer able to retain its shape or composition. These considerations do not apply to God. No external causes or conditions have brought Him into being or help to preserve His existence. He exists because He is perfect and is above the limitations of time. It is alleged that the human brain is incapable of comprehending how God can exist above the limitations of time when all matter is subject to those limitations. But the truth is that God exists in a sense different from that in which man or other material beings or substances exist and the resemblance between the two in the matter of existence is only apparent and superficial. God is Unique and does not share any of His attributes with any other being or thing. At another place the Quran says that God is the Creator of the heavens and of the earth. He has created man and animals and all things in couples and has made provision for the progress of the material universe through this means (42 : 12). This means that men and animals and vegetables and even solids have been created in couples which may be described as male and female, or positive and negative or by any other name and that the whole universe moves forward on the basis of everything having been created in couples. Again, the Quran says: "And of every thing have We created pairs, that haply you may reflect" (51 : 50). This means that man, by contemplating everything in the universe and observing that everything has been created in couples, can conclude that none of these created things can be God, for, each of them is imperfect in itself and can continue its existence and perform its functions adequately only with the aid of a mate.

In short, the Quran teaches that the Centre of the universe is a Being Unique in Himself and that no other being or thing bears any real resemblance to Him. The whole of the universe is dependent for its continuance and for the performance of its functions upon something else but the Being Who is the Centre of the whole universe is not dependent upon any other being or thing either for His existence or for the manifestation of His attributes. The Quran teaches that that Being is neither begotten nor begets. This distinguishes the teachings of the Quran on this point from the teachings of Christianity. Christianity as well as some other Aryan creeds attribute to God the begetting of children. The Quran, on the other hand, teaches that it is only those beings that are dependent or are liable to extinction that stand in need of children. Since God is neither dependent nor would cease to exist, He is in no need of children. Since He is Self-Existent, He has no father. Thus He is unique in that He is not begotten and does not beget and is also unique in that there is no other being possessing similar powers and attributes. That is to say, God was neither created nor He begets nor has He a peer. This last teaching of the Quran refutes the doctrine of the plurality of gods which is taught by religions like Zoroastrianism.

The Sūra Ikhlāṣ in its few laconic verses thus proclaims that the Centre of the whole universe is God, Who is a Unique Being. He is the only source of the universe and is not dependent for the manifestation of His attributes upon any other being or thing. He is not begotten nor does He beget. There is no parallel power that shares His attributes with Him nor is there any other being who possesses a rival position in opposition to Him. This very brief Sūra in a few simple words refutes the errors of the doctrines of all other religions relating to the Divine Being and proclaims the perfect Unity of God.

GOD OF ALL PEOPLES

The followers of some religions believe that God stands in a peculiar relationship towards them from which all other human beings are excluded. They believe that though God is the Creator of the whole universe He is in a special sense the God of a particular people, for instance, the Israelites or the Hindus or the Zoroastrians. The Quran rejects this doctrine and teaches that not only is God unique in His being but that He is the source of the whole universe. The word *Aḥad* occurring in the first verse of Sūra Ikhlāṣ means unique and also unity, that is to say, the source which is itself outside numbers but from which all numbers proceed. This verse indicates that God is equally the guide of the whole of mankind and entertains no special attachment to any particular people. Those who strive to attain nearness to Him He guides along the paths that lead to Him. Arabs, Jews, Persians, Indians, Chinese, Greeks and Africans are all equal in His sight, for He is the source of the creation of all of them. He alone is the unity which is the source of the multiplicity of the universe. By proclaiming that He is not begotten the Quran refutes the central doctrine of Christianity as well as of several Hindu creeds, for he who is himself begotten could not be God since he would be dependent for his own creation upon somebody else. By pointing out that He has no rival the Quran refutes the doctrine inculcated by some religions that light and darkness are distinct and opposing forces and thus in effect set up two parallel gods.

GOD—THE ULTIMATE CAUSE OF ALL CREATION

The Quran also teaches that God is the ultimate cause of all creation ; that is to say, that the whole of creation has proceeded from Him and reverts to Him. It says : "He is the First and the Last" (57 : 4). This means that everything in the universe owes its existence to God and that the extinction of everything is also brought about under divine laws. Had not God chosen to confer existence upon the universe, it could not have come into existence ; and had not God promulgated laws for its destruction it could not have been destroyed. All creation and destruction are thus controlled by divine laws and this is proof of the fact that the system of the universe has been established by an intelligent Being. The Quran says:

> The Originator of the heavens and the earth! How can He have a son when He has no consort, and when He has created everything and has knowledge of all things? Such is Allah, your Lord. There is no god but He, the Creator of all things, so worship Him. And He is Guardian over everything (6 : 102, 103).

These verses point out that as God is the source of all creation He has no need of a son. A son is procreated either by accident or to fulfil a certain need. The union of a male and a female even when the object is not procreation may result in the birth of a child. The possibility of this in the case of God is negatived in the verse quoted above by attention being drawn to the fact that He has no mate. It is, however, alleged by some that God might create a being and assign to him the position of a son. But a son is desired only for the purpose of assisting the father in the discharge of his functions and to perpetuate his name. The Quran points out that God, being the Creator and Controller of all things, needs no assistance, and being Eternal His name would endure for ever. No object would, therefore, be served by His creating or appointing a son. A man sometimes makes provision for the future against unknown contingencies, but the Quran points out that since God has perfect knowledge of all things, He is under no necessity to provide for unknown contingencies. He knows the past and the future and is under no need to take precautions with regard to the future. The Quran then goes on to draw attention to the fact that not only has God created man but that He also fosters and develops him from weakness and inferiority to strength and superiority. There is no god beside Him. He has created the whole universe. All mankind, whether Persians or Arabs, Jews or Hindus, are equal in His sight. He has created all of them and provided the means of progress for all. It is incumbent therefore upon all men that they should worship Him alone, for He alone controls the universe and man can escape ruin and destruction only by fostering his relationship with Him and can never find peace away from Him.

The Quran teaches that God knows all about everything in the universe. There is nothing that is outside His ken. It says: "His knowledge extends over the heavens and the earth" (2 : 256). Again, it says:

> And thou art not engaged in anything, and thou recitest not from Him any portion of the Quran, and you do no work, but We are Witnesses of you when you are engrossed therein. And there is not hidden from thy Lord even an atom's weight in the earth or in heaven. And there is nothing smaller than that or greater, but it is recorded in a clear Book (10 : 62).

These verses show that the condition of a man's mind and that which he utters by word of mouth and that which he does by the exercise of his limbs are all manifest to God. Objects even as minute as an atom or even smaller are not hidden from His sight. He perceives the minutest as well as the grossest object and not only is everything within His knowledge but all that is done or that happens is preserved in such manner as to produce its due result in its season. The verse says that all these things are recorded in an open Book. This means that whereas ordinary records are hidden from the eyes of men and after they are entered up they disappear even from the sight of the person making them, the divine record of all that occurs is such that it speaks for itself, that is to say, every action leads to its result in accordance with the divine law and the divine will. Again, the Quran says that since God is beyond physical perception, "Eyes cannot reach Him" (6 : 104), that is to say, God is by His nature different from all material objects and it is not therefore possible to perceive Him through any of the physical senses.

The Quran teaches that God has full power to carry out all His designs. It says: "Allah has the power to do all that He wills" (2 : 110). It should be noted that the verse does not merely say, God has power to do all things; for such phraseology would leave room for foolish people to raise absurd questions. It has, for instance, been asked whether God has power to destroy Himself or whether He has power to create another god like Himself. It is obvious that for God to do any such thing would be absurd and undesirable and it is incompatible with His Majesty and Perfection to indulge in anything absurd or undesirable. The Quran has, therefore, refrained from stating that God has power to do everything and has merely said that God has power to carry into effect all that He may determine to do. God, being perfect, determines only that which is perfect and it would be the height of folly to attribute to God a desire to destroy Himself or to create another god like unto Himself.

PRINCIPAL DIVINE ATTRIBUTES

The opening Chapter of the Quran (Sūra al-Fātiḥa) illustrates the operation of the attributes of God. It explains that the divine attributes, the operation of which affects man in any manner, branch out from four principal attributes.

Of these, the first is Rabb al-'Ālamīn (رب العالمين); that is to say, God creates everything and then fosters everything gradually towards perfection.

Secondly, He is Raḥmān (الرحمن). This means that without any effort on the part of His creatures He provides everything that is necessary for their development and progress.

Thirdly, He is Raḥīm (الرحيم). This means that when those of His creatures that are endowed with will and intelligence voluntarily choose to do good and to resist evil, God bestows upon them the highest reward and that reward continues indefinitely.

Fourthly, He is Mālik Yaum al-Dīn (مالك يوم الدين). This means that the ultimate judgement concerning everything rests with Him. Everything owes its origin to Him and the end of everything is also in His hands. Man and other creatures may bring about temporary and ephemeral changes but have not the power to effect any permanent change in the universe. For instance, man has no power to create either matter or soul. He is equally without power to destroy either, though he may be able to effect temporary changes in matter and to give it different shapes. As the attribute of creation belongs to God alone the attribute of destruction also is peculiar to Him,

Nothing can ultimately be destroyed till God decrees its destruction. This is an obvious truth and the Quran expresses it by stating that God is the Master of the time of judgement. That is to say, the final judgement regarding everything that is set in motion rests in His hands and these judgements are arrived at by Him in His capacity of Master of the universe and not merely as a judge who adjudicates upon the rights of the parties before him. A judge is bound to make an impartial adjudication upon the matter in dispute between the parties having regard to the rights and obligations of each. God is not so bound, for though when He pronounces His judgement no man is wronged or is cheated of his due, He is free to remit as much as He may choose out of what may be due to Himself. He does not insist upon the proverbial pound of flesh. As a master may treat his servants with mercy and act benevolently towards them and bestow favours upon them, so may God forgive the trespasses of His creatures and overlook their defaults and bestow His favours upon them. Failure to appreciate this attribute of God has led to the adoption by Christians of so untenable a doctrine as that of Atonement. The Christian doctrine is that God has, like a secular judge, no power to forgive any person his default. In making this erroneous assumption Christians overlook the fact that a judge is called upon to adjudicate between two parties and that he himself possesses no rights in respect of the subject-matter of the dispute. The relationship between God and His creatures is, however, very different from that between a judge and the parties to a dispute. God is both a claimant and the authority entitled to make the award. A judge is never himself a claimant. He is called upon merely to determine the rights of the parties before him. In other words, a judge has to arrive at a determination between two persons, one making a claim against the other. These persons may be both private individuals or one representing the State and the other a private individual. God determines between Himself and His creatures. He thus occupies dual position. He is both claimant and judge. As a claimant He is entitled to remit the whole or as much as He chooses of His claim. Such a remission would be mercy and not injustice, for the remission relates to God's own claim and does not operate to deprive any person of his right. This is in perfect accord with reason.

On the other hand the doctrine of Atonement is wholly opposed to reason. If belief in the crucifixion of Jesus is indispensable for the remission of sins, then how did the Prophets who appeared before Jesus and their followers attain salvation? Was it not necessary for the crucifixion to have taken place at the inception of the universe so that all mankind should have attained salvation? Again, how is it that sins may be remitted through belief in the crucifixion but not through repentance, which is the natural means of purification of the heart. Belief in an external matter is not a natural means of purification of the heart, whereas remorse and contrition, which inflict a kind of death upon a man's longings and desires and inspire him with a fresh determination to lead a virtuous life, are a natural and certain means of purification of the heart. It is surprising that Christians should believe that a sinner's heart is purified by belief in the crucifixion of Jesus and that God in consequence forgives him his sins, but they should refuse to accept the truth that when a sinner experiences remorse and admits his fault before God and asks His forgiveness, God forgives him his sins and errors.

We observe that in the transaction of their daily affairs Christians themselves follow this principle. When a man commits a fault and is then overtaken by true remorse and, admitting his fault, promises to make amends, they forgive him. For instance, this principle is followed in their schools. When a schoolmaster finds that a pupil has been at fault or has been negligent concerning his studies or his other duties and the former is convinced that the pupil is contrite and is prepared to make amends for the future, he forgives him. Yet, if the doctrine of Atonement were sustainable, all that should be necessary in such a case should be for the pupil to say that though he has been at fault he is a believer in the crucifixion of Jesus and that his fault should be overlooked. But this is not what happens. The master insists that to be forgiven the pupil must show that he is ashamed of his default and is ready to make amends for the future. He is not prepared to forgive merely on the assurance that the pupil believes in the crucifixion.

It may, however, be alleged that belief in the crucifixion is tantamount to purification of the heart. This is, however, belied by the conduct of Christians all over the world. The evils and the vices that prevail in Christian countries can scarcely be matched in any other part of the world.

Then what is it that the Christians have gained through belief in the Atonement? If they assert that they will attain salvation through belief in this doctrine, this would be untenable, as we have already shown that salvation can only be attained through true repentance and that the Prophets who appeared before Jesus and their followers attained salvation only by this means. If Christians claim that the Atonement brings about purity of heart, this has not been achieved by Christians in spite of their belief in the Atonement. We do not mean to imply that no Christian enjoys purity of heart, but we do assert that the purity of no Christian's heart is due to belief in the Atonement. If the heart of a Christian is purified it is purified, like the hearts of other people, through remorse and repentance or through the worship of God, *i.e.*, prayer and fasting as was said by Jesus himself: "This kind can come forth by nothing, but by prayer and fasting" (Mark 9 : 29).

OTHER ATTRIBUTES OF GOD

It is not possible to enter into a detailed explanation of the various attributes of God referred to in the Quran, either expressly or by inference, as stemming from the four principal attributes which have just been described. A brief mention of them may, however, be made here:

(1) Al-Mālik *i.e.* The Sovereign.
(2) Al-Quddūs *i.e.* The Holy One.
(3) Al-Salām *i.e.* The Source of Peace.
(4) Al-Mu'min *i.e.* The Bestower of Security.
(5) Al-Muhaimin *i.e.* The Protector.
(6) Al-'Azīz *i.e.* The Mighty.
(7) Al-Jabbār *i.e.* The Subduer.
(8) Al-Mutakabbir *i.e.* The Exalted.
(9) Al-Khāliq *i.e.* The Creator.
(10) Al-Bārī *i.e.* The Maker.

(11)	Al-Muṣawwir *i.e.*	The Fashioner.
(12)	Al-Ghaffār *i.e.*	The Great Forgiver.
(13)	Al-Qahhār *i.e.*	The Most Supreme.
(14)	Al-Wahhāb *i.e.*	The Bestower.
(15)	Al-Razzāq *i.e.*	The Great Sustainer.
(16)	Al-Fattāḥ *i.e.*	The Opener (of the doors of success for mankind) ; The Judge.
(17)	Al-'Alīm *i.e.*	The All-Knowing.
(18)	Al-Qābiḍ *i.e.*	The Controller ; He Who keeps all things within limits ; The Seizer.
(19)	Al-Bāsiṭ *i.e.*	The Enlarger ; He Who enlarges the means of subsistence.
(20)	Al-Khāfiḍ *i.e.*	The Depresser ; He Who brings low the proud.
(21)	Al-Rāfi' *i.e.*	The Exalter.
(22)	Al-Mu'izz *i.e.*	The Bestower of honour.
(23)	Al-Mudhill *i.e.*	The Abaser ; He Who abases the haughty.
(24)	Al-Samī' *i.e.*	The All-Hearing.
(25)	Al-Baṣīr *i.e.*	The All-Seeing.
(26)	Al-Ḥakam *i.e.*	The Wise Judge.
(27)	Al-'Adl *i.e.*	The Just.
(28)	Al-Laṭīf *i.e.*	The Incomprehensible ; The Knower of all subtleties ; The Benignant.
(29)	Al-Khabīr *i.e.*	The All-Aware.
(30)	Al-Ḥalīm *i.e.*	The Forbearing.
(31)	Al-'Aẓīm *i.e.*	The Great.
(32)	Al-Ghafūr *i.e.*	The Most Forgiving.
(33)	Al-Shakūr *i.e.*	The Most Appreciating.
(34)	Al-'Aliyy *i.e.*	The High.
(35)	Al-Kabīr *i.e.*	The Incomparably Great.
(36)	Al-Ḥafīẓ *i.e.*	The Guardian.
(37)	Al-Muqīt *i.e.*	The Preserver ; He Who preserves the faculties of all created things ; The Powerful.
(38)	Al-Ḥasīb *i.e.*	The Reckoner.
(39)	Al-Jalīl *i.e.*	The Lord of Majesty.
(40)	Al-Karīm *i.e.*	The Noble.

(41) Al-Raqīb *i.e.*	The Watchful.
(42) Al-Mujīb *i.e.*	The Answerer of prayers.
(43) Al-Wāsi' *i.e.*	The Bountiful ; The All-Embracing.
(44) Al-Ḥakīm *i.e.*	The Wise.
(45) Al-Wadūd *i.e.*	The Loving.
(46) Al-Majīd *i.e.*	The Lord of honour.
(47) Bā'ith *i.e.*	The Raiser (of the dead).
(48) Al-Shahīd *i.e.*	The Witness ; The Observer.
(49) Al-Ḥaqq *i.e.*	The True.
(50) Al-Wakīl *i.e.*	The Disposer of affairs ; The Keeper.
(51) Al-Qawiyy *i.e.*	The Powerful.
(52) Al-Matīn *i.e.*	The Strong.
(53) Al-Waliyy *i.e.*	The Friend.
(54) Al-Ḥamīd *i.e.*	The Praiseworthy.
(55) Al-Muḥṣī *i.e.*	The Recorder.
(56) Al-Mubdī *i.e.*	The Author (of life) ; The Beginner.
(57) Al-Mu'īd *i.e.*	The Repeater (of life).
(58) Al-Muḥyī *i.e.*	The Life-giver.
(59) Al-Mumīt *i.e.*	The Controller of the causes of death ; The Destroyer.
(60) Al-Ḥayy *i.e.*	The Living.
(61) Al-Qayyūm *i.e.*	The Self-Subsisting and All-Sustaining.
(62) Al-Wājid *i.e.*	The Discoverer ; The Finder.
(63) Al-Mājid *i.e.*	The Glorious.
(64) Al-Qādir *i.e.*	The Possessor of power and authority.
(65) Al-Muqtadir *i.e.*	The Omnipotent.
(66) Al-Muqaddim *i.e.*	The Provider (of the means of progress and advancement).
(67) Al-Mu'akhkhir *i.e.*	The Degrader ; The Postponer.
(68) Al-Awwal *i.e.*	The First.
(69) Al-Ākhir *i.e.*	The Last.
(70) Al-Ẓāhir *i.e.*	The Manifest ; He to Whose existence every created thing clearly points.
(71) Al-Bāṭin *i.e.*	The Hidden ; He through Whom the hidden reality of every thing is revealed.

(72) Al-Wālī *i.e.*	The Ruler.
(73) Al-Muta'ālī *i.e.*	The Most High; The Possessor of excellent attributes.
(74) Al-Barr *i.e.*	The Beneficent.
(75) Al-Tawwāb *i.e.*	The Oft-Returning with compassion; The Acceptor of repentance.
(76) Al-Mun'im *i.e.*	The Bestower of favours.
(77) Al-Muntaqim *i.e.*	The Awarder of appropriate punishment; The Avenger.
(78) Al'Afuww *i.e.*	The Effacer of sins.
(79) Al-Ra'ūf *i.e.*	The Compassionate.
(80) Mālik al-Mulk *i.e.*	The Lord of Sovereignty.
(81) Al-Muqsiṭ *i.e.*	The Equitable.
(82) Al-Jāmi' *i.e.*	The Gatherer; The Assembler.
(83) Al-Ghaniyy *i.e.*	The Self-Sufficient.
(84) Al-Mughnī *i.e.*	The Provider of the means of sufficiency; The Enricher.
(85) Al-Māni' *i.e.*	The Withholder, The Prohibitor.
(86) Al-Ḍārr *i.e.*	The Inflictor of punishment.
(87) Al-Nāfi' *i.e.*	The Benefactor.
(88) Al-Nūr *i.e.*	The Light.
(89) Al-Hādī *i.e.*	The Guide.
(90) Al-Badī' *i.e.*	The Originator.
(91) Al-Bāqī *i.e.*	The Survivor.
(92) Al-Wārith *i.e.*	The Inheritor.
(93) Al-Rashīd *i.e.*	The Director to the right way.
(94) Al-Ṣabūr *i.e.*	The Patient.
(95) Dhū'l 'Arsh *i.e.*	The Lord of the Throne.
(96) Dhū'l Waqār *i.e.*	The Possessor of staidness and gravity; He Who does everything with reason and to fulfil a certain purpose.
(97) Al-Mutakallim *i.e.*	The Speaker; He Who speaks to His servants.
(98) Al-Shāfī *i.e.*	The Healer.
(99) Al-Kāfī *i.e.*	The Sufficient.
(100) Al-Aḥad *i.e.*	The Unique; The Lord of Unity.
(101) Al-Wāḥid *i.e.*	The One.

(102) Al-Ṣamad *i.e.*	The Besought of all ; The Independent ; The Everlasting.
(103) Dhū'l Jalāl wa'l-Ikrām, *i.e.*	The Lord of Majesty and Bounty.

THREE CATEGORIES OF DIVINE ATTRIBUTES

These attributes are either expressly mentioned in the Quran or are deducible from Quranic verses. A consideration of these attributes helps to visualize the plan of the spiritual universe which the Quran puts forward. They may be roughly divided into three categories :

First, those that are peculiar to God and are not related in any way to His creatures *e.g.*,—Al-Hayy,—The Living ; Al-Qādir—The Possessor of power and authority ; Al-Majīd. —The Glorious.

Secondly, those that are related to the creation of the universe and indicate the relationship between God and His creatures and His attitude towards them *e.g.*, Al-Khāliq—The Creator ; Al-Mālik—The Sovereign, etc.

Thirdly, those that come into operation in consequence of the good or bad actions of such of God's creatures as are endowed with will *e.g.*, Al-Raḥīm—He rewards the voluntary good actions of man abundantly and repeatedly ; Mālik Yaum al-Dīn —The Master of the Day of Judgement ; Al-'Afuww—He overlooks faults ; Al-Ra'ūf—He is Compassionate, etc.

Some of these attributes appear to be repetitions but on consideration one finds fine distinctions between them. For instance, several of these attributes relate to creation as Khāliqu Kulli Shai'in, Al-Badī', Al-Fāṭir, Al-Khāliq, Al-Bārī, Al-Mu'īd, Al-Muṣawwir, Al-Rabb. At first sight they appear to overlap but in fact they signify different aspects.

Khāliqu Kulli Shai'in means that God has created all things and signifies that He is also the Creator of matter and of souls. Some people believe that God fashions but does not create. They do not, for instance, regard Him as the Creator of matter or of souls ; they believe that matter and souls are self-existing and eternal like God Himself. If God had been described in the Quran merely as the Creator, these people could have claimed that they too believe in God as the Creator in the sense that He brings about the union of the body and the soul and thus fashions and in a sense creates man. This interpretation would have left the real meaning of the Quran in this respect in doubt. By describing God as the Creator of all things, the Quran has enlarged the scope of the attribute of creation, so as to include the creation of matter and souls.

Badī' signifies that God has planned and designed the system of the universe and this system is not, therefore, accidental or copied from somewhere else.

Fāṭir means One Who extracts something by breaking the shell. The attribute Fāṭir, therefore, indicates that God has created matter with inherent faculties of development and that in due season He breaks open the shell or covering which confines the operation of these faculties and brings them into operation. For instance, a seed possesses the faculty of growing into a plant or a tree but this faculty comes into operation only at a certain season and under certain conditions. When those conditions arise and that season arrives, the seed begins to develop its faculty of growth. This attribute thus indicates that God has created the universe in accordance with a set of laws and that all sections of the universe continue to develop in accordance with those laws. All the time certain parts of the universe go on traversing preparatory stages and their inherent faculties come into play at certain seasons and then new forms of life become perceptible.

The attribute of *Khalq* (creation) also signifies planning. *Khāliq* (Creator) therefore also means that God has arranged all things in their proper order and that the universe is controlled by a system.

Bārī signifies that God starts different manifestations of creation and then appoints laws in obedience to which the thing created goes on repeating and multiplying its species. This is reinforced by the attribute *Mu'dī*, which signifies repetition.

Muṣawwir signifies that God has given each created thing a shape which is appropriate to its functions. This shows that the perfection of creation consists not merely in endowing the thing created with appropriate faculties but is achieved also by giving it appropriate shape.

Rabb signifies that God after creating goes on fostering the faculties of created things by stages and thus leads them to perfection.

All these attributes thus signify different aspects of creation. In the same way several other attributes which appear at first sight to be overlapping or mere repetitions are in fact intended to signify very fine distinctions. Once the significance of each attribute is clearly grasped, one is able to appreciate the beauty and the glory of the spiritual universe that the Quran describes.

The New Testament makes little mention of the attributes of God. Neither the Torah nor any other single Scripture describes all these attributes. If, however, all the Jewish Scriptures are taken together, one finds mention in them at different places of a good many of the attributes that we have set out above, but even then all are not mentioned. It is commonly thought by Muslims that God possesses ninety-nine attributes. This idea is related to certain Jewish traditions which are based upon the attributes of God mentioned in the Jewish Scriptures. The Quran makes mention of many more than the one hundred and three attributes we have mentioned above but those we have not set out. In fact many of the attributes of God, the operation of which is not connected with man, have not been mentioned in the Quran and it would therefore not be right to assign any particular number to the attributes of God. Wherever in Islamic literature any mention of a number is made in this connection it is only in contrast to the Jewish claim and not for the purpose of expressing the absolute reality.

The Vedas mention very few attributes of God and the same is the case with the Zend-Avesta. The truth is that as the Quran is the perfect book and contains complete guidance for all stages of spiritual development, it sets out all the attributes of God the knowledge of which is necessary for man, including those that have been mentioned in previous Scriptures and those that have not been so mentioned.

DIVINE ATTRIBUTES NOT CONTRADICTORY

It is sometimes alleged that some of these attributes are inconsistent with others. For instance, God is Merciful and yet He punishes. He is free from all needs and yet He creates and makes provision for the guidance of mankind which indicates a desire on His part to bring into existence man and other creatures. Such criticism often originates in minds that are not given to deep reflection. They do not realize that a large part of the real beauty of the universe is due to its diversity and that what they regard as conflict and inconsistency is evidence only of the richness of the pattern of the universe. Everything in the universe moves within its appointed sphere and may be regarded as a link in a huge chain.

It is true that God punishes, but this is done in accordance with His laws regulating punishments and penalties. When the operation of these laws demands the imposition of a penalty, God decrees punishment. As against this, God has promulgated laws through which his attributes of mercy and forgiveness find manifestation. When the operation of these laws necessitates the exercise of the attribute of mercy or of forgiveness, that attribute comes into operation. Thus at the same time His attribute of punishment manifests itself in accordance with His laws in respect of one person and His attribute of forgiveness or mercy or benevolence manifests itself in respect of another. One person is born in manifestation of God's attribute of creation and at the same moment another person dies in manifestation of God's attribute of destruction. The question is generally asked why God causes people to die when the Quran describes Him as Rabb al-'Ālamīn, which means that God creates and fosters and leads to perfection. This question indicates lack of reflection on the part of the persons who put it. The Quran does not describe God as the Rabb of this world alone but as the Rabb of all the worlds. Death means translation from one universe to another. When a person is so translated, the attribute of Rabūbiyyat (creation and fostering) makes itself manifest in respect of that person in the universe to which he is translated. Whatever exists in any universe is fostered under the attribute of Rabūbiyyat. If we are, however, to suppose that something has ceased to exist, then it has ceased to be part of any universe and the question of the manifestation of the attribute of Rabb al-'Ālamīn (Creator, Sustainer and Fosterer of all the worlds) in respect of that thing does not arise at all.

The Quran teaches that for the regulation and adjustment of the attributes which affect mankind God has set in motion two laws. The first of these is : "My mercy encompasses all things" (7 : 157) ; and the second is set out in the verse : "What has happened to you that you expect not wisdom and staidness from Allah" (71 : 14). The latter verse means that whatever God does is based upon wisdom. One of the attributes of God mentioned in the Quran is The Wise, which also indicates the same thing.

These two laws indicate that every manifestation of an attribute of God is for the achievement of a definite purpose or object. They also show that whenever there is a struggle between the laws demanding punishment and the laws necessitating the exercise of mercy, the latter will prevail and punishment will be subordinated to it. Contemplation of the operation of these two laws fills the heart of a Muslim with the love of God which pervades the whole of his being. A Muslim, for the purpose of creating love and devotion in his heart towards God, is not under the necessity of doing violence to his reason and of accepting the doctrine of Atonement and the crucifixion of a human being who bore the burden of all sins. It is enough for him that the Quran teaches that every manifestation of God's attributes is governed by wisdom and has a definite purpose and object and that, being human, if he is on occasion guilty of a weakness or commits a fault and is then overtaken by remorse and contrition and makes up his mind to eschew all manner of error in the future, the love and forgiveness of God will completely cover him. This knowledge melts his heart and it is dissolved in an ecstasy of love for God. A Muslim realizes that though God is the Creator and the Sovereign, He forgives the trespasses of His servants, overlooks their faults, and makes every manner of provision for their advancement. When He imposes a penalty, His object is not to inflict pain or to humiliate but to enable His erring servants to reform themselves and to march forward along the paths of progress. He realizes that God is ever ready to accept true repentance and covers up the faults of His servants and through remorse and repentance wipes them out altogether. He finds that God, Who is the Lord of Majesty and Exaltation hears the prayers of His servants and that His eagerness to draw near to His servants is many times greater than the eagerness of His servants to approach near to Him. Realizing all this, his heart is filled with the love of God and he is driven towards Him in a paroxysm of love and devotion even greater than that which drives an infant to the arms of its mother ; and God too inclines towards such a servant of His with love and tenderness many times greater than that of a mother who rushes to comfort her crying and distressed child.

MAN—THE CENTRE OF THE UNIVERSE

The Quran teaches that God desired to bring into existence a universe which should serve as a manifestation of His Majesty and His Light and that this was the cause of the creation of the universe. It says that God created the heavens and the earth in six periods. Before that God ruled over water. God's object in creating the heavens and the earth out of water was to bring into existence a being endowed with the will to choose between good and evil. These beings would pass through various trials and would seek to outstrip one another in doing good and thus show which of them had attained to perfection (11 : 8). This verse shows that before matter assumed its present form it existed in liquid shape, or, in other words, the creation of the material universe began with a pure atom of hydrogen and that the universe was gradually developed out of it. With regard to the pre-material stage the Quran says :

> Do not the disbeilevers see that the heavens and the earth were a closed up mass, then We opened them out ? And We made from water every living thing. Will they not then believe ? (21 : 31).

The verse purports to say that the heavens and the earth were at first an amorphous mass and God then split them and formed them into a solar system and from the beginning He has always created life out of water. The verse indicates that the spiritual universe would also develop as the material universe had developed. God, in accordance with the laws which He had set in motion, split the mass of matter, and its scattered bits became the units of the solar system. In the same way God brings about revolutions in the spiritual universe. When the spiritual condition of mankind degenerates and the spiritual atmosphere becomes dense and oppressive, God causes a light to appear which causes a disturbance in the darkness and shakes it up and out of this apparently lifeless mass a perpetually moving spiritual solar system is created which begins to reach out from its centre and eventually embraces whole countries or the whole earth, according to the impetus behind it. The creation of the material universe starts from water ; so also the spiritual universe comes into life with heavenly water which is revelation.

According to the Quran the universe passed from stage to stage till the earth assumed a shape and developed properties which could sustain human life. The Quran teaches that the creation of man was the ultimate object of the creation of at least our solar system. When that stage arrived, God created man in the material universe so that he should become the manifestation of divine attributes and should serve as a mirror to reflect the beautiful image of God and should become the foundation of a spiritual universe. God's creation comprises millions of species. The Quran says : "None knows the hosts of thy Lord but He" (74 : 32). Man, however, occupies a position of dignity and honour among created beings for the reason that he serves as a mirror for the attributes of God. That is why Muslim mystics have called man a microcosm meaning that man possesses the attributes of the whole of creation and may be regarded as an epitome of the universe As a survey map, though on a small scale, indicates all features of the country which it depicts, in the same way there are represented in the human body all the characteristics of the universe. Man is, therefore, the axis or centre of the created universe. The Quran says that the whole universe is created by God for the service of man and our observation confirms that man rules over the whole of creation and that no part of creation rules over him. He is no doubt affected by changes of climate, by the light of the planets and the stars, by thunder and lightning, by storms and blizzards, by epidemics and pestilences, but he is not in any way ruled by these phenomena. Those that rule are often affected by those over whom they rule and yet there is never any difficulty in determining who rules and who is ruled. Thus though man is affected by the other parts of creation, he nevertheless rules over them. He controls rivers, oceans, mountains, winds, thunder, rain, herbs and medicines and is manifestly the central point of creation or at least of that part of creation which is related to our universe. God's creation is vast and there may be worlds in existence of which we have no knowledge. We cannot therefore speculate with regard to them.

THE CULMINATION OF PROCESS OF EVOLUTION

The Quran, contrary to the accounts given in the Old and the New Testaments, teaches that man was created through a gradual process. We have adverted to this subject above and have cited Quranic authority for the proposition we have stated. There is another verse in the Quran which shows that the creation of man was the culmination of a gradual process and that it is not correct to say that God formed man out of clay and breathed His spirit into him. The Quran says : "And He has created you in different stages and different forms" (71 : 15). That is to say, God has created man by making him pass through stage after stage and condition after condition. According to the Quran, therefore, man was not created suddenly at one stroke but as the result of a gradual process. In the same way man's intellectual development also proceeded gradually. The Quran shows that human beings were in existence before Adam but that they were not yet able to bear the responsibility of revealed Law. They lived in caves and in mountain fastnesses. It is for this reason that the Quran has called them by the name of *Jinn*, which means literally those that dwell out of sight. Some people have applied this word to the genii of tales and fables, but the Quran does not support this interpretation. It expressly states that when Adam and his people went out of the garden (which again, according to the Quran, was a region of the earth and is not to be confused with Paradise) God warned them against *Iblīs* "who was one of the *Jinn*" and told them to be careful of him and his people as they would all have to live together upon the earth wherein they would spend their spans of existence and wherein they would die (7 : 26, 28). Again, addressing Adam and his people and *Iblīs* and his people God admonishes all of them to accept His Prophets when they should appear among them from time to time (2 : 39). All this shows that the *Jinn* of the time of Adam and their leader *Iblīs* were of the human race. The genii of the fables do not live in company with men nor are they in any other way connected with men. The Quran does not lend any support to the idea of the *Jinn* of the fables. Those whom the Quran describes as *Jinn* in connection with Adam were human beings who dwelt upon the earth but whose mental faculties were not yet fully developed. When the stage of the full development of the mental faculties of man was reached, God sent His revelation to the most perfect man of that generation, namely, Adam. This revelation was confined to a few social rules relating to the formation of a society and the provision of food and other means of maintenance for it. Those whose social sense was not yet fully developed refused to submit themselves to Adam. God punished them and gave Adam victory over them. For the future God decreed that Prophets would continue to appear and those who believed in them would identify themselves with Adam and his people and those who rejected them would identify themselves with the *Jinn* who had opposed Adam. Each Prophet is raised to help forward the intellectual and spiritual evolution of man. Those, who are opposed to the next stage of evolution and are not willing to submit to the limitations and regulations which God seeks to impose through His Prophet to help forward the process of evolution, reject the Prophet.

In short, the Quran teaches that man's physical creation and development are the result of a process of evolution and in the same way his intellectual development is also the result of a process of evolution. Adam was not the first human being but was the first human being whose intellect was capable of accepting and bearing the responsibility of revelation. The Quran nowhere states that God desired to create man and therefore created Adam. The Quran expressly states that God decided to appoint a "Vicegerent upon earth" and appointed Adam. This shows that at the time of the appointment of Adam as God's Vicegerent on earth there were human beings dwelling upon the earth but none of them had become the recipient of divine revelation since their mental faculties were not yet fully developed. When the development of human intellect arrived at the stage where man became capable of forming a society and living in accordance with an organized system, God sent His revelation to Adam, who possessed the most highly developed intellect in his own age, and he thus became the first Prophet. He was not the first man but the first Prophet, and the revelation received by him comprised a few clear and simple social laws and a simple explanation of some of the divine attributes.

At another place the Quran says: "And We did create you and then We gave you shape; then said We to the angels, 'Submit to Adam' " (7 : 12). The verse means that God created man and then gave shape to his faculties and then commanded the angels to bow down to Adam. This verse also clearly shows that man had been in existence prior to the time of Adam. The development of man's intellectual faculties indicates that before the appearance of Adam man had already passed through several stages of evolution. The verse indicates that after man was created his faculties developed from stage to stage and assumed different shapes and he began to be distinguished from the other animal creation around him and when his intellect was developed to a certain degree, Adam was created and God sent His revelation to him.

THE OBJECT OF MAN'S CREATION

The Quran teaches that man has been created to serve as a manifestation of God's attributes and to illustrate them in his life. It says, "And I have created the *Jinn* and men only that they may serve Me and receive the impress of My attributes"

(51 : 57). (As has already been explained the word *Jinn* does not mean some species of invisible creation but is intended to signify certain classes of people.) At another place the Quran says, "He it is Who made you vicegerents in the earth. So he who disbelieves, will himself suffer the consequences of his disbelief" (35 : 40). This means that if a man voluntarily abdicates the position that God has assigned to him, he does not thereby in any manner injure God but merely dislodges himself from a position of honour and will suffer the consequences himself. These verses show that man has been created to illustrate in his own life the attributes of God and that he is the vicegerent of God upon earth. He is, thus, the central point of the material universe. Since Prophets are raised for the reform of mankind and to remind them of the object of their life and to guide them rightly towards its achievement, they become in their spheres the centres for mankind. In other words, man is the sun round which the material universe revolves and each of the Prophets is a sun round which the men, for whose guidance that Prophet is sent, revolve.

LAW OF NATURE AND LAW OF SHARĪ'AT

The Quran shows that God has put into motion two kinds of laws for the purpose of reminding man of his duties and of helping him along the path of progress. One of these is the law of nature which is related to man's material progress. Since this law is not directly related to man's spiritual advancement, a contravention of this law results in material prejudice to man but does not involve God's displeasure or anger. The whole of the material universe is invested with the appropriate impetus of this law and is impelled by it. No direct revelation is made by God concerning the details of this law.

The second is the Law of Sharī'at which regulates man's spiritual progress. A contravention of this law involves divine displeasure, for it is only by conformity to this law that man can succeed in fulfilling the purpose for which he has been created and contravention of this law arrests his progress towards that objective. But every contravention of the Law of Sharī'at has not the effect of depriving a man altogether of his chances of achieving his objective. The Quran teaches that the Law of Sharī'at collectively helps a man to attain spiritual purity and exaltation. Just as every contravention of the law of nature does not involve a man in complete ruin and destruction nor does every carelessness in the matter of diet induce disease, in the same way not every contravention of the Law of Sharī'at draws upon man the wrath of God or deprives him of all chance of reaching his goal. The very object of the Law of Sharī'at is to help man to attain spiritual perfection. Where an extensive system is designed to bring about a certain result, its failure in one respect may be corrected or compensated for by its success in another and the desired result may yet be achieved. The human body, for instance, is a complex organization and human life depends for its healthy continuance upon various factors like food, water, air, etc. On occasion one or more of these factors become tainted but this does not necessarily result in the organism becoming diseased. The defect produced by deficiency in one factor may be overpowered by the healthy working of the other factors. The same is the case with the Law of Sharī'at. It comprises rules and principles which are collectively designed for the spiritual advancement of man. Short of the repudiation of the Kingdom of God or of the authority of His Prophets any defect that may be produced in human conduct by an error or weakness is remediable. If the defect is serious, it can be remedied only through true repentance and sincere prayer.

The Quran indicates that in addition to these two laws there are two other laws which are constantly in operation, namely, the social law and the moral law. But these are in reality the extensions of the boundaries of the law of nature and the Law of Sharī'at. The moral law is the extension of the Law of Sharī'at and the social law is the extension of the law of nature and they act and re-act upon each other to a large degree. Many rules of social law are based upon morality and many rules of moral law are based upon sociology. Since man has been intended to live as a member of society, he is in need of both these sets of laws. The social law being a continuation, as it were, of the law of nature, man has been permitted a very large choice in the framing of it. The moral law being related to the Law of Sharī'at, its fundamentals are governed by that law, though some of its details are left to man's choice. The whole system of the universe runs on the basis of these laws. The law of nature and the Law of Sharī'at are both appointed by God and man has no share in framing them. The social law and the moral law, however, are a combination of divine commandments and human regulations, and in this manner by associating human co-operation with the divine design the very best guidance is furnished for the running of the universe. So long as these two streams continue to run in parallel channels, the world goes on progressing in peace and man is able to set up a beneficent system upon the earth which is in accord with the Kingdom of God, but when these two streams begin to run in opposite directions, or in other words, when human reason is diverted from the course which runs parallel to divine guidance and is thus deprived of divine blessing, the world becomes a prey to conflict and discord. It is then ruled neither by God nor by man but becomes subject to the sway of satanic forces ; for man can claim to be human only so long as he follows divine guidance. When he ceases to do that, he descends to the level of the brutes.

To enable man to attain nearness to God it was necessary to leave him free to choose his course of action. The Quran teaches that man is free in one sphere and is subject to compulsion in another. He is free in the matter of the Law of Sharī'at and has no choice where the operation of the law of nature is concerned. He is subject to compulsion in this last sphere for the reason that his spiritual progress is not directly related to the operation of the law of nature. He has been given free choice of action in the sphere of the Law of Sharī'at inasmuch as he can become the object of divine favour and bounty only by acting upon the Law of Sharī'at and no reward can be earned unless there is free choice in the matter of action. What a man is under compulsion to do can earn him no reward.

The Quran recognizes that man's spiritual welfare and progress is affected by his material surroundings and to the extent to which it is so affected limitations are placed upon his actions, but it also teaches that man's actions are appraised by God with reference to his background and environment. For instance, if a millionaire spends a small fraction of his wealth in the service of humanity and a poor man possessing only the equivalent of that small fraction spends the whole of it in the service of his fellow-beings, they will not, in the eyes of God, be entitled to an equal reward. The millionaire devoted a thousandth or a hundred-thousandth part of his wealth to the winning of the pleasure of God and the poor man gave his all for that purpose. The reward earned by each will be in proportion to the sacrifice made by each. God looks not to the volume of a man's actions but appraises them against their true background. He does not overlook the handicaps to which a man is subject and which limit the scope of his actions nor the conveniences which a man enjoys and which facilitate his actions.

EVOLUTION OF SPIRITUAL UNIVERSE COMPLETED IN THE HOLY PROPHET

We learn from the Quran that as the material universe has developed gradually, a similar gradual process of development was prescribed for the spiritual universe. That is why the perfect code of laws was not revealed at the inception of the universe. Revelation was sent down to man in consonance with the stage of development reached by him. Eventually man arrived at a stage when he could bear the responsibility of the perfect Law of Sharī'at. God in His wisdom then caused to appear the most perfect human being in the person of the Holy Prophet of Islam and revealed to him the perfect Law of Sharī'at and the perfect Scripture. That perfect Law is Islam and that perfect Scripture is the Quran. The evolution of the spiritual universe was completed in the person of the Holy Prophet. As man is the central point of the material universe and the respective Prophets were the central points of the nations to which and the ages for which they were sent, the Holy Prophet of Islam is the central point for the whole of mankind. The plan of the universe, therefore, put forward by the Quran is that the first central point of the universe is man. In their different spheres mankind revolve around their respective Prophets, the Prophets revolve around the Holy

Prophet of Islam and he, in turn, revolves round and leads the whole universe to God and the spiritual universe is, thus, carried to its perfection.

QURAN—THE PERFECT SCRIPTURE

It has already been stated that God has through His Prophets provided for the progress and perfection of man by means of the Law of Sharī'at, the moral law and the social law. Since the Quran is the most perfect Scripture, it deals with all these three laws. It sets out the Law of Sharī'at and the moral law in full and states the fundamental principles of the social law leaving the rest of the field of social law to be developed and filled in by man himself. In the sphere of the moral law the Quran lays down this fundamental principle that it is the appropriate use of the natural faculties which constitutes high moral qualities. The suppression or stultification of natural faculties or desires is as much a moral offence as is complete submission to their domination. He who seeks to kill his natural faculties or completely to suppress his natural desires sets at defiance the law of nature. He whose mind is filled with, and whose energies are devoted to, the fulfilment of his natural desires sets the Law of Sharī'at at defiance and is heading towards spiritual destruction. Both courses are fatal to man's development. Neither the law of nature nor the Law of Sharī'at can be defied with impunity. That is why the Quran teaches that since all things are created for the service and benefit of man, their use is permissible to him save that he is restrained from putting them to uses which are definitely harmful. According to this principle, celibacy is viewed by Islam not as a virtue but as a vice. In the same way abstention from the use of clean articles of food, drink and dress is not a virtue but a vice, inasmuch as restrictions like this amount to a defiance of the law of nature and ingratitude in respect of divine bounties. It is equally a vice, however, to spend one's time wholly in the pursuit of these objects and to devote oneself completely to their enjoyment, for in this way a man neglects the development of his soul, which is the real object of human existence. As it is sinful for a man to go on working incessantly and to abstain from all nourishment—for thereby he will bring about his own death and will leave his work unfinished—in the same way it is sinful for a man to devote himself entirely to the fulfilment of his physical desires and to abstain from useful activities, for such a man spends his life in the pursuit of the means and neglects the end. No end can be achieved without the provision of means and appropriate means cannot be created without keeping the true end in view.

PRINCIPLES TO ESTABLISH SOCIAL ORDER

To establish order in the social sphere and to give it a beneficent direction the Quran has laid down the following principles:

(1) Absolute ownership vests in God alone and all things belong to Him.

(2) He has subjected everything to the control of man for the collective benefit of the whole of mankind.

(3) Since the object of man's existence is spiritual perfection, he must be given a certain amount of freedom of choice in his actions and must be provided with a field for his activities.

(4) Since the materials upon which human progress is based are the common heritage of the whole of mankind, the produce of human labour must be so distributed as to secure their proper share both to the individual and to the community.

(5) For the proper regulation of the human social system some person must be entrusted with executive authority who must be elected as the result of consultation among the members of the community over whom he is to exercise authority. His function is not to frame laws but to enforce divine laws.

(6) Keeping in view the possibility of diversity in the political systems of different communities the Quran teaches that:

(*a*) In case of a dispute arising between any two or more political States the others should combine to bring about a settlement of the dispute.

(*b*) If an amicable settlement is not arrived at between the parties to the dispute, the remaining States should pronounce an equitable award with reference to the matter which is the subject-matter of the dispute.

(*c*) If either of the parties to the dispute refuses to accept the award or, having accepted it, fails to give effect to it, the remaining States should combine to persuade the recalcitrant State to accept the award in the interests of international peace. If persuasion fails, they should compel the Government concerned by force to submit to the award.

(*d*) When the obdurate State has made its submission, the other Governments should refrain from going beyond the enforcement of the award relating to the original dispute and should not seek to secure any advantages for themselves, for this would lay the foundation of fresh disputes.

All this was prescribed by the Quran more than thirteen and a half centuries ago. The United Nations Organization has adopted some of these principles but is in danger of failing in its purpose for neglecting others. The League of Nations failed for the reason that it did not give effect to the Quranic principle that an intransigent Government should be compelled by force to submit to an international decision or award. The United Nations Organization does not appear to be anxious to secure that the powers that enforce a settlement should not seek any advantage for themselves at the expense of the vanquished nations and should confine their efforts to the enforcement of the settlement of the dispute which gave rise to the conflict. It is feared, therefore, that the United Nations Organization will experience the same fate which overtook the League of Nations ; for peace can only be established and maintained on the principles laid down in the Quran.

LIFE AFTER DEATH

The Quran teaches that on a man's death his soul enters a new universe and assumes a new body. That body is different from the physical body that is adjusted to the requirements of this life. It is a new kind of spiritual body possessing peculiar faculties for the perception of God's beautiful attributes. Perfect souls will be admitted immediately to the state described as Paradise. Those imperfectly developed in this life will encounter the state described as Hell which is a state of healing for spiritual ills. As the process of healing is completed in respect of each soul, it will attain Paradise ; till eventually all souls will have attained Paradise and the state of Hell will be altogether terminated. All, having proceeded from God, will eventually revert to Him. Their joys, their pleasures and their comforts will all be spiritual. The remembrance and the love of God will be their nourishment and the vision of God will be their highest reward. The Quran invites attention to this by saying that the extremities of this universe are in the hands of God (79 : 45). This means that the universe originated with God and will also terminate with Him. That which has proceeded from God will revert to God, as Jesus said : "And no man hath ascended up to heaven, but he that came down from heaven" (John 3 : 13).

AHMAD, THE PROMISED MESSIAH

THE Quran expounds the principle that, as the perfect code of spiritual laws has been revealed through the Holy Prophet of Islam, no Law-bearing Prophet shall appear after him. The Quran is the last revealed Scripture and is not liable to be superseded either wholly or in part by any subsequent revelation. The spiritual universe will continue to be ruled by the Quran and the Holy Prophet till the end of days. But man is liable to forget, is apt to fall into error and is prone to rebel. To maintain the dominion of the Quran it was necessary to provide a remedy for all these ills. Provision was necessary that the forgetful may be reminded, the erring set right and the rebellious brought to submission. We learn from the Quran that as in the material universe the moon obtains light from the sun and illumines the earth when the light of the sun is not directly available, in the same way men will continue to appear who will obtain spiritual light from the Holy Prophet and will continue to illumine the spiritual universe. These men, in accordance with the degree of the need which they are designed to fulfil, will appear in the shape of Reformers, but in the case of widespread disorder and mischief in the spiritual realm would be appointed as Prophets subordinate, and in strict obedience, to the Holy Prophet. The Quran indicates at various places the appearance of one such Prophet who would be the spiritual image of the Holy Prophet and whose advent would be regarded as the advent of the Holy Prophet himself. In the Traditions this image of the Holy Prophet has been given the name of Messiah and the Quran also at one place indicates the applicability of this name to him (43 : 58).

Another name mentioned in the Traditions for this Prophet is Mahdī. Both these names, however, are applicable to the same individual, though they express different capacities. The Gospels also refer to this second advent of the Holy Prophet by holding out the promise of the second advent of Jesus. The signs mentioned in the oldest Scriptures and in the Quran which should indicate the time of the advent of this Prophet have been fulfilled in this age and it is a mighty proof of the truth of the Quran that, in accordance with the prophecies made in it, a man was raised by God in this age who claimed to be the spiritual image of the Holy Prophet and in whose advent the prophecies contained in the Quran and other Scriptures were fulfilled. He explained that God had raised him for the purpose of re-establishing the dominion of Islam and to shed light upon the true teachings of the Quran. This claimant was the late Hazrat Mirza Ghulam Ahmad, Founder of the Ahmadiyya Movement. Nearly sixty years ago he was informed through divine revelation that he had been appointed to serve Islam and the Holy Prophet and to work for the exaltation of God's name in the universe. He was told that God had conferred upon him the dignity of prophethood with this proviso that he would continue to be a perfect follower of the Holy Prophet and of the Quran and that the revelation which was vouchsafed to him would be subordinate to the Quran and would contain no new Law. One of his revelations was, "Every blessing is from Muhammad and blessed is he who has taught," *i.e.*, the Holy Prophet, "and blessed is he who has learnt," *i.e.*, Ahmad, who was the recipient of this revelation (Ḥaqīqat al-Waḥy). Again, he received a revelation: "A Warner has appeared in the world but the world did not accept him. God will, however, accept him and will establish his truth through mighty convulsions" (Barāhīn Ahmadiyya). In the terminology of the Quran a warner means a Prophet and in one version of this revelation received by the Founder of the Ahmadiyya Movement the word used in place of "Warner" was Prophet (Ek Ghalaṭī Kā Izāla). His function was to bring man face to face with his Maker in this age of darkness and sow the seed of spiritual advancement in this material world through fresh Signs and revelations. When he first announced his claim he was alone and had no companion. He appeared in a small village of about one thousand four hundred or one thousand five hundred inhabitants which possessed no modern facility in the shape of a post-office, telegraph office or railway station. He announced then that God would establish his truth through mighty Signs and that his name would be carried to the farthest ends of the earth. In addition to the announcement that the Movement founded by him would be firmly established and would flourish and expand and that his followers would attain nearness to God, he further announced that within nine years of the date of the announcement a son would be born to him through whom many of his prophecies would be fulfilled and whose name would be carried to the ends of the earth. He would rapidly advance from success to success and would be blessed with the Holy Spirit. When Ahmad published his claims and the revelations received by him, he encountered a severe storm of opposition from all quarters and all communities. Hindus, Muslims, Sikhs and Christians all combined in opposition to him and resolved to compass his ruin. This opposition was in itself an indication that the Founder of the Ahmadiyya Movement was divinely inspired, for such universal opposition is normally encountered only by true Prophets. In spite of the fact that he was alone and was opposed by all communities, God began to strengthen his voice and by ones and twos people began to believe in him. Gradually his followers spread in the Punjab and then through the other provinces of India and even outside.

THE MESSIAH'S PROMISED SON

When the Founder of the Ahmadiyya Movement died in 1908, his opponents declared that the Movement would die a natural death. The Ahmadiyya Community, however, combined, in accordance with Islamic principles, to elect the late Maulawi Nūr 'ud-Dīn as the First Khalīfa. During the First Khilāfat some members of the Community who had been affected by Western ideas began to be critical of the institution of Khilāfat. Their views found some support among a certain section of the Community with the result that when Maulawī Nūr 'ud-Dīn died in 1914, a vigorous and concerted effort was made by this section to abolish the institution of Khilāfat altogether. I, who am the son of Ahmad, the Promised Messiah and Founder of the Ahmadiyya Movement, was then only twenty-five years of age and was utterly devoid of all material resources. The executive organization of the Community was dominated by the section who had revolted against the institution of Khilāfat. A very large majority of those members of the Community who were then present at Qadian and who were described as a mob by those who were in revolt against the Khilāfat were determined that they would maintain the institution in accordance with the principles laid down in the Quran and they insisted that I should take upon myself the burdens and responsibilities of the office of Khalīfa. In these circumstances I agreed to accept the allegiance of the Community as the Second Khalīfa and in that capacity began to serve the Community, Islam and humanity. Since the majority of those who were regarded as holding leading positions in the Community were opposed to the institution of Khilāfat, the Community was faced with a crisis. Outsiders began to speculate that the dissolution of the Community and its disintegration was a matter of only a few days. At that time God revealed to me that he would succour me and give me victory and create dissension among the ranks of my powerful opponents and would break them. A great miracle then came to pass.

The majority of those who were regarded as the educated and experienced section of the Community deserted it in the hour of its trial. Those who were regarded as men of substance and influence withdrew from it. Those who were looked upon as the intellect of the Community were cut off from it. Those who had revolted from the Khilāfat began to proclaim that since the direction of the affairs of the Community had been committed into the hands of an inexperienced youth, the Movement would soon disintegrate. But the decrees of Him, Who had revealed the Quran and Who is the Author of the spiritual universe in accordance with the laws of which the world is progressing and Who had revealed to Ahmad, the Promised Messiah and Mahdī, that within nine years from 1884 he would be blessed with a son who would, under the Grace and Mercy of God, be known unto the ends of the earth and who would through the propagation of Islam become the instrument of the release of those held in bondage and of bringing into life those that were spiritually dead, were fulfilled and His word was exalted. Every day that dawned brought with it fresh factors that contributed to my success and every day that departed left behind elements that hastened the failure of my opponents. God thus made me the instrument of the spread of the Ahmadiyya Movement in all parts of the earth. At each step He has blessed me with His guidance and on numerous occasions He has honoured me with His revelation. Then the day arrived when He revealed to me that I was the Promised Son, the tidings of whose advent had been proclaimed by the Promised Messiah in 1886, three years before my birth. From that day the volume of God's support and succour began to swell even faster and today Ahmadiyya Missionaries are fighting the battles of Islam in every continent. The Quran, which had become like a closed book in the hands of the Muslims, has again been made an open book for us by God through the blessings of the Holy Prophet and the instrumentality of the Promised Messiah. Fresh sources of knowledge are revealed to us through it. Whenever any teaching or doctrine contained in the Quran is made the target of criticism on the basis of some new scientific development, God reveals to me the true answer contained in the Quran. We have been chosen as the instrument for elevating the banner of the dominion of the Quran. Deriving faith and certainty from the words and the revelations of God we are demonstrating the superiority of the Quran to the world. Compared with the resources of the world our resources are pitiful. Yet we are assured that in spite of the severest opposition, the dominion of the Quran will be firmly established. The sun may move out of its course, the stars may leave their appointed places, the earth may stop in its revolution, but nothing and nobody can now obstruct the victory of Islām and the Holy Prophet. The dominion of the Quran will be established once more. Men will turn away from the worship of other men and of gods which they have fashioned with their own hands and will bow down in worship to the One God. In spite of the fact that the trend of human society appears to be in directions opposed to the teachings of the Quran, the Kingdom of Islam will be established again and so firmly that men will find it impossible to shake its foundations. God has sown a beneficent seed in the wilderness of the world that has been laid waste by Satan, and I proclaim that this seed will germinate and shoot up in the form of a tree which will spread and bring forth abundant fruit. The souls that aspire to soar high and are animated by longing to be united with God shall one day be roused and weaned from dreams of material prosperity and will be inspired with a passion to alight on the branches of this tree. All disorder shall then disappear and all travail shall be brought to an end. God's Kingdom shall be re-established on earth and God's love shall again become man's most valuable treasure. This revolution shall usher in an era of peace and order. All efforts to bring peace to the world and to remove disorder which are at variance with these principles shall be brought to nought.

TRANSLATIONS INTO OTHER LANGUAGES

The Quran directed the Prophet to carry on his greatest struggle with the help of the Quran, which was the most effective weapon for this purpose (25 : 53). It is in pursuance of this direction of the Quran that this volume of the English Translation is being published. It is expected that the publication of the remaining portion of the English Translation will not be long delayed. Besides the English Translation, translations in the following seven European languages have been completed and will be published as soon as post-war restrictions permit : Russian, German, Dutch, French, Italian, Portuguese and Spanish. Thereafter it is hoped that this series will be continued till it comprises translations into all the principal languages. A translation into Swahilī is already under preparation.

Missions of the Ahmadiyya Movement have been established in various parts of the world for the purpose of the propagation of Islam and the exposition of the teachings of the Quran. There is a central Mission in England and Missions are also working in France, Spain, Italy and Switzerland. On the American continent, there are Missions in U.S.A. and the Argentine, and plans are being pushed forward for opening Missions in Canada and Brazil. Missions have been established in all the countries of British West Africa and ten Missionaries are working in different parts of British East Africa. Missionary activities are also being carried on in Egypt, Sudan and Abyssinia. There are Missions in Palestine, Syria and Iran in the Middle East, and in Malaya, Java, Sumatra and Borneo in South East Asia. We believe that these translations and Missions will inaugurate a successful campaign for the triumph of Islam, for not only are our efforts directed towards carrying into effect that which has already been decreed by God, but have been undertaken in obedience to God's command.

In addition to offering this intellectual gift we invite the attention of all lovers of truth, to whatever religion they might profess allegiance, to the golden principle that a tree is known by its fruit. The Quran yields its fruits in every age and those who are devoted to it become the recipients of divine revelation and God manifests His powers through them. Why should we not, in our search for the truth, seek assistance not only from reason and reflection but also from our observation of the fruits that other Scriptures yield? The world would be materially assisted in its search for truth if Christians could persuade the Pope or other high Church dignitaries to put forward the revelations received by them as against those received by me for the purpose of determining which of them are true manifestations of God's power and knowledge. The Pope and other ecclesiastics whose predecessors, in defiance of the pacific teachings of Jesus, were ever eager to incite Christendom to undertake Crusades against Muslim States, should be only too eager to embrace the opportunity of participating in this spiritual crusade. If they were inclined to accept, or could be persuaded by their followers to accept, this invitation, it might prove an effective means for healing the spiritual ills from which mankind has so long suffered. The Majesty and Power of God would then manifest itself in an extraordinary manner and would help to establish the faith of man and guide his spiritual development.

ACKNOWLEDGEMENTS

In conclusion I desire to acknowledge the inestimable services rendered by Maulawī Sher 'Alī, B.A., who has, in spite of feeble and failing health, devoted so large a portion of his time to the translation of the text into English. I also wish to thank him along with Mirzā Bashīr Ahmad, M.A., Malik Ghulām Farīd, M.A., and the late Ch. Abu'l Hāshim Khān, M.A., for the labour they have devoted to extracting from my speeches and writings the material upon which the Explanatory Notes are based and to preparing these Notes. I have not had the opportunity of perusing these Notes but, having regard to the experience and devotion of these gentlemen, I am sure they must have interpreted correctly that which I have through divine grace been able to acquire in this behalf directly from the Quran or the teachings of the Promised Messiah. I would also like to take this opportunity of thanking Qāḍī Muhammad Aslam, M.A., Professor, Government College, Lahore, and Sir Muhammad Ẓafrullah Khān, who have rendered this General Introduction from Urdu into English. I pray that God may anoint all of them and their descendants with the perfume of His blessings and should watch over them and help them both in this life and the next. Amen!

I also desire to state that since I was a pupil of the late Maulawī Nur 'ud-Din, Khalīfatul Masīḥ I, a good deal of what I acquired from him is reflected in the Explanatory Notes. Thus these Notes are, in fact, based upon the interpretation of the Quran by the Promised Messiah, the First Khalīfa and myself. Since God had anointed the Promised Messiah with His Spirit and had honoured him by bestowing upon him such knowledge as was requisite for the development of this and succeeding generations, I trust that this Commentary will serve to heal many of their ills. By means of it the blind shall see, the deaf shall hear, the dumb shall speak, the lame and the halt shall walk and God's angels shall so bless it that it shall succeed in fulfilling the object for which it is being published. Do Thou, O Lord, ordain that it be so!

MIRZA BASHIR-UD-DIN MAHMUD AHMAD
(*Khalifatul Masih II*).

QADIAN,
28th February, 1947.
6th Rabīʻ al-Thānī, 1366.
28th Tablīgh, 1326.

INDEX

Abraham, God's promise to, 79 *et seq.*, 91, 278.
Abū 'Āmir, 290.
Abū Bakr, 144, 147, 167 *et seq.*, 299, 303, 310, 328 *et seq.*, 345.
Abū Jahl, 139 *et seq.*, 149 *et seq.*, 177; death, 184.
Abū Sufyān, 180, 188, 193, 219, 247, 268 *et seq.*, 286 *et seq.*
Abū Tālib, 139 *et seq.*, 151 *et seq.*, 156 *et seq.*, 324.
Abyssinia, emigration to, 152; Prophet's letter to Negus of, 253.
Ahmad, the Promised Messiah, 434; his son, 437.
'Ā'isha, 134, 303, 323, 345.
Arabia at the time of Muhammad's birth, 135.
Arabs, 136 *et seq.*
Arabic Language, 1.
Aus and Khazraj, 161, 290.

Badr, battle of, 180; prophesied, 94.
Baḥrain, Prophet's letter to Chief of, 256.
Banū Musṭaliq, 204.
Banū Quraiẓa, 161, 208 *et seq.*, 212, 220, 222.
Bilāl, 146 *et seq.*

Chosroes, 250 *et seq.*, 257.
Christianity, 24 *et seq.*
Civilisation and Culture, meaning of, 20; different periods, 23; Jewish and Christian, 24.
Confucianism, 9.

Egypt, Prophet's letter to Muqauqis, Ruler of, 254; Prophecy concerning, 114 *et seq.*
Ezra, 28 *et seq.*

Fasting, 393.

God, Biblical, 7;
- is one, 9;
- Quranic belief in 380;
- Worship of, 391;
- God of all peoples, 406;
- the Ultimate Cause, 406;
- Divine attributes, 409 *et seq.*

Habakkuk, 95 *et seq.*
Hebrew, 47 *et seq.*
Heraclius, 247 *et seq.*
Hijra, emigration to Medina, 167.
Hinduism, 68;
- Number of Vedic Gods, 78;
- Interpolations in Vedas, 68;
- Savage teachings in Vedas, 72;
- Superstitions and Contradictions 75 and 76.

Ḥirā, a place near Mecca, 142, 354.
Ḥudaibiya, Treaty of, 244.
Ḥunain, battle of, 282.

'Ikrima, 281.
Iran, the Prophet's letter to the King of, 250.
Isaiah, 101 *et seq.*, 145, 186 *et seq.*
Ishmael, 80 *et seq.*
- His descendants, 91;
- His sons, 92 *et seq.*

Ishmaelites, 121.
Islam, teaches Oneness of God, 16;
- Its message, 150;
- Islamic Fast, 393;
- Pilgrimage, 394;
- Zakāt, 395;
- Form of Government, 396;
- Prophesied, 109.
- Truthfulness, 347;
- Inquisitiveness, 349;
- Frank dealing, 349;
- Pessimism, 350;
- Cruelty to animals, 350;
- Patience in adversity, 346;
- Mutual co-operation, 346;
- Treatment of neighbours, 338;
- Treatment of women, 334;
- Treatment of slaves, 333;
- Treatment of the poor, 332;
- Tolerance in religion, 351;
- Bravery, 352.

Jesus, Not a universal teacher, 17
- His mission, 50;
- Teacher for Banu Isra'il, 7.

Jewish Scholars, 4, 30, 134
Jewish Tribes, Banished from Medina, 161, 175; 189, 206.
Jews, 13, 28, 47 *et seq.*, 100, 114 *et seq.*, 125 *et seq.*, 173, 198, 215 *et seq.*, 257 *et seq.*, 316.

Ka'ba, cleared of idols, 277.
Khadīja, 140 *et seq.*, 307, 323 *et seq.*
Khaibar, fall of, 257.

Man—The centre of the universe, 421
The object of man's creation, 425
Mecca—Prophet's birth-place, 135, 152 ;
Prophet leaves Mecca, 167 ;
Fall of Mecca, 267 *et seq.*
Medina—Islam spreads to, 161 ;
Emigration of Prophet to, 167 ;
Life unsafe at, 173 ;
Tribal pacts, 175 ;
Meccans prepare attack, 177.
Miracles, Quranic teaching, 385.
Moses, 30 *et seq.*, 35, 41 *et seq.*, 109, 122 *et seq.*, 328 ;
Prophesies in Deuteronomy, 83 *et seq.* ;
Mount Paran, 89, 94.
Mosques, 392.
Mount Paran (Faran). 89 *et seq.*, 94.
Muhammad—Prophecy in Deuteronomy, 83 *et seq.* ;
Prophecy in Habakkuk, 95 ;
Prophecy in Song of Solomon, 97 ;
Prophecy in Isaiah, 101 ;
Prophecy in Daniel, 116 ;
Prophecy in New Testament, 120 ;
Life Sketch, 130 ;
Early life, 138 *et seq.*;
Marriage with Khadīja, 140 ;
First revelation, 142 ;
First converts, 144 ;
Message of Islam, 150 ;
Persecution intensifies, 156 ;
Journey to Tā'if, 157 ;
First pledge of 'Aqaba, 165 ;
Emigration to Medina, pursuit and arrival, 167 *et seq* ;
Life unsafe at Medina, 173 ;
Tribal pacts at Medina, 175 ;
Battle of Badr, 180 ;
Battle of Uḥud, 188 ;
Banū Muṣṭaliq, 204 ;
Battle of Ditch, 207 ;
Leaves for Mecca, 240 ;
Treaty of Ḥudaibiya, 244 ;
Letters to various kings, 246 *et seq.* ;
Fall of Khaibar, 257 ;
Battle of Mūta, 263 ;
Marches on Mecca, 267 ;
Fall of Mecca, 270 ;
Entry of Prophet into Mecca, 272 ;
Enemies forgiven, 279 ;
Battle of Ḥunain, 282 ;
Expedition of Tabūk, 291 ;
The last pilgrimage, 294 ;
Last days, 300 ;
Death, 302 ;
Personality and character, 306 *et seq.* ;
Relationship with God, 313 ;
Disapproval of Penance, 321 ;
Attitude towards his wives, 323, 262 ;
High moral qualities, 324 ;
Self control, 325 ;
Justice and fair dealing, 327 ;
Regard for poor, 329 ;
Treatment of slaves, 333 ;
Treatment of women, 334 ;
Attitude towards the dead, 338 ;
Treatment of neighbours, 338 ;
Treatment of relatives, 339 ;
Other virtues, 342 *et seq.* ;
Evolution of spiritual universe completed in Muhammad, 429.
Mūta, Battle of, 263.

New Testament, 47 *et seq* ;
Testimony of Christian scholars, 51 ;
Contradictions, 57 ;
Superstitions in the Gospels, 59 ;
Doubtful ethics, 63.
Noah, 45.

Old Testament, 24, 28 *et seq.* ;
Contradictions, 33 ;
Savage teaching, 38 ;
Irrational teaching, 40.

Pilgrimage, 394.
Prophets, 11 ;
From among their own people, 11;
Their teachings, 13 *et seq.*
Prophets, defamed by Bible, 44.

Quraish, descendants of Ishmael, 91.
Quran—Translations, 1 ;
Commentaries, 3 ;
Need of, 6, 19 ;
Compilation, 354 ;
Devices adopted to safeguard text of, 355 ;
Instructors of, 357 ;
Reciters of, 359 ;
Committed to memory, 360, 365 ;
Collected into one volume, 362 ;
Standardised copies of, 363 ;
Arrangements of chapters and verses, 368 ;
Some prophecies of, 372 ;
Some characteristics of its teachings, 379 ;
Belief in living God, 380 ;
Salvation, 383 ;
Miracles, 385 ;

Worship of God, 391 ;
Mosques, 392 ;
Fasting, 393 ;
Pilgrimage, 394 ;
Zakāt, 395 ;
Form of Government, 396 ;
Slavery, 398 ;
Human soul, 399 ;
Plan of spiritual universe, 402 ;
God of all peoples, 406 ;
God the ultimate cause, 406 ;
God's attributes, 409 *et seq.* ;
Man, the Centre of universe, 421 ;
Culmination of process of evolution, 423 ;
Law of Nature and law of Shari'at, 426 ;
The perfect scripture, 430 ;
Social order, principles to establish, 431 ;
Translations into other languages, 440.

Religion, 10.
Revealed teachings, 13.

Sa'd bin Mu'adh, 177, 197, 217, 222 *et seq.*
Salvation, Quranic conception of, 383.
Seir, See Mount Paran.
Shari'at, the Law of, 426.
Sinai. See Mount Paran.
Slavery, 398.
Solomon, the Song of, 97.
Soul, 399.

Tabūk, 291.
Tā'if, Prophet's visit to, 157, 294.
Torah (see also Old Testament), 28, 44, 46, 344.

Uhud, battle of, 188.
'Umar, 153, 187, 192 *et seq.*, 303 *et seq.*, 313.
Accepts Islam, 154 ;
Prophecy concerning, 113.
'Uthman, 153, 243.

Vedas, 8.
Interpolations, 68 ;
Savage teaching of, 72 ;
Superstitions, 75 ;
Contradictions, 76.

War, the Prophet's policy, 176, 225 ;
Teachings of Judaism and Christianity, 228 ;
The Quranic teaching, 229 *et seq.* ;
The Prophet's precepts, 237.
Waraqa b. Naufal, 6, 144.
Women, in early Arabia, 137, 337 ;
The Prophet's treatment of, 334 *et seq.*

Zaid, 141, 142, 144 ;
Death, 202.
Zakāt, 395.
Zoroastrianism, 9.